X

only

SOURCES IN BRITISH POLITICAL HISTORY
1900-1951

Volume 2

Sources in British
Political History
1900 – 1951

compiled for the British Library of Political
and Economic Science by
CHRIS COOK

with

Philip Jones
Josephine Sinclair
Jeffrey Weeks

Volume 2

A Guide to the Private
Papers of Selected Public
Servants

© British Library of Political and
Economic Science 1975

First published 1975 by
THE MACMILLAN PRESS LTD
London and Basingstoke
Associated companies in New York
Dublin Melbourne Johannesburg and Madras

SBN 333 15037 6

Typeset by
COLD COMPOSITION LTD
Southborough, Tunbridge Wells

Printed in Great Britain by
Redwood Burn Limited
Trowbridge and Esher

Contents

Foreword

This is the second of four volumes reporting the results of a survey of twentieth-century British political archives. It has been undertaken by the British Library of Political and Economic Science with the support of the Social Science Research Council.

The project originated in a meeting of archivists, historians and librarians, held in October 1967 on the initiative of Nuffield College, Oxford, which appointed a Political Archives Investigation Committee (whose members are listed on p.viii) to explore the possibility of making a major effort to locate and list modern British political archives and encourage their preservation.

With the assistance of a grant from the Social Science Research Council a two-year pilot project, directed by Dr Cameron Hazlehurst, was begun at Nuffield College in 1968, with the object of locating the papers of Cabinet Ministers who held office between 1900 and 1951. The same Committee acted as a steering committee for the project. This enquiry was an undoubted success; Dr Hazlehurst's guide to the papers of Cabinet Ministers was published in 1974.*

In view of the favourable outcome of the pilot project, the Committee had no hesitation in recommending that a more comprehensive survey should be undertaken. Bearing in mind both the bibliographical facilities and the geographical convenience of London, as well as the number of scholars active in relevant fields working in the London School of Economics, it proposed that this phase of the investigation should be carried out under the auspices of the British Library of Political and Economic Science.

A generous grant was subsequently made to the British Library of Political and Economic Science by the Social Science Research Council; and on 1 October 1970 a research team directed by Dr C. P. Cook began work on a five-year project intended to locate the papers of all persons and organisations influential in British politics between 1900 and 1951, encourage their preservation, and publish guides.

The records of political parties, societies, institutions and pressure groups, with which the first volume was concerned, had, of necessity, to be treated with some degree of selectivity.† The same considerations have applied to this volume. The third volume will be devoted to reporting the findings of a comprehensive search that has been made for the papers of all Members of the House of Commons. The final volume will deal with the papers of writers, publicists, religious and trade union leaders etc. whose political influence was personal and intellectual rather than by virtue of their office.

D. A. Clarke

*C. Hazlehurst and C. Woodland, *A Guide to the Papers of British Cabinet Ministers, 1900-1951* (London: Royal Historical Society, 1974).

†C. Cook with Philip Jones, Josephine Sinclair and Jeffrey Weeks, *Sources in British Political History, 1900-1951*, vol. 1: *A Guide to the Archives of Selected Organisations and Societies* (London: Macmillan, 1975).

Acknowledgements

This book, like its predecessor, could not have been compiled without a large grant from the Social Science Research Council and the help and guidance of Derek Clarke, the Librarian of the British Library of Political and Economic Science. It would be impossible to thank by name all the people without whose help this volume either would not have appeared or would have looked very different. I am, however, especially indebted to the following:

Maurice Bond, O.B.E., Clerk of the Records at the House of Lords; D. S. Porter of the Bodleian Library, Oxford; Christine Kennedy of Nuffield College, Oxford; A. E. B. Owen of Cambridge University Library; Daniel Waley, Keeper of Manuscripts at the British Library; J. R. Ede and staff at the Public Record Office, Richard Bingle at the India Office Library; Sarah Graham-Brown of the Middle East Centre, St Antony's College, Oxford; Donald Brech of the Royal Air Force Museum, Hendon; Patience Empson of Rhodes House Library, Oxford; A. Pearsall of the National Maritime Museum, Greenwich; D. H. Simpson of the Royal Commonwealth Society; Roderick Suddaby of the Imperial War Museum; Julia Sheppard of the Liddell Hart Centre for Military Archives, King's College, London; B. Mollo of the National Army Museum; Clifton Child of the Cabinet Office; J. K. Bates, Secretary of the National Register of Archives (Scotland); J. S. Ritchie at the National Library of Scotland; Sir John Ainsworth, Bt, at the National Library of Ireland; and B. G. Owens at the National Library of Wales.

It will be evident from this book that a large debt is owed to Dame Margery Perham and the pioneer work done by the Oxford Colonial Records Project. Both the Civil Service Commission and the Public Record Office have co-operated closely in our work and their help has been much appreciated.

I have relied heavily on suggestions, advice and information supplied by colleagues and friends, both at the London School of Economics and elsewhere. I should like to thank especially Ken Bourne, David Bovey, Stephen Brooks, Philip Bull, Michael Dockrill, Mary Dysch, Cameron Hazlehurst, Catharine Hodges, Liz Hook, Stephen Inwood, George Jones, Elie Kedourie, Stephen Koss, Elizabeth Monroe, Ian Nish, Dame Margery Perham, Martin Sieff, Zara Steiner, Richard Storey, Paul Sturges, Christine Woodland, Philip Woods and Angela Raspin.

I have also received continual help and advice from members of the steering committee, both past and present, and especially from Mrs Strong and the staff of the Historical Manuscripts Commission, whose work is so closely associated with our own.

Last but by no means least, the compilation of this book has been a team effort, and my very warm thanks are due to my colleagues and co-authors, Philip Jones, Josephine Sinclair and Jeffrey Weeks. Most of the typing for the survey was done with unfailing energy and kindness by Eileen Pattison, with additional secretarial help from Jean Ali.

CHRIS COOK

Members of the Political Archives Investigation Committee

Mr John Brooke, Historical Manuscripts Commission (1967-) (Chairman, 1972-)
Mr D. A. Clarke, British Library of Political and Economic Science (1967-)
Dr C. P. Cook, British Library of Political and Economic Science (1970-)
Mr Martin Gilbert, Merton College, Oxford (1967-70)
Dr R. M. Hartwell, Nuffield College, Oxford (Chairman, 1967-72)
Dr Cameron Hazlehurst, Nuffield College, Oxford (1967-70)
Professor A. Marwick, The Open University (1972-)
Dr H. M. Pelling, St John's College, Cambridge (1967-)
Mrs Felicity Strong, formerly Historical Manuscripts Commission (1967-)
Dr John Roberts, Merton College, Oxford (1973-)
Mr A. J. P. Taylor, Magdalen College, Oxford (1972-)
Professor D. C. Watt, London School of Economics and Political Science (1967-)
Dr Edwin Welch, Churchill College, Cambridge (1967-71)

Introduction

1. Scope of the Survey

This volume is concerned with the private papers of some 1,500 senior public servants who were active and influential in British public life between 1900 and 1951. The main categories to be found within this volume are:

(a) *Diplomats*, including those who represented the British Government abroad, either as Ambassador or Minister.

(b) *Civil servants*, especially those who attained the rank of Permanent Secretary.

(c) *Colonial administrators*, especially Viceroys, Governors-General and Governors.

(d) *The armed forces*, including senior personnel of the Navy, Army and Air Force, not only field commanders but prominent members of the Board of Admiralty, the Army Council and the Air Council.

It would be wrong, in a book of this sort, to attempt to include people merely because of the rank they attained. Hence, this volume ranges more widely than the categories above and often includes people of lesser rank, but whose work in public service makes their papers of likely interest to historians. They include consular officials, military and naval attachés, private secretaries (particularly to Cabinet Ministers), staff officers in the armed forces, and senior officials of the Cabinet Office. Where information about papers has come to light, these persons have, where appropriate, been included in this volume.

The period covered by the survey is 1900 to 1951, but many of the persons covered by this book began their careers before 1900. Others stayed in public service after 1951. In most cases, papers prior to 1900 and for the period after 1951 are mentioned.

2. The Reports

The reports which appear in the following pages are necessarily brief. Biographical details are restricted to a concise note on particular aspects of what is often a very long and varied career. Researchers should, therefore, use entries in this Guide in conjunction with the lengthier entries in *Who's Who, Who Was Who* and the *Dictionary of National Biography*.

These reports attempt only to describe briefly the extent and nature of those collections of private papers which have survived. Where it has been found that no private papers exist, this information has often been included. Reference is not usually made to published biographies, memoirs or other such works, nor to official papers available in departmental files at the Public Record Office. In all cases, it must be assumed that official papers written by the individuals mentioned in this Guide will find their way into the public records.

Furthermore, relevant papers contained in the private collection of some other individual are not listed here. Researchers should consult the Personal Index to the National Register of Archives at the Historical Manuscripts Commission.

3. Research Procedure

No volume of this sort can ever be entirely comprehensive. Within this volume, most attention has been devoted to searching for the papers of senior diplomats and civil servants, partly because they had not been the subject of earlier systematic archive surveys. In the case of such categories as military and naval personnel, and colonial administrators, this volume has not attempted to duplicate the excellent work done by such specialist repositories as Rhodes House (for colonial administrators), the National Maritime Museum (for naval papers) and the Imperial War Museum, the National Army Museum and the Liddell Hart Centre for Military Archives (for the armed services). The information collected by the Middle East Centre, St Antony's College, Oxford, and by the India Office Library was also extensively consulted. These specialist archive centres are discussed in Appendix II (see pp. 287-91)

The research procedure has involved the collation of information on record at the National Register of Archives and at a number of repositories in this country, in the United States and the Commonwealth. Where papers were not known to be deposited, reference was made to the standard reference works, such as *Who Was Who* and *Burke's Peerage*. Where possible, a letter of enquiry was sent to a member of the family.

For certain categories, especially in the case of senior diplomats and civil servants, a visit was made to the Principal Probate Registry at Somerset House to consult wills and probate acts. In many cases, this enabled contact to be made with the surviving family, executor or solicitors. Lack of time and resources meant that a second visit to Somerset House to search for further contacts was not possible. For any number of reasons, it may not be possible to include details of papers of certain figures who should be included within this book. It may be impossible to trace a family; an address may change; illness or incapacity may prevent a reply to an enquiry; papers may be in store and details thus not available. Whilst every effort has been made to secure information about the papers of as wide and representative a range of public servants as possible, even so, faced with limited resources and a fixed period for research, certain omissions are inevitable. Equally, the information presented here may change; papers may be lost, destroyed, found or deposited. In particular, the addresses of custodians of papers will frequently change. For this reason, where the address of a person mentioned in the text can be obtained from the current *Who's Who* or similar sources, it is not cited in the text.

4. Availability of Papers

The inclusion of private papers in this volume in no way implies that these collections are necessarily available for research. Where papers are *known* to be closed to scholars, an attempt has been made to incorporate this information. For all collections in libraries and record offices, a preliminary letter to the appropriate archivist is very strongly advised. For collections in private hands, a letter is absolutely essential: no research worker should expect private collections necessarily to be opened up for his work. A letter of thanks to such custodians of private papers is also a matter of common courtesy. Scholars are reminded again of the law of copyright — and, in particular, that copyright lies with the writer of a letter not the recipient.

5. *Arrangement*

The entries in this guide are, in general, arranged alphabetically, under the last known name of the person concerned. Where a family name differs from the title subsequently chosen by a peer, the reader is referred to the index of such changes (see Appendix IV, p. 296 et seq.). Hyphenated names are usually found under the last half of the surname (e.g. for Talbot-Smith, see Smith).

6. *Abbreviations*

To save needless repetition, standard abbreviations have been used for ranks and appointments. A Life Peer has been styled Baron. Otherwise, titles have been abbreviated as follows: D (Duke); M (Marquess); E (Earl); Vt (Viscount); B (hereditary Baron); Bt (Baronet). The British Library of Political and Economic Science is referred to throughout as B.L.P.E.S.

Frequent reference is made in this volume to the survey of Cabinet Ministers' papers undertaken by Cameron Hazlehurst and Christine Woodland at Nuffield College, Oxford. This volume (*A Guide to the Papers of British Cabinet Ministers, 1900-1951*) is referred to in this book as Hazlehurst and Woodland, op. cit.

7. *Further Information*

Deposits of papers too recent to be included in this volume are recorded in the annual list of Accessions to Repositories published by H.M. Stationery Office for the Historical Manuscripts Commission. More detailed unpublished lists of archives both in repositories and libraries and in the custody of their originators may often be found in the National Register of Archives maintained by the Historical Manuscripts Commission, Quality House, Quality Court, Chancery Lane, London WC2A 1HP, where known alterations and additions to the information given in this volume will be recorded.

It is hoped that the information in this volume is correct at the time of going to press, but apart from the possible changes mentioned earlier, it must be remembered that many details of papers were often supplied by persons whose knowledge of the records was imperfect, by librarians who had not yet been able to catalogue records fully, or by scholars whose interests might be limited to certain aspects of their work. Both the British Library of Political and Economic Science and the Historical Manuscripts Commission would be grateful to be informed of alterations, additions and amendments.

CHRIS COOK

Private Papers

ABERDEEN AND TEMAIR, 1st M of
John Campbell Gordon (1847-1934)

Lord-Lieutenant of Ireland, 1886, 1905-15. Governor-General, Canada, 1893-98.

A collection of family papers and personal correspondence can be found in the King's College Library at Aberdeen University, and a further collection of letters survives in the Public Archives of Canada. N.R.A. (Scotland) has details of these and other relevant papers.

ABRAHALL, Sir (Theo) Chandos Hoskyns- (1896-   )

Colonial Service. Chief Commissioner, Western Provinces, Nigeria, 1946-51. Lieutenant-Governor, Western Region, Nigeria, 1951-52.

Papers at Rhodes House Library, Oxford, include personal diaries (1921-22 and 1946-52) and material relating to a mission to the Free French in 1940.

ABRAHAM, Edgar Gaston Furtado (1880-1955)

Assistant Secretary, War Cabinet, Jan. 1918; Supreme War Council, Versailles, May 1918; Supreme Council, Peace Conference, Jan. 1919-20.

A collection of papers survives at the Cambridge University Library consisting mainly of sets of minutes and memoranda of the War Cabinet, Supreme War Council and Peace Conference, 1918-19, with very little unofficial or personal material. There are also papers concerning the 'New Commonwealth' Society in which Abraham was active.

ABRAHAMS, Sir Lionel (1869-1919)

Assistant Under-Secretary, India Office, 1911-17.

The India Office Library holds papers accumulated by Sir Lionel Abrahams, including notes (1894-1919) on the powers of the Secretary of State for India and the Council of India, and copies of Acts of Parliament relating to India (1858-1909).

ACHESON, Captain Hon. Patrick George Edward Cavendish (1883-1957)

Naval career; served World War I. Commanded British Naval Flotilla on Rhine, 1919-21.

Papers covering Acheson's service in the Royal Navy, 1914-21, are available in the Imperial War Museum.

ACLAND, Lieutenant-General Arthur Nugent Floyer- (1885-   )

Served European War, 1914-18; India, 1936-38; War of 1939-45. Military Secretary to Secretary of State for War, 1940-42.

General Acland's papers will probably be placed in due course in the Imperial War Museum.

ACTON, 2nd B
Sir Richard Maximilian Dalberg-Acton, 2nd Bt (1870-1924)

Diplomat. Lord-in-Waiting, 1905-15. Consul-General, Zürich, 1917-19. Envoy to Finland, 1919-20.

The Dalberg-Acton family papers are in the care of the Hon. Richard Gerald Acton. One box file of papers, consisting of correspondence, memoranda, etc., relates to the 2nd Lord Acton's diplomatic career, particularly as Consul-General in Zurich, 1917-19. Enquiries should be directed to Lord Acton's daughter, Hon. Mrs Douglas Woodruff, Marcham Priory, near Abingdon, Oxon.

ADAM, Frederick Edward Fox (1887-1969)

Minister, Panama and Costa Rica, and Consul-General, Panama Canal Zone, 1934-39.

Mrs C. K. Adam, Blair Adam, Kinross-shire, states that certain papers survive in her care. The unsorted material consists of family and personal letters, and also letters, press cuttings and photographs relating to F. E. F. Adam.

ADAM, General Sir Ronald Forbes, 2nd Bt (1885-   )

Served European War, 1914-18, and War of 1939-45. Deputy Chief of Imperial General Staff, 1938-39. Commander, 3rd Army Corps, 1939-40. G.O.C.-in-C. Northern Command, 1940-41. Adjutant-General, 1941-46. Chairman and Director-General, British Council, 1946-54. Member, Executive Board UNESCO, 1950-54 (Chairman, 1952-54).

Certain memoranda relating to Adam's service as Adjutant-General (1941-46) have been deposited with the Liddell Hart Centre for Military Archives, King's College, London. Other papers will be placed at the Centre in due course.

ADAMS, Major Sir Hamilton John Goold (1858-1920)

Lieutenant-Governor, Orange River Colony, 1901-07; Governor, 1907-10. High Commissioner, Cyprus, 1911-14. Governor, Queensland, 1914-20.

A very small amount of material, including a few letters from Lord Milner, survives in the care of Mrs Elizabeth Main (daughter) of Ashcroft, Kilmalcolm, Renfrew-shire, who is currently compiling a biography of her father.

ADDISON, Sir Joseph (1879-1953)

Counsellor and Chargé d'Affaires, Berlin, 1920. Minister, Latvia, Lithuania and Estonia, 1927-30; Czechoslovakia, 1930-36.

Mr G. C. A. Doughty believes that his uncle, Sir Joseph Addison, left no papers.

AIREY, Lieutenant-General Sir Terence Sydney (1900-   )

Acting Deputy Supreme Allied Commander, Italy, 1946; Allied Commander and Military Governor, Trieste, 1947-51. Assistant Chief of Staff, Supreme H.Q. Allied Powers Europe, 1951-52. Commander, British Forces in Hong Kong, 1952-54.

British proclamations and press cuttings concerning the Free Territory of Trieste, Sept. 1947, are preserved at the Imperial War Museum. A few items only remain with Sir Terence Airey.

ALANBROOKE, 1st Vt
Field-Marshal Sir Alan Francis Brooke (1883-1963)

Served European War, 1914-18. Director of Military Training, War Office, 1936-37. Commander, Mobile Division, 1937-38; Anti-Aircraft Corps, 1938-39. G.O.C.-in-C., Anti-Aircraft Command, 1939; Southern Command, 1939 and 1940. Commander, 2nd Army Corps, British Expeditionary Force, 1939-40. C.-in-C., Home Forces, 1940-41. Chief of Imperial General Staff, 1941-46.

A collection of papers is held at the Liddell Hart Centre for Military Archives, whilst other papers remain with the biographer. Copies of some 20 personal letters (1940-46) with a few comments on the fall of France are at the Imperial War Museum. The Private Office Series (W.O. 216) at the Public Record Office contains correspondence from the office of the Chief of the Imperial General Staff to the Prime Minister, high-ranking officers, etc.

ALDERSON, Sir Edward Hall (1864-1951)

Private Secretary to Lord Chancellor, and Secretary of Commissions, 1895-1900. Reading Clerk and Clerk of Outdoor Committees, House of Lords, 1900-17. Clerk Assistant of the Parliaments, 1917-30. Clerk of the Parliaments, 1930-34.

Miss Pamela Alderson has not kept any of her father's papers, and no papers have been located elsewhere.

ALDRICH, Admiral Pelham (1844-1930)

Naval career, 1859-1908, including service in Arctic expeditions.

The material at the National Maritime Museum covers only a short period, but includes loose papers, maps and charts, and journals compiled whilst Aldrich was employed in the survey service (1877-85) in the Far East and off the African coast. Aldrich's Arctic papers are with the Scott Polar Research Institute at Cambridge.

ALEXANDER OF TUNIS, 1st E
Field-Marshal Sir Harold Rupert Leofric George Alexander (1891-1969)

Served European War, 1914-18. G.O.C.-in-C., Southern Command, 1940-42. G.O.C., Burma, 1942. C.-in-C., Middle East, 1942-43; 18th Army Group, North Africa, 1943; Allied Armies in Italy (15th Army Group), 1943-44. Supreme Allied Commander, Mediterranean Theatre, 1944-45. Governor-General, Canada, 1946-52. Minister of Defence, 1952-54.

A collection of papers is held at the Public Record Office (W.O. 214/1-69). The papers consist of official and semi-official correspondence, mostly for the years 1944-45. The Hon. Brian Alexander (son) knows of no further papers.

ALEXANDER, Brigadier-General Sir William (1874-1954)

Military Career; served European War, 1914-18. Controller of Aircraft Supply and Production, 1917-19. Director-General of Purchases, 1919-20. M.P. (Con.) Glasgow Central, 1923-45.

Efforts to trace the family have been unsuccessful. Further details may be available for Volume III of this Guide.

ALLARDYCE, Sir William Lamond (1861-1930)

Governor, Falkland Islands, 1904-14; Bahamas, 1915-20; Tasmania, 1920-22; Newfoundland, 1922-28.

The Library of the Royal Commonwealth Society holds twelve volumes of press cuttings collected by Allardyce.

ALLCHIN, Sir Geoffrey Cuthbert (1895-1968)

Head of Consular Department, Foreign Office, 1943-46; Inspector, 1947-49. Minister, Luxembourg, 1944-55; Ambassador, 1955.

Mrs Mildred Carr, Broomfield House, Longfield, Dartford, Kent DA3 7AE, executor to the estate, was unable to help with regard to her late brother's papers.

ALLENBY, 1st Vt
Field-Marshal Sir Edmund Henry Hynman Allenby (1861-1936)

C.-in-C., Egyptian Expeditionary Force, 1917-19. High Commissioner for Egypt, 1919-25.

The papers are in the possession of the 2nd Vt Allenby, and some photocopies are available at the Middle East Centre, St Antony's College, Oxford. This material includes family letters, extracts from official telegrams and other papers relating to the Palestine campaign, 1917-18; copies of letters to Sir Herbert Samuel, 1920-25; and further papers on service in Egypt, 1920-25.

ALLFREY, Lieutenant-General Sir Charles Walter (1895-1964)

Served European War, 1914-18. Commander, V Corps, North Africa and Italy, 1942-44. G.O.C., British troops in Egypt, 1944-48.

Lady Allfrey, Lower Hazel House, Rudgeway, Bristol BS12 2QP, has retained many papers and photographs relating to the career of her late husband, which cover most of his military activities.

ALSTON, Sir Beilby Francis (1868-1929)

Deputy High Commissioner, Siberia, 1918-19. Minister, Japan, 1919-20; China, 1920-22; Argentine Republic and Paraguay, 1923-25. Ambassador, Brazil, 1925-29.

At the Public Record Office the Private Office Series (F.O. 800/244-8) consists of Alston's correspondence (1908-15) as Senior Clerk in the Foreign Office Far Eastern Department, special envoy in Siam (1911) and acting Counsellor in China. Correspondence (1913-17) with Lord Hardinge of Penshurst can be seen in the Hardinge papers at Cambridge University Library.

ALTRINCHAM, 1st B
Sir Edward William Maclean Grigg (1879-1955)

M.P. (Lib.) Oldham, 1922-25; (Nat.Con.) Altrincham, 1933-45. Governor, Kenya, 1925-31. Parliamentary Secretary, Ministry of Information, 1939-40. Financial Secretary, War Office, 1940. Joint Parliamentary Under-Secretary, War Office, 1940-42. Minister Resident, Middle East, 1944-45.

Hazlehurst and Woodland, op.cit., pp.66-7, give details of the papers which survive with Mr John Grigg, Lord Altrincham's son, 32 Dartmouth Row, London SE10. Copies of many of these papers are available at the Bodleian Library, Oxford, and at the Douglas Library, Queen's University, Kingston, Ontario.

AMPTHILL, 2nd B
Arthur Oliver Villiers Russell (1869-1935)

Governor, Madras, 1899-1906. Acting Viceroy and Governor-General, India, 1904.

The collection at the India Office Library amounts to some 58 volumes of manuscript papers and 47 printed volumes, and relates to Ampthill's career in India. The principal correspondents include Lord George Francis Hamilton, the 1st E of Midleton, Vt Morley and Lord Kilbracken; and in India, Lords Curzon, Minto and Kitchener. Letters to Lord Rendel are in the National Library of Wales.

ANDERSON, Sir Alan Garrett (1877-1952)

M.P. (Con.) City of London, 1935-40. Controller of Railways, Ministry of War Transport, 1941-45, and chairman of Railway Executive.

A collection of papers is held at the Public Record Office (P.R.O. 30/68). This consists largely of papers relating to Anderson's work on government committees. Further material survives in the care of Sir Alan's son, Sir Colin Anderson, Admiral's House, Hampstead Grove, London NW3. The papers cover a wide range of subjects, including business affairs, his parliamentary career, educational matters, railways, food supply, hospitals, the Bank of England and personal affairs.

ANDERSON, Sir Alexander James (1879-1965)

Army career; served World War I. Member of the Burma Legislative Council, 1923-25.

Anderson's papers relating to the siege of Kut (1916), with maps and plans of Kut and material on the experiences of prisoners of war after the surrender of Kut, are available at the National Army Museum.

ANDERSON, Lieutenant-General Sir Desmond Francis (1885-1967)

Served European War, 1914-18. Major-General, General Staff, Home Forces, 1939-40. Commander, 45th Division, 1940. Assistant Chief of Imperial General Staff, 1940. Commander, 46th Division, 1940; III Corps, 1940-43; II Corps, 1943-44.

The Liddell Hart Centre for Military Archives has been informed that all papers were destroyed at the time of Anderson's death.

ANDERSON, Sir John (1858-1918)

Governor, Straits Settlements, and High Commissioner, Malay States, 1904-11. Permanent Under-Secretary, Colonial Office, 1911-16. Governor, Ceylon, 1916-18.

The Public Trustee who acted as Sir John's executor has no records which would be helpful in tracing Sir John Anderson's private papers.

ANDREWES, Admiral Sir William (1899-1974)

Naval career; Chief Staff Officer for administration and turnround invasion duties to the C.-in-C., Portsmouth, 1944. Chief of Staff to the Vice-Admiral, Pacific, 1944-45. Commander, British and Commonwealth Naval Forces in Korean War, 1950, and U.N. Task Force 95, 1951. Deputy Supreme Allied Commander, Atlantic, 1952-53.

The material on microfilm at the Imperial War Museum includes a diary and photographs (1925-26), records relating to Operation 'Overlord' (1944), and reports on British Commonwealth naval operations in Korea. (1950-51). The Korean papers remain closed.

ANDREWS, Sir Edwin Arthur Chapman- (1903-   )

Consular Service. Minister, Cairo, 1947-51. Ambassador, Lebanon, 1952-56 (Minister, 1951-52); Sudan, 1956-61.

Sir Edwin's secretary states that there is very little documentary or other material, apart from press cuttings, photographs and a number of personal letters.

ANSTEY, Brigadier Edgar Carnegie (1882-1958)

Military career; served European War, 1914-18. Chief Staff Officer, Armaments Sub-Commission of Inter-Allied Commission of Control, Germany, 1920-22. Brigadier, General Staff, Western Command, India, 1932-35. Military correspondent, 1942-45.

Two boxes of material relating to Anstey's career are housed at the Royal Artillery Institution.

ANTROBUS, Sir Reginald Laurence (1853-1942)

Assistant Under-Secretary, Colonial Office, 1898-1909. Senior Crown Agent, Colonies, 1909-18.

A collection of correspondence relating to West Africa and the period 1890-97 is held at Rhodes House Library, Oxford. Some other papers survive with Miss Eleanor Antrobus, Wall Hatch Country Hotel, Forest Row, Sussex.

APPLETON, Sir Edward Victor (1892-1965)

Secretary, Department of Scientific and Industrial Research, 1939-49. Academic and university vice-chancellor.

Lady Appleton states that her late husband's papers are in the University of Edinburgh Library, in the 'Appleton Room'. The papers were used by R. W. Clark for his biography of Appleton, and the material includes copies of speeches and broadcast texts, lantern slides, diaries, journals, and the valuable correspondence exchanged between Appleton and Van der Pol.

ARCHER, Sir Geoffrey Francis (1882-1964)

Colonial Civil Service, from 1902. Served in East Africa; Somaliland. Governor, Uganda, 1922-24. Governor-General, Sudan, 1924-26.

The Sudan Archive at Durham University has press cuttings and photographs of British Somaliland and East Africa, 1913-33; photographs of Morocco and Kashmir, 1928-29.

ARDAGH, Major-General Sir John Charles (1840-1907)

Private Secretary to Lord Lansdowne, 1888-94, and to Lord Elgin, Viceroy of India. Director of Military Intelligence, War Office, 1896-1901. British delegate to the Hague Peace Conference, 1899. H.M.G. Agent, South African Claims Commission, 1901.

Papers (1862-1908) at the Public Record Office (P.R.O. 30/40) comprise drafts and proof copies of War Office and Foreign Office memoranda, technical notes and monographs, diaries, collections of private memoranda, press cuttings, etc., and public and private correspondence. The material covers Ardagh's work as private secretary, at the D.M.I., and as a member of various commissions of enquiry and arbitration and as a delegate to international conferences.

ARMSTRONG, Edmond Arrenton (1899-1966)

Served War Office, Scottish Office, 1935-41; War Cabinet Office, 1941-47. Deputy Adviser to Viceroy on War Administration in India, 1943-44. Under-Secretary, Ministry of Transport and Civil Aviation, 1947. Controller, Civil Aviation Ground Service, 1957-60.

Mrs Mary Wilson, Flat 19, Clan House, Sydney Road, Bath, Avon, has a series of diaries and memoirs written by her father. Some of the material is purely personal, and some consists of comments on work and the people that Armstrong came into contact with.

ARNOLD, Sir Frederick Blackmore (1906-1968)

Secretary, Government of Burma Reconstruction Department, 1942-45; Commerce and Supply Department, 1946-47. Senior Trade Commissioner, Pakistan, 1950-58. Minister (Commercial) and Senior Trade Commissioner, Australia, 1958-66.

Papers (1939-47) relating to Arnold's career, as Controller of Prices, Imports and Civil Supplier, Government of Burma, 1939-42, etc., are deposited at the India Office Library.

ASHBOURNE, 3rd B
Vice-Admiral Edward Russell Gibson (1901-   )

Naval career; served World Wars I and II (specialising in submarine work). Commanded 3rd Submarine Flotilla, 1945. Served on Naval Staff, Admiralty, 1946-47. Naval Representative on Military Staff Committee, U.N., 1949-50. Flag Officer, Gibraltar, and Admiral Superintendent, H.M. Dockyard, Gibraltar, 1950-52.

Lord Ashbourne has kept no papers relating to his own career.

ASKWITH, 1st B
Sir George Ranken Askwith (1861-1942)

Chief Industrial Commissioner, 1911-19. Chairman, Industrial Council, 1911, and Fair Wages Advisory Committee, 1909-19. President, Middle Classes Union (National Citizens' League), 1921-29.

The Hon. Mrs Miller-Jones, 8 Egerton Terrace, London SW3, states that all her father's papers were returned after his death to the Board of Trade. These have not been traced. However, some papers of Lady Askwith remain with Mrs Miller-Jones. These consist of five volumes of press cuttings covering Lady Askwith's writing career, her work in World War I, her involvement with the Anti-Socialist League and the National Citizens' League in the 1920s, and her social work. There is also a series of day-to-day factual diaries (1880-92, 1907-40 and 1947-54), some of which relate to public affairs and to Lord Askwith's industrial work.

ASTON, Major-General Sir George Grey (1861-1938)

Served Sudan, 1884; South Africa, 1899-1900; European War, 1914. Employed with Naval Intelligence, 1887-90, 1892-95; Admiralty War Staff, 1913-14; War Cabinet Secretariat, 1918-19. Brigadier-General, General Staff, South Africa, 1908-12. Military historian.

The Liddell Hart Centre for Military Archives holds a collection of papers on temporary loan. The collection includes diaries (1899-1914); copies of articles, reviews, and drafts of his books; and correspondence (1899-1933). Some papers remain closed.

ATHLONE, 1st E of
Alexander Augustus Frederick William Alfred George Cambridge
(1874-1957)

Governor-General, South Africa, 1924-31; Canada, 1940-46.

It is believed that no papers survive. The Royal Archives at Windsor have no relevant information. However, the Blumenfeld papers now at the House of Lords Record Office include a few letters (c. 1911-14) mainly relating to charitable affairs.

AUCHINLECK, Field-Marshal Sir Claude John Eyre (1884-   )

Served World War I (Egypt, Aden, Mesopotamia), 1914-19. G.O.C.-in-C., Northern Norway, 1940; Southern Command, 1940. C.-in-C., India, 1941 and 1943-47; Middle East, 1941-42. War Member, Viceroy's Executive Council, 1943-46. Supreme Commander in India and Pakistan, 1947.

A large collection of papers is held at the John Rylands University Library of Manchester. Most of the papers date from the period after 1940, with correspondence, copies of official papers and notes on Norway (1940), Southern Command (1940), India (1941 and 1943-47), and Middle East Command (1941-43). There is also a series of dispatches and official accounts of military operations prepared by or under the supervision of Auchinleck. Principal correspondents include Lord Alanbrooke, L. S. Amery, W. S. Churchill, Sir J. G. Dill, the Marquess of Linlithgow, Sir N. M. Ritchie, Field-Marshal Smuts and Earl Wavell.

Documents of W. R. P. Ridgeway, private secretary to Auchinleck, dealing with Narvik (1940) and India (1941-47), are in the care of the National Army Museum.

AUSTEN, General Sir Alfred Reade Godwin- (1889-1963)

Served European War, 1915-19. Commander, 14th Infantry Brigade (Palestine), 1938-39; 8th Division, 1939; served in East Africa, Abyssinia, Libya; War Office, 1943-45, and India, 1945-47.

The Liddell Hart Centre for Military Archives holds certain papers relating to Godwin-Austen's appointment to command in Somaliland (1940).

AVELING, Arthur Francis (1893-1954)

Chargé d'Affaires to Belgium and Luxembourg in France and London, 1940-41.

The solicitors who acted in the estate were unable to give any help regarding papers or the present whereabouts of members of the family.

BACKHOUSE, Admiral of the Fleet Sir Roger Roland Charles (1878-1939)

Naval service; served World War I. Director of Naval Ordnance, 1920-22. Rear-Admiral Commanding 3rd Battle Squadron, Mediterranean Fleet, 1926-27. 3rd Sea Lord and Controller of the Navy, 1929-32. Vice-Admiral Commanding 1st Battle

Squadron, Mediterranean Fleet, 1932-34. C.-in-C., Home Fleet, 1935-38. 1st Sea Lord and Chief of Naval Staff, 1938-39.

It is believed that no papers survive.

BADEN-POWELL, 1st B
Lieutenant-General Sir Robert Stephenson Smyth Baden-Powell, 1st Bt (1857-1941)

Army career from 1876; active service in South Africa from 1897 (defence of Mafeking, 1899-1900). Inspector-General, South African Constabulary, 1900-03. Inspector-General of Cavalry, 1903-07. Founder of Boy Scouts and Girl Guides, 1908.

Four manuscript notebooks containing carbon flimsies of Baden-Powell's staff diaries kept during the siege of Mafeking, and covering the period Oct. 1899-May 1900, are deposited in the National Army Museum. Other material in the Museum includes correspondence, reports and other staff diaries for the early 1900s. The British Library also has papers relating to the siege of Mafeking, Add. MSS. 50255.

Certain papers of Baden-Powell also survive at Baden-Powell House, 25 Buckingham Palace Road, London SW1W 0PY. These include scrapbooks, photographs, original sketches and maps and certain correspondence. Some Baden-Powell material may also be found in the South African Library, Cape Town, Republic of South Africa. A scrapbook and diary (1895-96), kept during the Ashanti campaign, is in the museum at Kumasi, Ghana. The National Library of Scotland has further papers, viz daily orders issued at Mafeking.

BAILEY, Lieutenant-Colonel Frederick Marshman (1882-1967)

Served Younghusband Expedition, Tibet, 1903-04. British Trade Agent, Gyantse, Tibet, 1905-09. Political Officer, Indian Army, and Political Service, in Mesopotamia and Persia, 1917-18; Russian Turkestan, 1918-20; Sikkim, 1921-28. Political Agent, Central India, and Resident, Baroda, 1930-32; Resident, Kashmir, 1932-33. Minister, Nepal, 1935-38. Explorer.

The Hon. Mrs Eric Bailey has deposited many of her late husband's papers with the India Office Library. The unlisted material (1890-1965) relates to Bailey's career in India and to his parents. Further papers remain with the Hon. Mrs Bailey, Warborough House, Stiffkey, Wells-next-the-Sea, Norfolk. The collection includes diaries and letters to members of the family.

BAKER, Sir Edward Norman (1857-1913)

Financial Secretary, Government of India, 1902-05. Lieutenant-Governor, Bengal, 1908-11.

A visit to Somerset House produced no information useful in tracing the family or executors.

BALFOUR, Sir John (1894-   )

Minister, Lisbon, 1941-43; Moscow, 1943-45; Washington, 1945-48. Ambassador, Argentine Republic, 1948-51; Spain, 1951-54. Commissioner-General, Brussels International Exhibition, 1958.

Sir John Balfour kept no papers but retains his unpublished memoirs, a copy of which has been deposited with the Foreign Office Library, as has also a copy of a short essay entitled 'Encounters with the Windsors'. The Imperial War Museum has his letters from Ruhleben, when a civilian internee in Germany, 1914-18.

BAMFORD, Sir Eric St John (1891-1957)

Assistant Secretary, Treasury, 1938-39; Ministry of Information, 1939. Director-General, Information, 1945; Central Office of Information, 1946. Chairman, Board of Inland Revenue, 1948-55.

No contact with Lady Bamford could be established.

BANKS, Sir Donald T. M. (1891-1975)

Director-General, Post Office, 1934-36. Permanent Secretary, Air Ministry, 1936-38. Permanent Under-Secretary, Air, 1938-39. Director-General, Petroleum Warfare Department, 1940-45.

It is understood that Sir Donald Banks has kept some papers. Details are not available.

BANNATYNE, Sir Robert Reid (1875-1956)

Assistant Under-Secretary, Home Office. Served Industrial Health Research Board; Royal Commission on Workmen's Compensation, 1938; International Labour Organisation; Beveridge Committee on Social Insurance, 1941-42; Tomlinson Committee on Rehabilitation of Disabled Persons, 1942, etc.

Mr R. M. Robbins states that after the death of his father-in-law, Sir Robert Bannatyne, such papers and drafts as were at his home were returned by Lady Bannatyne to the government departments concerned, and that after her death none of Sir Robert's papers were found among her possessions.

BANNERMAN, Major Sir Alexander, 11th Bt (1871-1934)

Served South Africa, 1899-1902; Russo-Japanese War, 1904-05; European War, 1914-17.

Certain papers can be found at the Public Record Office (AIR 1/725/100/1-2). These documents and photographs relate to the Air Battalion of the Royal Engineers in the years up to 1914.

BARCLAY, Sir Colville Adrian de Rune (1869-1929)

Minister, Washington, 1918; Sweden, 1919-24; Hungary, 1924-28. Ambassador, Portugal, 1928-29.

Sir Colville Barclay, Bt, Pitshill, Petworth, Sussex, has retained a small collection of his father's papers. They include letters from Sir E. Monson, dated 1901; English and French magazines relating to the visit of King Edward VII to Paris in 1903, and various postcards of the visit; some press cuttings mostly about the Balkans (1912) and Sweden (1920); papers on Hungary (1924); and a number of personal family letters and a few from colleagues in the diplomatic service.

BARCLAY, Sir George Head (1862-1921)

Minister, Constantinople, 1908; Persia, 1908-12; Romania, 1912-21.

Efforts to trace the family and executors were not successful. The Hardinge papers at Cambridge University Library include some correspondence (c. 1906-19).

BARKER, General Sir Evelyn Hugh (1894-   )

Served European War, 1914-18, and War of 1939-45. Commander, VIII Corps,

1944-46; British Troops in Palestine and Transjordan, 1946. G.O.C.-in-C., Eastern Command, 1947-50.

At the Imperial War Museum, papers are available relating to British operations in northern France (1944-45).

BARLEY, Commander F., and WATERS, Lieutenant-General D. W.

The Barley-Waters MSS., in the Library of the Ministry of Defence (Naval Historical Branch), contain a mass of valuable papers and raw material on trade defence in World War I collected by the above.

BARLOW, Vice-Admiral Charles James (1848-1921)

Served in Egypt, 1882; Burma, 1885-86. Admiral Superintendent, Devonport Dockyard, 1906-08.

Logbooks and letters received (1863-1908) are available at the National Maritime Museum, together with a journal of the Naval Brigade in the Burma War (1885-86), papers relating to the opening of the Kiel Canal (1895) and a collection of dockyard papers (1899-1902, 1906-08).

BARLOW, Sir James Alan Noel, 2nd Bt (1881-1968)

Principal Private Secretary to the Prime Minister, 1933-34. Joint Second Secretary, Treasury, 1938-48.

Neither Sir Alan Barlow's widow, Lady Barlow, nor his sister, Miss Helen Barlow, were able to find any papers left by Sir Alan.

BARNARD, Vice-Admiral Sir Geoffrey (1902-1974)

Naval career; Deputy Chief of Staff to Naval C.-in-C. for North Africa Landings, 1942, and to C.-in-C. Mediterranean, 1942-43. Chief Staff Officer to Flag Officer (Air), 1946-47. Director, Royal Naval Tactical School, 1948-49. Assistant Chief of Naval Staff (Warfare), 1952-53. Deputy Chief of Naval Staff, 1953-54. Admiral, British Joint Services Mission, Washington, 1954-56. President of Royal Naval College, Greenwich, 1956-58.

There are some uncatalogued papers at the Imperial War Museum. These consist of a midshipman's journal covering the Prince of Wales' round-the-world tour (1921-22), and summary diaries of service, mostly in the Mediterranean, as a staff officer (1940-41).

BARNARDISTON, Major-General Nathaniel Walter (1858-1919)

Served South Africa, 1901-02; World War I; Military Attaché, Brussels, The Hague and Scandinavian Courts. Commander, British Forces in North China, 1914-15. Chief of British Military Mission to Portugal, 1916.

The Liddell Hart Centre for Military Archives holds Barnardiston's diaries relating to the Anglo-Japanese capture of Tsingtao in 1914, his command of the 39th Division (1915-16) and the British Military Mission to Portugal (1916-19). Other family papers survive at the Bury St Edmunds and West Suffolk Record Office.

BARNES, Sir George Stapylton (1858-1946)

Served Board of Trade; Joint Permanent Secretary, 1915. Member of Council of Viceroy of India, 1916-21.

Mrs A. C. Barnes, Foxholm, Cobham, Surrey, has a number of her father-in-law's papers. In the main these papers consist of a large book of letters and documents (1914-21), concerned with the period in India. Principal correspondents include Sir Thomas Holderness, Lords Buxton, Willingdon and Chelmsford, Sir George Lloyd and Mahatma Gandhi.

BARNES, Sir Hugh Shakespear (1853-1940)

Foreign Secretary, Government of India, 1900-03. Lieutenant-Governor, Burma, 1903-05. Member, Council of India, 1905-13.

The India Office Library holds a microfilm of Barnes's correspondence (1893-1903 and 1904) with his wife, and with Lords Curzon, Ampthill and Kilbracken.

BARNES, Sir James Horace (1891-1969)

Permanent Under-Secretary, Air Ministry, 1947-55.

Lady Barnes (widow) states that she has no papers that would be of interest.

BARNES, Sir Thomas James (1888-1964)

Solicitor, Board of Trade, 1920-33. Procurator-General and Treasury Solicitor, 1934-53.

Neither Mr J. F. Alexander, Sir Thomas's nephew, nor Mr H. C. Belk, an executor, know of any private papers which survive.

BARRINGTON, Hon. Sir William Augustus Curzon (1842-1922)

Minister, Argentina and Paraguay, 1896-1902; Sweden and Norway, 1902-04.

The Hon. R. E. S. Barrington, D.S.O., the only member of the Barrington family with whom the project managed to make contact, was unable to help in the survey.

BARTON, Sir Sidney (1876-1946)

Chinese Secretary, Peking, 1911-22. Consul-General, Shanghai, 1922-29. Minister, Abyssinia, 1929-37.

Certain papers, mainly concerned with family matters, survive with Mrs B. E. Kenyon Jones, Knowle House, Froxfield, near Marlborough, Wilts. These include three books of press cuttings relating to Ethiopia (1937-45). There are no papers relating to China.

BATEMAN, Sir Charles Harold (1892-   )

Minister, Cairo, 1938-40; Mexico, 1941-44. Ambassador, Mexico, 1944-47; Poland, 1950-52. Assistant Under-Secretary, Foreign Office, 1948-50.

Sir C. H. Bateman has retained no papers.

BATEMAN, Major-General Donald Roland Edwin Rowan (1901-1969)

Served India; War of 1939-45. Director of Military Training, India.

The Imperial War Museum holds certain official papers and post-war correspondence relating to service in North Africa and at Cassino in World War II.

BATTERBEE, Sir Harry Fagg (1880-   )

Assistant Secretary, Dominions Office, 1925-30; Assistant Under-Secretary,

1930-38. Deputy Secretary, Imperial Conferences, 1930 and 1937. High Commissioner, New Zealand, 1939-45.

It is understood that Sir Harry has kept some papers relating to his career.

BATTERSHILL, Sir William Denis (1896-1959)

Chief Secretary, Palestine, 1937-39. Governor, Cyprus, 1939-41; Tanganyika, 1945-49. Assistant Under-Secretary and Deputy Under-Secretary, Colonial Office, 1942-45.

Lady Battershill (widow) has no papers.

BAXTER, Charles William (1895-1969)

Minister, Iceland, 1947-50.

Mr Baxter's son, Mr R. L. Baxter, Quakers, Brasted Chart, Westerham, Kent, has only the letters which his father wrote as a young officer from Gallipoli and Iraq.

BAXTER, George Herbert (1894-1962)

Assistant Under-Secretary, India, 1943-47; Commonwealth Relations, 1947-55.

Mrs G. Baxter, 20 Woodcote Avenue, Wallington, Surrey, has a collection of unsorted material relating to her late husband. The papers include articles written by Baxter, correspondence in connection with these articles (especially over the Central African Federation), and travel diaries. A very small amount of political correspondence with such persons as Sir Roy Welensky and Lord Malvern on Central African affairs also exists.

BAYNES, Rear-Admiral Henry C. A. (1852-1922)

A gunnery and torpedo specialist, at one time connected with the revision of the Sea Fishery Manual.

Papers at the National Maritime Museum include career records (1866-1901), official papers and letters received (1888-95) and order books (1895-1901).

BEATTY, 1st E
Admiral of the Fleet Sir David Beatty (1871-1936)

Naval service from 1884. Naval Secretary to 1st Lord of the Admiralty, 1912. Commanded 1st Battle Cruiser Squadron, 1913-16. C.-in-C., Grand Fleet, 1916-19. 1st Sea Lord, 1919-27.

A substantial collection of uncatalogued papers survives in the care of Mrs Diane Nutting, Chicheley Hall, Newport Pagnell, Bucks., to whom all enquiries should be addressed. The papers include a large number of letters to his wife (1900-27), very few of which are entirely personal in character and which to a considerable extent take the place of a diary. There is also correspondence with the Duchess of Rutland (1925-30), and with public figures such as Balfour, Long, Fisher, Jellicoe and Wemyss. Other correspondents include Churchill, Hankey, Lloyd George and King George V. Subject files cover the actions of Heligoland Bight, Dogger Bank, the Scarborough Raid, Jutland, and the Armistice negotiations, also the historiography of Jutland, the battle cruiser and battle fleet tactics. Post-war files cover the Capital Ship controversy, Singapore, the Fleet Air Arm, marriage allowances, etc., but there is little on the Washington Conference, the so-called Cruiser Crisis, or the Geneva Conference.

BEAUCHAMP, 7th E
William Lygon, Viscount Elmley (1872-1938)

Governor, New South Wales, 1899-1901. Lord President of the Council, 1910 and 1914-15. 1st Commissioner of Works, 1910-14.

Hazlehurst and Woodland, op. cit., p. 94, found that the present (8th) Earl Beauchamp of Madresfield Court, Malvern, Worcs., has only a collection of scrapbooks relating to his father's career. The Mitchell Library, Sydney, has a diary kept while Governor of New South Wales and a substantial collection of correspondence relating to the question of Federation in 1900.

BEAUCLERK, William Nelthorpe (1849-1908)

Minister Resident and Consul General, Ecuador and Peru, 1898-1908, and Bolivia, 1903-08.

It was not possible to contact members of the family, which is a branch of the Duke of St Albans' family.

BEAUMONT, Sir Henry Hamond Dawson (1867-1949)

Chargé d'Affaires, Montenegro, 1909-10. Counsellor, Constantinople, 1914; Rome, 1915-16. Minister, Venezuela, 1916-23.

Mr C. A. W. Beaumont, 3 Gray's Inn Square, Gray's Inn, London WC1R 5AS, has retained his father's personal diaries and the only extant copy of an unpublished autobiography.

BEAVER, Sir Hugh Eyre Campbell (1890-1967)

Career in industry. Director-General and Controller-General, Ministry of Works, 1940-45. Member of Government Committees.

Sir Hugh Beaver's daughter, Mrs C. E. C. Lawson-Tancred, The Rectory, Wrington, Bristol BS18 7QD, has a collection of her father's papers. These include diaries, correspondence and press cuttings, and they are at present only roughly sorted.

BECKETT, Sir William Eric (1896-1966)

Legal Adviser, Foreign Office, 1945-53.

Lady Beckett, King-o-Mill, Keinton Mandeville, Somerton, Somerset, has retained the letters which her late husband wrote to her whilst attending conferences abroad, together with a diary of the Bretton Woods negotiations on Anglo-Egyptian relations in 1935.

BEDFORD, Admiral Sir Frederick George Denham (1838-1913)

Naval career from 1852. C.-in-C., Cape of Good Hope and West Coast of Africa, 1892-95. Lord of the Admiralty, 1889-92, 1895-99. C.-in-C., North American and West Indies Station, 1899-1903. Governor, Western Australia, 1903-09.

A small collection at the National Maritime Museum consists of logbooks, 1851-58, and diaries, 1875-79.

BEER, Harry (1896-1970)

Civil Service career: Board of Trade, Ministry of Supply. Permanent Under-Secretary, Board of Trade, 1946-56.

Mr David J. E. Beer, Orchard Way, Hurst Green, Oxted, Surrey, states that his mother has a small collection of letters written to his father, mostly letters of thanks or congratulation from Presidents of the Board of Trade from Oliver Stanley to Harold Wilson and Sir Hartley (Lord) Shawcross.

BELL, Sir Charles Alfred (1870-1945)

Assistant Political Officer, Sikkim, 1904-05. Political Officer, Sikkim, 1908. Adviser to Sir Henry McMahon, Simla Conference, 1913-14. Envoy to Tibet, 1920.

The collection of papers at the India Office Library consists of numerous files of notes, reports and letters, etc., mainly about Tibet but also containing a few papers on Bhutan and Sikkim. There is also a large number of photographs. The whole collection is carefully indexed.

BELL, Sir Gawain Westray (1909-   )

Served Middle East, Sudan Government, etc. Secretary-General, South Pacific Commission, 1966-70.

Sir Gawain Bell has retained a large collection of papers relating to his career, and a tape and transcript of interviews which he gave are held in Rhodes House Library.

BELL, Lieutenant-Colonel Sir Harold Wilberforce (1885-1956)

Political Secretary, Government of India, 1930-33. Resident, Punjab States, 1934-39.

Several scrapbooks and albums of newspaper cuttings have been deposited at the India Office Library. The scrapbooks include a number of private letters to Bell from friends and colleagues (1916-54).

BELLAIRS, Rear-Admiral Roger Mowbray (1884-1959)

Naval service from 1900. War Staff Officer to C.-in-C., Grand Fleet, 1916-19. Naval Assistant to 1st Sea Lord, 1919-25. Director of Plans Division, Admiralty, 1928-30. Representative on League of Nations Permanent Advisory Commission, 1939-46. Head of Historical Section, Admiralty, 1948-56.

Grand Fleet papers, 1917-18, of Bellairs, who was Beatty's War Staff Officer, are in the Naval Library, Ministry of Defence.

BENN, Captain Sir Ion Hamilton, 1st Bt (1863-1961)

Naval career. M.P. (Con.) Greenwich, Jan. 1910-22.

A small collection of papers relating to Sir Ion Benn's naval career, particularly during World War I, is available in the National Maritime Museum.

BENNETT, Sir Albert James, 1st Bt (1872-1945)

M.P. (Lib.) Mansfield, 1922-23; (Con.) Nottingham Central, 1924-30. Member of Mechanical Transport Board, War Office; Leather Control Board. Controller of Propaganda for South and Central America, Ministry of Information, in War of 1939-45.

Mr Michael Bennett and his brother, Sir Ronald Bennett, Bt, grandsons of Sir A. J. Bennett, have no papers relating to their grandfather.

BENNETT, Andrew Percy (1866-1943)

Minister, Panama, 1919-23; Costa Rica, 1920-23; Venezuela, 1923-27.

Mr Bennett's solicitors have been taken over by another firm, who have retained no papers which would enable them to contact surviving members of Mr Bennett's family.

BENNETT, Sir John Cecil Sterndale (1895-1969)

Head of Far Eastern Department, Foreign Office, 1940-42, 1944-46. British Political Representative, Bulgaria, 1947; Minister, 1947-49. Deputy Commissioner-General, South East Asia, 1950-53. Head of British Middle East Office, 1953-55.

Lady Sterndale Bennett, The Old Rectory, Netherfield, near Battle, Sussex, writes that her late husband kept no diary or letters of official importance. A collection of autobiographical notes remains in the care of Lady Sterndale Bennett.

BENSON, Lieutenant-Colonel Sir Reginald (1889-1968)

Served European War, 1914-18, and War of 1939-45. Military Secretary to Governor of Bombay, 1921-22. Military Attaché, Washington, 1941-44.

Some papers are held by the Liddell Hart Centre for Military Archives. The material includes papers relating to Benson's work as Liaison Officer with the Groupe des Armées du Nord and the Grand Quartier Général in France (1916-19). These papers include French and British casualty and strength figures, intelligence summaries, operational planning, and correspondence between the Commanders-in-Chief.

BENTINCK, Rev. Sir Charles Henry (1879-1955)

Consul-General, Munich, 1924. Minister and Consul-General, Ethiopia, 1925. Minister, Peru and Ecuador, 1929-33; Bulgaria, 1934-36; Czechoslovakia, 1936-37. Ambassador, Chile, 1937-40.

Lady Bentinck, Ash Tree Cottage, Upshire, Waltham Abbey, Essex, has only a few papers, including press cuttings, relating to her late husband.

BENTINCK, Victor Frederick William Cavendish- (1897-   )

Ambassador, Poland, 1945-47.

Mr Cavendish-Bentinck never kept a diary and has retained no papers relating to his Foreign Service career.

BERESFORD, 1st B
Admiral Lord Charles William de la Poer Beresford (1846-1919)

M.P. (Con.) Waterford, 1874-80; Marylebone East, 1885-89; York, 1897-99; Woolwich, 1902-03; Portsmouth, 1910-16. Junior Lord of the Admiralty, 1886-88. C.-in-C., Mediterranean Fleet, 1905-07; Channel Fleet, 1907-09.

A few papers are available in Duke University, North Carolina. Other papers concerning the Portsmouth Naval Reviews (1886-88) are at the National Maritime Museum. A further substantial amount of correspondence can be found in the Ardagh papers (PRO 30/40) at the Public Record Office.

BERTIE OF THAME, 1st Vt
Sir Francis Leveson Bertie (1844-1919)

Assistant Under-Secretary, Foreign Office, 1894-1903. Ambassador, Italy, 1903-5; France, 1905-18.

Private Office correspondence (1896-1918) is available at the Public Record Office (F.O. 800/159-91). Three small metal trunks of unsorted papers relating to Lord Bertie are deposited with the Pierpont Morgan Library, 29 East 36th Street, New York.

BESSBOROUGH, 9th E of
Sir Vere Brabazon Ponsonby (1880-1956)

M.P. (Con.) Cheltenham, Jan.-Dec. 1910; Dover, 1913-20. Governor-General, Canada, 1931-35.

The present (10th) Earl of Bessborough, Stansted Park, Rowlands Castle, Hants. PO9 6DX, son of the 9th Earl, has a substantial collection of his father's papers. This is not generally available and requests for access to the collection will be considered on their merits.

BETHELL, Admiral Hon. Sir Alexander Edward (1855-1932)

Naval career from 1869. Assistant Director, Torpedoes, 1903-07. Director, Naval Intelligence, 1909-12. C.-in-C., East Indies, 1912. Commanded Royal Naval War College, 1913-14. Commander, Channel Fleet, 1915. C.-in-C., Plymouth, 1916-18.

Bethell papers are in the care of Mrs Agatha Marsden-Smedley, 31 Draycott Place, London SW3. These are particularly important for the Duff and Jellicoe letters to Sir Alexander Bethell, 1917-18.

BETTS, Air Vice-Marshal Eric Bourne Coulter (1897-1971)

Royal Air Force career.

The Public Record Office has three folders of papers (1916-19) relating to air operations on the Belgian coast (AIR 1/2393/249/1-3). There is also an account of a flight from New York to Cairo during World War II, at the Imperial War Museum.

BEVERIDGE, 1st B
Sir William Henry Beveridge (1879-1963)

Director of Labour Exchanges, 1909-16. Assistant General Secretary, Munitions, 1915-16. 2nd Secretary, later Permanent Secretary, Food, 1916-19. Director, London School of Economics, 1919-37. Master, University College, Oxford, 1937-45. M.P. (Lib.) Berwick-on-Tweed, 1944-45. Chairman of Interdepartmental Committee on Social Insurance and Allied Services, 1941-42.

A substantial collection of Beveridge's papers is preserved at B.L.P.E.S. The papers have been catalogued with the aid of a grant from the Social Science Research Council, and a handlist and catalogue is available. The papers have been catalogued into a number of categories. Categories I and II consist of personal and family papers, and a substantial collection of family, general and personal correspondence. Category III relates to Unemployment and Labour Exchanges, and includes notes, correspondence, papers, lectures, memoranda, Government reports, etc. Category IV covers Beveridge's activities during World War I, and includes memoranda, correspondence, notes, drafts, office minutes, etc., relating to his work at the

Ministry of Munitions (1915-16), the Manpower Distribution Board, Reconstruction, the *History of the Ministry of Munitions*, and the Ministry of Food (1916-19). Category V covers Beveridge's work in the universities, as Director of the London School of Economics, as Vice-Chancellor of the University of London and as Master of University College, Oxford, and again includes a considerable amount of correspondence as well as lecture notes, business papers, memoranda, etc. Category VI relates to Beveridge's political activities. Category VII, 'Other Interests and Activities', brings together material relating to the Health Service and Old Age, New Towns, Population and Fertility, Weather Periodicity and World Government. Category VIII covers Beveridge's works on Government reports: the Royal Commission on the Coal Industry (1925); the Unemployment Statistics Committee (1934-44); the Sub-Committee of the Committee of Imperial Defence on Food Rationing (1936); the Manpower Survey (1940); Fuel Rationing Enquiry (1942); and, most important, the Interdepartmental Committee of 1941-42 which produced the Beveridge Report; and the Broadcasting Committee (1949-50). All these groupings include correspondence, papers, reports, memoranda, etc. Category IX covers Beveridge's published and unpublished works (including lectures and speeches). Category X covers pamphlets and offprints; Category XI 'Visits Abroad'; and Category XII covers a large collection of press cuttings, dating from 1870.

BEVERLEY, Vice-Admiral Sir (William) York La Roche (1895-)

Naval career; served World Wars I and II. Admiral Superintendent, Portsmouth, 1949-51. Director of Dockyards, 1951-54.

According to information received from the Imperial War Museum, it is believed that no papers survive.

BIGGE, Sir Lewis Amherst Selby-, 1st Bt (1860-1951)

Permanent Secretary, Board of Education, 1911-25.

It was not possible to contact the executors of Sir Lewis's son, Sir John Selby-Bigge, Bt.

BIGGS, Vice-Admiral Sir Hilary Worthington (1905-)

Naval career; served World War II. Commanding Officer, H.M.S. *Hero*. Captain (D.), 11th Destroyer Flotilla, Eastern Fleet, 1944-45. Deputy Chief of Naval Personnel (Personal Services), 1953-55. Flag Officer, Home Fleet Training Squadron, 1955-56. C.-in-C., East Indies Station, 1956-58.

The Vice-Admiral has retained a miscellaneous collection of papers, press cuttings, etc. He is also preparing, for the immediate interest of his family, a memoir of his naval career. This will not be made publicly available during the lifetime of the naval personnel Sir Hilary worked with.

BILNEY, Air Vice-Marshal Christopher Neil Hope (1898-)

Served European War, 1914-18; North Sea and Middle East; India, 1925-30; Air Ministry, War of 1939-45. Air Officer in Charge of Administration, Headquarters Maintenance Command, 1949-51. Director-General, Technical Service, Air Ministry, 1951-52. President, Ordnance Board, Ministry of Supply, 1953-54.

A collection of papers mainly relating to World War I is held at the Imperial War Museum. The material includes memoirs and a logbook covering service in the Eastern Mediterranean (1918) and the British Occupation Force on the Caspian Sea (1919). The Museum also holds a series of taped memoirs.

BINGHAM, Major-General Hon. Sir Francis Richard (1863-1935)

Deputy Director of Artillery, War Office, 1913-16. Member of Council, Ministry of Munitions, 1916. Chief of British Section and President of Sub-Commission for Armaments and Material, Military Inter-Allied Commission of Control, Germany, 1919-24. Lieutenant-Governor, Jersey, 1924-29.

Mr Humphrey Bingham states that his father's papers were destroyed during World War II.

BIRCH, Sir Ernest Woodford (1857-1929)

Colonial administrator. Secretary to Government of Perak, 1892-97. British Resident, Negri Sembilan, 1897-1900. Governor and C.-in-C. Labuan and North Borneo, 1901-04. British Resident, Perak, 1904-10.

A collection of papers covering the period 1889-1929 has been deposited in Rhodes House Library. The material includes correspondence, a diary and autobiographical notes.

BIRCH, General Sir James Frederick Noel (1865-1939)

Served European War, 1914-19. Artillery Adviser to C.-in-C., France, 1916-19. Director of Remounts, 1920-21. Director-General, Territorial Army, 1921-23. Master-General of Ordnance, 1923-27.

Lord Rhyl, the General's son, says that he has kept no papers relating to his father's career.

BIRCH, John Henry Stopford (d. 1949)

Minister, Central American Republics, 1933-38.

The family solicitors, Messrs Freshfields, and members of the family with whom they retain contact, know of no papers.

BIRCHALL, Sir Walter Raymond (1888-1968)

Deputy Director-General, Post Office, 1936-45; Director-General, 1946-49.

Mr J. V. R. Birchall, Eveleigh, 37 Essendene Road, Caterham, Surrey, has only a few papers relating to his father. There is an album from 1900 onwards, with press cuttings and one or two letters. The material is mainly of social and family interest.

BIRD, Sir Hugh Stonehewer- (1891-1973)

Agent and Consul, Jedda, 1927. Consul, Casablanca, 1930-36. Consul-General, Addis Ababa, 1937-39. Minister, Saudi Arabia, 1939-43. Consul-General, Morocco (French Zone), 1943-45. Ambassador, Iraq, 1945-48.

Sir Hugh wrote to Miss Elizabeth Monroe of the Middle East Centre at St Antony's College, Oxford, to say that he had no papers.

BIRDWOOD, 1st B
Field-Marshal Sir William Riddell Birdwood, 1st Bt (1865-1951)

Military Secretary to C.-in-C. (Lord Kitchener), South Africa, 1902; India, 1905-09. Secretary, Government of India (Army Department) and Member of the Governor-General's Legislative Council, 1912-14. G.O.C., Australian and New Zealand Army Corps, 1914-18, and Australian Imperial Force, 1915-20. C.-in-C., Army in India,

1925-30. Member of the Executive Council of the Governor-General, and Member of the Council of State of India.

Letters and papers (1888-1917), mainly relating to Birdwood's work with Lord Kitchener, his career in India, and to military administration there, have been deposited at the India Office Library. A few letters and other papers concerned with the activities of the Anzac forces in the Dardanelles and France (1915-17) are available at the Imperial War Museum. Further material is extant at the Australian War Memorial, Canberra, and at the National Army Museum where there are certain diaries, letters and papers relating to India and South Africa.

BIRKS, Major-General Horace Leslie (1897-)

Served European War, 1915-18, and War of 1939-45. Commander, 11th Armoured Brigade, 1941; 10th Armoured Division, 1942.

The Imperial War Museum holds a folder of correspondence with Sir Basil Liddell Hart and Major-General Sir Percy Hobart relating to tank warfare (1916-45).

BLACKBURNE, Sir Kenneth William (1907-)

Colonial Service. Director of Information Service, Colonial Office, 1947-50. Governor, Leeward Islands, 1950-56. Captain-General and Governor-in-Chief, Jamaica, 1957-62; Governor-General, 1962.

The Colonial Records Project found that Sir Kenneth Blackburne has retained many papers. They include weekly descriptive letters to his parents (1930-62); a detailed diary of the 'Arab rebellion' in Palestine (1936-38); the first major development plan produced in Africa (The Gambia), and a massive collection of press cuttings (Jamaica, 1957-62). Sir Kenneth has completed his autobiography and the manuscript remains with his papers. It is expected that the collection will be placed in due course in Rhodes House Library, Oxford.

BLACKETT, Sir Basil Phillott (1882-1935)

Secretary, Indian Finance and Currency Commission, 1913-14; Capital Issues Committee, 1915. Member, Anglo-French Financial Mission to the United States, 1915; National War Savings Committee, 1916. Treasury Representative in United States, 1917-19. Controller of Finance, Treasury, 1919-22. Finance Member, Viceroy's Council, India, 1922-28. Director, Bank of England.

A collection of papers owned by Mrs Brookbank cannot now be traced. Enquiries should be addressed to the National Register of Archives.

BLAKE, Vice-Admiral Sir Geoffrey (1882-1968)

Naval career from 1897; served World War I. Naval Attaché, U.S.A., 1919-21. Director, Royal Naval Staff College, 1926-27. Chief of Staff, Atlantic Fleet, 1927-29. 4th Sea Lord and Chief of Supplies and Transport, 1932-35. Vice-Admiral Commanding Battle Cruiser Squadron, 1936-38. Add. Assistant Chief of Naval Staff, 1940. Flag Officer Liaison, U.S. Navy in Europe, 1942-45.

Many of Vice-Admiral Sir Geoffrey Blake's papers are in the care of the National Maritime Museum. Other family letters and photographs remain with Mr J. P. W. Ehrman, Sloane House, 149 Old Church Street, London SW3 6EB.

BLAKE, Sir Henry Arthur (1840-1918)

Governor, Bahamas, 1884-87; Newfoundland, 1887-88; Jamaica, 1889-97; Hong Kong, 1897-1903; Ceylon, 1903-07.

It was not possible to trace persons mentioned in the Will and Act of Probate.

BLAND, Sir (George) Nevile Maltby (1886-1972)

Foreign Office career from 1911. Minister, Netherlands, 1938-42; Ambassador, 1942-48. Special Ambassador, Malagasy Republic, 1960. Special Representative of Secretary of State for Foreign Affairs, 1960-69.

Sir Nevile stated in 1971 that he had never kept a diary and that such letters as remained were inaccessible.

BLEDISLOE, 1st Vt
Charles Bathurst (1867-1958)

M.P. (Con.) Wilton, 1910-18. Parliamentary Secretary, Food, 1916-17. Parliamentary Secretary, Agriculture, 1924-28. Governor-General, New Zealand, 1930-35.

A collection of papers relating to Vt Bledisloe's career is retained at the family home, Lydney Park, Glos. It includes a box of political and general correspondence, 1900-1950s, covering topics such as Unionist agricultural policy, food supply, Imperial affairs, etc., with letters from a wide range of political contacts; a box of papers and pamphlets on the genealogy of the Bathurst family, and the history of the Lydney area; and smaller boxes containing notes on New Zealand affairs, notes on the military defence of the Gloucester area, 1940, agricultural matters, and personal affairs. Enquiries concerning these records should be directed to the present Vt Bledisloe.

BLOOD, Sir Hilary Rudolph Robert (1893-1967)

Governor, Gambia, 1942-47; Barbados, 1947-49; Mauritius, 1949-54. Constitutional Commissioner.

At Rhodes House Library, Oxford, there is a collection of correspondence, articles and reports, relating to service in Africa, the West Indies, Mauritius and Malta (1942-66).

BLYTHE, Wilfred Lawson (1896-   )

Colonial Service, Malaya. Colonial Secretary, Singapore, 1950-53.

A collection of papers is held at Rhodes House Library, Oxford. The material includes reports on Chinese affairs in Malaya, an account of the Changi internment camp (1942-45) and papers as Colonial Secretary of Singapore.

BODINNAR, Sir John Francis (1895-1958)

Commercial Secretary and Head of Supply Department, Ministry of Food, 1941-45. Commercial Adviser to Ministry of Food, 1946. President, Food Manufacturers Federation, 1947-49.

Lady Bodinnar, who now lives in Spain, states that some unsorted papers kept by her late husband may be among family possessions which are in store in England. A collection of Private Office papers will be included in series M.A.F. 8128 at the Public Record Office.

BOLS, Lieutenant-General Sir Louis Jean (1867-1930)

Chief Administrator, Palestine, 1919-20. Governor, Bermuda, 1927-30.

Major-General E. L. Bols states that he has no papers or diaries of his father's which would be of historical interest. All such material was lost during World War II.

BOND, Wiliam Linskill (1892-1950)

Consular Service. Agent and Consul, Jedda, 1929-30. Counsellor and Consul General, Cairo, 1943-48. Consul General, Marseilles, 1948-50.

The Middle East Centre at St Antony's College, Oxford, has found no papers.

BONHAM, Sir George Francis, 2nd Bt (1847-1927)

Minister, Serbia, 1900-03; Switzerland, 1905-09.

Major Sir A. L. T. Bonham, Bt, knows of no papers relating to his grandfather.

BOOTHBY, Sir Brooke, 11th Bt (1856-1913)

Counsellor, Vienna, 1905-07. Minister, Chile, 1907-13.

The Boothby family records are held at the Glamorgan County Record Office and with Sir Hugo Boothby, Bt, at Fonmon Castle, Barry, South Glamorgan. Some papers relate to Sir Brooke Boothby, and these include family correspondence, and a few business letters and letters arising from his career.

BOOTHMAN, Air Chief Marshal Sir John Nelson (1901-1957)

Assistant Chief of Air Staff, 1945-48. Air Officer Commanding, Iraq, 1948-50. Controller of Supplies (Air), Ministry of Supply, and Member of Air Council, 1950-53. Air Officer C.-in-C., Coastal Command, 1953-56.

Efforts to trace persons mentioned in the Will and Act of Probate were not successful.

BORASTON, Lieutenant-Colonel John Herbert (1885-1969)

Served European War, 1914-18. Private Secretary to Field-Marshal Haig, C.-in-C., France, 1919, and Great Britain, 1919-20.

The Imperial War Museum holds papers relating to Boraston's service with 8th Division, including a war diary of 8th Division to December 1915, and his service with G.H.Q. (1918) and then as Private Secretary to Haig, including correspondence with Haig (1919-20).

BORTON, Air Vice-Marshal Amyas Eden (1886-1969)

Served European War, 1914-18. Royal Air Force career.

A collection of papers at the Public Record Office consists of three folders of official and semi-official correspondence, memoranda and reports (1918-26). Some of the material refers to Palestine, and some to flights to India.

BOSANQUET, Captain Henry Theodore Augustus (1870-1959)

Naval career from 1883; served World War I. Secretary, Marine Society, 1898-1917. Admiralty War Staff, 1939-45.

A collection of papers is available at the National Maritime Museum, and includes notes, charts, etc., on his naval career, correspondence, notes and articles on the Marine Society, and cuttings albums, 1879-1955.

BOSWALL, Sir William Evelyn Houstoun- (1892-1960)

Acting Representative (H.M. Government), South Africa, 1930. Chargé d'Affaires, Budapest, 1932, 1933, 1934; Oslo, 1937, 1938; Baghdad, 1938, 1939, 1940. British Political Representative (Minister), Bulgaria, 1944-46. Minister, Lebanon, 1947-51.

Some press cuttings, photographs and a few letters (mainly of a formal nature) remain with Mrs C. R. Owen (*née* Houstoun-Boswall), c/o Coutts & Co., 1 Cadogan Place, London SW1.

BOTTOMLEY, Sir Cecil (1878-1954)

Assistant Under-Secretary, Colonial Office, 1927-38. Senior Crown Agent, Colonies, 1938-43.

Mr J. R. A. Bottomley, Sir Cecil's son, states that none of his father's papers relating to his Colonial Office career appear to survive in private hands.

BOTTOMLEY, Air Chief Marshal Sir Norman Howard (1891-1970)

Served European War, 1914-18, Assistant Chief of Air Staff (Operations), 1942-43. Deputy Chief of Air Staff, 1941, 1943-45. Air Officer C.-in-C., Bomber Command, 1945-47. Inspector-General, R.A.F., 1947-48.

The Royal Air Force Museum has a series of records, including subject files, speeches and publications, covering the period 1921-61. Subject matter includes India (1935-37), Bomber Command (1942-45), the British Bombing Survey Unit (1947) and the Manpower Economy Committee (1946-49).

BOURNE, Sir Frederick Chalmers (1891-   )

Indian Civil Service from 1920. Governor, Central Provinces and Berar, 1946-47; East Bengal, 1947-50.

Sir Frederick has kept some news cuttings and other papers stuck into scrapbooks.

BOVENSCHEN, Sir Frederick Carl (1884-   )

Deputy Under-Secretary, War Office, 1936-42. Joint Permanent Under-Secretary, War Office, 1942-45.

Sir F. C. Bovenschen states that he kept no records when he left the War Office.

BOWER, Sir Edmund Ernest Nott- (1853-1933)

Chairman, Board of Inland Revenue, 1914-18.

Sir Guy Nott-Bower, Sir Edmund's nephew, knows of no papers.

BOWER, Sir Graham John (1848-1933)

Imperial Secretary to High Commissioner, South Africa, 1884-97. Colonial Secretary, Mauritius, 1898-1910.

The papers (1888-1933) of Sir Graham and Lady Bower are held at the South African Library. A selection of letters from this collection is on microfilm at Rhodes House Library, Oxford, together with a series of further correspondence

(1898-1951), including photographs, reminiscences of the Jameson Raid by Maude L. Bower, and letters exchanged with Sir M. Ommaney (1905-06). Some five letters to A. P. Newton, about events in the Transvaal, 1894-96, are in the Royal Commonwealth Society Library.

BOWER, Lieutenant-General Sir Roger Herbert (1903-   )

Served World War II, 1939-45 (North-West Europe, Norway, Palestine, etc.). Commander, Hamburg District, 1948-49. Director, Land/Air Warfare, War Office, 1950-51. Director of Military Training and Director of Land/Air Warfare, 1951-57. Commander, East Anglian District, 1952-55. Chief of Staff, Allied Forces Northern Europe, 1955-56. G.O.C. and Director of Operations, Malaya, 1956-57. C.-in-C., Middle East Land Forces, 1958-60.

A collection of papers is housed at the Imperial War Museum. The collection is composed of official briefs and reports, with statistics, maps and similar related information, on operations in Holland, Norway, Palestine and Malaya, in which Bower was involved. Access to the papers is restricted under the Thirty-Year Rule. Sir Roger retains a small file of a few intelligence reports and propaganda leaflets.

BOWER, Sir (William) Guy Nott- (1890-   )

Under-Secretary, Mines, 1942. Deputy Secretary, Fuel and Power, 1942-48. Director of Public Relations, National Coal Board, 1948-54.

Sir Guy Nott-Bower has kept no papers.

BOWHILL, Air Chief Marshal Sir Frederick William (1880-1960)

Director of Organisation and Staff Duties, Air Ministry, 1929-31. Air Officer Commanding Fighting Area, R.A.F. Uxbridge, 1931-33; Transport Command, 1943-45. Air Member for Personnel, 1933-37. Air Officer C.-in-C., Coastal Command, 1937-41. Chief Aeronautical Adviser, Ministry of Civil Aviation, 1946-57.

Mr L. V. Pearkes, the solicitor who acted as Sir Frederick's executor, knows of no papers and has lost contact with members of the family. Relevant papers may, however, be found in the collection of Air Vice-Marshal E. J. Kingston-McCloughry at the Imperial War Museum.

BOWKER, Sir (Reginald) James (1901-   )

Minister, Cairo, 1945-47. High Commissioner, Burma, 1948-50. Assistant Under-Secretary, Foreign Office, 1950-53. Ambassador, Turkey, 1954-58; Austria, 1958-61.

Sir James Bowker has retained very few papers and did not keep a diary.

BOWMAN, Humphrey Ernest (1879-1965)

In charge of education, Iraq and then Palestine. Special Service under Foreign Office, 1941-45.

The Bowman papers comprise diaries ranging from 1904 to 1949 and documents relating to his thesis on the Wall of Jerusalem (1930) and evidence to the Peel Commission (1937), as well as personal papers relating to his career: letters to parents, 1904-05; correspondence regarding his appointment as Director of Education, Mesopotamia, 1917-20; journey to England escorting Sheikh Feisal, 1919; secondment to Government of Palestine, 1920; correspondence with the High

Commissioner, Palestine, 1934-36; correspondence (personal) on the Egyptian Government's pension, etc., 1922-25; proposed service in Egypt; lectures and book reviews, 1939-49; correspondence, 1918, about a visit to Jerusalem; lecture and papers on General Gordon; report on education in Palestine. The papers are at the Middle East Centre, St Antony's College, Oxford.

BOYD, Sir Alexander William Keown- (1884-1954)

Private Secretary (1917-19) and Oriental Secretary (1919-22) to High Commissioner, Egypt. Served Egyptian Government, 1922-37.

Copies of papers on Keown-Boyd's service in Egypt and the Sudan are available at the Middle East Centre, St Antony's College, Oxford.

BOYLE, Sir Courtenay Edmund (1845-1901)

Permanent Secretary, Board of Trade, 1893-1901.

Dr R. Davidson, University of Edinburgh, who attempted to locate records for his research, has failed to trace any papers left by Sir Courtenay Boyle.

BOYLE, Henry (Harry) (1863-1937)

Consul and Oriental Secretary, Cairo, 1899-1909. Consul-General, Berlin, 1909-14.

Boyle's correspondence with his wife and mother is deposited at St Antony's College, Oxford. Material on the Middle East is kept at the Middle East Centre, and other papers are in the College Library.
  The Middle East papers are mostly letters from Turkey and Egypt, 1884-1910, with copies of miscellaneous letters on Lord Cromer's retirement and drafts of dispatches to Sir Edward Grey. The correspondence goes on to 1936 and takes in letters to his wife while on special mission in Egypt, 1921. The Berlin papers are unsorted and consist almost entirely of personal and family letters of no political interest. One folder contains some interesting papers on the work of the Berlin consulate and its staff problems.

BRABOURNE, 5th B
Sir Michael Herbert Rudolph Knatchbull, 14th Bt (1895-1939)

M.P. (Con.) Ashford, 1931-33. Governor, Bombay, 1933-37; Bengal, 1937-39. Acting Viceroy of India, 1938.

The Knatchbull family archives are deposited on loan at the Kent Archives Office. This collection includes few papers relating to the 5th Lord Brabourne apart from some letters concerning his candidature at Ashford, his election success and his succession to the barony. Further papers are held by the India Office Library. This large collection includes papers and correspondence on Bombay and Bengal, and volumes of bound correspondence while Lord Brabourne was acting as Viceroy, files, bundles of miscellaneous papers, engagement books and copies of speeches. Principal correspondents include successive Viceroys and Secretaries of State for India, Lord Erskine, the 11th Earl of Scarbrough, Vt Waverley and R. A. Butler.

BRACKENBURY, General Sir Henry (1837-1914)

Director of Military Intelligence, 1886-91. Member of Council of Viceroy of India, 1891-96. President, Ordnance Committee, 1896-99. Director-General of Ordnance, War Office, 1899-1904.

A collection of papers survives at the Royal Artillery Museum, Woolwich. A further file of printed and manuscript notes, entitled 'Special Cases Collected', 1891-97, can be found at the India Office Library.

BRADBURY, 1st B
Sir John Swanwick Bradbury (1872-1950)

Joint Permanent Secretary, Treasury, 1913-19. Principal British Delegate to Reparation Commission, Paris, 1919-25. Chairman, National Food Council, 1925-29; Bankers' Clearing House Committee, and President, British Bankers' Association, 1929-30 and 1935-36.

The Bradbury Papers are available at the Public Record Office (T.170). The collection of some 144 folders includes working papers, memoranda and notes used by Bradbury at the Treasury. Topics covered include financial dealings with the United States, taxation, unemployment, etc.

BRADE, Sir Reginald Herbert (1864-1933)

Secretary, War Office, 1914-20.

Lady Brade was the sole executrix, and preliminary efforts to trace her were not successful.

BRADFIELD, Lieutenant-General Sir Ernest W. C. (1880-1963)

Served India; European War, 1914-18; Mesopotamia. Surgeon-General, Bombay, 1935-37. Medical Adviser to Secretary of State and President of Medical Board, India Office, 1939-46.

Diaries (1899-1944) relating to his career in the Indian Medical Service are housed at the National Army Museum, together with miscellaneous material, including a bound typescript of Service memoirs.

BRADFORD, Admiral Sir Edward Eden (1858-1935)

Naval service from 1872. Commanded Training Squadron, 1911-14. Rear-Admiral, Home Fleet, 1909-11. Commanded 3rd Battle Squadron, 1914-16.

Enquiries regarding papers should be directed to the Keeper of Documents, National Maritime Museum.

BRAITHWAITE, General Sir Walter Pipon (1865-1945)

Director, Staff Duties, War Office, 1914-15. Chief of General Staff, Mediterranean Expeditionary Force, 1915. G.O.C.-in-C., Western Command, India, 1920-23; Scottish Command, 1923-26; Eastern Command, 1926-27. Adjutant-General, 1927-31.

The trustees of Sir W. P. Braithwaite's widow state that no papers survive.

BRAITHWAITE, William John (1875-1938)

Assistant Secretary, Inland Revenue, 1910-12. Secretary, National Health Insurance Joint Committee, 1912. Commissioner for Special Purposes of Income Tax, 1913.

The manuscript and a typescript copy of Braithwaite's *Lloyd George's Ambulance Wagon*, together with papers collected during the preparation and operation of the Insurance Act (1911), are held at B.L.P.E.S.

BRAMLEY, Lieutenant-Colonel P. B.

Director of Public Security, Palestine.

The Library of the Royal Commonwealth Society holds Bramley's correspondence with British Government departments on the problems of security in Palestine and the Middle East, where he considered there was a danger of Russian agents working for political disruption (1923-25).

BRANCKER, Air Vice-Marshal Sir William Sefton (1877-1930)

Served European War, 1914-18. Director of Air Organisation, 1916-17. Controller-General of Equipment and Master-General of Personnel (Air Council), 1918. Director of Civil Aviation, Air Ministry, 1922-30.

The Imperial War Museum has a small collection of miscellaneous reports on the early organisation of supply and recruitment to the Royal Flying Corps (1914-17). Other papers survive at the Royal Air Force Museum.

BRAND, 1st B
Robert Henry Brand (1878-1963)

Served South Africa, 1902-09. Deputy Chairman, British Mission in Washington, 1917-18. Financial Adviser to Lord Robert Cecil, Paris, 1919; to German Government, 1922. Financial Representative of South Africa, Genoa Conference, 1922. Member of Macmillan Committee on Finance and Industry, 1930-31. Head of British Food Mission, Washington, 1941-44. Treasury Representative in Washington, 1944-46. Chairman, British Supply Council in North America, 1942, 1945-46. United Kingdom Delegate, Bretton Woods and Savannah Conferences.

Lord Brand's papers remain with Sir Edward and Lady Ford (Lord Brand's daughter), at Eydon Hall, Eydon, near Daventry, Northants NN11 6QE. The papers have been sorted and catalogued, and are assembled in some 180 box files. The collection covers the whole of Lord Brand's career. The section concerning Brand's relations with Sir William Flavelle and the Canadian Munitions Board in World War I has been microfilmed for the Public Archives of Canada.

BRASS, Sir Leslie Stuart (1891-1958)

Civil Service career. Legal Adviser, Home Office, 1947-56.

The Public Record Office has a collection of papers (HO 189) for the period 1935-39 relating to Brass's work at the Home Office, including the International Conference (1937) and the League of Nations Committee on the suppression of terrorism, and the Criminal Justice Bill of 1938.

BRICKELL, Daniel Francis Horseman (1893-1967)

Minister, Paraguay, 1940-43; Salvador, 1949-50. Consul General, Detroit, 1945-49, Ahwaz, 1950, and Philadelphia, 1951-53.

Brickell's widow is believed to live in Dublin, but no contact was secured.

BRIDGE, Admiral Sir (Arthur) Robin Moore (1894-1971)

Naval career. Director, Naval Air Divisions, Admiralty, 1941-43. Commander, Northern Naval Air Stations, 1944-45. Flag Officer (Air), East Indies, 1945-47. Flag Officer Commanding Reserve Fleets, 1948-50.

According to information supplied to the Imperial War Museum, Admiral Sir Robin Bridge kept no papers.

BRIDGE, Admiral Sir Cyprian Arthur George (1877-1924)

Director, Admiralty Intelligence Department, 1889-94. C.-in-C., Australian Station, 1895-98; China Station, 1901-04.

At the National Maritime Museum are letter books, journals and letters received, relating mainly to service in Australia and China.

BRIDGEMAN, 2nd Vt
Major-General Robert Clive Bridgeman (1896-   )

Served European War, 1915-18, and War of 1939-45. Deputy Director, Home Guard, 1941. Director-General, Home Guard and Territorial Army, 1941-44. Deputy Adjutant-General, 1944-45.

A collection of papers is housed at the Liddell Hart Centre for Military Archives. The papers are mainly concerned with the British Expeditionary Force in France and Belgium (1939-40), including Lord Gort's dispatches with maps and comments thereon. Other material relates to the 1928 Staff College study of the Italian campaign (1915), and armoured support for the infantry in the 7th Infantry Brigade (1933-34). Some papers by Major-General G. M. Lindsay are included in the collection. Viscount Bridgeman retains a further collection of notes relating to service with the 3rd Battalion, Rifle Brigade, in World War I and to the period 1939-40.

BRIDGEMAN, Admiral Sir Francis Charles Bridgeman- (1848-1929)

Naval career from 1862. C.-in-C., Home Fleet, 1907-09, 1911. 1st Sea Lord, 1911-12.

It is believed that no papers survive, although the papers of Sir Julian S. Corbett contain some Bridgeman letters.

BRIDGES, 1st B
Sir Edward Bridges (1892-1969)

Secretary to the Cabinet, 1938-46. Permanent Secretary, Treasury, 1945-56.

The present (2nd) Lord Bridges states that his father kept no diaries or other collections of official documents, and that the only scanty records which he has might be described as occasional personal mementoes. There are 22 files (1942-47) at the Cabinet Office. They cover India, Palestine, commercial and colonial policy, notes on the dissolution of the war and 'caretaker' governments.

BRIDGES, Lieutenant-General Sir George Tom Molesworth (1871-1939)

Served South Africa, 1899-1901; European War, 1914-18. Military Member, British Mission to the United States of America, 1917. Head of British War Mission in the United States, 1918. Head of British Mission, Allied Armies of the Orient, 1918-20. Governor, South Australia, 1922-27.

According to information received by the Liddell Hart Centre for Military Archives, the papers were destroyed during World War II.

BRISTOL, 5th M of
Lord Herbert Arthur Robert Hervey (1870-1960)

Consul-General, Madrid, 1914. Minister, Colombia, 1919-23. Minister and Special Envoy Extraordinary, Peru and Ecuador, 1923-29. Head of the South American

Diplomatic Station and Special Adviser on South American Affairs to the Foreign Office.

The Hervey family archive has been deposited with the Bury St Edmunds and West Suffolk Record Office. However, diaries, photographs and press cuttings of the 5th Marquess of Bristol, together with original documents of appointment from King George V, remain with the present Marquess. London residence: 15 Chapel Street, Belgrave Square, London SW1; seat: Ickworth, Bury St Edmunds, Suffolk.

BROAD, Lieutenant-General Sir Charles Noel Frank (1882-   )

Served South Africa, 1902; European War, 1914-18. G.O.C.-in-C., Aldershot Command, 1939-40; Eastern Army India, 1940-42.

The papers have been destroyed, but certain autobiographical fragments survive at the Liddell Hart Centre for Military Archives.

BROAD, Philip (1903-1966)

Foreign Service. Political Adviser to Allied Force Headquarters, Italy, 1943; Trieste, 1951-54. Consul-General, Istanbul, 1955-60.

Messrs Midland Bank Trust Company Ltd, Sheffield, have made enquiries of various members of the family regarding papers, but they have nothing to report.

BROMHEAD, Lieutenant-Colonel Alfred Claude (1876-1963)

Member, Special Mission to Russian Armies, 1916; Riga, Caucasus, Romania and Asia Minor, 1916-17. Commander, British Special Mission to Italian Armies, 1918-19. First Chairman, Gaumont British Film Corporation. Hon. Adviser to Film Division, Ministry of Information, 1939-45.

Bromhead's diaries (1916-17) survive at the University of London Library. Copies are also held at the Imperial War Museum.

BROOKE, Sir Charles Vyner (1874-1963)

Rajah of Sarawak, 1917-46.

There is a collection of papers at Rhodes House Library, Oxford. The material consists of letters to G. C. Gillan, Treasurer of Sarawak (1906-30); to C. P. Lowe (1922-35); and to others.

BROOKE, Sir John Reeve (1880-1937)

Secretary, Ministry of Transport, 1923-27; Central Electricity Board, 1927-29.

No members of the family, nor the solicitors, could be traced. Sir W. R. M. Lamb, one-time Secretary of the Royal Academy of Arts, was named one of the executors, but efforts to contact his widow were unsuccessful.

BROWETT, Sir Leonard (1884-1959)

Deputy Director, later Director, Ship Requisitioning, Shipping, 1917. Assistant Secretary, Inland Revenue, 1919-30. Principal Assistant Secretary, Board of Trade, 1932-35. Deputy, Chief Industrial Adviser, 1935-37. Secretary, Transport, 1937-41. Secretary-General, Army Staff/Supply, Mission to Washington, 1942-44.

A quantity of Sir Leonard's papers remains with his niece, Mrs G. I. G. Miller, 18 Hereward Avenue, Purley, Surrey CR2 2NN. They comprise press cuttings, articles by and about Sir Leonard, photographs and letters from a number of eminent people.

BROWN, Vice-Admiral Sir Harold Arthur (1878-1968)

Engineer-in-Chief of the Fleet, Admiralty, 1932-36. Director-General, Munitions Production, Army Council, War Office, 1936-39. Director-General, Munitions Production, Ministry of Supply 1939-41. Controller-General, Munitions Production, 1941-42. Senior Supply Officer and Chairman of Armament Development Board, 1942-46. Chairman, Fuel Research Board, 1947-50.

A few papers, 1894-1959, largely relating to Sir Harold Brown's naval activities, are available at the National Maritime Museum. Other papers, together with the papers of Sir George Turner, have been given to the Liddell Hart Centre for Military Archives, and the remainder of the collection will go there in due course.

BROWN, Sir Stuart Kelson (1885-1952)

Deputy Under-Secretary, India Office, 1940-42.

Papers (1917-33) relating to Brown's appointments as Joint Secretary in the Military Department (1924-34) and when attached to the Prime Minister for the Indian Round Table Conference (1930-31) survive at the India Office Library.

BROWN, Sir William Barrowclough (1893-1947)

Permanent Secretary, Board of Trade, 1937-40. Acting Secretary, Supply, 1940-42. Secretary, Petroleum Division, Fuel and Power, 1942-43; Home Security, 1943-45. Permanent Under-Secretary, Air, 1945-47.

Mr T. Swan, one of the executors, knows of no papers and has lost contact with members of the family.

BROWNE, Sir Granville St John Orde- (1883-1947)

Colonial Service, East Africa, etc. Substantive Member, Committee of Experts on Native Labour, International Labour Organisation, 1934-37. Adviser on Colonial Labour, Colonial Office, 1938-47.

Certain papers survive at Rhodes House Library, Oxford.

BROWNING, Lieutenant-General Sir Frederick Arthur Montague (1896-1965)

Served European War, 1914-18, and War of 1939-45. Chief of Staff, South East Asia Command, 1944-46. Military Secretary, War Office, 1946-48.

Lady Browning states that her husband left no papers.

BROWNING, Admiral Sir Montague Edward (1863-1947)

Naval career from 1876. Chief of Staff, Channel Fleet, 1908-09. C.-in-C., North America and West Indies, 1916-17. Commanding 4th Battle Squadron, Grand Fleet, 1918. President, Allied Naval Armistice Commission, 1918-19. 2nd Sea Lord, 1919-20. C.-in-C., Devonport, 1920-23.

Messrs Royal Exchange Assurance, executors to the estate, know of no papers and have lost contact with members of the family.

BROWNJOHN, General Sir Nevil Charles Dowell (1897-1973)

Served European War, 1916-18, and War of 1939-45. Deputy Military Governor,

Control Commission for Germany (British Element), 1947-49. Vice Quartermaster-General, War Office, 1949-50. Vice Chief of Imperial General Staff, 1950-52. Chief Staff Officer, Ministry of Defence, 1952-55. Quartermaster-General, 1956-58.

General Sir Nevil Brownjohn informed the Liddell Hart Centre for Military Archives that he had kept no papers.

BRUCE, Lieutenant-Colonel Charles Edward (1876-1950)

Resident, Waziristan, 1923-31.

An assortment of papers relating to the affairs and peoples of Waziristan, lecture notes, drafts of articles, maps and photographs, is available at the India Office Library. The collection also includes Bruce's diaries (1928 and 1930) and some papers amassed by his father, R. I. Bruce.

BRUTON, Charles Lamb (1890-1969)

Colonial Service. Commissioner, East African Refugee Administration, 1942-47.

Rhodes House Library, Oxford, has a collection of memoirs, with correspondence and letters (1937-68), relating to East Africa.

BRYCE, 1st Vt
James Bryce (1838-1922)

M.P. (Lib.) Tower Hamlets, 1880-85; Aberdeen South, 1885-1906. Parliamentary Under-Secretary, Foreign Affairs, 1886. Chancellor of the Duchy of Lancaster, 1892-94. President, Board of Trade, 1894-95. Chief Secretary, Ireland, 1905-07. Ambassador, United States, 1907-13.

Lord Bryce left a mass of papers relating to his career. The Bodleian Library, Oxford, has acquired certain parts of the collection. They have been listed, but are not fully catalogued and they remain in separate series. The American material is divided from the general English papers, and includes correspondence relating to the United States, and embassy papers. The other material covers political papers, records collected whilst in government office, pamphlets, photographs, and a mass of correspondence arranged in different series. Other papers and correspondence (1904-21) are available at the Public Record Office (F.O. 800/331-5), and papers relating to Irish affairs are held by the National Library of Ireland. For further details, readers should consult Hazlehurst and Woodland, op. cit., pp.21-2.

BUCHANAN, George (1890-1955)

M.P. (Lab.) Glasgow Gorbals, 1922-48. Joint Parliamentary Under-Secretary, Scotland, 1945-47. Minister of Pensions, 1947-48. Chairman, National Assistance Board, 1948-53.

Hazlehurst and Woodland, op. cit., p.22, were unable to find any surviving papers.

BUCHANAN, Sir George William (1854-1924)

Minister, Bulgaria, 1903-08; Netherlands, 1908-10. Ambassador, Russia, 1910-18; Italy, 1919-21.

Sir Charles Buchanan, Bt, states that he received some photographs and obituary notices after the death of Sir George's daughter, Mrs Meriel Knowling, but there were no other papers. Miss Buchanan, herself the author of several books, mentioned that her father had destroyed his remaining papers after completion of his memoir *My Mission to Russia* (1923). For this book, Sir George was helped by

Sir Edmund Gosse (1849-1928), and some 68 letters from Sir George survive in the Gosse collection at the Brotherton Library, Leeds.

BUCHER, General Sir Roy (1895-)

Served European War, 1914-18; India; Iraq. G.O.C., Bengal and Assam, 1946. G.O. C.-in-C., Eastern Command, 1946-47. Chief of Staff, India, 1947. C.-in-C., Army of India, 1948-49.

Sir Roy Bucher has kept a good many papers concerning the period as C.-in-C. of the Indian Army. Copies are with the Mountbatten archives and with the Nehru Memorial Library, Teen Murti House, New Delhi, India.

BULLARD, Sir Reader William (1885-)

Levant Consular Service after 1906. Military Governor, Baghdad, 1920. Minister, Saudi Arabia, 1936-39; Iran, 1939-44. Ambassador, Iran, 1944-46.

Sir Reader Bullard never kept a diary and has retained no papers.

BULLER, General Sir Redvers Henry (1839-1908)

Quartermaster-General, 1887. Under-Secretary, Ireland, 1887. Adjutant-General 1890-97. G.O.C., Natal, 1899-1900.

Some private papers survive at the Public Record Office (W.O. 132/25-6). The collection consists of official and semi-official correspondence, copies and lists of dispatches and telegrams sent and received, and copies of reports. The material relates to Zululand (1877-79), Ireland (1886-87) and South Africa (1899-1900).

BULLOCK, Sir Christopher Llewellyn (1891-1972)

Principal Private Secretary to successive Secretaries of State for Air, 1919, 1923-30. Permanent Secretary, Air Ministry, 1931-36.

A Private Office collection is available at the Public Record Office (AIR 19). The material covers the period 1917-45 and includes papers on relations with the Navy, the Geddes Committee on national expenditure, the Colwyn Committee on defence expenditure, civil aviation, and special quarterly reports of the Aeronautical Research Committee.

The Air Historical Branch of the Ministry of Defence holds a large collection of private papers, including photographs, notebooks used on flying trips abroad, maps and miscellaneous correspondence. This material is eventually to be transferred to the Imperial War Museum.

Other private papers remain with Sir Christopher's son, Mr R. H. W. Bullock, 17 Deodar Road, London SW15 2NP. Most of these papers remain confidential.

BURDETT, Scott Langshaw (1897-1961)

China Consular Service, after 1920. Consul-general, Tsingtao and Mukden, 1946-47; Tientsin, 1947-50; Shanghai, 1950-52.

Mrs S. L. Burdett says that her late husband kept no papers.

BURDON, Major Sir John Alder (1866-1933)

Colonial Service. Administrator, St Kitts and Nevis, 1915-25. Governor, British Honduras, 1925-31.

Rhodes House Library, Oxford, holds a series of letters (1902) relating to the slave trade, and an album of photographs and cuttings about the Niger campaign (1897) and service with the Coronation contingent of West African troops.

BURET, Captain Theobald John Claud Purcell- (1879-1974)

Commodore, Royal Mail Fleet, 1939-42 (active service in South American and Far Eastern waters), and lecturer with the Ministry of Information.

Diaries (1939-50) including press cuttings and photographs, and copies of Ministry of Information lectures, are available at the National Maritime Museum.

BURGIS, Lawrence Franklin (1892-1972)

Private Secretary to Viscount Esher, 1909-13. Assistant Secretary, War Cabinet, 1918, 1939-45. Military Assistant Secretary, Committee of Imperial Defence, 1919-21. Assistant Secretary, Cabinet Office.

A copy of Burgis's unpublished memoirs is held at Churchill College, Cambridge. This remains closed to researchers.

BURNETT, Air Chief Marshal Sir Charles Stuart (1882-1945)

Served South African War, 1900-01; European War, 1914-18. Director of Operations and Intelligence, Air Ministry, and Deputy Chief of Air Staff, 1931-33. Air Officer Commanding, Iraq Command, 1933-35; Training Command, 1936-39. Inspector-General, R.A.F., 1939-40. Chief of Air Staff, Royal Australian Air Force, 1940-42.

Mrs Sybil-Jean Swann, Heathbank, Cambus o'May, Ballater, Aberdeenshire, has a few papers left by her father. There is a diary kept when in Nigeria, and a few letters. Further papers may survive with other members of the family.

BURNEY, Admiral of the Fleet Sir Cecil, 1st Bt (1858-1929)

Naval career; served World War I, Commanding 1st Battle Squadron, and 2nd-in-Command, Grand Fleet, 1914-16. 2nd Sea Lord, 1916-17. C.-in-C., Scotland, 1917; Portsmouth, 1919-20.

Sir Cecil Burney, Bt, 5 Lyall Street, London SW1, has certain papers in his care, while others remain with his mother in Bermuda.

BURNS, Sir Alan Cuthbert (1887-   )

Governor, British Honduras, 1934-40. Assistant Under-Secretary, Colonial Office, 1940-41. Governor, Gold Coast, 1941-47 (and Acting Governor, Nigeria, 1942). Permanent United Kingdom Representative, United Nations Trusteeship Council, 1947-56.

According to information given to the Colonial Records Project, Sir Alan has no papers apart from a rough diary of the 1914-15 Cameroons campaign.

BURROUGH, Admiral Sir Harold Martin (1888-   )

Naval career; served World War II, with commands at Gibraltar, Mediterranean Approaches, etc. Assistant Chief of Naval Staff, 1939-40. Allied Naval C.-in-C., Expeditionary Force, 1945. British Naval C.-in-C., Germany, 1945-46. C.-in-C., The Nore, 1946-48.

A microfilm of papers, 1916-46, is available at the Imperial War Museum. The material relates to the Battle of Jutland, relief work in northern Spain during the

Civil War, the Vaagso Raid, the convoys to Russia and Malta, and the surrender and occupation of Germany after World War II. The collection also includes copies of speeches and unpublished articles.

BURROWS, Lieutenant-General Montagu Brocas (1894-1967)

Served European War, 1914-18; North Russia Expeditionary Force, 1918-19. General Staff, War Office, 1935-38. Military Attaché, Rome, Budapest and Tirana, 1938-40. Head of British Military Mission, Soviet Union, 1944. G.O.C.-in-C., West Africa, 1945-46.

The Liddell Hart Centre for Military Archives has been informed that there are no surviving private papers.

BUTLER, Sir Frederick George Augustus (1873-1961)

Deputy Comptroller-General, Overseas Trade, 1917-22. Finance Officer, Foreign Office, 1922-38; Assistant Under-Secretary, 1933-38.

Miss Margot Butler has no papers relating to her father's career.

BUTLER, Sir Nevile Montagu (1893-1973)

Private Secretary to Prime Minister, 1930-35. Counsellor, Tehran, 1936-39; Berne, 1939; Washington, 1940. Minister, Washington, 1940-41. Head of North American Department, Foreign Office, 1941-44; Assistant Under-Secretary, 1944-47. Ambassador, Brazil, 1947-51; Netherlands, 1952-54.

A small collection has been passed by Lady Butler to the Public Record Office. The papers include a couple of letters from Arthur Ponsonby, M.P., about the Zinoviev letter (1924), a record of a private talk with Lord Robert Cecil (1928), papers dealing with disarmament (1925-28), one or two papers about the Middle East (1935), and a collection of newspaper reports and photographs relating to the period in Washington (1940-41), at the San Francisco Conference (1945), in Rio de Janeiro and at The Hague. Papers dating from the years when Butler was Private Secretary to the Prime Minister, J. R. MacDonald (1929-35), are to join the MacDonald Collection at the Public Record Office.

A Private Office collection (1945-47) in ten bundles of files will be made available at the Public Record Office.

BUTLER, Lieutenant-General Sir Richard Harte Keatinge (1870-1935)

Served South Africa, 1899-1902; European War, 1914-18. Deputy Chief of General Staff, 1916-18. G.O.C.-in-C., Western Command, 1924-28.

The Imperial War Museum has two boxes of papers relating to Butler's service as Brigade Commander (1914-15) and later as Deputy Chief of the General Staff, B.E.F. (1916-18), on the Western Front.

BUTLER, Sir Spencer Harcourt (1869-1938)

Foreign Secretary, Government of India; Lieutenant-Governor, Burma, 1915-17; Agra and Oudh, 1918. Governor, Agra and Oudh, 1921-23; Burma, 1923-27.

The papers deposited at the India Office Library contain a very large number of letters from Butler, mostly kept by his family and close friends, with a few groups of official papers and letters sent to Butler. Some of this correspondence is arranged chronologically by subject. There is also an assortment of speeches, notebooks and printed reports. A further collection of letters to Mrs Joan Oglander (1910-27) can be found in the Isle of Wight Record Office.

BUTLER, Major General Stephen Seymour (1880-1964)

Military career from 1897, South Africa; Egyptian Army; European War. Head of Naval Intelligence, Constantinople, 1919-20. Military Attaché, Bucharest, 1923-26. Served India; Royal West African Frontier Force; Kaid Sudan Defence Force. G.O.C., 48th Division Territorial Army, 1935-39. Head of Military Mission to Turkey, 1939-40; Ethiopia, 1941-43.

The Sudan Archive at Durham University has Butler's letters to his family, 1909-15; a 1911 account of a camel corps patrol; a Sudan Intelligence journal, 1911-12; travel diaries; and a typescript memoir of the Egyptian Army, 1909-15; and photographs.

BUXTON, 1st E
Sir Sydney Charles Buxton (1853-1934)

M.P. (Lib.) Peterborough, 1883-85; Poplar, 1886-1914. Under-Secretary of State, Colonial Office, 1892-95. Postmaster-General, 1905-10. President, Board of Trade, 1910-14. High Commissioner and Governor-General, South Africa, 1914-20.

A collection of papers survives in the care of Lord Buxton's granddaughter, Mrs E. Clay, Newtimber Place, Hassocks, Sussex. A full description of these papers, including those relating to Buxton's term in South Africa, is given by Hazlehurst and Woodland, op. cit., pp.26-7.

BYATT, Sir Horace Archer (1875-1933)

Lieutenant-Governor and Chief Secretary, Malta, 1914-16. Governor, Tanganyika, 1920-24 (and Administrator, 1916-20); Trinidad, 1924-29.

A diary (1900-09, 1916-29) survives with the family. Copies of part of the diary and further information about these papers are available at Rhodes House Library, Oxford.

BYNG OF VIMY, 1st Vt
Field-Marshal Julian Hedworth George Byng (1862-1935)

G.O.C., Egypt, 1912-14. Commander, 3rd Army, France, 1917-19. Governor-General, Canada, 1921-26. Commissioner, Metropolitan Police, 1928-31.

Members of the family could not be contacted. According to information available at the Imperial War Museum, the papers of Viscount Byng and his wife were destroyed to comply with instructions in their wills.

BYRNE, Brigadier-General Sir Joseph Aloysius (1874-1942)

Governor, Seychelles, 1922-27; Sierra Leone, 1927-31; Kenya, 1931-37.

Messrs Lloyds Bank, Salisbury, who acted in the estate, know of no papers.

BYRNE, Sir William Patrick (1859-1935)

Assistant Under-Secretary, Home Office, 1908-13. Under-Secretary to Lord-Lieutenant, Ireland, 1916-18.

Sir William Byrne lived in retirement at Monte Carlo, and he died intestate — a single man without issue. It has not proved possible to trace the solicitor, Peter Byrne, who acted as administrator to the estate.

CACCIA, Baron
Sir Harold Anthony Caccia (1905-   )

Foreign Service after 1929. Minister, Athens, 1945. Anbassador, Austria, 1951-54 (and High Commissioner, Austria, 1950-54); United States, 1956-61. Assistant Under-Secretary, 1946; Deputy Under-Secretary, 1949, 1954-56; Permanent Under-Secretary, Foreign Office, 1962-65. Head of Diplomatic Service, 1964-65.

Lord Caccia says that he has kept no papers which he considers of historical value.

CADELL, Sir Patrick Robert (1871-1961)

Indian Civil Service, 1891-1926. Commissioner in Sind, 1925-26.

A collection of papers has been placed in the National Army Museum. The material includes correspondence, mostly relating to Indian military history; notes for lectures and articles; a typescript of a short biographical study by Cadell; and newspaper cuttings relating to his ninetieth birthday.

CADOGAN, Sir Alexander George Montagu (1884-1968)

Minister, China, 1933-35; Ambassador, 1935-36. Deputy Under-Secretary, 1936-37; Permanent Under-Secretary, Foreign Office, 1938-46. Permanent Representative, United Nations, 1946-50.

The papers of Sir Alexander Cadogan have been deposited in Churchill College, Cambridge. There is a diary for each year (1933-67), some scrap-books, a few personal letters for the period of Cadogan's official life, and a considerable bulk of private correspondence from the time of his retirement. Two volumes of Private Office papers (1934-39) are available at the Public Record Office (F.O. 800/293-4).

CALDECOTT, Sir Andrew (1884-1951)

High Commissioner, Malay States, 1934. Governor, Hong Kong, 1935-37; Ceylon, 1937-44.

Copies of speeches and addresses given whilst Caldecott was Governor of Ceylon are available at Rhodes House Library, Oxford.

CALLANDER, Lieutenant-General Sir Colin Bishop (1897-   )

Served European War, 1914-18, and War of 1939-45. G.O.C., 4th Division (Greece), 1945-46; 2nd Division, British Army of the Rhine, 1949-51. Director-General, Military Training, 1948, 1952-54. Military Secretary to Secretary of State for War, 1954-56.

General Callander has kept no papers.

CALTHORPE, Admiral of the Fleet Hon. Sir Somerset Arthur Gough- (1864-1937)

Naval career from 1878. Naval Attaché, Russia, Norway and Sweden, 1902-05. 2nd Sea Lord, 1916. C.-in-C., Mediterranean, 1917-19; High Commissioner, Constanti-nople, 1918-19. C.-in-C., Portsmouth, 1920-23. Principal A.D.C. to the King, 1924-25. Admiral of the Fleet, 1925.

Family papers are retained in the Hampshire Record Office. These, however, contain no material relating to the Admiral.

CAMERON, Lieutenant-General Sir Alexander Maurice (1898-   )

Served European War, 1916-18, and War of 1939-45. Deputy Quartermaster-General, 1945-48. Major-General in Charge of Administration, Middle East Land Forces, 1948-51. G.O.C., East African Command, 1951-53.

Certain unsorted papers have been kept by Sir Alexander.

CAMERON, General Sir Archibald Rice (1870-1944)

Served South Africa, 1899-1902; European War, 1914-18. Military Secretary to Governor, Cape of Good Hope, 1904-07. Director of Staff Duties, War Office, 1925-27. G.O. C.-in-C., Scottish Command, 1933-37.

Two volumes of Cameron's South African diary (1899-1902) are housed at the Black Watch Regimental Museum in Perth.

CAMERON, Sir Donald Charles (1872-1948)

Governor, Tanganyika, 1925-31; Nigeria, 1931-35.

The Colonial Records Project found that Sir Donald's trustees hold no papers, and that Lady Cameron's solicitors had found no papers.

CAMPBELL, Major-General Sir (Alexander) Douglas (1899-   )

Military career; served World War I. Chief Engineer, IX Corps, North Africa, 1943; I Corps, Normandy, 1944; 2nd Army, 1944-45; 14th Army, 1945; Middle East Land Forces, 1947-48. Engineer-in-Chief, War Office, 1948-52. Vice Adjutant-General to the Forces, 1952-54. Commander, Aldershot District, 1954-57. Colonel Commandant, Royal Engineers, 1958-64.

Sir Douglas has retained a collection of papers. This includes papers relating to his service in France, 1918; and material relating to World War II (e.g. documents relating to the evacuation of British forces through St Malo in 1940; operations in North Africa; the planning and execution of the engineering work in the assault on Normandy in June 1944, etc.).

CAMPBELL, General Sir David Graham Muschet (1869-1936)

Served South Africa, 1899-1902; European War, 1914-18. Military Secretary to Secretary of State for War, 1926-27. G.O.C.-in-C., Aldershot Command, 1927-31. Governor and C.-in-C., Malta, 1931-36.

Sir David Campbell kept no diary and letters written to his wife were burnt after her death at his request. Rhodes House Library, Oxford, has information about certain biographical writings and diaries by Lady Campbell, dating from the 1920s in Tanganyika to the period in Malta.

CAMPBELL, Sir Ian Vincent Hamilton, 7th Bt (1895-   )

Served European War, 1914-18. Home Civil Service: Air Ministry after 1919. Assistant Under-Secretary, Air Ministry, 1945-55.

According to information available at the Imperial War Museum, Sir Ian Campbell kept no papers.

CAMPBELL, Sir Ronald Hugh (1883-1953)

Minister, Paris, 1929-35; Belgrade, 1935-39. Ambassador, France, 1939-40; Portugal, 1940-45.

Mr R. F. Campbell says that his father left no papers or records of his official life.

CAMPBELL, Sir Ronald Ian (1890-   )

Counsellor, Cairo, 1931-34; Foreign Office, 1934-38. Minister, Paris, 1938-39; Belgrade, 1939-41; Washington, 1941-45. Assistant Under-Secretary, 1945-46; Ambassador, Egypt, 1946-50.

Sir Ronald Campbell has no papers relating to his government service, and he never kept a diary.

CAMPION, Sir Harry (1905-   )

Director of Central Statistical Office, Cabinet Office, until 1967. Director, Statistical Office, United Nations, 1946-47. Member of Statistical Commission, United Nations, 1947-67.

Sir Harry states that he retains few papers in his possession. Material dealing with official business was left at the Cabinet Office and in the United Nations Archives, New York, and papers relating to the affairs of the Statistical Societies, etc., have been placed with the records of the Royal Statistical Society.

CAMPION, Lieutenant-Colonel Sir William Robert (1870-1951)

M.P. (Con.) Lewes, 1910-24. Governor, Western Australia, 1924-31.

Papers of Campion's when he was Governor of Western Australia are included in the Danny MSS. at the East Sussex Record Office (ref. 2191-2196). These consist of five volumes of journals (1924-31).

CANNY, Sir Gerald Bain (1881-1954)

Chairman, Board of Inland Revenue, 1938-42.

Information available at Somerset House was not helpful in tracing papers.

CANTLIE, Lieutenant-General Sir Neil (1892-1975)

Served European War, 1914-18; Egypt and Sudan; War of 1939-45. Director-General, Army Medical Services, 1948-52.

There is a collection of papers at the Museum of the Royal Army Medical Corps.

CAPPER, Major-General Sir Thompson (1863-1915)

Commandant, Indian Staff College, 1906-11; 13th Infantry Brigade, 1911-14 Inspector of Infantry, 1914.

A collection of family papers is with the Liddell Hart Centre for Military Archives. The material includes papers relating to the Indian Staff College (1908-11), with a series on the question of tactics in the war in Manchuria (1904-07); Somaliland (1913); and a lecture on the effect of aircraft on war (1913).

CARDEN, Sir Lionel Edward Gresley (1851-1915)

Consular Service. Minister, Cuba, 1902-05; Guatemala, 1905-11; Central America, 1911-13; Mexico, 1913-14.

The Will and Act of Probate names Lady Carden as the sole executrix and mentions no children or solicitors.

CARMICHAEL, 1st B
Sir Thomas David Gibson-Carmichael, 11th Bt (1859-1926)

M.P. (Lib.) Midlothian, 1895-1900. Governor, Victoria, 1908-11; Madras, 1911-12; Bengal, 1912-17.

Only distant members of the family were traced. It was not possible to contact Sir David Gibson-Craig-Carmichael, Bt, the head of the family. Some correspondence is to be found in the Hardinge papers at Cambridge University Library.

CARNEGIE, Sir Lancelot Douglas (1861-1933)

Minister, Paris, 1911-13; Lisbon, 1913-24. Ambassador, Portugal, 1924-28.

Mr James Carnegie says that his father left no papers, and that his diaries were unfortunately lost. Some correspondence (1908-18) with Hardinge is to be found in the Hardinge papers at Cambridge University Library.

CARNOCK, 1st B
Sir Arthur Nicolson, 11th Bt (1849-1928)

Minister, Morocco, 1895-1904. Ambassador, Spain, 1904-05; Russia, 1905-10. Permanent Under-Secretary, Foreign Office, 1910-16.

A large collection of correspondence (1889-1916) is deposited at the Public Record Office (F.O. 800/336-81). Personal papers are at Sissinghurst Castle, Kent. Application to view should be made to Mr Nigel Nicolson at that address.

CARR, Lieutenant-General Lawrence (1886-1954)

Served European War, 1914-18. Assistant Chief of Imperial General Staff, 1939-40. G.O.C., I Corps, 1940-41. G.O.C.-in-C., Eastern Command, 1941-42. Senior Military Assistant, Ministry of Supply, 1942-44.

Mrs L. Carr, Leys Cottage, Crathes, Banchory, Kincardineshire AB3 3QD, states that most of her late husband's papers were destroyed, but some personal letters have survived, including material on Palestine (1936-37). The papers have been given to the Liddell Hart Centre for Military Archives.

CARRINGTON, Major-General Sir Frederick (1844-1913)

Commanded Native Levies in Zulu Rebellion; served Transvaal, 1878-79. Commanded Colonial Force in Basuto War, 1881; Bechuanaland Police, 1893. Military Adviser to High Commissioner during Matabele War, 1893. G.O.C. Rhodesian Rebellion. Commander, Gibraltar, 1895-99; Belfast; 1899-1900; Rhodesian Field Force in Boer War.

Papers (1876-1901) on military service in South Africa and Rhodesia are housed in the South African Government Archives, Transvaal Archives Depot, Pretoria.

CARTER, General Sir Charles Bonham- (1876-1955)

Director of Staff Duties, War Office, 1927-31. Director-General, Territorial Army, 1933-36. Governor, Malta, 1936-40.

The material at Churchill College, Cambridge, is not open to general inspection. Two volumes of correspondence and four diaries (1914-15, 1918, 1919, 1920) relate to World War I. A typescript journal (1936-40), correspondence, some official Council of Government papers, photographs, speeches and newspaper cuttings relate to the period in Malta.

CARTER, Sir Richard Henry Archibald (1887-1958)

Private Secretary to Secretary of State for India, 1924-27. Assistant Secretary, Indian Statutory Commission, 1927-30. Secretary-General, Round Table Conference, 1930-31. Assistant Under-Secretary, India Office, 1936. Permanent Secretary, Admiralty, 1936-40. Chairman, Board of Customs and Excise, 1942-47. Permanent Under-Secretary, India, 1947. Joint Permanent Under-Secretary, Commonwealth Relations, 1948. Chairman, Monopolies and Restrictive Practices Commission, 1949-53.

The executor of Lady Carter (widow) knows of no surviving papers. However, H.M. Customs and Excise Library holds a number of files relating to Sir R. H. A. Carter.

CARTER, Admiral Sir Stuart Sumner Bonham- (1889-1972)

Naval career; served World War I. Naval Secretary to 1st Lord of the Admiralty, 1939. Commodore of Convoys, 1944-45.

The Imperial War Museum understands that Sir Stuart kept no papers.

CARTWRIGHT, Sir Fairfax Leighton (1857-1928)

Minister-Resident, Munich, 1906-08. Ambassador, Austria-Hungary, 1908-13.

A vast collection of family papers is deposited at the Northamptonshire Record Office. The material is not fully catalogued, and for Sir Fairfax Cartwright consists of both diplomatic papers and private correspondence. Apart from certain bound volumes of correspondence with the Permanent Under-Secretaries, Hardinge and Nicolson, after 1908, the diplomatic papers are arranged in bundles in boxes. Personal papers are in a separate series. Miss Elizabeth Cartwright, Iford Mill, Bradford-on-Avon, Wiltshire, has a number of typed copies of her grandfather's letters to Sir Edward Grey (1909-13), and several German press cuttings (1912).

CARVELL, John Eric Maclean (1894-   )

Consular Service. Consul-General, Munich, 1938-39; Algiers, 1942-45; Los Angeles, 1945-47. Ambassador, Ecuador, 1950-51 (and Minister, 1947-50). Minister, Bulgaria, 1951-54.

No contact could be established.

CASEY, Baron
Sir Richard Gardiner Casey (1890-   )

Australian diplomat and Cabinet Minister. Minister of State Resident, Middle East, and Member of War Cabinet, 1942-43. Governor, Bengal, 1944-46. Governor-General, Australia, 1965-69.

Lord Casey has retained a large number of papers relating to his career. Copies of his diaries, 1944-46, are housed at the India Office Library. Further details are given by Hazlehurst and Woodland, op. cit., pp.29-30.

CASH, Sir Thomas James (1888-   )

Entered War Office as Higher Division Clerk, 1912. Director of Finance and Assistant Under-Secretary of State, 1936. Deputy Under-Secretary of State for War, 1945-54.

Sir Thomas Cash kept neither diaries, private papers, letters nor press cuttings relating to his service in the War Office.

CASLON, Vice-Admiral Clifford (1896-1973)

Naval career; served World War I. Commanded 4th, 18th and 6th Destroyer Flotillas, 1938-42. Chief of Staff, Plymouth, 1943-44. Flag Officer, Malaya, 1947-50.

Vice-Admiral C. Caslon's personal recollections of the Battle of Jutland have been deposited at the Imperial War Museum.

CASSELS, General Sir Robert Archibald (1876-1959)

Served European War, 1914-18. Adjutant-General, India, 1928-30. G.O.C.-in-C., Northern Command, India, 1930-34. C.-in-C., Army in India, 1935-41. Member, Executive Council of Governor-General of India, 1935-41.

It is understood that Cassels destroyed his papers when he left India.

CASTLETOWN, 2nd B
Bernard Edward Barnaby Fitz-Patrick (1849-1937)

M.P., Portarlington Borough, 1880-83. Assistant Adjutant-General, South Africa, 1899-1902.

Papers concerning the South African war survive in the South African Government Archives, at the Orange Free State Archives Depot, Bloemfontein.

CATLING, Sir Richard Charles (1912-   )

Served Police forces, Palestine, 1935-48; Malaya and Kenya.

Sir Richard has retained miscellaneous dispatches, memoranda, etc., mainly on Jewish affairs, which are now held at Rhodes House, Oxford.

CATTO, 1st B
Sir Thomas Sivewright Catto, 1st Bt (1879-1959)

Company Director, and member of Government missions and commissions. Director-General of Equipment and Stores, and member of Supply Council, Ministry of Supply, 1940. Financial Adviser to the Chancellor of the Exchequer, 1940-44. Governor, Bank of England, 1944-49.

The present (2nd) Lord Catto, 41 William Mews, London SW1, states that he has a copy of his father's unpublished autobiography, and that some other papers survive with his mother, the Dowager Lady Catto.

CAVAN, 10th E of
Field-Marshal Frederic Rudolph Lambart (1865-1946)

Served South Africa, 1907; European War, 1914-18. C.-in-C., Aldershot, 1920-22. Chief of Imperial General Staff, 1922-26.

A collection of papers (1916-37) is available at the Public Record Office (W.O. 79). The papers mainly cover Cavan's career in Belgium and the Middle East (1916-17), Italy (1917-19), and the period 1920-23. A copy of Cavan's unpublished memoirs is kept at Churchill College, Cambridge.

CAVE, Wing Commander Thomas Reginald Cave-Browne- (1895-1969)

Royal Air Force career.

There is an important collection of papers relating to aeronautics (1914-30) at the

Imperial War Museum. The material has particular reference to the development of the airship.

CAZALET, Vice-Admiral Sir Peter Grenville Lyon (1899-)

Naval career from 1918; served War of 1939-45. Deputy Director of Plans, Naval Staff, 1946-47. Commodore, R.N. Barracks, Chatham, 1949-50. Chief of Staff to Flag Officer, Central Europe, 1950-52. Allied Chief of Staff to C.-in-C., Mediterranean, 1953-55. Flag Officer Commanding Reserve Fleet, 1955-56. Chairman, Navy League, 1960-67.

Papers relating *inter alia* to the fall of Singapore, the Russian convoys and the invasion of France, 1940-44, are available at the Imperial War Museum. A microfilm of papers relating to the Yangtse incident, 1949, and to the Nevada atom bomb test, 1955, is also available at the museum.

CHALMERS, 1st B
Sir Robert Chalmers (1858-1938)

Chairman, Board of Inland Revenue, 1907-11. Permanent Secretary, Treasury, and Auditor of Civil List, 1911-13. Governor, Ceylon, 1913-16. Joint Secretary, Treasury, 1916-19. Under-Secretary, Ireland, 1916.

Lt.-Col. M. C. Stevenson, White Shutters, Exlade, near Woodcote, Reading, Berks., retains the majority of papers which survive in connection with his grandfather, Lord Chalmers. There is some useful correspondence in the Asquith papers at the Bodleian Library, Oxford.

CHALMERS, Sir Mackenzie Dalzell (1847-1927)

Permanent Under-Secretary, Home Office, 1903-08. Member of several Royal Commissions, Government committees, conference delegations, etc.

A representative of Messrs Parker, Garrett & Co., the solicitors who acted in Sir M. D. Chalmers's estate, was unable to provide information about any surviving members of the family.

CHAMPION, Rev. Sir Reginald Stuart (1895-)

Served Palestine, Aden and Transjordan. Governor, Aden, 1944-51.

Sir Reginald has retained a large collection of photographs and series of personal letters to his wife, many of which contain accounts of his activities and travels.

CHANCELLOR, Lieutenant-Colonel Sir John Robert (1870-1952)

Assistant Secretary (Military), Committee of Imperial Defence, 1904. Secretary, Colonial Defence Committee, 1906. Governor, Mauritius, 1911-16; Trinidad and Tobago, 1916-21; Southern Rhodesia, 1923-28. High Commissioner, Palestine, 1928-31.

A large collection of papers (31 boxes) is held at Rhodes House Library, Oxford. Most of the papers relate to the period in Palestine. Telegrams and dispatches exchanged with the Secretary of State, Lord Passfield, especially after the disturbances of August 1929, are especially interesting. A wide range of subjects is covered in the Palestine papers. Other material in the collection relates to the Army and defence matters (1880-1936); Mauritius (1905-48); Trinidad and Tobago (1915-29); Southern Rhodesia (1923-55); Chancellor's activities after retirement (1931-52); and committees, councils and commissions on which Chancellor served.

CHAPMAN, Sir Sydney John (1871-1951)

Professor of Political Economy, Manchester University, 1901-18. Permanent Secretary, Board of Trade, 1920-27. Chief Economic Adviser to the Government, 1927-32; British Plenipotentiary to various international conferences, etc.

The Hon. Sir Stephen Chapman, The Manor House, Ware, Herts., states that his father kept no papers but that in later life he wrote a series of memoirs. Copies of this unpublished autobiography are lodged at the John Rylands University Library of Manchester and at B.L.P.E.S.

CHARLES, Lieutenant-General Sir James Ronald Edmonston (1875-1955)

Served South Africa, 1899-1900; European War, 1914-18. Commandant, Royal Military Academy, Woolwich, 1924-26. Director of Military Operations and Intelligence, War Office, 1926-31. Master-General of the Ordnance, 1931-34.

Papers and diaries relating to the Boer War can be found at the National Army Museum.

CHARLES, Sir Noel Hughes Havelock, 3rd Bt (1891-   )

Minister, Portugal, 1940-41. Ambassador, Brazil, 1941-44. High Commissioner, Italy, 1944-47. Served Foreign Office, 1947-49.

No contact could be established.

CHARRINGTON, Brigadier H. V. S. (1886-1965)

Served War of 1939-45.

Some papers are held by the Liddell Hart Centre for Military Archives. The collection includes World War II papers and material relating to operations in Eritrea, Abyssinia and Greece (1940-41). There are also papers on his book *Where Cavalry Stands Today* (1927).

CHARTERIS, Brigadier-General John (1877-1946)

M.P. (Con.) Dumfriesshire, 1924-29. Military career from 1896; served European War, 1914-18; India, 1920-22.

Certain papers are in the care of the Intelligence Corps Museum. These include five books of newspaper cuttings, copies of letters written by the General to the press (1920-41), assorted notes and commentaries on military subjects, photographs and published material.

CHATER, Major-General Arthur Reginald (1896-   )

Served European War, 1914-18. Senior Royal Marines Officer, East Indies, 1931-33; Home Fleet, 1935-36. Commander, Sudan Camel Corps, 1927-30; Somaliland Camel Corps, 1937-40. Military Governor and Commander, British Somaliland, 1941-43. Director of Combined Operations, India and South East Asia, 1944-45.

Papers and photographs relating to the Somaliland Camel Corps and the Military Command of the colony (1937-40) are housed at the Liddell Hart Centre for Military Archives. Further miscellaneous military papers remain with Major-General Chater.

CHATFIELD, 1st B
Admiral of the Fleet Sir (Alfred) Ernle Montacute Chatfield (1873-1967)

Naval career from 1886; served World War I. 4th Sea Lord, 1919-20. Assistant Chief of Naval Staff, 1920-22. 3rd Sea Lord and Controller of the Navy, 1925-28. C.-in-C., Atlantic Fleet, 1929-30; Mediterranean, 1930-32. 1st Sea Lord and Chief of Naval Staff, 1933-39. Minister for Co-ordination of Defence, 1939-40.

The bulk of Chatfield's papers are deposited in the National Maritime Museum. These cover, in seven groups, all aspects of Chatfield's career, from his early naval service, his Atlantic and Mediterranean commands, to his tenure of office as 1st Sea Lord and as a Minister. For further details see Hazlehurst and Woodland, op. cit., p.38.

CHEETHAM, Sir Milne (1869-1938)

Counsellor, Cairo, 1911-19. Minister, Peru and Ecuador, 1919-20; Paris, 1921-22; Switzerland, 1922-24; Athens, 1924-26; Copenhagen, 1926-28.

The Middle East Centre at St Antony's College, Oxford, holds a collection of private letters to Consuls-General Sir Eldon Gorst and Lord Kitchener on British policy in Egypt (1910-15), and copies of telegrams to and from Cheetham (1912-13). Sir N. J. A. Cheetham knows of no private papers relating to the latter part of his father's career.

CHELMSFORD, 1st Vt
Frederic John Napier Thesiger (1868-1933)

Governor, Queensland, 1905-09; New South Wales, 1909-13. Viceroy of India, 1916-21. First Lord of the Admiralty, 1924. Agent-General for New South Wales, 1926-28.

Chelmsford's papers as Viceroy of India are held at the India Office Library. The large collection includes correspondence with the King, with the Secretary of State for India, and with prominent persons in India and in Britain, copies of official dispatches, political papers, memoranda and minutes. Further details are given in Hazlehurst and Woodland, op. cit., p.143.

CHETWODE, 1st B
Field-Marshal Sir Philip Walhouse Chetwode, 7th Bt (1869-1950)

Served South Africa, 1899-1902; European War, 1914-18. Military Secretary, War Office, 1919-20. Deputy Chief of Imperial General Staff, 1920-22. Adjutant-General, 1922-23. C.-in-C., Aldershot, 1923-27. Chief of General Staff, India, 1928-30. C.-in-C., Indian Army, 1930-35. Chairman, Executive Committee of Red Cross and St John Joint War Organisation, 1940-47.

The Imperial War Museum has a collection of miscellaneous papers relating to Chetwode's service in the Egyptian Expeditionary Forces (1916-18). It consists chiefly of official memoranda and battle orders, with some official and semi-official correspondence, and a few personal letters. It is understood that Chetwode's diaries were destroyed, according to instructions in his will.

CHILSTON, 2nd Vt
Aretas Akers-Douglas (1876-1947)

Secretary of Embassy, Vienna, 1909-14. Chargé d'Affaires, Montenegro, 1911,

1912, 1913; Romania, 1914. Minister, Austria 1921-27; Hungary, 1928-33. Ambassador, U.S.S.R., 1933-38.

A small collection of papers is retained by the present Vt Chilston at Chilston Park, near Maidstone, Kent. The few letters which remain concern Chilston's appointment at Moscow, and most of the photographs, press cuttings and film also cover the period in Russia. Two five-year diaries (1931-41) are extant, and a copy of the unpublished *Memoirs of Lady Chilston*.

CHILTON, Sir Henry Getty (1877-1954)

Minister, Washington, 1924-28; Holy See, 1928-30. Ambassador, Chile, 1930-33; Argentine Republic, 1933-35; Spain, 1935-38. Served Ministry of Economic Warfare, 1939-40; Information, 1940.

Messrs Burton, Yeates & Hart, Solicitors, undertook to make enquiries of members of the family with whom they remain in contact. However, they have had nothing to report.

CHILTON, Lieutenant-General Sir Maurice Somerville (1898-1956)

Served European War, 1916-18, and War of 1939-45. Chief of Staff, 2nd Army, and Deputy Adjutant-General, 21 Army Group, British Liberation Army, 1944-46. Director of Air, War Office, 1946-48. G.O.C.-in-C., Anti-Aircraft Command, 1953-55. Quartermaster-General, 1955-56.

Lady Chilton states that her late husband's diaries have not survived, and all the letters General Chilton wrote to her remain private.

CHRISTIE, Group Captain Malcolm Grahame (1881-1971)

Air Attaché, Washington, 1922-26; Berlin, 1927-30.

A substantial collection of papers (1929-44) has been placed in the archives centre at Churchill College, Cambridge. These papers relate mainly to Christie's activities in Germany and Central Europe where he undertook an investigation of the political situation on behalf of Sir Robert Vansittart. Christie acted as an intermediary between Henlein and the Sudeten German parties, and interested circles in Britain.* The correspondence and papers are arranged in several sections, according to subject or date. For example, there are papers on Germany in 1932, on Hermann Göring, on the Luftwaffe, and on the question of the Sudeten Germans; there are also series of Chatham House papers, notes on the Balkans, Italy and Poland, and war-time memoranda and papers. The questions of air power and the development of air forces are particularly well covered.

CHRISTIE, Walter Henry John (1905-   )

Deputy Private Secretary to Viceroy, 1939-43; Joint Private Secretary, 1947. Adviser in India to Central Commercial Committee, 1947-52.

Certain diaries and papers (1931-47) are held at the India Office Library. The collection includes diaries of Christie's tours when Deputy Commissioner in the Chittagong Hill Tracts (1936-37), and diaries and other papers relating to his period as Deputy Private Secretary to the Viceroy (1939-43) and Joint Private Secretary (1947).

---

*P. Conwell Evans, *None so Blind* (London, 1947).

CHRISTISON, General Sir Alexander Frank Philip, 4th Bt (1893-   )

Served war of 1939-45. C.-in-C., Allied Land Forces, South East Asia, 1945. Allied Commander, Netherlands East Indies, 1945-46. G.O.C.-in-C., Northern Command, 1946; Scottish Command, 1947-49.

General Sir Philip Christison has kept no papers, but has a series of unpublished memoirs.

CHRYSTAL, Sir George William (1880-1944)

Secretary, Ministry of National Service, Ministry of Reconstruction, and Demobilisation Section of the War Cabinet, 1918-19; Ministry of Pensions, 1919-35. Permanent Secretary, Ministry of Health 1935-40.

Sir George's sister, Miss Marjorie Janet Margaret Chrystal, was the sole executrix. Efforts to trace her were not successful.

CLAGUE, Sir John (1882-1958)

Chief Secretary, Government of Burma (Home and Political Department), 1928-31. Commissioner, Shan States, 1933-42. Adviser, Secretary of State for Burma, 1937-42.

The papers at the India Office Library include material relating to the Sino-British Joint Commission for the Investigation of the Yunnan-Burma Frontier (1936), papers, reports and correspondence collected in Burma and the Shan States. Many of the reports relate to conditions among the peoples of Nagaland. There are also several Government Officer's diaries kept by Clague (1915, 1918-19, 1925, 1932, 1935, 1936); correspondence with Sir Harcourt Butler (1923-28), and a collection of material on Burma during World War II.

CLARENDON, 6th E of
George Herbert Hyde Villiers, Baron Hyde (1877-1955)

Captain, Gentleman-at-Arms, 1922-25. Parliamentary Under-Secretary, Dominion Affairs, and Chairman of Overseas Settlement Committee, 1925-27. Governor-General, South Africa, 1931-37. Lord Chamberlain, 1938-52.

The surviving papers of the 6th Earl of Clarendon are in the care of his grandson, the present (7th) Earl, at 8 Chelsea Square, London SW3. No detailed list of contents is at present available, but it appears that the bulk of the papers consists of material of a largely social nature, particularly relating to the Earl's activities as Governor-General in South Africa.

CLARK, Sir Ernest (1864-1951)

Assistant Under-Secretary, Ireland, 1920-31. Secretary, Northern Ireland Treasury, 1921-25. Member, Australian Economic Mission, 1928-29; Joint Exchequer Board, Great Britain and Northern Ireland, 1930. Governor, Tasmania, 1933-45.

A collection of personal diaries and papers (c. 1900-50) is held at the Northern Ireland Public Record Office (Accession No. D.1022).

CLARK, Sir William Henry (1876-1952)

Member, Viceroy's Council, India, 1910-16. Comptroller-General, Department of

Overseas Trade, 1917-28. High Commissioner, Canada, 1928-34; South Africa, 1934-39.

One folder of papers (*c.* 1928-39) is held at B.L.P.E.S. The collection consists mainly of correspondence between Clark and Sir Harry Batterbee (1935-39), with other letters relating to Clark's appointment to South Africa and his proposed appointment to Kenya (1936).

CLARKE, Sir Charles Noble Arden- (1898-1962)

Governor, Sarawak, 1946-49; Gold Coast, 1949-57. Governor-General, Ghana, 1957.

It is understood that a collection of personal papers and letters has survived in private hands. Information is available at Rhodes House Library, Oxford.

CLARKE, Major-General Sir Edward Montagu Campbell (1885-1971)

Director of Artillery, 1938-42; Director-General, 1942-45.

A small collection of papers has been deposited at the Imperial War Museum. The material consists of papers relating to Clarke's service at the War Office as Director of Artillery (1938-42) and as Director-General of Artillery, and is most useful on the subject of anti-tank measures.

CLARKE, Sir Selwyn Selwyn- (1893-   )

Colonial Medical Service, Gold Coast, Hong Kong, etc. Governor, Seychelles, 1947-51. Principal Medical Officer, Ministry of Health, 1951-56. Author.

Sir Selwyn Selwyn-Clarke has given a collection of books to the University of Sussex, but he retains an extensive range of books, pamphlets, printed reports, etc., relating to his interests in the Commonwealth and medicine. He has also kept an assortment of lecture notes, letters, press cuttings, engagement diaries and other papers. These were used for the writing of an autobiography, which is to be published. The original draft of this memoir remains with Sir Selwyn.

CLAY, Sir Henry (1883-1954)

Economic Adviser, Bank of England, 1930-44.

The papers at Nuffield College, Oxford, relate to the Bank of England, to war-time financial problems and Board of Trade reconstruction policy.

CLAYTON, Brigadier-General Sir Gilbert Falkingham (1875-1929)

Director of Intelligence, Egypt, 1914-17. Brigadier-General, General Staff, Hejaz Operations, 1916-17. Chief Political Officer, Egyptian Expeditionary Force, 1917-19. Adviser to Ministry of the Interior, Egypt, 1919-22. Chief Secretary, Palestine, 1922-25. High Commissioner and C.-in-C., Iraq, 1929.

The papers in the Sudan Archive at the School of Oriental Studies, University of Durham, include diaries (1901-29, with gaps), correspondence with Sir Reginald Wingate (1908-16), and general correspondence, etc., (1917-22).

CLEMENTI, Sir Cecil (1875-1947)

Governor, Hong Kong, 1925-30. Governor, Straits Settlements, and High Commissioner, Malay States, 1930-34.

It is understood that papers have survived in the care of Mrs R. F. Overell, Sir Cecil's daughter. Correspondence for the period 1903 to 1926 can also be found in the Nathan papers (see N.R.A. List 8981).

CLERK, Sir George Russell (1874-1951)

Minister, Czechoslovakia, 1919-26. Ambassador, Turkey, 1926-33; Belgium, 1933-34; France, 1934-37.

Sir George Clerk left instructions in his will that all papers, letters, official and private documents should be burnt. His books were left to Lady Jeanne Malcolm, whose daughter, Mrs M. McFadyean, has been unable to find any of Sir George's papers.

CLIFF, Eric Francis (1884-1969)

Assistant Under-Secretary, Air Ministry, 1938-43. Principal Assistant Secretary, Treasury, 1943. Treasury Establishment Representative, Washington, 1943-45.

The Imperial War Museum found that Mr Cliff had kept no papers of historical interest.

CLIFFORD, Captain Hon. Sir Bede Edmund Hugh (1890-1969)

Imperial Secretary and U.K. Representative, South Africa. Governor, Bahamas, 1932-37; Mauritius, 1937-42; Trinidad and Tobago, 1942-46.

It is understood that some papers have survived in private hands. The material, about which no details are available, is to be placed in the care of the Rt Hon. Lord Clifford, Ugbrooke Park, Chudleigh, near Newton Abbot, Devon.

CLIFFORD, Sir (Geoffrey) Miles (1897-   )

Military and Colonial Service. Governor, Falkland Islands, 1946-54.

Tape recordings and the transcript of an interview given by Sir Miles are held at Rhodes House Library. It is understood that Sir Miles retains a number of papers relating to his career.

CLIFFORD, Sir Hugh Charles (1866-1941)

Governor, Gold Coast, 1912-19; Nigeria, 1919-25; Ceylon, 1925-27. Governor, Straits Settlements and High Commissioner, Malay States, 1927-29.

Correspondence as Governor of Nigeria to Sir William Gowers (1920-24) is at Rhodes House Library, Oxford. Sir Hugh's press cuttings and official correspondence files are held by his grandson, Mr H. Clifford Holmes, Dennington, Ridgeway, Woking, Surrey.

CLIVE, Lieutenant-General Sir George Sidney (1874-1959)

Served South Africa, 1899-1902; European War, 1914-18. Military Governor, Cologne, 1919. British Military Representative, League of Nations, 1920-22. Military Attaché, Paris, 1924-27. Director of Personal Services, War Office, 1928-30. Military Secretary to Secretary of State for War, 1930-34.

A letter book and personal diaries (1914-18) are housed at the Liddell Hart Centre for Militay Archives. The material relates to Clive's service as head of the British Mission at the French General Headquarters. Other material was destroyed in a fire.

CLIVE, Sir Robert Henry (1877-1948)

Minister, Persia, 1926-31; Holy See, 1933-34. Ambassador, Japan, 1934-37; Belgium (and Minister, Luxembourg), 1937-39.

Lady Harrison, Timbers, Plummers Plain, near Horsham, Sussex, retains some papers relating to her father's career. The material includes correspondence (c. 1926-39) exchanged between Clive and Lord Stamfordham, Private Secretary to King George V, together with a collection of press cuttings (mostly of a social nature), and copies of lectures and articles about Japan written by Clive during World War II.

CLUTTERBUCK, Sir Peter Alexander (1897-   )

Colonial Office and Dominions Office service. Assistant Under-Secretary, Dominions Office, 1942-46. High Commissioner, Canada, 1946-52; India, 1952-55. Ambassador, Eire, 1955-59. Permanent Under-Secretary, Commonwealth Relations Office, 1959-61.

It is understood that Sir Alexander Clutterbuck has destroyed his papers.

CLYDESMUIR, 1st B
Sir David John Colville (1894-1954)

M.P. (Con.) Midlothian North, 1929-43. Parliamentary Secretary, Department of Overseas Trade, 1931-35. Parliamentary Under-Secretary, Scotland, 1935-36. Financial Secretary, Treasury, 1936-38. Secretary of State for Scotland, 1938-40. Governor, Bombay, 1943-48. Viceroy and Governor-General (Acting), India, 1945, 1946, 1947.

The present (2nd) Lord Clydesmuir retains no papers relating to his father's political career. Further information is given in Hazlehurst and Woodland, op. cit., pp.40-1.

COBBOLD, 1st B
Cameron Fromanteel Cobbold (1904-   )

Governor, Bank of England, 1949-61. Lord Chamberlain, 1963-71.

A number of unsorted personal papers remain with Lord Cobbold, whilst papers relating to the office of Lord Chamberlain are in the Royal Archives, and those relating to the Bank of England are with the Bank.

CODRINGTON, Lieutenant-General Sir Alfred Edward (1854-1945)

Served South Africa, 1899-1900, 1901-02; European War, 1914-18. G.O.C., London District, 1909-13. Military Secretary to Secretary of State for War, 1914.

General Codrington's son, the late Col. Sir G. R. Codrington, stated that his father kept no papers.

COLLER, Frank Herbert (1866-1938)

Director-General, Ministry of Food, 1919-21. Secretary, Board of Trade (Food Department), 1921-25.

Mr Coller's solicitors, Messrs Gepp & Sons, have no documents relating to Mr Coller and do not know where such papers might be located.

COLLIER, Sir Laurence (1890-   )

Counsellor, Foreign Office, from 1932. Minister, Norway, 1941; Ambassador, 1942-50.

Sir Laurence kept no diary and retains very few papers relating to his career. Copies of two papers, relating to Sir Eyre Crowe and appeasement respectively, have been deposited with the B.L.P.E.S.

COLVILLE, Sir John (1915-   )

Assistant Private Secretary to Neville Chamberlain, 1939-40; Private Secretary to Winston Churchill, 1940-41 and 1943-45. 1st Secretary, British Embassy, Lisbon, 1949-51. Principal Private Secretary to Prime Minister, 1951-55.

It is believed that the papers retained by Sir John have been promised to Churchill College, Cambridge.

COLVIN, Brigadier-General Sir Richard Beale (1856-1936)

Military career; Commander, 20th Battalion, Imperial Yeomanry, South Africa, 1900-01; Essex Yeomanry, 1901-09, etc. M.P. (Con.) Epping, 1917-23.

A collection of papers (1900-02) at the Public Record Office (W.O.136) includes reports of operations, patrols, orders and a diary. Eight volumes of scrapbooks have been deposited by the Brigadier-General's son at the Essex Record Office. All volumes contain photographs, cartoons and Christmas cards, newspaper cuttings, etc., as well as correspondence, from military and political colleagues, election literature, and formal notices of appointments. The volumes cover the years 1877-1936.

COLYTON, 1st B
Sir Henry Lennox d'Aubigné Hopkinson (1902-   )

Diplomatic Service from 1924. Diplomatic Assistant to Minister of State, Cairo, 1941-43. Minister, Lisbon, 1943-44. Deputy High Commissioner, Italy, 1944-46. Head, Conservative Party Parliamentary Secretariat, and Joint Director, Conservative Research Department, 1946-49. M.P. (Con.) Taunton, 1950-56. Secretary, Overseas Trade, 1951-52. Minister of State, Colonial Affairs, 1952-55.

Lord Colyton states that he has very little left in the form of papers since most papers which he had during the war and afterwards at the Conservative Research Department were destroyed in error. Certain papers on the Middle East have been promised to the Middle East Centre at St Antony's College, Oxford.

CONGREVE, General Sir Walter Norris (1862-1927)

Entered Rifle Brigade, 1885; served South African and European Wars, and in Egypt and Palestine. C.-in-C., Southern Command, 1923-24. Governor and C.-in-C., Malta, 1924-27.

Major A. C. J. Congreve, Westering, Newtown, Newbury, Berks., writes that his father's diaries and letters have survived. The diaries after 1914 are of particular interest. The collection will be placed in due course in either the Imperial War Museum or with the family archives at the Staffordshire Record Office. Letters to and from Sir Henry Wilson (1919-22) are at the Imperial War Museum.

CONNAUGHT, Arthur Frederick Patrick Albert, Prince Arthur of (1883-1938)

Governor-General, South Africa, 1920-24.

The Royal Archives, Windsor, have no knowledge of any papers.

CONNAUGHT, 1st D of
Prince Arthur William Patrick Albert (1850-1942)

Governor-General, Canada, 1911-16.

Certain papers are held at the Royal Archives, Windsor. Access is restricted.

COOK, Vice-Admiral Eric William Longley- (1898-   )

Naval career; served World Wars I and II. Director of Naval Intelligence, 1948-51.

According to information available at the Imperial War Museum, the Vice-Admiral has retained certain papers which are now in store.

COOKE, Air Marshal Sir Cyril Bertram (1895-1972)

Served European War, 1914-18; India, 1922-25; Iraq, 1931-33; War of 1939-45 (Middle East, North Africa and Italy). Air Officer Commanding, No. 43 Group, Maintenance Command, 1945-46. Director-General, Servicing and Maintenance, Air Ministry, 1946-47. Air Officer C.-in-C., Maintenance Command, 1947-49.

The Imperial War Museum has a few papers (1942), mainly concerning the transport of prisoners of war on board H.M.T. *Queen Elizabeth.*

COOKE, Sir John Fletcher- (1911-   )

Colonial Service. Under-Secretary, Palestine Government, 1946-48. Counsellor (Colonial Affairs), U.K. Delegation to United Nations, 1949-51. Colonial Secretary, Cyprus, 1951-55. Served Tanganyika. M.P. (Con.) Southampton Test, 1964-66.

Sir John has in his possession a large collection of papers and documents covering, roughly, the period 1934 to date. These papers are at present in store, but Sir John intends to assemble them at his home in France. The material relates to the period 1934-37 at the Colonial Office; 1937-41 in Malaya and Singapore; 1942-45 when a prisoner of war in Japan; 1946, Malta; 1946-48, Palestine; 1948-51, the United Nations; 1951-55, Cyprus; 1956 to date, Africa; 1964-66, the House of Commons; and 1969, New Hebrides. Tape recordings made by Sir John are held at Rhodes House Library, Oxford, and at the Middle East Centre, St Antony's College, Oxford.

COOPER, Colonel Harry (1847-1928)

Vice-Consul, Bosnia, 1877-78; Asia Minor, 1879-80. Chief Staff Officer, Egypt, 1896-98. Served South African War, 1899-1902; World War I.

Papers (1877-1922), including reports and letters written when Cooper was Vice-Consul in Bosnia, are available at the National Army Museum.

COPE, Sir Alfred (d. 1954)

Assistant Under-Secretary for Ireland and Clerk of Privy Council (Ireland), 1920-22. General Secretary, National Liberal Organisation, 1922-24.

It is understood that a few papers remain in the care of Mrs T. R. South, 51 Fitzjames Avenue, Croydon, Surrey.

CORBETT, Sir Julian Stafford (1854-1922)

Director of Historical Section, Committee of Imperial Defence.

A collection of papers has survived. The material includes letters from Lord Keynes on the Dardanelles; documents on National Service (1912-13); Admiral Sir Edmond Slade's letters on the Committee of Imperial Defence Sub-Committee on Invasion, and the appearance of Lord Roberts and Colonel Repington before it (1907-08); general remarks on war with Germany prepared for Lord Fisher (1903-07); and papers on the War Council of 5-6 August 1914. A full report, and details regarding access, are held at the National Register of Archives.

CORBETT, Sir Vincent Edwin Henry (1861-1936)

Financial Adviser, Egyptian Government, 1904-07. Minister Resident, Venezuela, 1907-10; Bavaria and Württemberg, 1910-14.

Sir Vincent Corbett had no descendants, and no near relation was traced. *Reminiscences — Autobiographical and Diplomatic* (London, 1927) should be consulted. Some correspondence (1898-1909) is in the Hardinge papers at Cambridge University Library.

CORNWALL, General Sir James Handyside Marshall- (1887-   )

Served European War, 1914-18. Military Attaché, Berlin, Stockholm, Oslo and Copenhagen, 1928-32. Chief of British Military Mission to the Egyptian Army, 1937-38. Director-General, Air and Coast Defence, War Office, 1938-39. Special employment, War Office, 1939-40. G.O.C., British Troops in Egypt, 1941; G.O.C.-in-C., Western Command, 1941-42.

General Marshall-Cornwall has agreed to leave his papers to the Liddell Hart Centre for Military Archives.

CORNWALLIS, Sir Kinahan (1883-1959)

Adviser, Ministry of Interior, Iraq Government, 1921-35. Ambassador, Iraq, 1941-45. Chairman, Foreign Office Middle East Committee, 1945-46.

It is understood that no papers survive apart from a few letters at the Middle East Centre, St Antony's College, Oxford.

CORYNDON, Sir Robert Thorne (1870-1925)

Governor, Uganda, 1917-20; Kenya, 1923-25 (and High Commissioner, Zanzibar, 1923-25).

A collection of papers survives at Rhodes House Library, Oxford. The 18 boxes contain material mostly relating to East Africa; Uganda; the administration of Kenya, with special emphasis on the Indian controversy and Coryndon's interests in transport, agriculture and veterinary advances. The other papers consist of unofficial correspondence relating to the British South Africa Company, copies of Coryndon's articles and biographical material collected together after Coryndon's death. The collection also includes papers of Major Eric Dutton, Coryndon's private secretary (1920-25).

COTTON, Sir (Harry) Evan Auguste (1868-1939)

M.P. (Lib.) East Finsbury, July-Nov. 1918. Member, London County Council. Journalist in India. President, Bengal Legislative Council, 1922-25.

A collection of papers is in the care of Col. H. E. M. Cotton, 2 Grotes Place, Blackheath, London SE3 0QH. Many of the papers have been microfilmed for the India Office Library. The microfilm covers a series of letters from Lord Lytton (1922-29) and Lord Curzon (1924-25); letters to Sir Evan Cotton (1878-1932); and a collection of newspaper cuttings (1906-34) on Cotton's career in India. A further collection of papers relating to Cotton's historical research, and in particular a proposed book on Thomas and William Daniel, has been deposited at the India Office Library.

COTTON, Sir Henry John Stedman (1845-1915)

Chief Secretary, Government of Bengal, 1891-96. Acting Home Secretary, Government of India, 1896. Chief Commissioner, Assam, 1896-1902. M.P. (Lib.) Nottingham East, 1906-10.

A collection of papers remains in the care of Col. H. E. M. Cotton, 2 Grotes Place, Blackheath, London SE3 0QH. A microfilm of most of the papers is held at the India Office Library. The material includes letters to Sir Henry Cotton (1889-1915), correspondence (1899-1902) with prominent figures including Lord Curzon, press cuttings and copies of articles on India written by Sir Henry and by Sir Evan Cotton.

COUCHMAN, Admiral Sir Walter Thomas (1905-)

Director of Naval Air Organisation and Training, 1947. Deputy Controller of Supplies (Air), Ministry of Supply, 1955-56. Vice Chief of Naval Staff, 1960.

According to information supplied by the Imperial War Museum, Sir Walter has retained no papers.

COUPLAND, Professor Sir Reginald (1884-1952)

Historian of the British Empire. Member of Peel Commission, 1936-37.

Coupland destroyed most of his personal papers before his death, but some material survives at Rhodes House Library. These papers consist of travel diaries and albums (1913-42), and papers relating to the history of the British Empire and Commonwealth (1904-48).

COURTHOPE, William John (1842-1917)

1st Civil Service Commissioner, 1892-1907.

Efforts to trace members of the family were not successful.

COURTNEY, Air Chief Marshal Sir Christopher Lloyd (1890-)

Chief Staff Officer, Iraq Command, 1931-33. Director of Training, Air Ministry, 1933-34. Director of Staff Duties, 1934-35. Director of Operations and Intelligence and Deputy Chief of Air Staff, 1935-36. Air Officer Commanding, British Forces in Iraq, 1937-38. Air Member for Supply and Organisation, Air Council, 1940-45.

There is a small amount of material at the Royal Air Force Museum, Hendon. No details are available.

COVELL, Major-General Sir Gordon (1887-   )

Military career; Army Medical Service.

Rhodes House Library, Oxford, holds a journal relating to the military campaign in East Africa (1914-17), and a series of reminiscences of the campaign, together with a collection of letters sent home (1914-20).

COWAN, Admiral Sir Walter Henry, 1st Bt (1871-1956)

A.D.C. to Lord Kitchener and Naval A.D.C. to Earl Roberts, South African War, 1901. Naval service, World War I. Captain, H.M.S. *Princess Royal*, during Battle of Jutland, 1916. C.-in-C., North America and West Indies Station, 1926-28.

A collection of papers is available at the National Maritime Museum. This consists of the journals kept by Cowan when a junior officer, and a captain's order book, a few official papers, and photographs. The collection contains little detailed information concerning Cowan's later naval career. Correspondence with Vt Cunningham (1939-55) is in the British Library (Add. MSS. 52562).

COWANS, General Sir John Steven (1862-1921)

Served India, 1906-10. Director-General, Territorial Forces, 1910-12. Quartermaster-General, 1912-19.

The Imperial War Museum holds a collection of letters, newscuttings and photographs (1916-20). Cowans' letters to Asquith are included in the Asquith Collection at the Bodleian Library, Oxford.

COX, Lieutenant-Colonel Sir (Charles) Henry (1880-1953)

British Resident, Transjordan, 1924-39.

Lady Cox states that she has none of her late husband's papers. However, Mrs Patricia Sparrow, Bottle Lane Cottage, Shottesbrooke, Maidenhead, Berks., Sir Henry's daughter, feels that her brother, presently in Zambia, has some papers.

COX, Dame Marjorie Sophie (1893-   )

Member, Beveridge Committee on Social Security. Deputy Secretary, Pensions and National Insurance, 1946-54.

Dame Marjorie Cox states that she has destroyed her private diaries, papers, letters and press cuttings. She retains a few papers only, including a memorandum to the Beveridge Committee and subsequent correspondence and press cuttings regarding proposals for workmen's compensation.

COX, Major-General Sir Percy Zachariah (1864-1937)

Consul and Political Agent, Muscat, 1899-1904. Consul-General, Bushire, 1904. Political Resident, Persian Gulf, 1909. Foreign Secretary, Government of India, 1914. Chief Political Officer, Indian Expeditionary Force, 'D', 1914-18. Acting Minister, Persia, 1918-20. High Commissioner, Mesopotamia, 1920-23.

Messrs Child & Child, successors to the solicitors who acted for Sir Percy, have retained no papers from the estate and cannot provide the addresses of any surviving members of the family. Some papers relating to Sir Percy Cox are contained in the Philby Collection at the Middle East Centre, St Antony's College, Oxford.

CRACE, Admiral Sir John Gregory (1887-1968)

Naval career from 1902; served World War I. Commanded Australian Squadron (Coral Sea), 1939-42. Admiral Superintendent, H.M. Dockyard, Chatham, 1942-46.

The Imperial War Museum has a collection of Crace's midshipman's journals, logs and diaries (1939-42), various reports on important naval engagements during the war and photograph albums.

CRAIGIE, Sir Robert Leslie (1883-1959)

Assistant Under-Secretary, Foreign Office, 1934-37. Ambassador, Japan, 1937-41. U.K. Representative, United Nations War Crimes Commission, 1945-48.

Papers remain with Mr Robert Craigie (son), but no further details were available at the time of writing.

CRAVEN, Commander Sir Charles Worthington, 1st Bt (1884-1944)

Air Council Civil Member for Development and Production and Chairman, Air Supply Board, 1940. Controller-General, Ministry of Aircraft Production, 1941-42. Industrial Adviser to Minister of Production, 1943-45.

Lady Craven, St Andrews Cottage, Donhead St Andrew, near Shaftesbury, Dorset, was unable to help in the survey.

CREASE, Captain Thomas E. (1875-1942)

Naval career.

Certain records of Captain Crease, as Naval Secretary to Lord Fisher during his two appointments as 1st Sea Lord and in the first year of his chairmanship of the Board of Invention and Research (1915-16), are available at the Naval Library, Ministry of Defence. One volume includes the 'inside story' of Fisher's resignation in May 1915; another volume consists of the proceedings of the Beresford Inquiry of 1909.

CREASY, Admiral of the Fleet Sir George Elvey (1895-1972)

Naval career from 1908. Director of Anti-Submarine Warfare, 1940-42. Chief of Staff to Allied Naval C.-in-C., 1943-44. 5th Sea Lord and Deputy Chief of Naval Staff (Air), 1948-49. Vice Chief of Naval Staff, 1949-51. C.-in-C., Home Fleet, and Eastern Atlantic (NATO), 1952-54; Portsmouth, and Channel Command (NATO), 1954-57.

Sir George Creasy's surviving papers, few in number, have been given to the National Maritime Museum.

CREASY, Sir Gerald Hallen (1897-   )

Governor, Gold Coast, 1947-49; Malta, 1949-54.

Rhodes House Library, Oxford, has xerox copies of a West African diary (1943-44), a few nineteenth-century family papers and a tape recording and transcript of an interview conducted by Sir G. H. Creasy. He himself retains a collection of unsorted papers.

CREEDY, Sir Herbert James (1878-1973)

Private Secretary to successive Secretaries of State for War, 1913-20. Permanent Under-Secretary for War, 1924-39. Member and Secretary, Army Council, 1920-39.

Sir Herbert Creedy held very clear views on the retaining of papers by senior civil servants and at no time kept any private notes or diaries. However, a few useful letters and miscellaneous newscuttings and papers, mostly relating to Creedy's service as Private Secretary to Lord Kitchener in World War I, survive at the Imperial War Museum. The Private Office Collection (W.O. 159) at the Public Record Office includes material collected by Creedy.

CREWE, 1st M of
Robert Offley Ashburton Crewe-Milnes, 2nd Baron Houghton (1858-1945)

Lord President of the Council, 1905-08, 1915-16. Secretary of State for the Colonies, 1908-10. Lord Privy Seal, 1908-11, 1912-15. President, Board of Education, 1916. Ambassador, France, 1922-28. Secretary of State for War, 1931.

Although many of Crewe's papers were destroyed during his lifetime, a large collection survives at Cambridge University Library. The papers comprise general correspondence, personal papers, copies of speeches (1908-39), miscellaneous papers, India Office papers and printed material. At the Public Record Office a volume of reports to Crewe (1926) from the Press Attaché in France is included in the Foreign Office Private Office series (F.O. 800/330). For further details, readers should consult Hazlehurst and Woodland, op. cit., pp. 106-7.

CRIPPS, Sir Richard Stafford (1889-1952)

M.P. (Lab.) Bristol East, 1931-50; Bristol South East, 1950. Solicitor-General, 1930-31. Ambassador, U.S.S.R., 1940-42. Lord Privy Seal and Leader of the House of Commons, 1942. Minister, Aircraft Production, 1942-45. President, Board of Trade, 1945-47. Minister, Economic Affairs, 1947. Chancellor of the Exchequer, 1947-50.

Many of Cripps's papers remain with his widow, Dame Isobel Cripps, but these are not available for research. However, other material has been deposited in the Library of Nuffield College, Oxford. These papers cover the period 1930-50 and are divided into speech files and special subject files, which include constituency and Labour Party papers. For further details, readers should see Hazlehurst and Woodland, op. cit., p. 42.

CROFT, Sir William Dawson (1892-1964)

Chief Civil Assistant to Minister of State in Cairo, 1943-45. Chairman, Board of Customs and Excise, 1947-55.

Certain files relating to Sir W. D. Croft survive in H.M. Customs and Excise Library. Efforts to contact members of the family were unsuccessful.

CROMER, 1st E of
Sir Evelyn Baring (1841-1917)

Agent and Consul-General, Egypt, 1883-1907.

Private and official correspondence and papers (1872-1929), covering Cromer's career as Chief Secretary to the Viceroy of India (1872-76), as Commissioner of the Egyptian Public Debt (1877-79) and Minister Plenipotentiary in Egypt, are available at the Public Record Office (F.O. 633). The papers also deal with Cromer's activities in parliamentary and political affairs in Britain, and some personal and literary correspondence is included in the collection. Miscellaneous papers for the period 1892-1915 are in the British Library (Add. MSS. 44093-11) ·

CROSBY, Sir Josiah (1880-1958)

Consul General, Saigon, 1920; and Batavia, 1921-31. Minister, Panama, 1931-34, and Siam, 1934-41.

Crosby's sister, Mrs E. Porter of Southport could not be contacted. The Hong Kong and Shanghai Banking Corporation, Crosby's representatives, know of no papers.

CROWE, Sir Eyre Alexander Barby Wichart (1864-1925)

Permanent Under-Secretary, Foreign Office, 1920-25.

A very large collection of letters, covering Crowe's early life between the ages of eighteen and twenty, remains in the possession of Miss Sybil Crowe in Oxford. These papers are not available for inspection. Private Office correspondence (1907-25) covering Crowe's work at the Foreign Office is held at the Public Record Office (F.O. 800/243). Correspondence (1919) concerning Italy and the Adriatic can be found in the Lothian papers at the Scottish Record Office.

CROWE, Brigadier-General John Henry Verinder (1862-1948)

Commander, Royal Artillery in East Africa, 1915-17. General Staff, 1917-18.

Duke University, Durham, North Carolina, holds a series of eight letters (1917-42) from Field-Marshal Smuts to Crowe, concerning publication of Crowe's history of the East African campaign.

CRUTCHLEY, Ernest Tristram (1878-1940)

British Representative in Australia, 1931-35. Assistant Under-Secretary, Dominions Office, 1936, 1937. Public Relations Officer, Post Office, 1935-39; Ministry of Home Security, 1939-40.

Mr Brooke Crutchley, 2 Courtyards, Little Shelford, Cambridge, states that E. T. Crutchley kept a diary in five notebooks from 1932 until his death. These diaries remain with Mr Brooke Crutchley.

CULLEN OF ASHBOURNE, 1st B
Sir Brien Cokayne (1864-1932)

Governor, Bank of England, 1918-20.

The Hon. Miss D. Cokayne, Windy Brae, Rectory Farm, Finchampstead, Berks., has a good collection of family papers, including some relating to her father, Lord Cullen of Ashbourne. The papers are mainly letters written to Cullen by members of his family, and correspondence between Cullen and his wife about their children.

CUNLIFFE, 1st B
Walter Cunliffe (1855-1919)

Governor, Bank of England, 1913-18

The Hon. Geoffrey Cunliffe says that his father did not keep a diary or any papers which would be of value.

CUNNINGHAM, General Sir Alan Gordon (1887-   )

Served European War, 1914-18, and War of 1939-45. G.O.C., East Africa Forces, 1940-41; Northern Ireland, 1943-44. G.O.C.-in-C., 8th Imperial Army in Middle

East, 1941; Eastern Command, 1944-45. High Commissioner and C.-in-C., Palestine, 1945-48.

A full collection of Palestine papers has been deposited with the Middle East Centre at St Antony's College, Oxford. General Cunningham will leave his military papers to the Liddell Hart Centre for Military Archives.

CUNNINGHAM OF HYNDHOPE, 1st Vt
Admiral of the Fleet Sir Andrew Browne Cunningham, 1st Bt
(1883-1962)

Naval career from 1898, including active service in World War I. Deputy Chief of Naval Staff, 1938-39. C.-in-C., Mediterranean, 1939-42. Head of British Admiralty Delegation, Washington, 1942. 1st Sea Lord and Chief of Naval Staff, 1943-46.

Twenty-eight volumes of correspondence and papers kept by Vt Cunningham are in the care of the British Library (Add. MSS. 52,557-52,584). The collection includes his family correspondence from 1898; general correspondence (1898-1962); correspondence with senior naval colleagues from 1939; naval telegrams (1940-46); diaries (1944-46); speeches, with related correspondence (1946-58); a draft of *A Sailor's Odyssey*, with related correspondence (1949); and papers relating to the demolition of Heligoland (1919-26). This collection is reserved for thirty years from the date of writing. A few documents only relating to Vt Cunningham are retained by the National Maritime Museum. Churchill College, Cambridge, has a quantity of correspondence and materials gathered from various sources (1928-67) for a biography.

CUNNINGHAM, Sir George (1888-1964)

Political Agent, North Waziristan, 1922-23. Counsellor, Kabul, 1925-26. Private Secretary to Viceroy of India, 1926-31. Governor, North West Frontier Province, 1937-46, 1947-48.

Papers deposited at the India Office Library are not available for inspection. The collection consists of papers, letters, notes and reports, mainly concerning the North West Frontier Province and Waziristan (1937-48), e.g. correspondence with the External Affairs Department regarding propaganda through Mullahs (c. 1941-42), and reports on the work of Congress governments in the North West Frontier Province and elsewhere (1937-42). There is also a collection of early diaries, letters and papers (1911-62), including several letters from Gandhi (1930-39), copies of official papers, texts of speeches and copies of published articles. Further papers are at Churchill College, Cambridge.

CUNNINGHAM, Sir Graham (1892-   )

Chief Executive and Controller-General, Munitions Production, Ministry of Supply, 1941-46. Chairman, Shipbuilding Advisory Committee, 1946-61. Deputy Chairman, Royal Commission on the Press, 1961-62.

Sir Graham has not kept a diary but has retained certain papers including some letters, mostly of a personal nature, and press cuttings.

CUNNINGHAM, Admiral of the Fleet Sir John Henry Dacres
(1885-1962)

Naval career. Director of Plans Division, Admiralty, 1930-32. Assistant Chief of Naval Staff, 1936-37; Assistant Chief of Naval Staff (Air), 1937-38. Chief of Naval

Air Services, 1938. Chief of Supplies and Transport, 1941-43. C.-in-C., Levant, 1943; Mediterranean, 1943-46. 1st Sea Lord and Chief of Naval Staff, 1946-48.

It is understood that no papers survive, except for some correspondence with Vt Cunningham of Hyndhope at the British Library.

CUNNISON, Sir Alexander (1879-1959)

Permanent Secretary, Pensions, 1941-45.

It is believed that no papers survive.

CURRIE, 1st B
Sir Philip Henry Wodehouse Currie (1834-1906)

Permanent Under-Secretary, Foreign Office, 1889. Ambassador, Turkey, 1893-98; Italy, 1898-1902.

Certain papers (1893-96), relating to the Turkish embassy, survive at the Public Record Office (F.O. 800/114). It was not possible to trace a surviving member of Lord Currie's family. There is correspondence on financial relations with Ireland and the Gold Standard Defence Association in the Welby papers at B.L.P.E.S.

CURRIE, Brigadier Douglas Hendrie (1892-1966)

Served European War, 1914-18; India. Military Secretary to Viceroy, 1944-48.

The solicitors who acted in Currie's estate were unable to find any information that would lead to the whereabouts of his papers.

CURTIS, Major-General Alfred Cyril (1894-1971)

Served Indian Army. Commander, Lucknow District, 1946.

A collection of papers relating to Curtis's service during World War II is held at the Imperial War Museum. There is a report on the 14th Indian Division (1943-45), and a farewell address by Curtis (9 Jan. 1946) to the Division.

CURTIS, Lionel George (1872-1955)

Served South African War, 1899-1902. Member, Transvaal Legislative Council. Secretary, Irish Conference, 1921. Adviser on Irish Affairs, Colonial Office, 1921-24. Author.

The papers of Lionel Curtis, together with some papers of the Round Table organisation, were given to the Bodleian Library in 1973. Many of Curtis's papers were destroyed in a fire in the early 1930s, so what remains of his own papers consists for the most part of about 150 boxes of correspondence from between 1930 and his death in 1955, with some correspondence from the late nineteenth and early twentieth centuries. Virtually nothing survives for the World War I period and the immediate post-war years. A substantial collection of papers of the Round Table organisation came to the Bodleian with the Curtis papers. These consist of about 50 boxes of correspondence and papers for the period 1910-20, with a few similar papers for the 1930s and 1940s. They include many memoranda on various subjects and correspondence of the Round Table office.

CURZON, 1st M
George Nathaniel Curzon, 5th Baron Scarsdale (1859-1925)

M.P. (Con.) Southport, 1886-1898. Under-Secretary of State, India, 1891-92;

Foreign Affairs, 1895-98. Viceroy and Governor-General of India, 1898-1905. Lord Privy Seal, 1915-16. President, Air Board, 1916. Lord President of the Council, 1916-19, 1924-25. Member, War Cabinet, 1916-19. Secretary of State for Foreign Affairs, 1919-24.

The India Office Library holds a large collection of Curzon's papers, covering his Indian activities and also the rest of his private and public life. Other papers, relating to Curzon's work at the Foreign Office, are included in the Private Office series (F.O. 800/28, 147-158) at the Public Record Office. A few electoral and political papers are retained by Southport Public Library. All these collections are described in further detail by Hazlehurst and Woodland, op. cit., pp.44-5.

CUSTANCE, Admiral Sir Reginald Neville (1847-1935)

Naval career. Naval Attaché, Washington and Paris, 1893-95. Director of Naval Intelligence, 1899-1902. Rear Admiral, Mediterranean Fleet, 1902-04. 2nd in Command, Channel Fleet, 1907-08.

Churchill College, Cambridge, has a collection of letters, 1909. The NRA has details of papers in other collections.

CUTHBERT, Vice-Admiral Sir John Wilson (1902-)

Naval career. Served on Joint Planning Staff, 1942-44. Deputy Controller, Admiralty, 1951-52. Flag Officer, Flotillas, 1953-55. Admiral Commanding Reserves, 1955-56. Flag Officer, Scotland, 1956-58.

According to information supplied to the Imperial War Museum and confirmed by the Vice-Admiral, no papers survive.

D'ABERNON, 1st Vt
Sir Edgar Vincent (1857-1941)

M.P. (Con.) Exeter, 1899-1906. Ambassador, Germany, 1920-26.

Forty-one volumes of papers are available in the British Library (Add. MSS. 48,922-48,962). These include papers relating to D'Abernon's Special Mission to Warsaw (1920); to his period as Ambassador in Berlin (1920-26); letters to Lady D'Abernon; general correspondence; diaries (1876-98); Berlin diaries (1920-23); and a manuscript of a proposed book on Egypt. Extracts from a diary (June-July 1922), kept whilst in Berlin, are in the Balfour papers (see NRA List 10026). There is also extensive correspondence in the Lloyd George papers now housed at the House of Lords Record Office.

DANE, Sir Louis William (1856-1946)

Resident, Kashmir after 1901. Envoy to Kabul, 1904-05. Foreign Secretary, Government of India, 1902-08. Lieutenant-Governor, Punjab, 1908-13.

Reports, letters and papers relating to the British Mission to Kabul (1904-05) are deposited at the India Office Library. The collection also includes a copy of the papers and diary of Lieutenant-General Sir Francis Booth Norman (1830-1901), and articles by Dane on the history of the Griffiths family in India. ·

DANIEL, Admiral Sir Charles Saumarez (1894-   )

Naval career; served World War I. Director of Plans, Naval Staff, Admiralty, 1940-41. 3rd Sea Lord and Controller of the Navy, 1945-49.

Papers deposited at Churchill College, Cambridge, include diaries covering Daniel's naval service during World War I.

DANNREUTHER, Sir Sigmund (1873-1965)

Controller of Finance and Accounting Officer, Munitions, 1917; Joint Secretary, 1920-21. Accounting Officer and Joint Secretary, Disposal and Liquidation Commission, 1921-24. Deputy Secretary, Air Ministry, 1923-34.

Mrs K. Goldsworthy, Sir Sigmund's daughter, states that her father left no diaries, memoirs or other private papers concerning his career in the Civil Service.

DARLING, Sir Malcolm Lyall (1880-1969)

Colonial administrator. Financial Commissioner, Punjab, 1936-39. Indian Editor, BBC, 1940-44.

The Cambridge South Asian Archive has a number of papers, including notes (1930s) relating to rural conditions; periodical articles written 1921-59, reprints and reviews; notes and drafts of published works; notes on a mission to Yugoslavia (1951) and on land reform and co-operation in Egypt and Italy (1955) and correspondence (1960s).

DARLINGTON, Colonel Sir Henry Clayton (1877-1959)

Served European War, 1914-18 (Egypt, Gallipoli and France).

Some papers relating to training for the Gallipoli campaign are at the Liddell Hart Centre for Military Archives.

DAVIDSON, Major-General Alexander Elliott (1880-1962)

Secretary, Mechanical Transport Committee, War Office, 1910-14. Served European War, 1914-18. Chief Inspector, Royal Engineers Stores, 1920-24. Deputy Assistant Director of Fortification and Works, 1924-25. Chairman, Technical Committee, Mechanical Warfare Board, 1927-31. Assistant Director of Works, War Office, 1931-35. Director of Mechanisation, War Office, 1936.

Mr I. S. Davidson, Torton Grove, Hartlebury, Worcs., writes that any papers left by his father would be with his sister, Miss M. E. Davidson.

DAVIDSON, Major-General Francis Henry Norman (1892-1973)

Served European War, 1914-18. Director of Military Intelligence, War Office, 1940-44. Deputy Head, British Army Staff, Washington, 1944-46. Colonel Commanding, Intelligence Corps, 1952-60.

The Liddell Hart Centre for Military Archives holds a series of narratives on the Moscow Allied Military Mission of 1939, and on Davidson's service with I Corps (1939) and as Director of Military Intelligence. The Centre also has certain maps on the war produced by Davidson.

DAVIDSON, Major-General Sir John Humphrey (1876-1954)

General Staff, European War, 1914-18, and Director of Military Operations in France. M.P. (Con.) Fareham, 1918-31.

A slim file of papers has been given to the National Library of Scotland (Acc. 3679). The papers include copies of articles, pamphlets and maps relating to World War I, a speech by Sir Archibald Sinclair on Earl Haig, and certain notes and reviews relating to Davidson's book and other books on Haig.

DAVIDSON, Sir Walter Edward (1859-1923)

Governor, Seychelles, 1904-12; Newfoundland, 1913-17; New South Wales, 1918-23.

Rhodes House Library, Oxford, holds certain papers, including the transcript of diaries (1907-12) kept while Governor of the Seychelles.

DAVIES, Sir Alfred Thomas (1861-1949)

Permanent Secretary, Welsh Department of Board of Education, 1907-25.

Certain papers from Sir A. T. Davies's library have been deposited in the National Library of Wales. These include: material relating to British Prisoners of War Book Scheme (Educational) (1914-18), comprising copies of two booklets by Sir Alfred, *Student Captives, I* and *Student Captives, II* (1917-18), a fully documented typescript history of the whole movement, an index and files of notes and copies used in the compilation of the work; three bound volumes of a magazine produced by prisoners, printed prospectus of study and other papers, at Ruhleben Camp, near Berlin; press cuttings relating to the scheme; official publications on treatment of prisoners, and letters of support for the scheme. Other papers relate to the publication by Sir Alfred of a book entitled *Robert Owen ... A Memoir* (1948); and typescript copies of a booklet entitled *Owned of God: or Moody and Sankey, 1875 and 1883; Some Memoirs and a Tribute,* which Sir Alfred proposed to publish, together with a Welsh translation.

DAVIES, General Sir Francis John (1864-1948)

Served South African War, 1899-1901. Assistant Director of Military Operations, from 1904. Brigadier-General, General Staff, Aldershot Command, 1910-13. Director of Staff Duties, War Office, 1913-14. G.O.C., 8th Division, 1914-15; VIII Corps, Middle East Force, 1915-16. Military Secretary, War Office, 1916-19. G.O.C.-in-C., Scottish Command, 1919-23.

Lt.-Col. H. R. H. Davies can trace none of his father's papers.

DAVIES, Major-General Henry Rudolph (1865-1955)

Commanded 3rd Brigade, 1915-16; 33rd Brigade, 1917; 11th Division, 1917-19; 49th Division, 1919-23.

A collection of papers survives at the Worcestershire Record Office. The papers consist of letters and journals: 52nd Light Infantry (1884-1915); Burma (1887-88); North West Frontier (1897-98); China (1900-01); South Africa (1901-02); and the European War.

DAVIES, Major-General Llewelyn Alberic Emilius Price- (1878-1965)

Served South Africa, 1899-1902, European War, 1914-18. President, Standing Committee of Enquiry regarding Prisoners of War, 1918-19. Assistant Adjutant-General, Aldershot Command, 1920-24. Commanding 145th Infantry Brigade, 1924-27. Assistant Adjutant and Quartermaster-General, Gibraltar, 1927-30.

A collection of papers has been deposited at the National Army Museum. The diaries relate to Price-Davies's career in the Boer War, in World War I when Price-Davies was a Staff Officer and a Brigade Commander, and with the Home Guard (1940-44).

DAVIS, Sir Charles Thomas (1873-1938)

Permanent Under-Secretary, Dominions Office, 1925-30.

Efforts to trace the family were unsuccessful. Apart from Lady Davis, only the solicitors, Messrs Stanley Attenborough & Co., Dorland House, Regent Street, London SW1, were mentioned in the Will and Act of Probate. Contact with the solicitors was not secured.

DAVIS, Admiral Sir William Wellclose (1901-)

Naval career. Deputy Director of Plans and Cabinet Offices, 1940-42. Commander, H.M.S. *Mauritius*, 1943-44. Director of Under-Water Weapons, 1945-46. Naval Secretary, Admiralty, 1950-52. Vice Chief of Naval Staff, 1954-57. C.-in C., Home Fleet, and Eastern Atlantic (NATO), 1958-60.

Lady Davis (widow) has retained certain of her husband's papers.

DAWKINS, Sir Horace Christian (1867-1944)

Clerk of the House of Commons, 1930-37.

Mr C. R. V. Holt, Sir Horace's nephew and executor to the late Lady Dawkins, knows of no surviving papers.

DAWNAY, Major-General Guy Payan (1878-1952)

Served South Africa, 1899-1902; European War, 1914-18 (Gallipoli and Palestine).

An important collection of papers survives at the Imperial War Museum. The material includes official and private manuscripts, typescripts, letters and documents, maps, reports and photographs, relating to (1) the Dardanelles (1915); (2) Egypt, Palestine and the Egyptian Expeditionary Force (1916-17); (3) France (1918); and (4) personal and literary matters. Dawnay was Chief of Staff to Hamilton in the Dardanelles, to Allenby in Egypt, and to Haig in France.

DAWSON, Rear-Admiral Sir Oswald Henry (1882-1950)

Naval career from 1898. Director of Navigation, Admiralty, 1927-30. Flag Captain and Chief Staff Officer, 2nd Battle Squadron, 1930-31. Commander, Navigation School, Portsmouth, 1932-41. Commodore responsible for Mercantile Convoys, 1939-45.

The Imperial War Museum has a brief autobiography covering the years 1898-1919, and a diary, 1939-45.

DE BARTOLOME, Admiral Sir Charles Martin (1871-1941)

Naval career from 1885. 3rd Sea Lord and Controller of the Navy, 1918-19. Director-General of Development, Ministry of Transport, 1919-22.

The Admiral's son reports that no papers relating to his father's career were found after his death.

DE BUNSEN, Sir Maurice William Ernest (1852-1932)

Minister, Paris, 1902-05; Portugal, 1905. Ambassador, Spain, 1906-13; Austria-Hungary, 1913-14. Special Ambassador, South America, 1918.

A collection of papers has been catalogued by the National Register of Archives. The papers include diaries and notebooks and a mass of letters written by De Bunsen to his family. There is also some diplomatic material. Enquiries should be directed to the N.R.A.

DE BURGH, General Eric (1881-1948)

Army career; active service in World War I, and in India (North West Frontier, 1936-37).

A photostat copy (39 pp.) of a typescript autobiography of de Burgh, covering the years 1881 — 1948, and including accounts of his active service, is in the care of the National Army Museum.

DE CHAIR, Admiral Sir Dudley Rawson Stratford (1864-1958)

Naval service from 1878, including active service in World War I. Assistant Controller of the Navy, 1910-12. Naval Secretary to 1st Lord of the Admiralty, 1912-14. Naval Adviser to Foreign Office on Blockade Affairs, 1916-17. President, Inter-Allied Commission on Enemy Warships, 1921-23. Governor, New South Wales, 1923-30.

A collection of Sir Dudley de Chair's papers has been donated to the Imperial War Museum. The material includes diaries (1882, 1894, 1900-01, 1922); papers relating to the 10th Cruiser Squadron (Northern Patrol) which Admiral de Chair commanded between 1914-16; correspondence from other prominent naval figures of World War I; press cuttings; and draft copies of Admiral de Chair's memoirs, covering his years in Australia (1924-30).

DEEDES, Brigadier-General Sir Wyndham Henry (1883-1956)

Military Attaché, Constantinople, 1918-19. Director-General, Public Security, Egypt, 1919-20. Chief Secretary, Palestine, from 1920.

A collection of papers survives with Rt Hon. W. F. Deedes, New Hayters, Aldington, Kent, and copies are held at the Middle East Centre, St Antony's College, Oxford. The papers include letters home during service in the Ottoman Gendarmerie (1910-14), the Gallipoli campaign, Palestine campaign, etc., and a few letters received and sent during his term in Palestine (1920-23) and his subsequent relations with the Zionists. One letter from Sir M. Hankey argues against a separate peace with Turkey. Other papers concern the conflict of British and French interests (1916).

DE GUINGAND, Major-General Sir Francis W. (1900-)

Military Assistant, Secretary of State for War, 1939-40. Director of Military Intelligence, Middle East, 1942. Chief of Staff, 8th Army, 1942-44; 21st Army Group, 1944-45.

The Liddell Hart Centre for Military Archives holds miscellaneous papers (mainly 1942-45), covering De Guingand's work as Chief of Staff to the 8th Army and 21st Army Group.

DE LA FERTE, Air Chief Marshal Sir Philip Bennet Joubert (1887-1965)

Served European War, 1914-18. Air Officer Commanding, Fighting Area, 1934-36. R.A.F. India, 1937-39. Air Officer C.-in-C., Coastal Command 1936-37, 1941-43. Assistant Chief of Air Staff. Deputy Chief of Staff (Information and Civil Affairs), South East Asia Command, 1943-44. Director of Public Relations, Air Ministry, 1946-47.

The Royal Air Force Museum has a collection of diaries, files, logbooks, letters and photographs for the period 1908-62. Some of the material relates to work with the B.B.C. (1940-41).

DEMPSEY, General Sir Miles Christopher (1896-1969)

Served European War, 1914-18; Iraq operations, 1919-20; War of 1939-45. Commander, 13th Infantry Brigade, Dunkirk; XIII Corps, Sicily and Italy; 2nd Army, Normandy and North West Europe; 14th Army, Singapore and Malaya. C.-in-C., Allied Land Forces in South East Asia, 1945-46; Middle East, 1946-47; (designate) United Kingdom Land Forces, 1951-56.

A complete set of 2nd Army Planning Intelligence Summaries and 2nd Army Intelligence Summaries (1944-45) have been given to the Liddell Hart Centre for Military Archives.

DENHAM, Sir Edward Brandis (1876-1938)

Governor, Gambia, 1928-30; British Guiana, 1930-34. Captain-General and Governor-in-Chief, Jamaica, 1934-38.

Rhodes House Library, Oxford, has a collection of miscellaneous papers (1911-32) and diaries, relating to service in Mauritius (1921-23), Kenya (1923-28), Gambia (1928-30), British Guiana (1930-34) and Jamaica (1934-38).

DENING, Sir Maberly Esler (1897-)

Chief Political Adviser to Supreme Allied Commander, South East Asia, 1943-46. Assistant Under-Secretary, Foreign Office, 1946-50. U.K. Political Representative, Japan, 1951-52; Ambassador, 1952-57.

Sir Esler Dening's niece, Miss Fenella C. Dening, has written that many of her uncle's possessions, including any papers which survive, are in store and therefore unavailable for inspection. Sir Esler did not keep a diary or press cuttings.

DENMAN, 3rd B
Thomas Denman (1874-1954)

Governor-General, Australia, 1911-14.

A collection of letters, telegrams and other documents (1909-14) can be found in the National Library of Australia.

DENNY, Admiral Sir Michael Maynard (1896-1972)

Naval career. Chief of Staff to C.-in-C., Home Fleet, 1942-43. 3rd Sea Lord and Controller of the Navy, 1949-53. C.-in-C., Home Fleet, 1954-55.

Messrs Lloyds Bank Ltd, Trust Division, of Richmond, Surrey, state that most of Admiral Denny's papers and naval records were destroyed after his death.

DE NORMANN, Sir Eric (1893-   )

Served European War, 1914-19; Army Service Corps, Salonika. Civil Service career from 1920. Deputy Secretary, Ministry of Works, 1943-54. Chairman, Ancient Monuments Board for England, 1955-64.

Sir Eric donated to the Imperial War Museum his letters to his mother during World War I. The correspondence relates to the feelings of the British Forces in Salonika during this period. Sir Eric has no private papers covering his Civil Service career.

DERBY, 17th E of
Edward George Villiers Stanley, Baron Stanley (1865-1948)

M.P. (Con.) Westhoughton, 1892-1906. Financial Secretary, War Office, 1900-03. Postmaster-General, 1903-05. Under-Secretary of State for War, 1916; Secretary of State, 1916-18, 1922-24. Ambassador, France, 1918-20.

The Derby family papers at Liverpool City Library include a very large collection of papers relating to the 17th Earl. The material is divided into five main series, relating to Liverpool, Lancashire, government offices, public life and domestic life. A mass of correspondence up to 1947, and papers connected with each of Derby's public offices, have survived, and a good number of subject files, memoranda and minutes, and correspondence files relate to the period at the Paris embassy. Further details are given in Hazlehurst and Woodland, op. cit., pp.138-9.

DERING, Sir Henry Nevill, 9th Bt (1839-1906)

Agent and Consul-General, Bulgaria, 1892-94. Minister, Mexico, 1894-1900; Brazil, 1900-06.

Lady Dering, Bellings, Midhurst, Sussex, has some papers relating to the 9th Bt, *A Day to Day Diary of the Berlin Congress, 1878.*

DERING, Sir Herbert Guy Nevill (1867-1933)

Counsellor, Rome, 1911-15. Minister, Siam, 1915-19. High Commissioner, Bulgaria, 1919-20. Minister, Romania, 1920-26.

Lady Dering, Bellings, Midhurst, Sussex, has some papers relating to Sir Herbert. The bulk of the small collection consists of private letters written to Sir Herbert Dering and his wife in Siam and Romania, and private letters from (among others) King Gustav of Sweden and the King of Siam. Other papers include a few press cuttings and drafts of dispatches to the Foreign Office. A copy of an unpublished autobiography also survives.

DE ROBECK, Admiral of the Fleet Sir John Michael, 1st Bt (1862-1928)

Naval career from 1875. Admiral of Patrols, 1912-14. Commanded Naval Force in Dardanelles, 1915. C.-in-C., Mediterranean, 1919-22; Atlantic Fleet, 1922-24.

The papers of Sir John de Robeck are located in Churchill College, Cambridge. They include letters (1901-27), material relating to the Dardanelles (1915-17) and papers on the Mediterranean (1918-22).

DE SALIS, Sir John Francis Charles, Count de Salis (1864-1939)

Minister, Montenegro, 1911-16; Holy See, 1916-23.

Efforts to contact the present Count de Salis were not successful.

DES GRAZ, Sir Charles Louis (1860-1940)

Charge d'Affaires, Tehran, 1902; Athens, 1903-04; Rome, 1905, 1906, 1907; Montenegro, 1906. Minister, Bolivia, 1908-10; Peru and Ecuador, 1908-13; Serbia, 1914-20.

A collection of papers is retained at Cambridge University Library. The four items comprise correspondence and papers (1893-1940), a diary (1914-16), papers relating to his appointment as K.C.M.G. (1915), and domestic papers, (1933).

DEVERELL, Field-Marshal Sir Cyril John (1874-1947)

General Staff, India, 1913-14. Served European War, 1914-18. Commanded United Provinces District, India, 1921-25. Quartermaster-General, India, 1927-30. Chief of General Staff, India, 1930-31. G.O.C.-in-C., Western Command, 1931-33; Eastern Command, 1933-36. Chief of Imperial General Staff, 1936-37.

The papers of Brigadier Harold Richard Sandilands, at the Liddell Hart Centre for Military Archives, include correspondence (1945-60) by Deverell and others about his ceasing to be C.I.G.S. No further papers were traced.

DEVONSHIRE, 9th D of
Victor Christian William Cavendish (1868-1938)

M.P. (Lib. Un.) Derbyshire West, 1891-1908. Financial Secretary, Treasury, 1903-05. Civil Lord of the Admiralty, 1915-16. Governor-General, Canada, 1916-21. Secretary of State, Colonies, 1922-24.

A small collection of papers, mainly relating to the period in Canada, survives with the present (11th) Duke of Devonshire, at Chatsworth House, Bakewell, Derbyshire DE4 1PN (Hazlehurst and Woodland, op. cit., p.31).

DEWAR, Vice-Admiral Kenneth Gilbert Balmain (1879-1964)

Naval career. Assistant Director of Plans Division, Naval Staff, 1917. Deputy Director, Naval Intelligence Division, 1925-27.

The papers of Dewar are in the care of the National Maritime Museum, and include collected papers relating to his work at the Admiralty during World War I; material relating to the inter-war years, and to World War II; and a diary, including engagements and personal notes.

DE WIART, Lieutenant-General Sir Adrian Carton (1880-1963)

Served South Africa, 1901; East Africa, 1914-15; European War, 1915-18. Commander, British Military Mission to Poland, 1918-24. British Military Mission with Polish Army. Commander, Central Norwegian Expeditionary Force, 1940. Special Military Representative to Generalissimo Chiang Kai-shek, 1943-46.

Lady Carton de Wiart states that her late husband kept no papers.

DEWING, Major-General Richard Henry (1891-   )

Served Mesopotamia and Persia, 1915-19. Director of Military Operations, 1939-40. Chief of Staff, Far East, 1940-41. Military mission, Washington, 1942. Chief of Army-R.A.F. Liaison Staff, Australia, 1943-44. SHAEF Mission to Denmark, 1945.

The Major-General states that there are no papers or diaries which would be of interest.

D'EYNCOURT, Sir Eustace Henry William Tennyson-, 1st Bt (1868-1951)

Director of Naval Construction and Chief Technical Adviser to Admiralty, 1912-23.

Certain papers are preserved at the National Maritime Museum.

DICKEN, Admiral Charles Gauntlett (1854-1937)

Naval career from 1867. Commodore at Hong Kong, 1903-05.

A collection of papers is housed at Trinity College, Cambridge.

DICKENS, Admiral Sir Gerald Charles (1879-1962)

Naval career; active service, World War I. Deputy Director, Plans Division, Admiralty, 1920-22. Director of Naval Intelligence Division, 1932-35. Commander, Reserve Fleet, 1935-37. Naval Attaché, The Hague, 1940. Principal Liaison Officer with Allied Navies, 1940. Flag Officer, Tunisia, 1943-45; Netherlands, 1945-46.

Captain Peter Dickens, R.N., Lye Green Forge, Crowborough, Sussex TN6 1UU, has retained a small collection of his father's papers. This contains a number of interesting letters and documents relating to public events.

DICKSON, Lieutenant-Colonel Harold Richard Patrick (1881-1959)

Colonial administrator. Political Agent, Kuwait, 1929-36.

The Middle East Centre at St Antony's College, Oxford, has a collection of papers (1915-19) relating to service in Mesopotamia; papers (1920, 1922) about negotiations with Ibn Saud; reports (1918-31) from Kuwait; and correspondence (1934-36).

DICKSON, John (d.1906)

Consul, Damascus, 1884-90; Jerusalem, 1890-1906.

The Middle East Centre of St Antony's College, Oxford, holds a collection of diaries.

DICKSON, Marshal of the Royal Air Force Sir William Forster (1898-   )

Director of Plans, Air Ministry, 1941-42. Commander, Nos. 9 and 10 Groups, Fighter Command, 1942-43; No. 83 Group, Tactical Air Force, 1943-44; Desert Air Force, 1944. Assistant Chief of Air Staff (Policy), Air Ministry, 1945-46. Vice-Chief of Air Staff, 1946-48. C.-in-C., Middle East Air Force, 1948-50. Member for Supply and Organisation, Air Council, 1950-52. Chief of the Air Staff, 1953-56. Chairman, Chiefs of Staff Committee, 1956-59. Chief of Defence Staff, 1958-59.

It was not possible to make contact.

DIGBY, Sir Kenelm Edward (1836-1916)

Permanent Under-Secretary, Home Office, 1895-1903.

Efforts to contact members of the family were not successful.

DILL, Field-Marshal Sir John Greer (1881-1944)

Served South Africa, 1901-02; European War, 1914-18. Director of Military Operations and Intelligence, War Office, 1934-36. Commander, British Forces in

Palestine, 1936-37. G.O.C.-in-C., Aldershot Command, 1937-39. Commander, 1st Army Corps in France, 1939-40. Chief of Imperial General Staff, 1940-41. Head of British Joint Staff Mission, United States, 1941-44.

The Liddell Hart Centre for Military Archives have undertaken enquiries regarding papers. No information was available at the time of writing.

DIMOLINE, Major-General William Alfred (1897-1965)

Served European War, 1914-19; India, 1920-22, 1935-36; Iraq, 1921; Nigeria, 1922-28; Staff College, 1933-34; Northern Rhodesia, 1937-39; War of 1939-45 in Abyssinia, Madagascar and Burma. G.O.C., East Africa, 1946-48. Commander, Aldershot District, 1948-51. U.K. Representative on Military Staff Committee, United Nations, 1951-53.

A collection of papers (1914-62) is housed at the Liddell Hart Centre for Military Archives. The material covers Dimoline's service with the Royal Signals in France during World War I, in India and Africa between the wars and during World War II, and also his subsequent career. Some of the later papers relate to Dimoline's work with the Inter-Parliamentary Union and with the Army Cadet Force. The collection includes a large number of photographs.

DIXON, Sir Pierson John (1904-1965)

Principal Private Secretary to Foreign Secretary, 1943-48. Ambassador, Czecho-slovakia, 1948-50. Deputy Under-Secretary, Foreign Office, 1950-54. Permanent Representative, United Nations, 1954-60. Ambassador, France, 1960-64.

Mr Piers Dixon, M.P., says that his father left a large number of papers and diaries, and that these are in due course to be deposited at Churchill College, Cambridge.

DOBBIE, Lieutenant-General Sir William George Sheddon (1879-1964)

Served South Africa, Ireland, European War, etc. Brigade Commander, Egypt, 1928-32. Inspector of the Royal Engineers, Commander of Chatham area, etc., 1933-35. G.O.C., Malaya, 1935-39. Governor, Malta, 1940-42.

A collection of papers survives with Colonel O.C.S. Dobbie, M.B.E., c/o Goodman, Brown & Warren, 30 John Street, London WC1.

DOBBS, Sir Henry Robert Conway (1871-1934)

Political Officer, Mesopotamia, 1915-16. Foreign Secretary, Indian Government, 1919. Head of British Mission, Kabul, 1920-21. High Commissioner and Consul-General, Iraq, 1923-29.

Contact with the solicitors mentioned in the Will and Act of Probate was not established.

DODDS, Sir James Leishman (1891-1972)

Minister, Bolivia, 1940-43; Cuba, 1944-49. Ambassador, Peru, 1949-51.

Sir J. L. Dodds left no papers relating to his career.

DODDS, Sir James Miller (1861-1935)

Under-Secretary, Scottish Office, 1909-21.

The late Sir J. L. Dodds had no papers relating to his father.

DOMVILLE, Admiral Sir Barry Edward (1878-1971)

Naval service from 1892. Assistant Secretary, Committee of Imperial Defence, 1912-14. Director of Plans Division, Admiralty, 1920-22. Director of Naval Intelligence Division, 1927-30.

A collection of papers at the National Maritime Museum includes diaries (1894-1970, 72 volumes), autobiographical notes and assorted press cuttings.

DON, Air Vice-Marshal Francis Percival (1886-1964)

Served European War, 1914-18, then Iraq, Egypt and Air Ministry. Air Attaché, Berlin, 1934-37. Head of Mission to French Air Forces, 1939. Air Officer in Charge of Administration, British Air Forces in France, 1940.

The Liddell Hart Centre for Military Archives found that Air Vice-Marshal Don had kept no papers.

DONALD, Air Marshal Sir Grahame (1891-   )

Served European War, 1914-18, and War of 1939-45. Air Officer C.-in-C., Maintenance Command, 1942-47.

Sir Grahame Donald has kept no papers of value.

DORMER, Sir Cecil Francis Joseph (1883-   )

Assistant Private Secretary to Secretary of State for Foreign Affairs, 1915-19. Chargé d'Affaires, Venezuela, 1919-21. Secretary of Legation. Holy See, 1921-25. Counsellor, Tokyo, 1926-29. Minister, Siam, 1929-34; Norway, 1934-40. Ambassador, Polish Government, 1941-43.

Sir Cecil Dormer kept few papers relating to his career, but retains one box of assorted records. The subject-matter includes Lord Northampton's accession mission to Paris, Racconigi, Athens and Constantinople (1910); the Abyssinia Mission to Britain for the Coronation of King George V; the Balfour Mission to the United States (1917); the affairs of the Vatican and of Japan; and there is an account of the German invasion of Norway in 1940.

DORRIEN, General Sir Horace Lockwood Smith- (1858-1930)

Served Zulu War, 1879; Egypt and the Sudan; India and South Africa, 1899-1901. Adjutant-General, India, 1901-03. C.-in-C., Aldershot, 1907-12; Southern Command, 1912-14; East African Forces, 1915-16. Commander, 2nd Army Corps and 2nd Army, 1914-15. Governor, Gibraltar, 1918-23.

Two volumes of papers are available at the British Library (Add. MSS. 52,776-7). The papers consist of a statement of Smith-Dorrien's activities in 1914-15, relating to Sir John French and the Battle of Le Cateau. The Imperial War Museum has records of correspondence between the General and the official historian, Major Becke, relating to the battle of Le Cateau and its background.

DOUGHERTY, Sir James Brown (1844-1934)

M.P. (Lib.) Londonderry, 1914-18. Under-Secretary to Lord-Lieutenant of Ireland, 1908-14.

The solicitors, Messrs Wells & Hind of Nottingham, retain no contact with the family. A son and daughter, John Gerald Dougherty and Miss Mary Dougherty, were named in the Will. Three letters can be found in the Plunkett papers (see NRA List 16228 p.21).

DOUGLAS OF BARLOCH, 1st B
Sir Francis Campbell Ross Douglas (1889-   )

M.P. (Lab.) Battersea North, 1940-46. Governor, Malta, 1946-49.

Lord Douglas has retained few records relating to his membership of the House of Commons. Most of his correspondence of this period dealt with constituency matters and was subsequently destroyed. He has retained a few papers relating to his Governorship of Malta, but no official correspondence. A collection of material relating to the period when Lord Douglas was Deputy Chairman of the Corby Development Corporation (1950-62) is to be deposited in the Northamptonshire Record Office.

DOUGLAS OF KIRTLESIDE, 1st B
Marshal of the Royal Air Force William Sholto Douglas (1893-1969)

Director of Staff Duties, Air Ministry, 1936-37. Assistant (then Deputy) Chief of Air Staff, 1938-40. Air Officer C.-in-C., Fighter Command, 1940-42; Middle East Command, 1943-44; Coastal Command, 1944-45. Air C.-in-C., British Air Forces of Occupation, Germany, 1945-46. C.-in-C. and Military Governor, British Zone of Germany, 1946-47.

An extensive collection of papers is held at the Imperial War Museum. Series of official and service papers relate to Douglas's career in World War I and later; to the Leros operation (1943); 'Overlord' (1944); Coastal Command questions (1948-49); and Douglas's service with B.E.A. Other material includes notes, drafts and correspondence relating to Douglas's published works, especially *Years of Combat* (1963); also House of Lords speeches; miscellaneous correspondence; photographs and news cuttings. Other papers (1914-18) are at the Royal Air Force Museum, Hendon.

DOUGLAS, General Sir Charles Whittingham Horsley (1850-1914)

Served Afghan War, 1879-80; South Africa, 1880-81, 1899-1901. Adjutant-General, 1904-09. G.O.C.-in-C., Southern Command, 1909-12. Inspector-General, Home Forces, 1912-14. Chief of Imperial General Staff, 1914.

Efforts to trace members of the family were not successful.

DOUGLAS, Sir William Scott (1890-1953)

Secretary, Department of Health, Scotland, 1937-39. Under-Secretary, Treasury, 1939-42. Permanent Secretary, Ministry of Supply, 1942-45; Ministry of Health, 1945-51.

Mrs M. Hutchinson, 3 Cavendish Road, Birkenhead, Merseyside L41 8AX, states that her father kept no detailed diaries, but there may be some press cuttings and a little correspondence amongst the unsorted papers of the late Lady Douglas.

DOWDING, 1st B
Air Chief Marshal Hugh Caswall Tremenheere Dowding (1882-1970)

Director of Training, Air Ministry, 1926-29. Air Member for Supply and Research, 1930-35; Research and Development, Air Council, 1930-36. Air Officer C.-in-C., Fighter Command, 1936-40. Special Duty (with Ministry of Aircraft Production) in United States, 1940-41.

A collection of papers is deposited in the Royal Air Force Museum. It covers his

R.A.F. career, and spans the years 1928-65. The records include files of papers and press cuttings, covering Palestine (1928-29), Fighter Command (1939-42), and his American visit (1940-41).

DOWNE, 8th Vt
Major-General Hugh Richard Dawnay (1844-1924)

Special Envoy, Persia, 1902-03.

The Dawnay family archive is held at the County Record Office, Northallerton, Yorkshire. Other unsorted papers remain with Vt Downe at Wykeham Abbey, Scarborough, Yorkshire.

DRAKE, Sir (John Henry) Eugen Vanderstegen Millington- (1889-1972)

Minister, Uruguay, 1934-41. Chief Representative, British Council in Spanish America, 1942-46.

Sir Eugen's papers remain in the care of Lady Effie Millington-Drake, and a biography is being undertaken by a member of the family. Enquiries should be addressed to Sir Eugen's elder son, Mr J. Millington-Drake, 40 St Mary Axe, London EC3. Certain papers relating to a book on the Battle of the River Plate are held in the Imperial War Museum.

DRAX, Admiral Hon. Sir Reginald Aylmer Ranfurly Plunkett-Ernle-Erle- (1880-1967)

Naval career from 1896. Director, Royal Naval Staff College, Greenwich, 1919-22. President, Naval Allied Control Commission (Berlin), 1923 and 1924. Director, Manning Department, Admiralty, 1930-32. C.-in-C., America and West Indies Station, 1932-34; Plymouth Station, 1935-38; The Nore, 1939-41. Commodore of Ocean Convoys, 1943-45.

The papers housed at Churchill College, Cambridge, are arranged in three groups: early files (1912-18); files from 1932-1939; and articles and papers. Early papers include war records, files on particular naval engagements, on education, battle cruisers, etc. The later material takes in 'war plans', articles by Admiral Drax, and records of overseas visits. The other naval papers comprise files on A. H. Pollen, H.M.S. *Lion*, miscellaneous printed papers, and intelligence reports (1915-19, 1941-45). The literary papers cover copies of published articles and drafts, copies of lectures given at the Naval Staff College and training pamphlets. Miscellaneous printed material completes the collection.

DREW, John Alexander (1907-   )

Assistant Secretary, Cabinet Office, 1945-48; Board of Trade, 1948-50. Assistant Under-Secretary, Ministry of Defence, 1951-67.

Mr Drew has no documents of any kind relating to his career in Crown Service.

DREYER, Admiral Sir Frederick Charles (1878-1956)

Naval career. Assistant Director, Anti-Submarine Division, Admiralty, 1916-17. Director of Naval Ordnance, 1917-18. Director of Naval Artillery, 1918-19. Assistant Chief of Naval Staff, 1924-27; Deputy Chief, 1930-33. C.-in-C., China Station, 1933-36. Inspector of Merchant Navy Gunnery, 1941-42. Chief of Naval Air Services, 1942-43.

The Private Office series (Adm. 205, First Sea Lord: Papers, 1939-45) at the Public Record Office includes papers relating to the career of Sir F. C. Dreyer. The family was not contacted by the survey.

DROGHEDA, 10th E of
Henry Charles Ponsonby Moore (1884-1957)

Director-General, Economic Warfare, 1942-45.

Lord Drogheda left no papers relating to his career.

DUBOULAY, Sir James Houssemayne (1868-1945)

Colonial Administrator. Private Secretary to Lord Hardinge (Viceroy), 1910-16. Secretary to the Home Department, Government of India, 1916.

His correspondence as Hardinge's private secretary, his notes and memoranda concerning Indian affairs, 1910-14, and correspondence with prominent Indian Civil Servants are with the Hardinge papers at Cambridge University Library.

DU CANE, General Sir John Philip (1865-1947)

Served South Africa, 1899-1902; European War, 1914-18. British Representative with Marshal Foch, 1918. Master-General of Ordnance, 1920-23. G.O.C.-in-C., Western Command, 1923-24; British Army of the Rhine, 1924-27. Governor and C.-in-C., Malta, 1927-31.

No papers survive, but a copy of Ducane's privately printed biography of Marshal Foch is held at the Imperial War Museum Library.

DUCKHAM, Sir Arthur McDougall (1879-1932)

Member, Council of Ministry of Munitions; Air Council, 1919. Director-General, Aircraft Production.

Lady Duckham, who was the sole executrix and only person mentioned in the Will and Act of Probate, was not traced.

DUFF, Lieutenant-Colonel Adrian Grant- (1869-1914)

Assistant Secretary (Military), Committee of Imperial Defence, 1910-13.

A diary covering the years whilst with the Committee of Imperial Defence is held at Churchill College, Cambridge, together with some correspondence (1912 and 1914), mostly about the *War Book*. A microfilm of the diaries is kept at the Imperial War Museum. The diaries, which are concerned entirely with administrative and political matters, are an invaluable account of the compilation of the *War Book*, which was largely the work of Grant-Duff.

DUFF, Admiral Sir Alexander Ludovic (1862-1933)

Director of Mobilisation Division, Admiralty War Staff, 1911-14. Rear-Admiral, 4th Battle Squadron, 1914-17. Director, Anti-Submarine Division, 1917. Assistant Chief of Naval Staff, 1918-19. C.-in-C., China Station, 1919-22.

Certain papers of Sir Alexander Duff are now in the care of the National Maritime Museum. These include correspondence between Duff and Jellicoe (1916-33); Duff's notes on the removal of Jellicoe (1917-18); Duff's correspondence with Admiral Bethell (1917-18), and miscellaneous correspondence (1917-37); and Admiralty and Ministry of Shipping papers (1918). Admiral Sir Alexander Duff's private diary (Oct. 1914-Nov. 1916) and certain other papers are also in the care of the National Maritime Museum.

DUFF, Sir Arthur Cuninghame Grant- (1861-1948)

Minister, Cuba, 1906-09; Dresden and Coburg, 1909-14; Peru and Ecuador, 1920-23; Chile, 1923-24; Sweden, 1924-27.

No papers could be located.

DUFF, General Sir Beauchamp (1855-1918)

Military Secretary to C.-in-C., India, 1895-99. Assistant Military Secretary (India), War Office, 1899. Served South Africa, 1899-1901. Adjutant-General, India, 1903-06. Chief of Staff, India, 1906-09. Military Secretary, India Office, 1910. C.-in-C., India, 1913-16.

Contact was not established with members of the General's family, and his solicitors, who were contacted, were unable to locate any papers. Relevant material is available in the Hardinge papers at Cambridge University Library.

DUFF, Sir (Charles) Patrick (1889-1972)

Private Secretary to successive Presidents of the Board of Trade, 1919-23, and to successive Prime Ministers, 1923-33. Secretary, Office of Works, 1933-41. Deputy High Commissioner, Canada, 1941-44. High Commissioner, New Zealand, 1945-49.

Lady Duff states that she destroyed all her late husband's diaries and papers, according to his wishes.

DUFF, Sir Evelyn Grant- (1863-1926)

Minister, Venezuela, 1910; Switzerland, 1913-16. Consul-General, Hungary, 1911-13.

A few letters to Sir Evelyn Grant-Duff, and from him to his father, are included in the collection of papers of Sir Mountstuart Elphinstone Grant-Duff (1829-1906), c/o Messrs Farrer & Co., 66 Lincolns Inn Fields, London WC2A 3CH.

DUKE, Sir Frederick William (1863-1924)

Lieutenant-Governor, Bengal, 1911. Member, Council of India, 1914-19. Permanent Under-Secretary, India, 1919-24.

The Private Office collection (D.714) at the India Office Library includes some material from Duke's time as Permanent Under-Secretary. Some relevant papers are also to be found in the Hardinge collection at Cambridge University Library.

DUMAS, Admiral Philip Wylie (1868-1948)

Naval career from 1881. Naval Attaché, Germany, Denmark and Netherlands, 1906-08. Assistant Director, Torpedoes, at Admiralty, 1914.

Certain papers are in the possession of Mrs Dumas, Woodpeckers, Snakey Lane, Preston Park, Brighton, Sussex. These include diaries (1905-14), mainly of family interest, but with entries on the pre-war Fisher regime at the Admiralty and on the German Navy.

DUNCAN, Sir Patrick (1870-1943)

Private Secretary to Lord Milner. Colonial Secretary, Transvaal, 1903-06. Minister of Interior, Public Health and Education, South Africa, 1921-24; Mines, 1933-36. Governor-General, South Africa, 1937-43.

A very large collection of papers is held in the Library of the University of Cape Town, South Africa. There is a considerable quantity of Sir Patrick Duncan's administrative and political papers, e.g. Transvaal Executive Council minutes (1903-04); material on railways, education, industry, and white labour; correspondence with Lionel Curtis and the Round Table; documents on Imperial relations, the South African Parliament, racial questions and 'native affairs'. Other categories of records consist of copies of speeches and articles, literary papers, private papers, diaries and notebooks, and several series of correspondence with prominent South Africans and with political figures outside South Africa. Further correspondence includes letters exchanged with the Countess Selborne (1907-43), and letters on particular subjects. The whole Patrick Duncan collection is supplemented by a further mass of Duncan family material (including letters exchanged between Sir Patrick and Lady Duncan and their children), and a quantity of scrapbooks, newspaper cuttings, photographs and mementoes.

DUNDONALD, 12th E of
Douglas Mackinnon Baillie Hamilton Cochrane (1852-1935)

Served Nile Expedition, 1884-85; South Africa, 1899-1902; Canadian Militia, 1902-04; European War, 1914-18.

The papers (1897-1923) consist of general correspondence, diaries, memoranda, speeches, reports and some printed material. Correspondents include Lord Roberts, Sir Henry Wilson, Baden-Powell, General Maude, Sir John French, General Gough, Lord Kitchener and Sir Garnet Wolseley. The original papers are with the Scottish Record Office, and the Douglas Library at Queen's University, Kingston, Ontario, holds a microfilm copy.

DUNLOP, Brigadier Sir John Kinninmont (1892-1974)

Served European War, 1914-18. Military historian. Regional Commissioner, etc., in Italy, 1943-45, and Germany, 1946-52; (Sardinia, 1943; Lazio and Umbria, 1944; Southern Italy, 1944; Venezia, 1945). Control Commission for Germany, 1946. Deputy Regional Commissioner, Hamburg, 1947. Land Commissioner, Lower Saxony, 1948; Hamburg, 1949. Consul-General, Hamburg, 1952-56.

The Imperial War Museum holds some letters and diaries, and a mass of official reports, correspondence and press cuttings covering his entire military career. These contain special reference to his service on the Military Mission to the U.S.A. (1917-18), his recruiting work on behalf of the Territorial Army in the 1930s, his service on the Allied Commission for Italy (1943-46) and, to a lesser extent, in Germany in a number of capacities after the Second World War.

DUNNELL, Sir Robert Francis, 1st Bt (1868-1960)

Secretary, Naval Mission to America, 1918; Demobilisation Section of the War Cabinet, 1919; Ministry of Transport, 1919-21.

Mr A. J. V. Merritt, a member of Sir Francis's family, states that no papers survive other than a very few personal papers.

DUNRAVEN AND MOUNT-EARL, 6th E of
Richard Southwell Windham Robert Wyndham-Quin (1887-1965)

Master of the Horse and Military Secretary to Lord-Lieutenant of Ireland, 1918-21.

There is a collection of Lord Dunraven's papers at the National Library of Ireland.

DURAND, Sir Henry Mortimer (1850-1924)

Foreign Secretary, Government of India, 1884-94. Minister, Persia, 1894-1900. Ambassador, Spain, 1900-03; United States of America, 1903-06.

Papers at the India Office Library consist of letter books and papers (1876-1908). The correspondence includes letters written to the Viceroy of India, Lord Lansdowne, by Durand during his mission to the Emir of Afghanistan in 1893, and letters written whilst Minister at Tehran. A further important collection of Durand papers is available at the School of Oriental and African Studies. The material, purchased from the Durand family in 1969, includes 15 diaries for the period 1870-1907, miscellaneous personal papers, letters on the 1874/5 Persia expedition, letters from Lansdowne on Afghanistan and Morocco, correspondence and press-cuttings relating to America, and four bound volumes of letters sent 1902-09. A more detailed inventory is available at the National Register of Archives (Report 14595).

EADY, Sir Crawfurd Wilfrid Griffin (1890-1962)

Secretary, Unemployment Assistance Board, 1934-38. Deputy Under-Secretary, Home Office, 1938-40. Chairman, Board of Customs and Excise, 1941-42. Joint 2nd Secretary, Treasury, 1942-52.

Messrs Parker Garrett & Co., London, stated that Sir Wilfrid's son, Mr David Max Eady, might be able to help. A few files relating to part of Sir Wilfrid's career survive at H.M. Customs and Excise Library.

EARLE, Sir Lionel (1866-1948)

Permanent Secretary, Office of Works, 1912-33.

Colonel Charles Earle, Sir Lionel's nephew and heir, states that he inherited no papers or letters. The papers used for the autobiography *Turn Over the Page* (1935) were destroyed during World War II. A little relevant material may be found in the Asquith papers at the Bodleian Library, Oxford.

EASTWOOD, Christopher Gilbert (1905-   )

Colonial Office service. Principal Assistant Secretary, Cabinet Office, 1945-47. Assistant Under-Secretary, Colonial Office, 1947-52, 1954-66. Commissioner of Crown Lands, 1952-54.

Mr Eastwood feels that he has kept few papers which would be of much interest. There are, however, a number of rough diaries and notes of visits abroad, etc., which were used for the compilation of official reports.

EATON, Vice-Admiral Sir John Willson Musgrave (1902-)

Naval career; active service in World War II. Director of Royal Naval Staff College, 1949-51. C.-in-C., America and West Indies, 1955-56. Deputy Supreme Allied Commander, Atlantic, 1955-57.

According to information given to the Imperial War Museum, Sir John Eaton has retained no papers.

EDELSTEN, Admiral Sir John Hereward (1891-1966)

Naval career from 1908; active service in World Wars I and II. Deputy Director of Plans Division, Admiralty, 1938. Assistant Chief of Naval Staff (U-Boat Warfare and Trade), 1942-44. Vice-Chief of Naval Staff, 1947-49. C.-in-C., Mediterranean Station, 1950-52; Portsmouth, 1952-54. Allied Naval C.-in-C., Channel Command, 1952-54. Vice-Admiral of the United Kingdom and Lieutenant of the Admiralty, 1962-66.

Papers at Churchill College, Cambridge, include letters (1936-51), speeches (1947-55), and assorted miscellaneous papers.

EDMOND, Colin Alexander (1888-1956)

Minister, Ecuador, 1946-47.

Mrs Anne Bidwell states that her father's papers were destroyed in 1940 just before the German invasion of Norway, where Edmond was serving as Consul at Bergen. No later papers survive.

EDMONDS, Cecil John (1889-)

Levant Consular Service, from 1910. Minister, Foreign Service, 1948-50.

The material deposited at the Middle East Centre, St Antony's College, Oxford, relates to Mr Edmonds' career with the Government of Iraq (1915-45). The use of these papers is restricted at present.

EDMONDS, Brigadier-General Sir James Edward (1861-1956)

Served South Africa, 1901-02; European War, 1914-19. Officer in Charge of Military Branch, Historical Section, Cabinet Office (formerly Committee of Imperial Defence), 1919-49.

The Liddell Hart Centre for Military Archives holds papers concerning Edmonds' military service and subsequent career as Cabinet Office official historian of World War I.

EDWARDS, Admiral Sir Ralph Alan Bevan (1901-1963)

Naval service from 1914; served World Wars I and II. Assistant Chief of Naval Staff, 1948-50. 3rd Sea Lord and Controller of the Navy, 1953-56. C.-in-C. Mediterranean Station, and Allied Forces, Mediterranean, 1957.

Material deposited at Churchill College includes diaries (1939-45) and files of papers (1938-55).

EGERTON, Sir Edwin Henry (1841-1916)

Minister, Greece, 1892-1903. Ambassador, Spain, 1903-05; Italy, 1905-08.

Persons mentioned in the Will and Act of Probate, Lady Egerton and a son, John Frederic Egerton, were not traced.

EGERTON, Major-General Granville George Algernon (1859-1951)

Military career from 1879; served European War, Dardanelles, 1915. Inspector of Infantry, 1916.

The Imperial War Museum holds Egerton's diary as G.O.C. in Sicily (1915-16) and a large number of notebooks relating to his service as Inspector-General of Infantry Training (1916-17).

EGERTON, Vice-Admiral Wion de Malpas (1879-1943)

Naval career; served in Harwich Force, 1911-17. Convoy Commodore, Royal Naval Reserve, 1942.

Two diaries, kept while Egerton was serving as a Commodore of transatlantic convoys (July-Nov. 1942), are available at the Imperial War Museum.

ELDRIDGE, Lieutenant-General Sir William John (1898-   )

Served European War, 1916-18; Iraq, 1919-20; War of 1939-45. Director-General of Artillery, Ministry of Supply, 1945-48. G.O.C., Aldershot District, 1951-53. Controller of Munitions, Ministry of Supply, 1953-57.

Lt.-Gen. Eldridge has no papers. However, a few items, retained as war souvenirs, were given to the Royal Artillery Institution.

ELIOT, Sir Charles Norton Edgcumbe (1862-1931)

High Commissioner, Samoa, 1899; British East African Protectorate (and Agent and Consul-General, Zanzibar), 1900-04; Siberia, 1918-19. Ambassador, Japan, 1919-26.

A volume of correspondence (1924-25) is available at the Public Record Office (F.O. 800/255). Ten letters from Eliot to Granville Bantock can be found at Birmingham University Library. It has not proved possible to contact any surviving member of Sir Charles Eliot's family.

ELKINS, Vice-Admiral Sir Robert Francis (1903-   )

Naval career; active service, World War II, with various commands. Flag Officer, 2nd-in-Command, Far Eastern Station, 1955-56. Admiral, British Joint Staff Mission, Washington, 1956-58.

Sir Robert states that he has given his papers to the National Maritime Museum.

ELLENBOROUGH, 6th B
Colonel Cecil Henry Law (1849-1931)

Served Afghan War, 1878-79; South African War, 1899-1902.

A diary of the South African War, kept by Colonel C. H. Law, survives at the Dorset Military Museum, The Keep, Dorchester, Dorset.

ELLERTON, Admiral Walter Maurice (1870-1948)

Naval career; active service, World War I. Director of Training and Staff Duties, Admiralty, 1919-21. C.-in-C., East India Station, 1925-27.

The Admiral left no personal private papers.

ELLINGTON, Marshal of the Royal Air Force Sir Edward Leonard (1877-1967)

Director-General of Supply and Research, Air Ministry, 1919-21. Commanded R.A.F. in Middle East, 1922-23; India, 1923-26; Iraq, 1926-28. Air Officer C.-in-C., Air Defence of Great Britain, 1929-31. Air Member for Personnel on Air Council, 1931-33. Chief of Air Staff, 1933-37. Inspector-General, R.A.F., 1937-40.

Messrs Dickson Ward & Co., Richmond, Surrey, the solicitors who acted for Sir Edward Ellington's executors, understand that there were very few papers in the estate. The present location of those papers is uncertain.

ELLIOT, Sir Francis Edmund Hugh (1851-1940)

Agent and Consul-General, Bulgaria, 1895-1903. Minister, Greece, 1903-17.

Mr B. H. Moloney, Dunton Lodge, Herongate, Brentwood, Essex, retains some family papers, but they relate mainly to Sir Francis's father, Sir Henry George Elliot, an Ambassador in Turkey and Austria-Hungary during the nineteenth century. Sir Francis Elliot appears to have left no private papers, although a very little relevant material may be found in the Hardinge papers.

ELLIOT, Air Chief Marshal Sir William (1896-1971)

Served European War, 1914-18; South Russia, 1919. Assistant Secretary, Committee of Imperial Defence, 1937-39; War Cabinet, 1939-41. Director of Plans, Air Ministry, 1942-44. Air Officer Commanding, Gibraltar, 1944; Balkan Air Force, 1944-45. Assistant Chief Executive, Ministry of Aircraft Production, 1945-46. Assistant Chief of Air Staff (Policy), 1946-47. C.-in-C., Fighter Command, 1947-49. Chief Staff Officer to Minister of Defence and Deputy Secretary (Military) to Cabinet, 1949-51. Chairman, British Joint Services Mission, Washington, and U.K. Representative, NATO, 1952-54.

The Liddell Hart Centre for Military Archives has been in touch with Sir William Elliot's son, Simon, who retains some unsorted papers relating to his father.

ELLIOTT, Harold William (1905-   )

Controller of Road Transport, Ministry of Supply, 1941. Director of Transport, Middle East Supply Centre, Cairo, 1943.

Mr Elliott was seconded by his company, Pickfords, to four different Ministries at various times, and did advisory work with the Board of Trade from early 1939. The only surviving private papers concern the Middle East Supply Centre, an Anglo-American organisation sponsored on the British side by the Ministry of War Transport. The papers comprise the agenda, papers and minutes of a Transport Conference (8-10 April 1943); Mr Elliott's report on transport developments (1944); copy of a paper presented to the Institute of Transport in London (1945); and booklets describing the activities of the Middle East Supply Centre and the U.K. Commercial Corporation. The Middle East Supply Centre papers have been deposited with the Middle East Centre at St Antony's College, Oxford.

ELLIOTT, Sir Thomas Henry, 1st Bt (1854-1926)

Secretary, Agriculture and Fisheries, 1892-1913. Deputy Master and Comptroller of the Mint, 1913-17. Boundary Commissioner, and Commissioner for the Experimental Application of Proportional Representation, 1917-18.

Mr Hugh Elliott, 173 Woodstock Road, Oxford, holds a small collection of papers relating to his grandfather. There are several dispatch cases and drawers full of papers. These are sorted into chronological order and stored away in bundles but not catalogued.

ELLISON, Lieutenant-General Sir Gerald Francis (1861-1947)

Secretary, War Office Reconstruction Committee, 1904. Principal Private Secretary to Secretary of State for War, 1905-08. Director of Organisation, Army Headquarters, 1908-11. Staff Officer to Inspector-General, Overseas Forces, 1911-14. Deputy Quartermaster-General, Gallipoli, 1915; War Office and Inspector-General of Communications, 1917-23. Major-General in Charge of Administration, Aldershot, 1916-17.

A collection of papers remains in the care of Ellison's step-grandson, Mr Simon Spencer, The Red House, Burnham, Bucks. Details are not available.

ELMHIRST, Air Marshal Sir Thomas Walker (1895-   )

Air Attaché, Ankara, 1937-39. Deputy Director, Intelligence Section, Air Ministry, 1940. Assistant Chief of Air Staff (Intelligence), 1945-47. Chief of Inter-Service Administration, India, 1947. C.-in-C., Indian Air Force, 1947-50. Lieutenant-Governor, Guernsey, 1953-58.

A collection of papers, not all of them open to public inspection, is deposited at Churchill College, Cambridge. Official files relate to Sir Thomas Elmhirst's early career, his activities during World War II, Indian affairs and Guernsey. Personal correspondence includes letters to Lady Elmhirst (1941-49) and family letters. The collection is completed with an assortment of typescript memoirs, edited letters (1940-45), draft articles, lectures and miscellaneous papers.

EMBRY, Air Chief Marshal Sir Basil Edward (1902-   )

Served War of 1939-45. Assistant Chief of Air Staff (Training), Air Ministry, 1945-48. Air Officer C.-in-C., Fighter Command, 1949-53. Commander, Allied Air Forces, Central Europe, 1956.

Contact was not established with the Air Chief Marshal, who now lives in Australia.

EMMERSON, Sir Harold Corti (1896-   )

Civil Servant. Secretary, Royal Commission on Unemployment Insurance, 1930-32. Under-Secretary, Home Security, 1940-42. Chief Industrial Commissioner, Labour, 1942-44. Deputy Secretary and Director-General, Manpower, 1944-46. Permanent Secretary, Works, 1946-56; Labour, 1956-59.

Sir Harold Emmerson has no papers of interest, except for copies of official reports of those Courts of Inquiry, Commissions and Councils of which he was a member.

ERROLL, 21st E of
Victor Alexander Sereld Hay, Baron Kilmarnock (1876-1928)

Chargé d'Affaires, Germany, 1920. High Commissioner, Inter-Allied Rhineland High Commission, 1921-28.

The project failed to secure contact with Lord Kilmarnock, younger son of the 21st Earl of Erroll.

ERSKINE, Lord*
John Francis Ashley Erskine (1895-1953)

M.P. (Con.) Weston-super-Mare, 1922-23, 1924-34; Brighton, 1940-41. Parliamentary Private Secretary to Postmaster-General, 1923. Principal Private Secretary to Home Secretary, 1924. Governor, Madras, 1934-40.

Papers kept whilst Governor of Madras are deposited at the India Office Library. The collection includes official and personal correspondence with the Viceroy of India, and files on specific problems.

ERSKINE, General Sir George Watkin Eben James (1899-1965)

Served European War, 1918, and War of 1939-45. G.O.C., Land Forces, Hong Kong, 1946. Director-General, Territorial Army, 1948-49. G.O.C., British Troops, Egypt and Mediterranean Command, 1949-52. G.O.C.-in-C., Eastern Command, 1952-53; Southern Command, 1955-58. C.-in-C., East Africa Command, 1953-55. Lieutenant-Governor and C.-in-C., Jersey, 1958-63.

A large collection of papers has been given to the Imperial War Museum.

ERSKINE, Sir William Augustus Forbes (1871-1952)

Minister, Cuba, Haiti and Dominican Republic, 1919-21; Bulgaria, 1921-27; Poland, 1928. Ambassador, Poland, 1929-34.

Efforts to contact members of the family were not successful.

ESHER, 2nd Vt
Reginald Baliol Brett (1852-1930)

M.P. (Lib.) Penryn and Falmouth, 1880-85. Secretary, Office of Works, 1895-1902. Chairman, War Office Reconstruction Committee, 1903. Permanent Member, Committee of Imperial Defence.

The archives are deposited at Churchill College, Cambridge. The papers are arranged in seven main groups in bound volumes, and a catalogue of the collection is available. The journals cover the years 1870-1922, letters and memoranda 1898-1919 (11 volumes). The mass of official and personal correspondence includes 54 volumes of political letters alone, arranged by subject (e.g. India, Army Reform) or by the name of correspondents. Further subject files of papers deal with the affairs of different geographical areas, for example the Sudan (1881-85), the Indian Army, the South African War Commission (1902-04); other papers cover Army reform, the War Office Reconstruction Committee (1903-05), the Committee of Imperial Defence, and the Navy and Lord Fisher. The collection is completed with literary papers, newspaper cuttings and miscellaneous printed material.

Another assortment of papers and diaries relating to the period 1914-17 is at the British Library, at present closed for research purposes. Further papers again may be found at the Imperial War Museum. These consist of documents relating to the Committee investigating the performance of the British Army during the Boer War. They include correspondence of Esher with King Edward VII on the progress of the Committee proposals for the reorganisation of the Army, and confidential findings

---

*Son of the 12th Earl of Mar and 14th Earl of Kellie

and secret printed papers by the Committee of Imperial Defence (Defence Committee Colonies) (1907), and a typescript memorandum of Mr Beit's audience with the Kaiser in January 1906.

A number of Esher's letters are included in the Brett family collection at Liverpool University Library.

EVANS, Sir Francis Edward (1897-   )

Consular Service. Assistant Under-Secretary, Foreign Office, 1951. Ambassador, Israel, 1952-54 (and Minister, 1951-52); Argentine, 1954-57.

Sir Francis Evans has retained no papers likely to be of value to the project.

EVANS, Sir Geoffrey (1883-1963)

Colonial Service.

Rhodes House Library, Oxford, has a large collection of diaries, relating to agricultural service in India, Australia, Trinidad, Fiji and New Guinea (1906, 1909-63). There are also letters written to Lady Evans.

EVANS, Lieutenant-General Sir Geoffrey Charles (1901-   )

Served War of 1939-45. G.O.C., 5th and 7th Indian Division, Burma, 1944-45; Allied Land Forces, Siam, 1945-46; 42nd (Lancashire) Division and North West District, 1947-48; 40th Division, Hong Kong, 1949-51. Director of Military Training, War Office, 1948-49. Temporary Commander, British Forces, Hong Kong, 1951-52. Assistant Chief of Staff (Organisation and Training), Supreme Headquarters Allied Powers Europe, 1952-53. G.O.C.-in-C., Northern Command, 1953-57.

A collection of papers is to be placed at the Imperial War Museum. The material consists of diaries, minutes of conferences, reports and memoirs relating to World War II; the Western Desert (Dec. 1940); Keren in Eritrea (Feb.-Mar. 1941); Sidi Omar (Nov. 1941-Jan. 1942); Burma (1944-45); and Siam (1945-46).

EVERETT, Major-General Sir Henry Joseph (1866-1951)

Army career from 1885; served South African War and World War I.

The personal diaries of Everett are in the care of the Light Infantry Office in Taunton. They cover the years 1893-1937, and are factual diaries of each day, in small volumes.

EVETTS, Lieutenant-General Sir John Fullerton (1891-   )

Served European War, 1914-18, and War of 1939-45. Assistant Chief of Imperial General Staff, 1942. Senior Military Adviser, Ministry of Supply, 1944-46.

Sir John has a large number of photographs concerning the Arab rebellion of 1939, also of the Woomera project in Australia. There is a complete diary of the first five years of the Woomera project, 1946-51.

EVILL, Air Chief Marshal Sir Douglas Claude Strathern (1892-1971)

Served European War, 1914-19; War of 1939-45. Head of R.A.F. Delegation, Washington, 1942. Vice Chief of Air Staff, 1943-46.

The Royal Air Force Museum has a collection of logbooks, diaries, files, letters, photographs and publications, for the period 1910-67. The subject matter includes war organisation (1934-35), the German Air Force (1937-38), Bomber Command (1936-39), the Supreme War Council (1939-40), Royal Air Force service in France (1940), and the air defence of Egypt (1941-42).

EWART, Lieutenant-General Sir John Spencer (1861-1930)

Served Egypt, 1882; Nile Expedition, 1884-85; Sudan Frontier Field Force, 1885-86; Sudan, 1898; South Africa, 1899-1901. Military Secretary, War Office, 1904-06; Director of Military Operations, 1906-10. Adjutant-General, 1910-14. G.O.C., Scottish Command, 1914-18.

A collection of papers held by Mr Hector Monro, M.P., has been catalogued by the N.R.A. (Scotland). The material includes a series of unpublished memoirs and a diary.

EWART, Major-General Sir Richard Henry (1864-1928)

Military career from 1883. Served Central Prisoner of War Committee, European War, 1914-18. Chief of British Military Mission, Berlin, and President, Inter-Allied Commission for Repatriation of Russian Prisoners of War, 1919.

A good autobiographical document is held at the Imperial War Museum. It covers Ewart's military service (1883-1925), with special reference to France (1914-15) and East Africa (1915-18), and there is a diary as President of the Commission for the Repatriation of Prisoners of War (1919-20).

EWING, Vice-Admiral Sir (Robert) Alastair (1909-   )

Naval career; commanded destroyers, 1939-45. Director of Naval Staff College, 1954-56. Admiral Commanding Reserves and Inspector of Recruiting, 1960-62.

A diary, 1939-40, kept whilst 1st Lieutenant of the destroyer *Imogen*, is held on microfilm at the Imperial War Museum.

EYRES, Sir Harry Charles Augustus (1856-1944)

Consul-General, Constantinople, 1896-1914. Minister, Albania, 1922-26.

Messrs Waltons & Co., the solicitors who acted for Sir Harry's family, have no information which would be helpful.

FANSHAWE, Lieutenant-General Sir Hew Dalrymple (1860-1957)

Military career; India, Sudan, South Africa, etc. Served European War, 1914-18.

Major General Sir Evelyn Fanshawe, C.B., C.B.E., D.L., Guilsborough House, Northampton, has his father's diaries covering his military career, mostly with the cavalry, from Winchester to his death.

FARQUHAR, Sir Harold Lister (1894-1953)

Consul-General, Barcelona, 1941-45. Minister, Ethiopia, 1946-48. Ambassador, Sweden, 1948-51.

Messrs Walters Vandercom & Hart, acting on behalf of Sir Harold Farquhar's family, state that there are no papers which would be of interest.

FAULKNER, Sir Alfred Edward (1882-1963)

Director of Sea Transport, Admiralty, 1920-27. Under-Secretary, Mines and Petroleum, 1927-42. Chairman, Traffic Commissioners, Eastern Area, 1943-51.

Sir Eric Faulkner, c/o Lloyds Bank Ltd, 71 Lombard Street, London EC3P 3BS, has in his care a few papers relating to his father.

FAWCETT, Edmund Alderson Sandford (1868-1938)

Secretary, Manpower Distribution Board and Ministry of National Service, World War I. Chief Engineer, Ministry of Health, 1921-30.

Mr P. Fawcett, grandson of E. A. S. Fawcett, made enquiries among the family and colleagues of his grandfather. No collection of private papers is known to survive.

FEDDEN, Sir (Alfred Hubert) Roy (1885-1973)

Aeronautical Engineer. Special Technical Adviser, Ministry of Aircraft Production, 1942-45. Research work for Ministry of Supply, 1945-47. Aeronautical Adviser to North Atlantic Treaty Organisation, 1952-53.

The Imperial War Museum has papers relating to many aspects of his long connection with British aircraft development in the twentieth century. They include, in particular, schedules and detailed drawings for a number of his engine designs — including the Jupiter, Hercules, Taurus and Centaurus — as well as correspondence and reports concerned with post-war British and NATO air developments, especially reflecting his interest in the training of scientists and technologists for the British aircraft industry.

FELL, Lieutenant-General Sir Matthew Henry Gregson (1872-1959)

Served South Africa, 1899-1902, and European War, 1914-18. Director, R.A.F. Medical Service, 1919-21. Director-General, Army Medical Service, 1926-29.

A collection of papers survives in the library of the Royal Army Medical College. The material relates to Fell's career in the R.A.F. (1918-21), at Constantinople (1922-23) and in the European War (1914-18).

FERGUSSON, Brigadier Sir Bernard Edward (1911-) (created Baron Ballantrae in 1972)

Served Palestine, 1937, and War of 1939-45. Director of Combined Operations (Military), 1945-46. Assistant Inspector-General, Palestine Police, 1946-47. Colonel Intelligence, Supreme Headquarters Allied Powers Europe, 1951-53. Governor-General, New Zealand, 1962-67.

The Brigadier kept no papers, but the Liddell Hart Centre for Military Archives has on loan Field Marshal Wavell's Staff College papers, notes and copies of lectures.

FERGUSSON, General Sir Charles, 7th Bt (1865-1951)

Adjutant-General, Egyptian Army, 1901-03. Inspector of Infantry, 1909-13. Served European War, 1914-18. Military Governor, Occupied German Territory, 1918-19. Governor-General and C.-in-C., New Zealand, 1924-30.

Family papers survive with the present (9th) baronet, Sir Charles Fergusson, Kilkerran, by Maybole, Ayrshire KA19 7SJ. The papers include private material of General Sir Charles Fergusson, including letters written to his father from the

Sudan (1896-1900) and to his wife from Flanders, France and Germany (1914-19); diaries for the years 1896-99 and 1918-19; and a small file of papers on the Curragh incident of 1914.

FERGUSSON, Sir John Donald Balfour (1891-1963)

Private Secretary to successive Chancellors of the Exchequer, 1920-36. Permanent Secretary, Agriculture and Fisheries, 1936-45; Fuel and Power, 1945-52.

Mr J. A. Fergusson, 7 Birchin Lane, London EC3V 9DD, has a collection of his father's papers. The material is largely of a personal nature.

FESTING, Field-Marshal Sir Francis Wogan (1902-   )

Served War of 1939-45. G.O.C., Land Forces, Hong Kong, 1945-46; British Troops in Egypt, 1952-54. Director of Weapons and Development, War Office, 1947-49. Commander, British Forces, Hong Kong, 1949. Assistant Chief of Staff (Organisation and Training), Supreme Headquarters Allied Powers in Europe, 1951-52. G.O.C.-in-C., Eastern Command, 1954-56. Commander-in-Chief, Far East Land Forces, 1956-58. Chief of Imperial General Staff, 1958-61.

The Field-Marshal has kept no papers of interest relating to his career. A collection of photographs is with the Imperial War Museum.

FIDDES, Sir George Vandeleur (1858-1936)

Secretary to High Commissioner, South Africa, 1897-1900. Political Secretary to C.-in-C., South Africa, 1900. Secretary, Transvaal Administration, 1900-02. Permanent Under-Secretary, Colonial Office, 1916-21.

Efforts to contact members of the family were not successful.

FIELD, Admiral of the Fleet Sir Frederick Laurence (1871-1945)

Naval career from 1884. Commanded H.M.S. *King George V* at Battle of Jutland, 1916. Director of Torpedoes and Mining, 1918-20. 3rd Sea Lord and Controller of the Navy, 1920-23. Deputy Chief of Naval Staff, 1925-28. C.-in-C., Mediterranean, 1928-30. 1st Sea Lord and Chief of Naval Staff, 1930-33.

No papers were located.

FIELDING, Sir Charles William (1863-1941)

Director and Chairman, Rio Tinto Zinc. Chairman, Economy of Metals and Materials Committee, Ministry of Munitions, 1917. Member, Ministry of Reconstruction Council; Non-Ferrous Metals Committee, Board of Trade; Restriction of Imports Committee; Committee on the Production of Food, 1915. Director-General of Food Production, 1918-19.

Sir Charles's daughter, Mrs W. W. B. Scott, Folly House, Bampton, Oxford, and her sister-in-law, Mrs Fielding, have been unable to find any papers of Sir Charles Fielding, apart from a typescript copy of his published work *Food* (1923). Material relating to Sir Charles Fielding's career may, however, be found in the archives of Rio Tinto Zinc. Application should be made to the Company Secretary at R.T.Z., 6 St James's Square, London SW1.

FIENNES, Hon. Sir Eustace Edward Twisleton-Wykeham-, 1st Bt (1864-1943)

M.P. (Lib.) Banbury, 1906-Jan 1910, Dec. 1910-18. Governor, Seychelles, 1918-21; Leeward Islands, 1921-29.

Lady Fiennes, Sir Eustace Fiennes's daughter-in-law, knows of no papers.

FINDLAY, Sir Mansfeldt de Cardonnel (1861-1932)

Diplomatic Service. Minister, Bulgaria, 1909-11; Norway, 1911-23.

Commander Noel Findlay, Court Lodge, Hastingleigh, Ashford, Kent, states that a collection of his father's papers has survived. The collection is quite extensive, and papers are arranged according to stages in Findlay's career.

FISHER OF KILVERSTONE, 1st B
Admiral of the Fleet Sir John Arbuthnot Fisher (1841-1920)

Entered Navy, 1854. Director, Naval Ordnance, 1886-91. Controller of the Navy, 1892-97. C.-in-C., North America and West Indies, 1897-99. C.-in-C., Mediterranean, 1899-1902. 2nd Sea Lord, 1902-03. C.-in-C., Portsmouth, 1903-04. 1st Sea Lord, 1904-10, 1914-15.

The Kilverstone MSS. in the care of the present Lord Fisher contain personal and family papers relating to Fisher's life. The Fisher papers in the care of the Duke of Hamilton, at Lennoxlove, Haddington, East Lothian, are the major source. The collection comprises about 6,000 items, and includes official and family correspondence, correspondence collected by Nina, Duchess of Hamilton, concerning Fisher; naval papers, drafts, notes, memoranda, proofs; papers relating to the Oil Commission (1912-14); material relating to the Board of Invention and Research; Fisher's private and personal notes, including material for his memoirs; and press cuttings. A copy of the catalogue of these papers prepared by R. F. Mackay may be consulted at the National Register of Archives (List 16615) and at major libraries. Enquiries should be directed to the Duke of Hamilton.

FISHER, Lieutenant-General Sir Bertie Drew (1878-1972)

Served South African War, 1900-02; European War, 1914-18. Director of Recruiting and Organisation, War Office, 1932-34. G.O.C.-in-C., Southern Command, 1939-40.

Sir Bertie Fisher kept no papers of public interest.

FISHER, Major-General Donald Rutherford Dacre (1890-1962)

Served European War, 1914-18. Director-General, Army Requirements, War Office, 1942-46.

Mr Donald Fisher states that his father kept no papers.

FISHER, Sir Godfrey Arthur (1885-1969)

Consul General, Naples, 1930-37; Antwerp, 1937-40; San Francisco, 1941-45.

Sir Godfrey's son-in-law, Sir David H. Burnett, Bt., Tandridge Hall, near Oxted, Surrey, has a collection of papers, most of which relate to Sir Godfrey's historical research on the Barbary States and his published works. However, there are also some unsorted letters from various people such as visiting statesmen for the period when Sir Godfrey was at Antwerp and San Francisco.

FISHER, Sir Norman Fenwick Warren (1879-1948)

Chairman, Board of Inland Revenue, 1918-19. Permanent Secretary, Treasury, and Head of Civil Service, 1919-39.

Mr R. W. Fisher (son) states that his father kept no papers. Certain papers collected for a biographical study have been placed in B.L.P.E.S. Relevant material may be found in the Lloyd George papers now at the House of Lords Record Office.

FISHER, Admiral Sir William Wordsworth (1875-1937)

Naval career; served at Jutland, 1916. Director of Anti-Submarine Division, Admiralty, 1917-18. Chief of Staff, Mediterranean Fleet, 1919-22; Atlantic Fleet, 1922-24. 4th Sea Lord, 1927-28. Deputy Chief of Naval Staff, 1928-30. C.-in-C., Mediterranean, 1932-36; Portsmouth, 1936-37.

A collection of papers is in the care of the National Maritime Museum. It includes papers relating to naval policy up to 1918; certain material on the situation in the Mediterranean (1919-22); papers relating to Disarmament (1929-31); papers on discipline and organisation (1931-33); and miscellaneous papers on general policy, shipbuilding, tactics, treaty discussions, etc.

FITZGERALD, Lieutenant-Colonel Brinsley J. H. (1859-1931)

Military career. Private Secretary to Sir John French during World War I.

Mr Adrian Fitzgerald, 16 Clareville Street, London SW7, has what remains of Fitzgerald's papers, which include correspondence, diaries and press cuttings.

FITZMAURICE, Sir Gerald Gray (1901-)

Legal Adviser, Ministry of Economic Warfare, 1939-43; 2nd Legal Adviser, Foreign Office, 1945-53; Legal Adviser, 1953-60. Judge of the International Court of Justice, 1960-73.

Sir Gerald Fitzmaurice has retained some papers of legal rather than general interest.

FITZROY, Sir Almeric William (1851-1935)

Clerk of the Privy Council, 1899-1923.

A copy of an unpublished autobiography can be found at the British Library. Other material (1896-1926) at Duke University, North Carolina, consists of correspondence relating to Fitzroy's duties as Clerk of the Privy Council, education, the government of London, the Fashoda crisis (1898) and the Cabinet crisis of 1903.

FLETCHER, Sir (Arthur George) Murchison (1878-1954)

Governor, Fiji (and High Commissioner, Western Pacific), 1929-36; Trinidad and Tobago, 1936-38.

Mr D. G. M. Fletcher, Sir Murchison's son, knows of no papers.

FLOUD, Sir Francis Lewis Castle (1875-1965)

Permanent Secretary, Agriculture and Fisheries, 1920-27; Labour, 1930-34. Chairman, Board of Customs and Excise, 1927-30. High Commissioner, Canada, 1934-38. Chairman, Bengal Land Revenue Commission, 1938-40; Appeal Tribunal for Conscientious Objectors, 1940-46; Road Haulage Central Wages Board, 1941-47.

Dr R. C. Floud, Birkbeck College, London, Sir Francis Floud's grandson, has possession of his grandfather's papers. There are some interesting mementoes of his early life — school essays, etc. — together with copies of speeches, official reports, and press cuttings concerned with his work in Canada and India in the late 1930s and 1940s. A collection of letters written by Sir Francis and Lady Floud to their children from Canada and India has also survived, together with Lady Floud's manuscript autobiography. One file at H.M. Customs and Excise Library also refers to Sir F. L. C. Floud.

FLOWER, Sir Cyril Thomas (1879-1961)

Deputy Keeper, Public Records, 1938-47.

A certain amount of correspondence survives with Lady Flower, 2 Lammas Park Gardens, London W5. These letters are mostly of a private nature.

FOGARTY, Air Chief Marshal Sir Francis (1899-1973)

Served European War, 1918; War of 1939-45. Air Officer in Charge of Administration, Mediterranean Allied Air Forces, 1945; Mediterranean and Middle East, 1946-47. Air Officer Commanding, Italy, 1946. C.-in-C., Far East Air Force, 1949-52. Air Member for Personnel, 1952-56.

Lady Fogarty states that her late husband never kept much correspondence or diaries, but that she retains certain press cuttings and photographs which would be of interest. Unfortunately, a logbook of World War I was lost.

FOLEY, Sir Ernest Julian (1881-1966)

Under-Secretary, Mercantile Marine Department, Board of Trade, 1929-39. Secretary, Ministry of Shipping, 1939-42.

The National Westminster Bank Trustee Department was unable to provide any useful information.

FORBER, Sir Edward Rodolph (1878-1960)

Deputy Secretary, Ministry of Health, 1925-30. Chairman, Board of Customs and Excise, 1930-34; Board of Inland Revenue, 1934-38.

Efforts to contact members of the family were not successful. Certain files relating to Sir E. R. Forber survive at H.M. Customs and Excise Library.

FORBES, Admiral of the Fleet Sir Charles Morton (1880-1960)

Naval career from 1894; served World War I. Director of Naval Ordnance, 1925-28. 3rd Sea Lord, 1932-34. C.-in-C., Home Fleet, 1938-40; Plymouth, 1941-43.

Certain relevant material may be found in the Cunningham papers at the British Library (Add. MSS. 52565).

FORBES, Sir George Arthur D. Ogilvie- (1891-1954)

Minister, Cuba, 1940-44. Ambassador, Venezuela, 1944-48.

The papers are included in the Ogilvie-Forbes of Boyndlie family collection in King's College Archives, Aberdeen. The relevant papers fill two boxes, and consist of private and personal material, mainly for the years 1919-20 and the mid-1930s when Sir George was in Spain and Germany.

FORSTER, 1st B
Sir Henry William Forster (1866-1936)

M.P. (Con.) Sevenoaks, 1892-1919. Financial Secretary, War Office, 1915-19. Governor-General, Australia, 1920-25. Member of Army Council.

The Rt Hon. Dorothy Lady Wardington, Lepe House, Exbury, Southampton SO4 1AD, Lord Forster's daughter, states that her family has very few records or personal papers of her father's. Lepe House suffered bomb damage during the war, and many of its contents were put in store. Also Lady Forster has destroyed many old papers. It may be that two or three boxes of old letters have survived.

FORSTER, Major-General John Burton (1855-1938)

Army service from 1872. Served 27 years in 18th, The Royal Irish Regiment (in Nile Expedition, 1884-85; at Tirah, 1897-98; in India during World War I).

Certain papers relating to the Royal Irish Regiment, the Tirah campaign and World War I are available in the National Army Museum.

FOULDS, Linton Harry (1897-1952)

Minister, Philippines, 1946-51.

Mrs C. M. Foulds has retained none of her late husband's papers.

FOULKES, Major-General Charles Howard (1875-1969)

Served South Africa, 1899-1900; West Africa, 1903 (Anglo-French Boundary Commission east of River Niger); European War, 1914-18 (G.O.C. Special Brigade, Chemical Warfare, and Director of Gas Services, G.H.Q.). Chief Engineer, Aldershot Command, 1926-30.

Maj.-Gen. T. H. F. Foulkes, The Warren, Fitzroy Road, Fleet, Hants., has retained many of his father's papers. These include an unpublished book covering the period 1897-1903, and 70 years of manuscript diaries.

FOWLER, Rees John (1894-1974)

Minister, Honduras, 1945-50. Consul-General, Genoa, 1950-55.

Mr Fowler stated that he retained no papers relating to his career.

FRANCIS, Herbert William Sidney (1880-1968)

Civil Service career, Ministry of Health, etc. Secretary and Comptroller-General, National Debt Office, 1938-46.

Mr P. A. Francis states that his father kept no papers.

FRANKLYN, General Sir Harold Edmund (1885-1963)

Served European War, 1914-19; Sudan Defence Force. G.O.C., British troops in Northern Ireland, 1941-43. C.-in-C., Home Forces, 1943-45.

Brigadier T. E. Southwell states that General Franklyn left no private papers or records bearing upon his career.

FRANKS, Baron
Sir Oliver Shewell Franks (1905-   )

Permanent Secretary, Supply, 1945-46. Ambassador, United States, 1948-52.

Lord Franks has retained some of his papers, including two suitcases filled with papers, press cuttings and speeches relating to his time at Washington. Lord Franks has no papers relating to his work at the Ministry of Supply.

FRASER OF NORTH CAPE, 1st B
Admiral of the Fleet Sir Bruce Austin Fraser (1888-   )

Naval career. 3rd Sea Lord and Controller, 1939-42. C.-in-C., Home Fleet, 1943-44; Eastern Fleet, 1944; British Pacific Fleet, 1945-46; Portsmouth, 1947-48. 1st Sea Lord and Chief of Naval Staff, 1948-51.

It is understood that Lord Fraser has a number of his papers, but that the material is not available.

FRASER, Sir Andrew Henderson Leith (1848-1919)

Home Secretary, Government of India, 1898-99. Chief Commissioner, Central Provinces, 1899. Lieutenant-Governor, Bengal, 1903-08.

It was not possible to trace members of the family.

FRASER, Sir Robert Brown (1904-   )

Leader writer, *Daily Herald*, 1930-39. Director of Publications Division, Ministry of Information, 1941-45; Controller of Production, 1945-46. Director-General, Central Office of Information, 1946-54; Independent Television Authority, 1954-70. Chairman, Independent Television News, 1971-74.

Sir Robert has kept few notes and papers earlier than 1954. He has kept all his published articles and all his speeches and addresses, published and unpublished, for his Independent Television period, together with some correspondence.

FRASER, Brigadier Hon. William (1890-1964)

Served European War, 1914-18, and War of 1939-45. Military Attaché, Brussels and The Hague, 1931-35; Paris, 1938-39. Chief of United Nations Relief and Rehabilitation Administration Mission, Paris, 1945-47.

A collection of family papers exists. The material includes Brigadier Fraser's diaries (1913-19) and a personal account of the Norwegian campaign (1940). The papers are in the possession of Lt.-Gen. Sir David Fraser, K.C.B., O.B.E., Vallenders, Isington, Alton, Hants.

FRASER, Major-General William Archibald Kenneth (1886-1969)

Served European War, 1914-19; India. Military Attaché, Kabul, 1922-24; Tehran, 1924-28. Military Secretary to Governor, Bengal, 1930-32.

A collection of papers at the Imperial War Museum consists of Fraser's World War I diaries, papers relating to his command of the South Persia Rifles from 1919 to 1921, and two photograph albums of India and Persia during the inter-war years. General Fraser served with the 9th and 16th Lancers on the Western Front (1914-17), taking part in the retreat from Mons and the battles of Neuve Chapelle (March 1915) and Arras (April 1917).

FREEMAN, Air Chief Marshal Sir Wilfred Rhodes, 1st Bt (1888-1953)

Served European War, 1914-18. Air Officer Commanding, Palestine and Trans-jordan, 1930-33. Commandant, R.A.F. Staff College, 1933-36. Member of Air

Council for Research, Development and Production, 1936-40. Vice Chief of Air Staff, 1940. Chief Executive, Ministry of Aircraft Production, 1942-45.

A collection of papers (42 files), relating to Sir Wilfred Freeman's work at the Air Ministry is included in the unregistered papers series AVIA 10 at the Public Record Office. No further papers remain in private hands.

FREMANTLE, Admiral Hon. Sir Edmund Robert (1836-1929)

Naval career from 1849. C.-in-C., East Indies, 1888-91; China, 1892-95; Plymouth, 1896-99.

Papers at the National Maritime Museum include material relating to the Maori War (1864-66); the Ashanti War (1873); logs kept by Fremantle when he was a junior officer; and letter books covering the later years of the nineteenth century.

FREMANTLE, Admiral Sir Sydney Robert (1867-1958)

Naval career from 1881; active service in World War I. Deputy Chief of Naval Staff, 1918-19. C.-in-C., Portsmouth, 1923-26.

Minute books covering Fremantle's period as Deputy Chief of Naval Staff (1918-19), and some lecture notes, articles and essays (c. 1916-19), are in the custody of the National Maritime Museum.

FRENCH, Sir Henry Leon (1883-1966)

Secretary, Ministry of Food, 1939-45.

Contact with Lady French could not be established.

FREWEN, Captain Oswald M. (d. 1958)

Naval career.

Papers at the British Library (Add. MSS. 53738) include letters received by Frewen regarding the Battle of Jutland, from Lord Jellicoe (1920-25) and Admiral Sir Hugh Evans-Thomas (1927). Mrs Lena Frewen, Sheephouse, Brede, Sussex, has in her care 55 volumes of diaries (1903-57), of which the first 44 are indexed.

FREYBERG, 1st B.
Sir Bernard Freyberg (1889-1963)

Served European War, 1914-18. G.O.C., Salisbury Plain, 1939; New Zealand Forces, 1939-45. C.-in-C., Allied Forces, Crete, 1941. Governor-General, New Zealand, 1946-52.

Efforts to contact members of the family were not successful.

FULLER, Admiral Sir Cyril Thomas Moulden (1874-1942)

Naval career from 1887. Director of Plans Division, Admiralty, 1917-20. Head of British Naval Section, Paris Peace Conference, 1919-20. Assistant Chief of Naval Staff, 1922-23. 3rd Sea Lord and Controller of the Navy, 1923-25. C.-in-C., America and West Indies, 1928-30. 2nd Sea Lord and Chief of Naval Personnel, 1930-32.

Papers at the National Maritime Museum include volumes of material relating to the campaigns in Togoland and Cameroons (1914-17), and miscellaneous notes and printed material.

FULLER, Major-General John Frederick Charles (1878-1966)

Served South Africa, 1899-1902; European War, 1914-18. Military historian and theorist.

A collection of papers has been deposited at the Liddell Hart Centre for Military Archives. The papers include letters to his parents (1892-1922), pocket diaries (1900-02, 1909, 1918-63), two volumes on the Battle of Cambrai (1917), some material on tank strategy and tactics (1916-18), and papers on Tank Corps operations in World War I. A further, more substantial collection of Fuller's papers is held in the library of Rutgers State University. This includes correspondence (1893-1966); drafts of published works, and scrapbooks of newspapers and periodicals, cuttings, reviews and articles (1920-1960s).

FULLERTON, Admiral Sir Eric John Arthur (1878-1962)

Naval career. Naval Secretary to 1st Lord of the Admiralty, 1927-29. C.-in-C., East Indies, 1929-32; Plymouth, 1932-35.

Certain papers, including diaries, are housed at the National Maritime Museum.

FURSE, Lieutenant-General Sir William Thomas (1865-1953)

Served India; South Africa, 1899-1900; European War, 1914-18. Master-General of Ordnance, 1916, and Member of Army Council. Director, Imperial Institute, 1925-34.

It is understood that the papers were destroyed shortly after General Furse's death.

GAINER, Sir Donald St Clair (1891-1966)

Consul-General, Mexico City, 1931-32; Munich, 1932-38; Vienna, 1938-39. Minister, Venezuela, 1939-44. Ambassador, Venezuela, 1944; Brazil, 1944-47; Poland, 1947-50. Permanent Under-Secretary, Foreign Office (German Section), 1950-51.

Lady Gainer has none of her late husband's papers, apart from some press cuttings relating to the Munich appointment and to the expulsion from Vienna in 1939.

GAIRDNER, General Sir Charles Henry (1898-)

Military career from 1916. G.O.C., 6th Armoured Division, 1942; 8th Armoured Division, 1943. Chief of General Staff, North Africa, 1943. Head of U.K. Liaison Mission, Japan, 1945-46. Prime Minister's Special Representative in Far East, 1945-48. Governor, Western Australia, 1951-63; Tasmania, 1963-68.

Sir Charles has kept no private papers or diary.

GAISFORD, Hugh William (1874-1954)

Minister, Central America, 1920-22. Consul-General, Munich, 1925-32.

Messrs Corbould, Rigby & Co., who dealt with Mr Gaisford's estate in Italy, believe that Mr Gaisford left no papers.

GALE, Lieutenant-General Sir Humfrey Myddelton (1890-1971)

Served European War, 1914-18. Deputy Chief of Staff and Chief Administrative Officer under General Eisenhower, 1942-45. Personal Representative in Europe of the Director-General, United Nations Relief and Rehabilitation Administration, 1945-47.

The Liddell Hart Centre for Military Archives holds some papers relating to Gale's service with Supreme Headquarters, Allied Expeditionary Force (1942-45).

GALLIENNE, Wilfred Hansford (1897-1956)

Consular Service. Chargé d'Affaires, and Consul, Dominican Republic, 1929-30; Estonia, 1935-40. Minister, Guatemala, 1947-54. Ambassador, Cuba, 1954-56.

Messrs Midland Bank Trust Company (Channel Islands) Ltd contacted Mr Gallienne's widow who was unable to help.

GALLOWAY, Lieutenant-General Sir Alexander (1895-   )

Served European War, 1914-18; War of 1939-45. G.O. C.-in-C., Malaya, 1946-47. High Commissioner and C.-in-C., British Troops in Austria, 1947-50.

No contact was established. Information available at the Imperial War Museum indicates that Sir Alexander has kept some papers.

GALWAY, 8th Vt
Sir George Vere Arundell Monckton-Arundell (1882-1943)

Military career. Assistant Adjutant and Quartermaster-General, 1917-19. Governor-General, New Zealand, 1935-41.

There is a collection of papers at Nottingham University Library.

GAME, Air Vice-Marshal Sir Philip Woolcott (1876-1961)

Served South Africa, 1901-02; European War, 1914-18. Director of Training and Organisation, Air Ministry, 1919-22. Air Member for Personnel, 1923-28. Governor, New South Wales, 1930-35. Commissioner, Metropolitan Police, 1935-45.

Mr Philip Game, Oldbury Farmhouse, Ightham, Sevenoaks, Kent TN15 9DE, states that some of his father's private papers survive with him. These include private letters written by Sir Philip Game to his wife from France during World War I, press-cutting books relating to the period in Australia, family letters from that time, and photographs. The cream of Sir Philip Game's papers on his service in New South Wales has been deposited in the Mitchell Library, Macquarie Street, Sydney, Australia. No private papers relating to the period with the Metropolitan Police are extant.

GAMMELL, Lieutenant-General Sir James Andrew Harcourt (1892-   )

Served European War, 1914-18, and War of 1939-45. G.O.C.-in-C., Eastern Command, 1942-43. Chief of Staff to Supreme Allied Commander, Mediterranean Theatre, 1944. Representative, British Chiefs of Staff with the Soviet Union, and Head of British Military Mission in Moscow, 1945.

Some papers (1914-45) are held at the Imperial War Museum. The collection includes copies of letters from France and Gallipoli where Sir James Gammell served with the Royal Field Artillery, and a report on motorised operations in the Western Desert (1917). Papers concerning the British Military Mission in Moscow (1945) are also in the collection, but these remain under restriction.

GARDENER, Sir Alfred John (1897-   )

Ambassador, Afghanistan, 1949-51; Syria, 1953-56.

Sir John Gardener has retained no papers relating to his career.

GARDINER, Sir Thomas Robert (1883-1964)

Director-General, Post Office, 1936-45. Secretary, Ministry of Home Security, 1939-40.

Efforts to contact members of the family were not successful.

GASCOIGNE, Sir Alvary Douglas Frederick (1893-1970)

Consul-General, Tangier and Spanish Morocco, 1939-44. Political Representative, Hungary, 1945-46; Japan, 1946-51. Ambassador, Soviet Union, 1951-53.

Contact with members of the family could not be secured.

GASELEE, Sir Stephen (1882-1943)

Librarian and Keeper of the Papers, Foreign Office, 1920-43.

Lady Gaselee has kept a few papers only relating to the career of her late husband. The material includes a diary of the royal wedding in Spain of Queen Ena, kept by Sir Stephen Gaselee when he was tutor to her brother, Lord Leopold Mountbatten.

GATER, Sir George Henry (1886-1963)

Permanent Under-Secretary, Colonial Office, 1939-47. Joint Secretary, Home Security, 1929-40. Secretary, Supply, 1940; Home Security, 1940-42.

Lady Gater states that she destroyed many of her late husband's private letters and that there are no papers of interest among the material which survives.

GAUSSEN, Major-General Charles de Lisle (1896-1971)

Served European War, 1914-18, and War of 1939-45. Engineer-in-Chief, India, 1947. Deputy Engineer-in-Chief, War Office, 1948-49.

Some papers have been deposited at the Imperial War Museum. The collection includes a diary of service with the Royal Engineers in India in the 1920s, and a photograph album (1913-23).

GEDDES, 1st B
Sir Auckland Campbell Geddes (1879-1954)

M.P. (Con.) Basingstoke, 1917-20. Minister, National Service, 1917-19. President, Local Government Board, 1918-19. Minister, Reconstruction, 1919. President, Board of Trade, 1919-20. Ambassador, United States, 1920-24.

The present (2nd) Baron Geddes states that none of his father's papers have survived (Hazlehurst and Woodland, op. cit., p.58).

GELL, Air Vice-Marshal William Charles Coleman (1888-1969)

Served European War, 1914-19, War of 1939-45. Air Officer Commanding, Balloon Command, 1944-45.

A collection of papers and photographs relating to Gell's career is deposited at the Imperial War Museum.

GENT, Sir (Gerard) Edward (1895-1948)

Military career; served European War, 1914-18. Assistant Under-Secretary, Colonial Office, 1942-46. Governor, Malaya, 1946-48; High Commissioner, Malayan Federation, 1948.

Lady Gent, Little Paddock, Fairmile Lane, Cobham, Surrey, states that her late husband kept no diary and that no papers have survived apart from press cuttings and commemorative notes concerning Sir Edward.

GIBBS, Sir Frank Stannard (1895-   )

Consul-General, Saigon, 1947-51. Ambassador, Philippines, 1954-55 (Minister, 1951-54).

Sir Frank S. Gibbs kept no diary, and retains only a few press cuttings and private papers dealing mainly with social rather than political events.

GIBSON, Sir Henry James (1860-1950)

Comptroller and Auditor-General, 1911-21.

Mrs Joan M. Glynn, 5 Lipton Road, Chichester, Sussex, Sir Henry's daughter, has only a few papers relating to her father's career. Mrs Glynn feels that these would not be of interest to historians.

GIFFARD, General Sir George James (1886-1964)

Served East Africa, 1913-14; European War, 1914-18; War of 1939-45. Inspector-General, African Colonial Forces, 1938-39. Military Secretary to Secretary of State for War, 1939. G.O.C., British Forces in Palestine and Transjordan, 1940; West Africa, 1940. G.O. C.-in-C., Eastern Army, India, 1943. C.-in-C., 11th Army Group, South East Asia, 1943-44.

The Liddell Hart Centre for Military Archives understands that none of Sir George Giffard's papers have survived.

GILBERT, Sir Bernard William (1891-1957)

Joint 2nd Secretary, Treasury, 1944-56.

Lady Gilbert states that her late husband left no papers.

GILL, Thomas Patrick (1858-1931)

M.P. (Nat.) Louth South, 1885-92. Secretary, Department of Agriculture and Technical Instruction for Ireland, 1900-23; Commissioner for Intermediate Education, 1909-23.

The letters and papers of T. P. Gill at the National Library of Ireland relate, *inter alia*, to the Plan of Campaign (1886-90), the Parnell crisis, the co-operative movement, the Irish Convention (1917) and the Government of Ireland Bill (1920). Correspondents include Archbishop Croke and Horace Plunkett.

GILLETT, Sir George Masterman (1870-1939)

M.P. (Lab.) Finsbury, 1923-31; (Nat. Lab.) 1931-35. Parliamentary Secretary, Overseas Trade, 1929-31; Transport, 1931. Commissioner for the Special Areas (England and Wales), 1936-39.

Sir George Gillett's son, Mr E. S. Gillett, Marsh Lock House, Wargrave Road, Henley-on-Thames, Oxon., has retained a collection of papers relating to his father's career. This includes the following: family and personal letters, including those written by Gillett at school, in the early 1880s; political letters (1924-39), including some from J. R. MacDonald and others; copies of speeches (1929-39); a case of press cuttings (1929-39); letters received by Sir George after his resignation from the Government in 1931, and after his retirement as Commissioner for the Special Areas in 1939; and letters of condolence following his death in 1939.

GILLMAN, General Sir Webb (1870-1933)

Career in Royal Artillery from 1889; served South Africa, Nigeria and European War. Inspector of Artillery, War Office, 1924-27. Master-General of Ordnance and Member of Army Council, 1927-31. Colonel Commandant, Royal Artillery, from 1930, and G.O.C.-in-C., Eastern Command, from 1931.

Two boxes of material, much of it relating to World War I, are available at the Royal Artillery Institution.

GIMSON, Sir Franklin Charles (1890-   )

Governor, Singapore, 1946-52.

Rhodes House Library, Oxford, has a diary and papers, mainly relating to internment in Hong Kong (1942-45).

GLADSTONE, 1st Vt
Sir Herbert John Gladstone (1854-1930)

M.P. (Lib.) Leeds, 1880-85; Leeds West, 1885-1910. Financial Secretary, War Office, 1886. Under-Secretary of State, Home Affairs, 1892-94. 1st Commissioner of Works, 1894-95. Secretary cf State for Home Affairs, 1905-10. Governor-General, South Africa, 1910-14.

Hazlehurst and Woodland, op. cit., pp.61-2, describe the Herbert Gladstone papers in the British Library (Add. MSS. 45985-46118, 46474-46486), and the family collection at St Deiniol's Library, Hawarden, Clwyd.

GLADSTONE, Admiral Sir Gerald Vaughan (1901-   )

Naval career. Vice-Controller of Navy, 1952-53. C.-in-C., Allied Naval Forces, Northern Europe, 1955-57; Far Eastern Station, 1957-66.

It is understood that the Admiral's papers will be donated to the National Maritime Museum.

GLADSTONE, Samuel Steuart (1837-1909)

Governor, Bank of England, 1899-1902.

Mr John Gladstone, Capenoch, Penpont, Dumfriesshire, retains a number of letters from S. S. Gladstone to his parents, mostly written from Calcutta when he was in business (1858-68), and also a diary (1883-1908), relating mainly to sporting activities.

GLADWYN, 1st B
Sir Hubert Miles Gladwyn Jebb (1900-   )

Head of Reconstruction Department, 1942; Counsellor, Foreign Office, 1943-46. Acting Secretary-General, United Nations, 1946. Assistant Under-Secretary and U.N. Adviser, 1946-47. U.K. Representative, United Nations, 1950-54. Ambassador, France, 1954-60.

Lord Gladwyn's papers and records have been promised to Churchill College, Cambridge.

GLEICHEN, Major-General Lord Albert Edward Wilfred, Count Gleichen (1863-1937)

Served Nile Expedition, 1884-85; South Africa, 1899-1900; Belfast, 1911-15; European War, 1914-18. Military Attaché, Berlin, 1903-06; Washington, 1906. Director, Intelligence Bureau, Department of Information, 1917-18.

General Gleichen's nephew and executor, Mr R. V. Machell, states that there are no papers.

GLOUCESTER, Duke of
Prince Henry William Frederick Albert (1900-1974)

Governor-General, Australia, 1945-47.

Records which survive would be placed in the Royal Archives, Windsor.

GLUBB, Lieutenant-General Sir John Bagot (1897-)

Military career. Administrative Inspector, Iraq and Transjordan. Officer Commanding, Desert Area, 1932; Arab Legion, Transjordan, 1939. Chief of General Staff, Arab Legion, 1939-56.

A collection of memoranda and reports (1920-30) relating to Iraq is deposited at the Middle East Centre, St Antony's College, Oxford. Other papers of Lt.-Gen. Glubb are included in the Philby collection at St Antony's. Sir John has retained other papers in his own care, mainly memoranda and reports relating to Transjordan.

GODDARD, Air Marshal Sir Robert Victor (1897-)

Served European War, 1914-19; War of 1939-45. Director of Military Co-operation, Air Ministry, 1940-41. Chief of Air Staff, New Zealand, and Commander, Royal New Zealand Air Forces, South Pacific, 1941-43. Air Officer in Charge of Administration, South East Asia Air Command, 1943-46. R.A.F. Representative, Washington, 1946-48. Air Member for Technical Services, Air Council, 1948-51.

Air Marshal Sir Victor Goddard has few papers, but retains copies of an unpublished book relating to the antecedents of World War II and the 'phoney war'. The material is of particular interest regarding the Dunkirk evacuation.

GODFREY, Admiral John Henry (1888-1971)

Naval career. Deputy Director, Royal Naval Staff College, 1929-31; Plans Division, Admiralty, 1933-35. Director of Naval Intelligence, 1939-42. Flag Officer Commanding, Royal Indian Navy, 1943-46.

The Naval Library, Ministry of Defence, has Godfrey's Naval Staff College Jutland lectures and supplementary papers, and a collection of Mediterranean papers (1917-18). Copies of Godfrey's naval memoirs (1902-46) are available.

GODFREY, General Sir William Wellington (1880-1952)

Served European War, 1914-18. Adjutant-General, Royal Marines, 1936-39, 1940.

A good collection of papers survives at the Imperial War Museum. The papers consist of official documents relating to naval aspects of the Dardanelles campaign covering convoy orders, the landings and the evacuation.

GODLEY, General Sir Alexander John (1867-1957)

Military career; served European War, 1914-18. Military Secretary to Secretary of State for War, 1920-22. C.-in-C., Army of the Rhine, 1922-24. G.O.C.-in-C., Southern Command, 1924-28. Governor, Gibraltar, 1928-33.

Colonel A. S. Godley (nephew) now lives in Rhodesia. Contact was not established.

GOMM, Lieutenant Mark Culling Carr- (1883-1963)

Military service, World War I (Cameroons Expeditionary Force, 1914) and World War II.

Papers and letters relating to the Anglo-French conquest of the Cameroons (1914-16) are available at the Imperial War Museum.

GOODALL, Sir Stanley Vernon (1883-1965)

Director of Naval Construction, Admiralty, 1936-44. Assistant Controller (Warship Production), 1942-45.

There is a collection of diaries and papers at the British Library (Add. MSS. 52785-97). The diaries cover the years 1932-46, and the other material consists of correspondence and papers (1934-56); a copy of the report of the Buckhill Committee on the loss of H.M.S. *Prince of Wales*, and related papers (1942-45); and a diary kept by Goodall's secretary, F. O. Barnford (1939-45).

GOODDEN, Lieutenant-Colonel R. B.
Military career.

The Imperial War Museum has an important collection of letters, diaries and papers relating to Goodden's service in the British Adriatic Mission and as a liaison officer, with the Serbian Army (1915-18), and as Military Attaché in Eastern Europe and the Baltic States in the 1920s.

GOODE, Sir William Allmond Codrington (1907-   )

Colonial Service. Governor, Singapore, 1957-59; North Borneo, 1960-63.

Sir William Goode has a collection of papers relating to service in Malaya. At Rhodes House Library, Oxford, there is a tape and transcript of an interview given, covering service, 1931-63.

GORDON, James Scott (1867-1946)

Permanent Secretary, Northern Ireland Ministry of Agriculture, 1921-33.

A collection of papers can be found at the Northern Ireland Public Record Office.

GORST, Sir John Eldon (1861-1911)

Assistant Under-Secretary, Foreign Office, 1904-07. Agent and Consul-General, Egypt, 1907-11.

Some autobiographical notes and four volumes of press cuttings relating to Sir Eldon Gorst's service in Egypt etc. (1890-1911) have been deposited in the Middle East Centre at St Antony's College, Oxford.

GORT, 6th Vt
Field-Marshal John Standish Surtees Prendergast Vereker (1886-1946)

Served European War, 1914-18. Chief of Imperial General Staff, 1937-39. C.-in-C., British Field Force, 1939-40. Inspector-General to the Forces for Training, 1940-41. Governor and C.-in-C., Gibraltar, 1941-42; Malta, 1942-44. High Commissioner and C.-in-C., Palestine, and High Commissioner, Transjordan, 1944-45.

The papers which are in private possession are not available for research. Reference to papers is made in J. R. Colville's *Man of Valour.*

GOSCHEN, 2nd Vt
George Joachim Goschen (1866-1952)

M.P. (Con.) East Grinstead, 1895-1906. Joint Parliamentary Secretary, Agriculture and Fisheries, 1918. Governor, Madras, 1924-29. Viceroy and Acting Governor-General, India, 1929.

Papers relating to Goschen's career in India have been deposited in the India Office Library, by Hon. Mrs F. Balfour. The principal correspondents include successive Viceroys and Secretaries of State for India (1921-31), and the collection consists of correspondence, speeches and lectures. Hon. Mrs Balfour knows of no further papers remaining with the family.

GOSCHEN, Sir William Edward, 1st Bt (1847-1924)

Minister, Serbia, 1898-1900; Denmark, 1900-05. Ambassador, Austria-Hungary, 1905-08; Germany, 1908-14.

Sir Edward C. Goschen, Bt, 5 Queen Victoria Street, London EC4N 8DX, retains his grandfather's engagement diaries which are of social rather than political interest.

GOSLING, Sir Audley Charles (1836-1913)

Minister, Central American Republics, 1890-97; Chile, 1897-1902.

Madame Teresa Preyre has been unable to trace any papers relating to her grandfather.

GOSLING, Cecil William Gustaf (1870-1944)

Minister, Bolivia, 1910-16. Consul-General, Gothenburg, 1916-18; Frankfurt-am-Main, 1919-24. Chargé d'Affaires, Czechoslovakia, 1918.

Madame Teresa Preyre, 5 rue de Russie, Tangier, Morocco, has a few speeches, addresses and reports relating to her father's career. The papers include notes on the Amazon, a copy of Gosling's long official report from La Paz (22 Dec. 1913), and speeches made in Germany and Czechoslovakia. Copies of the papers are held at B.L.P.E.S.

GOSSAGE, Air Marshal Sir Leslie (1891-1949)

Served European War, 1914-18. Air Attaché, Berlin, 1930-31. Air Officer Commanding, British Forces in Aden, 1935-36; No. 11 Group, 1936-40; Balloon Command, 1941-44. Air Member for Personnel, 1940. Chief Commandant and Director-General of Air Training Corps, 1944-46.

Attempts to trace the family were unsuccessful, and the solicitors mentioned in the Act of Probate no longer appear in the *Law List.*

GOUGH, General Sir Hubert de la Poer (1870-1963)

Served South Africa, 1899-1902; European War, 1914-1918; Commanded 1st Army Corps, 1916; 5th Army, 1916-1918; Chief of Allied Mission, Baltic, 1919.

An extensive collection of family records, including papers of General Sir Hubert Gough, is described in the biography *Goughie*, by Anthony Farrar-Hockley (1975).

GOWERS, Sir Ernest Arthur (1880-1966)

Principal Private Secretary to Chancellor of the Exchequer, 1911-12. Permanent Under-Secretary, Mines, 1920-27. Chairman, Board of Inland Revenue, 1927-30. Chairman, Coal Mines Reorganisation Commission, 1930-35; Coal Commission, 1938-46.

Mr W. R. Gowers, The Picks, Aston Upthorpe, Didcot, Berks. OX11 9HQ, has found few papers of any public interest among his father's surviving records. He kept no diary and his collection of press cuttings related only to the books which he wrote.

GOWERS, Sir William Frederic (1875-1954)

Governor, Uganda, 1925-32. Senior Crown Agent for Colonies, 1932-38.

A collection of papers is held at Rhodes House Library, Oxford. The papers consist of correspondence (1927-32), a diary of a visit to the Belgian Congo (1931), and miscellaneous notes on African affairs.

GOWRIE, 1st E
Brigadier-General Sir Alexander Gore Arkwright Hore-Ruthven (1872-1955)

Military Secretary to Viceroy of Ireland, 1905-08; to Governor General, Australia, 1908. Served European War, 1914-18. Governor, South Australia, 1928-34; New South Wales, 1935. Governor-General, Australia, 1936-44.

Information regarding papers was not forthcoming.

GRAHAM, Admiral Sir Angus Edward Malise Bontine Cunninghame (1893-   )

Naval career. World War I; China, 1936-38. Commodore, Royal Naval Barracks, Chatham, 1943-45. Admiral Superintendent, H. M. Dockyard, Rosyth, 1947-50.

The National Library of Scotland has a number of papers. These include notes on life in the Grand Fleet (1914-16); a xerox of his 'Essay on signalling at the Battle of Jutland' (1929); copies of correspondence with Professor Marder; a catalogue of his naval library; and other papers.

GRAHAM, Sir Henry John Lowndes (1842-1930)

Clerk of the Parliaments, 1885-1917.

Mrs Virginia Thesiger has no papers relating to her grandfather.

GRAHAM, Sir Ronald William (1870-1949)

Minister, Egypt, 1916; Holland, 1919-21. Ambassador, Italy, 1921-33.

Neither Mrs V. Thesiger, nor her last surviving aunt, know of any private papers relating to Sir Ronald Graham. A single letter to Graham from Benito Mussolini (1926), with a covering letter from Graham to Sir John Forsdyke (1945), is held at the British Library (Add. MSS. 46362). The Hardinge papers contain some of Graham's correspondence and minutes for the period 1903-20.

GRAHAME, Sir George Dixon (1873-1940)

Minister, Luxembourg, 1922-28. Ambassador, Belgium, 1920-28; Spain, 1928-35.

Messrs Gregory, Rowcliffe & Co., solicitors, referred us to the son of one of Sir George Grahame's executors. He, Mr M. R. Allsopp, stated that his late mother had destroyed those papers of Sir George Grahame which had passed into her care. No member of Sir George's family, nor his other executor, were traced.

GRANT, Sir Alfred Hamilton, 12th Bt (1872-1937)

Foreign Secretary, Government of India, 1914-19. Chief Commissioner, North West Frontier Province, 1919-21.

A collection of Hamilton Grant's letters and papers (1903-30) has been given to the India Office Library.

GRANT, General Sir Charles John Cecil (1877-1950)

Served South Africa, 1899-1902; European War, 1914-18; Egypt, 1921-25. Brigadier-General, General Staff, 1918-19. G.O.C., London District, 1932-34. G.O.C.-in-C., Scottish Command, 1937-40.

A collection of papers survives in the care of Mrs Oliver Colthurst, Pitchford Hall, Shrewsbury. The material includes letters to Lord Rosebery (1914-18).

GRANT, General Sir Henry Fane (1848-1919)

Military career from 1868. Governor, Malta, 1907-09.

A visit to Somerset House brought forward no information useful in tracing executors or members of the family.

GRANTHAM, Sir Alexander William George Herder (1899-   )

Colonial Service. Governor, Fiji (and High Commissioner, Western Pacific), 1945-47; Hong Kong, 1947-57.

Sir Alexander Grantham has kept no papers, but a tape recording and transcript of an interview is held at Rhodes House Library, Oxford.

GRANTHAM, Admiral Sir Guy (1900-   )

Naval career; served World War II. Vice Chief of Naval Staff, 1951-54. C.-in-C., Mediterranean, 1954-57; Portsmouth, 1957-59. Governor and C.-in-C., Malta, 1959-62.

According to information supplied to the Imperial War Museum, no papers survive.

GRANVILLE, 3rd E
Granville George Leveson Gower (1872-1939)

Lord-in-Waiting, 1905-15. Counsellor, Berlin, 1911-13; Paris, 1913-17. Diplomatic Agent, Salonika, 1917. Minister, Greece, 1917-21; Denmark, 1921-26; Netherlands, 1926-28. Ambassador, Belgium, 1928-33.

No information regarding papers was secured. A few letters (c. 1916-19) are in the Hardinge papers at Cambridge University Library.

GREENE, Sir (W.) Conyngham (1854-1934)

Agent and Chargé d'Affaires, Pretoria, 1896-99. Minister, Switzerland, 1901-05; Romania, 1905-10; Denmark, 1910-12. Ambassador, Japan, 1912-19.

Mrs D. Conyngham Greene, widow of Sir W. Conyngham Greene's son Geoffrey, and Lord Courtown, who was one of Lady Greene's executors, had no knowledge of any papers left by Sir W. Conyngham Greene. Mrs Conyngham Greene stated that her father-in-law did not want any of his papers kept.

GREENE, Sir (William) Graham (1857-1950)

Permanent Secretary, Admiralty, 1911-17; Munitions, 1917-20.

An important collection at the National Maritime Museum includes letters, extracts, notes and memoranda on departmental administration; correspondence and memoranda relating to the Controller's Department (1916-17), Munitions (1915-18), and the financial system; papers on the Dardanelles campaign and Commission (1915-16); correspondence and notes (1914-35); and articles and correspondence on the lives of admirals and statesmen.

GREENLY, Major-General Walter Howorth (1875-1955)

Served South Africa, 1899-1902; European War, 1914-18. Commander, 2nd Cavalry Division, 1916-18. Chief of Military Mission to Romania, 1918-20.

Major-General Greenly kept no papers.

GREENWAY, John Dee (1896-1967)

Minister, Panama, 1946-50; Iceland, 1950-53.

A visit to Somerset House produced no useful information. Mr Greenway's publishers, Faber & Faber Ltd, were also unable to give any help.

GREG, Sir Robert Hyde (1896-1953)

Minister, Siam, 1921-26; Romania, 1926-29. British Commissioner, Egyptian Public Debt, 1929-40.

Mr M. Maclagan, Trinity College, Oxford, states that his godfather had an extensive private correspondence and kept a letter book. However, the present whereabouts of these papers is not known.

GREGG, Sir Cornelius Joseph (d. 1959)

Chairman, Board of Inland Revenue, 1942-48.

Executors to the estate could not be contacted, and it proved impossible to trace the family, who lived in Ireland.

GREGORY, John Duncan (1878-1951)

Assistant Under-Secretary, Foreign Office, 1925-28.

Mr Gregory's executors could not be traced, and his literary agents, Messrs Curtis Brown Ltd, were unable to provide the name and address of any surviving heir or member of Mr Gregory's family. Two books by Gregory, *On the Edge of Diplomacy* (1929) and *Dollfuss and His Times* (1935), have appeared.

GRENFELL, 1st B
Field-Marshal Sir Francis Wallace Grenfell (1841-1925)

Military career from 1859. Governor, Malta, 1899-1903. C.-in-C., Ireland, 1904-08.

Members of the family could not be contacted. Relevant papers can be found in the Cromer collection at the Public Record Office and the Wolseley papers at Hove Central Library. Grenfell's correspondence with Sir F. R. Wingate is at Duke University.

GREVILLE, Sir George (1851-1937)

Minister, Siam, 1896-1900; Mexico, 1900-05.

Miss Carmelita Greville has found no papers relating to her father's career.

GREY, 4th E
Sir Albert Henry George Grey (1851-1917)

M.P. (Lib.) Northumberland South, 1880-85; Tyneside, 1885-86. Administrator, Rhodesia, 1896-97. Director, British South Africa Company, 1898-1904. Governor-General, Canada, 1904-11.

A collection of papers is held in the Palaeography Department at the University of Durham.

GREY OF FALLODON, 1st Vt
Sir Edward Grey, 3rd Bt (1862-1933)

M.P. (Lib.) Berwick-on-Tweed, 1885-1916. Parliamentary Under-Secretary, Foreign Affairs, 1892-95. Secretary of State for Foreign Affairs, 1905-16. Ambassador, United States, 1919-20.

The Private Office collection of correspondence and papers (1892-95, 1905-16) is available at the Public Record Office (F.O. 800/35-113), and no further private papers have been found. Details are given in Hazlehurst and Woodland, op. cit., pp.64-5.

GRIER, Sir Selwyn MacGregor (1878-1946)

Colonial Service. Governor, Windward Islands, 1935-37.

Rhodes House Library, Oxford, holds three boxes of correspondence relating to service in Nigeria (1906-25).

GRIERSON, Lieutenant-General Sir James Moncrieff (1859-1914)

Served Egypt, 1882; South Africa, 1900; China, 1900-01. Military Attaché, Berlin, 1896-1900. Director of Military Operations, 1904-06. Commander, 1st Division, Aldershot Command, 1906-10. G.O. C.-in-C., Eastern Command, 1912-14.

The papers were destroyed by Grierson's biographer, D. S. MacDiarmid.

GRIGG, Sir (Percy) James (1890-1964)

Principal Private Secretary to successive Chancellors of the Exchequer, 1921-30. Chairman, Board of Customs and Excise, 1930; Board of Inland Revenue, 1930-34. Finance Member, Council of the Viceroy of India, 1934-39. Permanent Under-Secretary, War Office, 1939-42. M.P. (Nat.) Cardiff East, 1942-45. Secretary of State for War, 1942-45.

A collection of papers is held at Churchill College, Cambridge. Most of the papers relate to Grigg's period in India, with a few papers from the early 1940s when Grigg was in the Government and a good deal of material relating to the publication of the autobiography, *Prejudice and Judgement* (1948). Details are given by Hazlehurst and Woodland, op. cit., p.67.

GROHMAN, Vice-Admiral Harold Tom Baillie- (1888-   )

Naval career from 1902; served World War I (Grand Fleet, Dover Patrol in destroyers and minesweepers). Head of British Naval Mission to China, 1931-33. Commanded 1st Destroyer Flotilla, Mediterranean, 1934-36. Attached to H.Q. Mid-East in Cairo, 1941. Commanded H.M.S. *Ramillies*, 1939-40. Rear-Admiral, Combined Operations, 1942. Flag Officer in Charge, Harwich, 1944; Kiel and Schleswig-Holstein, 1945-46.

An unpublished autobiography, 'Flashlights on the Past', is preserved at the National Maritime Museum, together with the unpublished 'Flashlights on German Naval Disarmament, 1945-46', and certain papers relating to the naval mission to China (1931-33) and to the Dieppe raid.

GROVES, Air Commodore (Brigadier General) Robert Marsland (1880-1920)

Director of Operations and Intelligence, Air Ministry, 1918-1919, and Deputy Chief of Air Staff.

The Imperial War Museum has Groves' diaries (2 volumes) for the period April 1918 to November 1919.

GUILLEMARD, Sir Lawrence Nunns (1862-1951)

Chairman, Board of Customs and Excise, 1909-19. Governor, Straits Settlements, and High Commissioner, Malay States, 1919-27.

Sir John Mellor, Bt, who was one of Sir Lawrence Guillemard's executors, states that he has no knowledge of the whereabouts of relevant papers. The firm of solicitors who acted for Sir Lawrence no longer appears in the *Law List* and it did not prove possible to contact Sir Lawrence's other executors. A number of files relating to Sir Lawrence survive in H.M. Customs and Excise Library.

GURNEY, Sir Henry Lovell Goldsworthy (1898-1951)

Chief Secretary, Palestine, 1946-48. High Commissioner, Malayan Federation, 1948-51.

The Middle East Centre at St Antony's College, Oxford, has a series of Sir Henry Gurney's notes on the last two months of the Palestine Mandate.

GURNEY, Sir Hugh (1878-1968)

Minister, Denmark, 1933-35. Ambassador, Brazil, 1935-39.

Lady Gurney has found no papers relating to her late husband which would be of interest.

GWATKIN, Frank Trelawny Arthur Ashton- (1889-   )

Counsellor, Foreign Office, from 1934. Policy Adviser, Economic Warfare, 1939. Assistant Under-Secretary and Chief Clerk, Foreign Office, from 1940.

Mr Ashton-Gwatkin has retained a few papers only, relating to his career.

GYE, Ernest Frederick (1879-1955)

Minister, Tangier, 1933-36; Venezuela, 1936-39.

Messrs Radcliffes & Co., solicitors in the estate, were unable to provide any information regarding papers or members of the family.

HAGGARD, Sir Godfrey Digby Napier (1884-1969)

Chargé d'Affaires, Bolivia, 1915; Cuba, 1921. Consul-General, Brazil, 1924; Chicago, 1928-32; Paris, 1932-38; New York, 1938-44. Director, American Forces Liaison Division, Ministry of Information, 1944-45.

The papers are retained by Mr D. Corley-Smith, 49 Sheering Road, Old Harlow, Essex CM17 0JN. The material includes notes, photographs, press cuttings and various drafts of an unpublished autobiography. The memoirs consist of biographical sketches, anecdotes and an account of political affairs in Venezuela (1902-03), Bolivia, etc.

HAGGARD, Admiral Sir Vernon Henry Stuart (1874-1960)

Naval career from 1888; served European War, 1914-18. Director of Training and Staff Duties, Admiralty, 1921-23. Chief of Submarine Service, 1925-27. 4th Sea Lord and Chief of Supplies and Transport, 1928-30. C.-in-C., America and West Indies Station, 1930-32.

Commander H. A. V. Haggard, Orchard Cottage, Moreton Pinkney, Daventry, Northants., states that his father kept a diary all his life and used these diaries to write an autobiographical narrative (5 vols.). Commander Haggard retains a copy of this memoir.

HAGGARD, Sir William Henry Doveton (1846-1926)

Minister, Venezuela, 1897-1902; Argentine Republic and Paraguay, 1902-06; Brazil, 1906-14.

Members of the family who were contacted know of no papers, except for the letters to Lady Holland (1874-85) available at the British Library (Add. MSS. 52133).

HAIG, 1st E
Field-Marshal Sir Douglas Haig (1861-1928)

Served Sudan, 1898; South Africa, 1899-1902. Chief of Staff, India, 1909-12. G.O.C., Aldershot, 1912-14. Commander, 1st Army, 1914-15. C.-in-C., Expeditionary Force in France and Flanders, 1915-19; Forces in Great Britain, 1919-20.

A collection of papers (1882-1928) in 336 volumes is held in the National Library of Scotland. The papers consist of letters, diaries, military notebooks and textbooks, photographs, maps, copies of daily orders, albums of press cuttings, and other papers. The material relates to the various periods of Haig's military career, and to the work of Lord and Lady Haig with the British Legion. A copy of the Haig memorandum, an account of operations on the Western Front (1916-18), compiled by members of Haig's staff, is available at the British Library (Add. MSS. 52460).

HAIG, Sir Harry Graham (1881-1956)

Home Secretary, Government of India, 1926-30. Home Member, Executive Council of Governor-General, India, 1932-34. Governor, United Provinces, 1934-39.

The collection at the India Office Library consists of correspondence, including copies of telegrams and secret letters between Haig and the Viceroy (c. 1937-39), relating to political affairs in the United Provinces.

HAIG, Lieutenant-Colonel Sir Thomas Wolseley (1865-1938)

Indian Political Service and Consular Agent. Consul-General and Agent of Indian Government, Khivasah, Persia, 1914-16; Isfahan, 1916; Tehran, 1919.

An unpublished autobiographical record is held at the Middle East Centre, St Antony's College, Oxford.

HAILEY, 1st B
Sir William Malcolm Hailey (1872-1969)

Governor, Punjab, 1924-28; United Provinces, 1928-30, 1931-34. Member, Permanent Members Commission, League of Nations, 1935-39.

The Indian papers of Lord Hailey are deposited at the India Office Library. The collection includes papers relating to Hailey's work as Chief Commissioner at Delhi (1912-18) and as President of the committee in charge of the construction of New Delhi, also to the Indian Round Table Conference of 1930-31. Other material consists of correspondence accumulated and speeches made when Hailey was a provincial governor, some printed reports and a collection of press cuttings. A further collection of papers survives at Rhodes House Library, Oxford. There is a typescript diary, relating to South Africa (1935) and the United States (1942-43 and 1944), with copies of addresses given (1912-58) and other miscellaneous papers. In addition, the Library holds correspondence relating to an African journey (1940-41), and papers on the Colonial Research Committee (1940-43), South West Africa (1946), British Council lectures (1946-47) and the United States (1952-53).

HAINING, General Sir Robert Hadden (1882-1959)

Director of Military Operations and Intelligence, War Office, 1936-38. G.O.C., British Forces in Palestine and Transjordan, 1938-39. G.O.C.-in-C., Western Command, 1939-40. Vice Chief, Imperial General Staff, 1940-41. Lieutenant-General, Middle East, 1941-42.

The papers at the Middle East Centre, St Antony's College, Oxford, relate to the Arab revolt of 1938-39, and there is correspondence between Haining and Sir Charles Tegart on Palestine affairs (1938-39), dispatches on British operations at that time, a statement to Jewish leaders on bloodshed and a reply by Ben-Gurion (1939), and two cuttings on Haining's success in Palestine.

HALDANE, General Sir James Aylmer Lowthorpe (1862-1950)

Served India; South Africa, 1899-1900; European War, 1914-19. Military Attaché with Japanese Army, 1904-05. G.O. C.-in-C., Mesopotamia, 1920-22.

The National Library of Scotland holds a collection of papers (1890-1950), including letters and diaries, and material on World War I and Mesopotamia (1920-22).

HALIFAX, 1st E of
Edward Frederick Lindley Wood, 1st B Irwin (1881-1959)

M.P. (Con.) Ripon, 1910-25. Parliamentary Under-Secretary, Colonies, 1921-22. President, Board of Education, 1922-24, 1934-35. Minister, Agriculture and Fisheries, 1924-25. Viceroy of India, 1926-31. Secretary of State for War, 1935. Lord Privy Seal, 1935-37. Lord President of the Council, 1937-38. Secretary of State, Foreign Affairs, 1938-40. Ambassador, United States, 1941-46.

The present Earl of Halifax, of Garrowby, Yorkshire, retains many of his father's papers. A microfilm of some of the papers relating to 1938-39 and to the period in Washington is kept at Churchill College, Cambridge, and the Indian papers are deposited in the India Office Library. Foreign Office correspondence (1938-40) remains at the Public Record Office (F.O. 800/309-28). Researchers should consult Hazlehurst and Woodland, op. cit., pp.153-4, for further details.

HALL, Sir Alfred Daniel (1864-1942)

Permanent Secretary, Agriculture and Fisheries, 1917-20.

Mr Robert Orwin, O.B.E., son of Sir Daniel's executor, knows of no papers. It was not possible to trace members of the Hall family. Correspondence (1915-30) with Sir Horace Plunkett concerning wartime food production and agricultural co-operation can be found in the Plunkett MSS. Further correspondence on food production may be found in the Lloyd George papers.

HALL, Sir John Hathorn (1894-   )

Chief Secretary, Palestine, 1933-34. British Resident, Zanzibar, 1937-40. Governor, Aden, 1940-44; Uganda, 1944-51.

The Colonial Records Project found that Sir John Hathorn Hall has kept no papers.

HALL, Admiral Sir (William) Reginald (1870-1943)

Director of Intelligence Division, Admiralty War Staff, 1914-18. M.P. (Con.) Liverpool West Derby, 1919-23; Eastbourne, 1925-29.

Commander R. A. Hall has presented all his father's papers to Churchill College, Cambridge. These consist of memoirs and papers, 1915-33.

HALLETT, Vice-Admiral Sir (Cecil) Charles Hughes- (1898-   )

Naval career from 1914. Director of Administrative Plans and Joint Planning Staff, 1942-44. Chief of Staff to C.-in-C., Home Fleet, 1950-51. Admiral, British Joint Services Mission, Washington, 1952-54.

It is believed that Sir Charles Hughes-Hallett kept no papers.

HALLETT, Vice-Admiral John Hughes- (1901-1972)

Naval career; active service in World War II. Commodore commanding Channel Assault Force and Naval Chief of Staff (X), 1942-43. Vice-Controller of the Navy, 1950-52. M.P. (Con.) Croydon East, 1954-55; Croydon North East, 1955-64. Parliamentary Secretary, Transport, 1961-64.

A collection of papers at the Imperial War Museum relates to Operation 'Jubilee' (the raid on Dieppe, Aug. 1942) and other operations conducted by Combined Operations Headquarters.

HALLETT, Leslie Charles Hughes- (1887-1966)

Minister, Ecuador, 1941-45; Guatemala, 1946-47.

Mrs M. Langford knows of no papers relating to her uncle, Mr L. C. Hughes-Hallett.

HALLETT, Sir Maurice Garnier (1883-1969)

Home Secretary, Government of India, 1932-36. Governor, Bihar, 1937-39; United Provinces, 1939-45.

The papers (1907-47) at the India Office Library are arranged in ten sections. The correspondence and minutes consist mainly of Hallett's fortnightly reports (1938-39), and notes made whilst Governor of the United Provinces. These are supplemented by miscellaneous papers and printed reports from the United Provinces, and other papers about agriculture in the area. Further series of papers relate to Jamshedpur, the Tata Iron and Steel Company, to war work in the United Provinces, and revolutionary movements in India. Series of miscellaneous pamphlets, speeches, newspaper cuttings and photographs complete the collection.

HALSEY, Admiral Sir Lionel (1872-1949)

Naval career. 3rd Sea Lord, 1917-18. Commander, Royal Australian Navy, 1918-20.

Certain papers in the care of the Halsey family, Golden Parsonage, Hemel Hempstead, Herts., are relevant to the career of Sir Lionel, including material in a scrapbook of photographs, letters and speeches. Further Halsey family material is deposited at Hertfordshire Record Office.

HAMILTON, Sir Edward Walter (1847-1908)

Private Secretary to W. E. Gladstone, 1873-74, 1880-85. Joint Permanent Secretary, Treasury, 1902-08.

The Private Office collection (1858-1909) at the Public Record Office (T.168) consists of correspondence, printed papers (including some Cabinet papers), memoranda, etc., relating to Hamilton's work at the Treasury and as private secretary to Chancellors of the Exchequer and to the Prime Minister, W. E. Gladstone. A large proportion of the papers described as 'Financial notes' and 'Financial papers' are the Budget papers of the day.

A further large collection of private papers can be found at the British Library (Add. MSS. 48599-699). Special correspondents include King Edward VII, Queen Alexandra, King George V, and their private secretaries; Sir Henry Ponsonby, W. E. Gladstone and members of his family, Lord Rosebery, H. H. Asquith, H. A. D. Seymour, Lord Kilbracken, G. W. S. Littleton. There are also a number of diaries for the years 1867, 1880-1906 and 1890-1906.

HAMILTON, Admiral Sir Frederick Huw George Dalrymple- (1890-1975)

Naval career from 1905. Naval Secretary to 1st Lord of Admiralty, 1942. 2nd-in-Command, Home Fleet, 1944-45.

The Admiral's papers are to be given to the National Maritime Museum.

HAMILTON, Vice-Admiral Sir Frederick Tower (1856-1917)

Naval career from 1869. 2nd Sea Lord, 1914-16. C.-in-C., Rosyth, 1916-17.

Papers, including private and official correspondence, and a diary for Oct.

1915-June 1916, are now in the care of the National Maritime Museum. The private correspondence dates from *c.* 1880 to 1917, and covers a large number of important correspondents. Official papers include correspondence (1914-16) on policy, and material on the resignation of Fisher in 1915. Six volumes of journals cover the years 1870-1916.

HAMILTON, Sir George Rostrevor (1888-1967)

Private Secretary to Chairman, Board of Inland Revenue, 1913. Secretary, Committee on National Debt and Taxation, 1926. Assistant Secretary, Board of Inland Revenue, 1929. Special Commissioner, Income Tax, 1934. Poet, writer and Civil Servant.

The papers at the Bodleian Library consist of letters to Sir George (1911-66) with a few to his wife Marion. The letters are arranged by correspondent (both literary and political figures), in alphabetical order. Further papers about Hamilton are in the Erica Marx collection at Washington University Library, St Louis.

HAMILTON, Sir Horace Perkins (1880-1971)

Private Secretary to Chancellor of the Exchequer, 1912-18. Chairman, Board of Customs and Excise, 1919-27. Permanent Secretary, Board of Trade, 1927-37. Permanent Under-Secretary, Scotland, 1937-46.

Some papers (1912-18) of Sir H. P. Hamilton survive in the Treasury Private Office series (T.171) at the Public Record Office. This class of papers, entitled 'Chancellor of the Exchequer's Office: Budget and Finance Bill papers' (1859-1925), consists of material accumulated during the preparation of Budgets and finance bills.
　Sir H. P. Hamilton's daughter Mrs B. Henderson, 25 Christchurch Hill, London NW3, has none of her father's papers, apart from one or two odd letters from colleagues.

HAMILTON, Major-General Hubert Ian Wetherall (1861-1914)

Served Burma, 1886-88; Egypt, 1897-99; South Africa, 1899-1902; India. Military Secretary to Lord Kitchener, 1900-05.

A collection of papers is held at the National Army Museum. The material consists of letters and documents relating to the Boer War, and correspondence of General Hamilton with the Marker family. Letters (1904-09) to R. J. Marker are in the British Library (Add. MSS. 52278)

HAMILTON, General Sir Ian Standish Monteith (1853-1947)

Served South Africa, 1881, 1899-1901; Egypt and Sudan, 1884-85; Burma, 1886-87. Chief of Staff to Lord Kitchener, 1901-02. Military Representative of India with Japanese Army in Manchuria, 1904-05. G.O.C.-in-C., Southern Command, 1905-09; Mediterranean, 1910-15. Adjutant-General, 1909-10. Commander, Mediterranean Expeditionary Force, 1915.

A large collection of papers is available at the Liddell Hart Centre for Military Archives. The papers are particularly strong on the Gallipoli campaign (1915) and the South African War (1899-1902). The material subsequent to 1916 includes a great bulk of private papers and diaries.

HAMILTON, Admiral Sir Louis Henry Keppel (1890-1957)

Naval career; served World Wars I and II. 1st Naval Member and Chief of Naval Staff, Commonwealth Naval Board, 1945-48.

A substantial collection of papers is deposited at the National Maritime Museum, including correspondence, a diary dating from 1908, papers relating to naval events in World War I and the inter-war years, lecture notes (1914-47) and personal papers.

HAMPTON, 4th B
Major Herbert Stuart Pakington (1883-1962)

Military career.

The Imperial War Museum has a diary (1917-19), being a personal account based on the official diary of D Squadron of the Worcestershire Yeomanry, relating to the conquest of Palestine, Jordan and Syria.

HANCOCK, Sir Henry Drummond (1895-1965)

Permanent Secretary, National Insurance, 1949-51; Food, 1951-55. Chairman, Board of Inland Revenue, 1955-58.

Lady Hancock states that her late husband left no papers at all.

HANKEY, 1st B
Sir Maurice Pascal Alers Hankey (1877-1963)

Secretary, Committee of Imperial Defence, 1912-38; War Cabinet, 1916; Imperial War Cabinet, 1917-18; Cabinet, 1919-38; and Clerk of the Privy Council, 1923-38. Minister without Portfolio, 1939-40. Chancellor of the Duchy of Lancaster, 1940-41. Paymaster-General, 1941-42.

A large collection of papers and diaries has been deposited with Churchill College, Cambridge. Another set of papers is available at the Public Record Office (Cab. 63). Details are given by Hazlehurst and Woodland, op. cit., pp.70-1.

HANKEY, 2nd B
Sir Robert Maurice Alers Hankey (1905-)

Chargé d'Affaires, Spain, 1949-51. Minister, Hungary, 1951-53. Ambassador, Sweden, 1954-60.

Lord Hankey states that he has given such family papers and letters as he has retained to the Archives Centre at Churchill College, Cambridge. As a public official himself, he did not keep papers.

HARCOURT, Admiral Sir Cecil Halliday Jepson (1892-1959)

Naval career. Naval Secretary to 1st Lord of the Admiralty, 1944-45. C.-in-C., Hong Kong, 1945-46. 2nd Sea Lord, 1948-50. C.-in-C., The Nore, 1950-52.

The Admiral's stepdaughter, Mrs Yehudi Menuhin, 2 The Grove, London N6, has a collection of photograph albums and press cuttings.

HARDING OF PETHERTON, 1st B
Field-Marshal Sir Allan Francis John Harding (1896-)

Served European War, 1914-19, and War of 1939-45. G.O.C.-in-C., Southern Command, 1947-49. C.-in-C., Far East Land Forces, 1949-51; British Army of the Rhine, 1951-52. Chief of Imperial General Staff, 1952-55. Governor and C.-in-C., Cyprus, 1955-57.

Lord Harding has retained a few papers only and these are not made available.

HARDING, Sir Edward John (1880-1954)

Permanent Under-Secretary, Dominions Office, 1930-40. High Commissioner, South Africa, and Basutoland, Bechuanaland and Swaziland, 1940-41.

The Library of the Royal Commonwealth Society holds a collection of diary letters (1913-16) from Harding to members of his family. These were written while he was Secretary of the Dominions Royal Commission. A collection of press cuttings kept by Miss Eva Harding relating to Sir Edward Harding survives with Mr W. J. Willcocks, F.C.A., of Messrs Capel-Cure Carden & Co., Bath House, Holborn Viaduct, London EC1A 2EU. Sir John Burrows, who was one of Sir Edward Harding's executors, knows of no further private papers.

HARDINGE OF PENSHURST, 1st B
Sir Charles Hardinge (1858-1944)

Permanent Under-Secretary, Foreign Affairs, 1906-11, 1916-20. Ambassador, Russia, 1904-06; France, 1920-23. Viceroy of India, 1910-16.

The main collection of Hardinge's papers is housed in Cambridge University Library. The material includes some 40 volumes of semi-official correspondence: letters to Hardinge (1880-1911, 1916-20), with some typescript copies of replies. Another section of the material relates to the Indian Viceroyalty, and further items include official correspondence with Lord Lansdowne (1904-06), and a letter book and diary (1904-05). The Private Office papers at the Public Record Office include one volume of Hardinge's correspondence (F.O. 800/192) for the years 1906-11. The Hardinge family papers at Kent Archives Office include some material relating to Lord Hardinge of Penshurst. The collection at Cambridge University Library is fully indexed.

HARDINGE, Sir Arthur Henry (1859-1933)

Commissioner and Consul-General, East Africa Protectorate, 1896-1900. Minister, Persia, 1900-05; Belgium, 1906-11; Portugal, 1911-13. Ambassador, Spain, 1913-19.

A certain amount of correspondence survives in the Lord Hardinge of Penshurst collection at Cambridge University Library.

HARDMAN, Air Chief Marshal Sir James Donald Innes (1899-)

Served European War, 1916-19. Air Officer in Charge of Administration, South East Asia Air Command, 1946-47. Assistant Chief of Air Staff (Operations), 1947-49. Air Officer C.-in-C., Home Command, 1951-52. Chief of Air Staff, Royal Australian Air Force, 1952-54. Air Member for Supply and Organisation, 1954-57.

It is understood that there are certain papers and that these may be given to the Imperial War Museum.

HARFORD, Frederic Dundas (1862-1931)

Minister, Venezuela, 1911-16.

Lady Bannerman believes that her father destroyed all his papers before his death.

HARINGTON, General Sir Charles Harington (1872-1940)

Served South Africa, 1899-1900; European War, 1914-18. Deputy Chief of Imperial General Staff, 1918-20. G.O.C.-in-C., Army of the Black Sea, 1920-21. Allied

Occupation Forces in Turkey, 1921-23; Northern Command, 1923-27; Western Command, India, 1927-31; Aldershot Command, 1931-33. Governor and C.-in-C., Gibraltar, 1933-38.

A small collection of papers covering the years 1916-35 survives at the Museum of the King's Regiment (Liverpool), City of Liverpool Museum, William Brown Street, Liverpool 3. The papers relate mainly to the Chanak crisis of 1922-23, and there are a number of photographs, memorabilia and obituary notices. Harington records in his biography of Lord Plumer of Messines that he destroyed most of his papers when he left Constantinople.

HARMAN, Sir Charles Anthony King- (1851-1939)

Governor, Sierra Leone, 1900-04. High Commissioner, Cyprus, 1904-11.

Captain R. D. King-Harman, Sir Charles's son, believes that no private papers have survived.

HARPER, Sir Charles Henry Hasler (1876-1950)

Governor, St Helena, 1925-32. Served Ministry of Food, 1939-41.

A collection of papers is held at Rhodes House Library, Oxford. The material consists of notes on Ashanti law and history (1902-22), Gold Coast diaries and correspondence (1914-20), notes on the history of Ascension, St Helena and Guinea, and miscellaneous papers.

HARPER, Vice-Admiral John Ernest Troyte (1874-1949)

Naval career from 1888. Director of Navigation, Admiralty, 1919-21.

Papers of Vice-Admiral Harper, regarding the *Official Record of the Battle of Jutland,* completed by him in 1919 and published in amended form in 1927, are available at the British Library (Add. MSS. 54477-54480). These include a draft and printed proof (1920); copies of Admiralty minutes (1919-21); lithographed diagrams and charts; and a statement of facts dealing with the official record and the reason for its non-publication (1924, 1928, 1935), together with relevant correspondence.

HARRELL, Sir David (1841-1939)

Under-Secretary, Ireland, 1893-1902.

Sir David Harrell's granddaughter, Miss G. M. Orme, states that her grandfather's papers do not survive. However, a copy of an autobiography, written in 1926 for family circulation only, has been placed in B.L.P.E.S.

HARRIES, Air Vice-Marshal Sir Douglas (1893-1972)

Royal Air Force career. Director-General of Personnel, Air Ministry, 1943-46.

Miscellaneous papers (1939-45), including a 1938 Report of the Transjordan Frontier Force are available at the Imperial War Museum.

HARRIS, Marshal of the Royal Air Force Sir Arthur Travers, 1st Bt (1892-   )

Served European War, 1914-19. Air Officer Commanding, Palestine and Trans-jordan, 1938-39; 5 Bomber Group, 1939-41. Deputy Chief of Air Staff, 1940-41. Head of R.A.F. Delegation, United States, 1941. C.-in-C., Bomber Command, 1942-45.

The Liddell Hart Centre for Military Archives found that Sir Arthur Harris has kept no military papers.

HARRIS, Sir Charles (1864-1943)

Civil Service career from 1886. Joint Secretary of the War Office 1920-24, and Permanent Head of the Finance Department, War Office.

Mr Alan Harris, 15 Blenheim Road, London NW8, has a certain amount of material relating to his father's career.

HARRIS, Sir Percy Wyn- (1903-   )

Colonial service, Kenya. Governor, Gambia, 1949-58.

The Oxford Colonial Records Project found that Sir Percy has kept only a few papers, relating to the plebiscite in the Northern Cameroons.

HART, Captain Sir Basil Liddell (1895-1970)

Served European War 1914-18. Military theorist, writer and publicist. Military correspondent, *Daily Telegraph*, 1925-35; *The Times*, 1935-39.

A very large and important collection of correspondence, memoranda, lectures and other papers on military matters is to be housed at the Liddell Hart Centre for Military Archives, King's College, London. At present the papers remain with Lady Liddell Hart at States House, Medmenham, Bucks. A detailed list is now available at N.R.A. Apart from innumerable files of correspondence, notes and drafts of published works, there is a large collection of press cuttings.

HARTLEY, Brigadier-General Sir Harold (1878-1972)

Controller of Chemical Warfare Department, Ministry of Munitions, 1918-19. Chairman, Fuel Research Board, 1932-47. Hon. Adviser, Ministry of Fuel and Power, 1939-47.

A collection of papers is held at Churchill College, Cambridge. The material relates to scientific affairs, railways and air. There are also a number of personal papers.

HARVEY OF TASBURGH, 1st B
Sir Oliver Charles Harvey, 4th Bt (1893-1968)

Principal Private Secretary to Secretary of State, Foreign Affairs, 1936-39, 1941-43. Assistant Under-Secretary, 1943-46; Deputy Under-Secretary (Political), Foreign Office, 1946-47. Minister, France, 1940; Ambassador, 1948-54.

The diaries and papers of Lord Harvey have been deposited in the British Library (Add. MSS. 56412-8). Much of the collection remains closed to researchers.

HARVEY, Sir Henry Paul (1869-1948)

Financial Adviser to Egyptian Government, 1907-12, 1919-20. Director, Prisoners of War Information Bureau, 1914-16. Secretary, Air Board, 1916-18.

The Public Record Office holds one volume of correspondence (F.O. 800/194) relating to Harvey's work as British Delegate on the International Commission at Paris for the Settlement of Financial Questions arising out of the Balkan War (1913). Surviving members of the family were not traced.

HAWKINS, Admiral Sir Geoffrey Alan Brooke (1895-   )

Naval career; served World Wars I and II. Flag Officer, Malta, 1950-52.

Certain papers in the care of the Imperial War Museum include Hawkins's midshipman's journal (1913-15), kept while he was serving in the cruiser *Natal;* copies of the *Natal Newsletter* (Aug. 1914-May 1915); two scrapbooks of press cuttings relating to Hawkins's appointment as Flag Officer, Malta (1950-52); and various letters of appointment.

HAWTREY, Sir Ralph George (1879-   )

Served Admiralty, 1903; Treasury, 1904-45. Director of Financial Enquiries, 1919-45. Economist and author.

A collection of Private Office papers is to be made available at the Public Record Office, and a further extensive accumulation of papers remains with Sir Ralph Hawtrey. This material mainly relates to his work as an economist, and includes notes and the drafts of several unpublished works. There are also: (1) drafts and copies of Treasury papers; (2) correspondence with economists; (3) voluminous correspondence with J. M. Keynes; (4) papers relating to a proposed financial history of World War II; (5) notes and copies of published articles and reviews; and (6) a fairly complete set of letters to the press, and a quantity of press cuttings.

HAY, Lord Edward Douglas John (1888-1944)

Served European War, 1914-18; Paris Peace Conference, 1918-19; and on special missions to Austria, Hungary and Bulgaria, 1919-21. Military Secretary to High Commissioner, Palestine, 1921-23.

A fair-sized collection of papers, covering various aspects of his career, is held at the Middle East Centre, St Antony's College, Oxford.

HAYTER, Sir William Goodenough (1906-   )

Minister, France from 1949. Ambassador, U.S.S.R. 1953-57. Deputy Under-Secretary, Foreign Office, 1957-58.

Sir William Hayter has retained very few private papers, almost none of any significance. The papers will probably be deposited in due course with New College, Oxford.

HEADLAM-MORLEY, Sir James Wycliffe (1863-1929)

Staff Inspector, Board of Education, 1902-14. Assistant Director, Political Intelligence Bureau, Department of Information, 1914-18; Political Intelligence Department, Foreign Office, 1918-20. Member of Political Section, British Delegation, Paris Peace Conference, 1919. Historical Adviser, Foreign Office, from 1920.

Professor Agnes Headlam-Morley, 29 St Mary's Road, London SW19 7BT, states that her father's papers remain in her care. The collection consists of a diary and notes written at Paris in 1919 (published as *A Memoir of the Paris Conference,* edited by Agnes Headlam-Morley, 1972); a large collection of letters written by Headlam-Morley at Paris to friends and colleagues at the Foreign Office; copies of correspondence between Headlam-Morley and Sir Lewis Namier; a series of printed Foreign Office memoranda (1919-29) covering the Peace Conference and later problems arising from the settlement (such as the Saar Valley, Fiume and the Adriatic, and eastern Galicia); and letters (1919-29) on political topics. Some of the

Peace Conference notes are now at the New University of Ulster, Coleraine, but copies remain with Professor Agnes Headlam-Morley. The whole collection is to be placed in due course in the archive centre at Churchill College, Cambridge.

HEATH, Sir (Henry) Frank (1863-1946)

Secretary, Department of Scientific and Industrial Research, 1916-27.

Professor O. V. S. Heath, F.R.S., 10 St Peter's Grove, London W6 9AZ, has a few letters and papers relating to his father's plan for the setting up of the Department of Scientific and Industrial Research, when he was Director of Special Enquiries and Reports at the Board of Education.

HEATH, Sir Thomas Little (1861-1940)

Joint Permanent Secretary, Treasury, 1913-19. Comptroller-General, National Debt Office, 1919-20.

Miss V. Heath, 77 Cambridge Gardens, London W10, states that her father kept no diaries or correspondence, but that she retains certain material relating to her father's classical studies and publications.

HELM, Sir Alexander Knox (1893-1964)

Consul, Addis Ababa, 1937-39. Counsellor, Washington, 1939-42; Ankara, 1942-46. Political Representative, Hungary, 1946-47. Minister, Hungary, 1947-49; Israel, 1949-51. Ambassador, Turkey, 1951-54. Governor-General, Sudan, 1955-56.

Lady Helm has retained no papers relating to her late husband's career. Some papers (1953-55) remain with the Foreign and Commonwealth Office Library. They include copies of dispatches and letters to the Foreign Office, some private letters of no historical interest and copies of printed lectures.

HEMMING, (Arthur) Francis (1893-1964)

Principal Private Secretary to Chief Secretary for Ireland, 1920-22. Secretary, Economic Advisory Council, 1930-39. Principal Assistant Secretary, War Cabinet Offices, 1939-41; Administrative Head (Economic Section), War Cabinet Secretariat, 1939-40, and Central Statistical Office, 1941. Principal Assistant Secretary (Fire Guard), Home Security, 1941-44. Director of Petrol Rationing, Fuel and Power, 1944-45. Principal Assistant Secretary (Economics and Statistics), Fuel and Power, 1945-46; Under-Secretary, 1946-53.

A good collection of papers is held at Corpus Christi College, Oxford. The two series of papers relate to the Irish Troubles and the subsequent treaty in the period 1920-23, and to the work of the International Council for Non-Intervention in Spain (1936-49), to which Hemming acted as Secretary. The second series includes a number of diaries written by Hemming (1938-39, with gaps).

HENDERSON, Lieutenant-General Sir David (1862-1921)

Served South Africa, 1899-1900; European War, 1914-18. Director-General, Military Aeronautics, 1913-18. Vice-President of Air Council, 1918.

A collection of papers, including a mass of family material, is held at the Royal Air Force Museum. Subject matter includes the Royal Flying Corps in World War I, and the amalgamation in 1917-18 of the R.F.C. and the Royal Naval Air Service.

HENDERSON, Sir Hubert Douglas (1890-1952)

Editor, *The Nation* and *Athenaeum*, 1923-30. Joint Secretary, Economic Advisory Council, 1930-34. Economic Adviser, Treasury, 1939-44. Drummond Professor of Political Economy and Fellow of All Souls College, Oxford, 1944-51. Warden Elect of All Souls, 1951-52.

Sir Hubert Henderson's correspondence and papers, and drafts of his published works, are held in the Library at Nuffield College, Oxford.

HENDERSON, Sir Ian Leslie (1901-1971)

Consular and Diplomatic Service: Innsbruck, 1933-38; Prague. Ambassador, Paraguay, 1952-53 (Minister, 1949-52); Panama, 1954-60. Consul-General, Rotterdam, 1953-54.

Lady Henderson, c/o Messrs Kitson, Dymond & Easterbrook, 2 Vaughan Parade, Torquay TQ2 5EF, has retained the drafts of a few of her late husband's lectures and of a short treatise, *Prelude to War*.

HENDERSON, Lieutenant-Colonel Kenneth (1875-1955)

Military career; Indian Army; served World War I.

The Imperial War Museum has a series of memoirs by Henderson covering his active life from birth and his service in the Indian Army (1895-1923); diaries kept while serving in East Africa (1900), South Africa (1902) and India (Durbar and manoeuvres, 1903). The memoirs cover service on the Western Front (1914-16). A copy of the East African diary is also held in the Library of Rhodes House, Oxford.

Sir Malcolm Henderson, 32 Cadogan Place, London SW1X 9RX, retains two further collections of his father's papers. These consist of letters to his mother and his wife whilst on active service, particularly during World War I. There is also an elaborate and minutely detailed family history, illustrated with photographs and original documents. These papers are not available at present.

HENDERSON, Sir Nevile Meyrick (1882-1942)

High Commissioner (Acting), Constantinople, 1922-24. Minister, Egypt, 1924-28; France, 1928-29; Yugoslavia, 1929-35. Ambassador, Argentine Republic, and Minister, Paraguay, 1935-37. Ambassador, Germany, 1937-39.

The Private Office correspondence (1924-41) is available at the Public Record Office (F.O. 800/264-71). It did not prove possible to contact Mr Raymond Savage, Sir Nevile's literary executor. Other correspondence may be found in the Hardinge, Lloyd, Londonderry and Lothian papers.

HENDERSON, Vice-Admiral Sir William Hannam (1845-1930)

Naval career from 1859. Admiral-Superintendent, Devonport Dockyard, 1902-06.

Papers at the National Maritime Museum include letters written to his parents and family, articles and memoranda on naval topics, and scrapbooks of press cuttings.

HENNESSY, Sir Patrick (1898-   )

Joint Head of Production and Member of Advisory Council, Aircraft Production, 1940-41.

Sir Patrick Hennessy has no papers which he considers of any consequence.

HENNIKER, Sir Brydges Powell, 4th Bt (1835-1906)

Registrar-General, 1880-1900.

Brigadier Sir Mark Henniker, Bt, states that he has no papers relating to the 4th Baronet. He was unable to suggest any other person who might have such papers.

HERBERT, Sir Arthur James (1855-1921)

Diplomatic Service. Minister, Norway, 1905-11.

Sir Arthur Herbert's grandson, Mr Robin Herbert of Llanover, near Abergavenny, Gwent, has a collection of private papers relating to Sir Herbert's Ministry at Oslo, including papers regarding his resignation. These papers are currently not available.

HERBERT, Sir John Arthur (1895-1943)

M.P. (Con.) Monmouth, 1934-38. Governor of Bengal, 1939-43.

Sir John Herbert's son, Mr Robin Herbert, of Llanover, near Abergavenny, Gwent, possesses some private papers of his father. The material includes newspaper scrapbooks and correspondence with Lady Herbert, the Marquess of Linlithgow and Field-Marshal Earl Wavell, regarding his father's resignation as Governor of Bengal. These papers are not currently available.

HERBERT, Hon. Mervyn Robert Howard Molyneux (1882-1929)

Diplomatic Service, 1907-26.

Two volumes of Herbert's diary (1912-17 and 1917-23), covering his service in Cairo and Spain, are available at the Middle East Centre, St Antony's College, Oxford.

HERBERT, Hon. Sir Michael Henry (1857-1903)

Ambassador, United States, 1902-03.

A considerable volume of correspondence, both diplomatic and personal, of Sir Michael Herbert is held in the Muniment Room, Wilton House, near Salisbury, Wiltshire. Enquiries regarding the papers should be addressed to the Earl of Pembroke.

HERVEY, Lord Francis (1846-1931)

M.P. (Con.) Bury St Edmunds, 1874-80, 1885-92. 1st Civil Service Commissioner, 1907-09.

The family papers, deposited at the Suffolk Record Office, Bury St Edmunds, include some material of Lord Francis Hervey, such as correspondence on family matters and genealogy, on local history, on the County of Suffolk Bill (1904), and on Hervey's literary works. The papers of Lady Augustus Hervey include correspondence, mainly of a family nature, with Lord Francis Hervey. Other papers relate to Hervey's literary and historical work, and to excavations on the site of Bury Abbey (1902-05).

HEWITT, Air Chief Marshal Sir Edgar Rainey Ludlow- (1886-1973)

Served European War, 1914-19. Air Officer Commanding, Iraq, 1930-32; India, 1935-37. Director of Operations and Intelligence, Air Ministry, 1933-35. Air Officer C.-in-C., Bomber Command, 1937-40. Inspector-General, R.A.F., 1940-45.

At the Public Record Office (AIR 1/725/97/1-10) ten folders relate to Ludlow-Hewitt's work (1916-18).

HICKLING, Vice-Admiral Harold (1892-1969)

Naval career from 1905.

A microfilm in the care of the Imperial War Museum includes documents relating to naval battles during World War I in which Hickling was involved. The largest part of the material, however, covers Hickling's work during World War II, particularly relating to his period as the Naval Officer in charge of the artificial harbour, Mulberry B, at Arromanches, Normandy.

HIGGINS, Air Marshal Sir John Frederick Andrews (1875-1948)

Served South Africa, 1899-1902; European War, 1914-18. Air Officer Commanding, Iraq, 1924-26. Air Member for Supply and Research, 1926-30. Air Officer C.-in-C., India, 1939-40.

Efforts to contact the family were not successful.

HIGHTON, John Elborn (1884-1937)

Secretary, Department of Health for Scotland, 1933-37. Permanent Under-Secretary, Scotland, 1937.

Mr John Henderson of Messrs Crawford, Herron & Cameron, Glasgow, states that J. E. Highton died without issue and that his collaterals are all deceased. No papers are known to have survived.

HILDRED, Sir William Percival (1893-   )

Director-General, Civil Aviation, 1941-46.

Sir William Hildred has kept no papers relating to his period in the Civil Service. However, he has a considerable number of papers relating to his long service as Director-General of the International Air Transport Association (1946-66). Also, Sir William has kept some press cuttings and a private and personal diary, first started in 1914. These papers are not available for study.

HILL, Sir Reginald Herbert (1888-1971)

Deputy Secretary, Ministry of Transport, 1940; War Transport, 1941-45. Deputy Director General (Inland Transport), Ministry of War Transport, 1941-47. Chairman, Docks and Inland Waterways, British Transport Commission, 1948-54.

Mr A. H. C. Hill states that his father left no papers.

HILL, Major-General Robert Charles Cottrell- (1903-1965)

Served War of 1939-45. Chief of Staff, Malaya, 1950-53. Director of Military Training, War Office, 1953-55. G.O.C., Berlin (British Sector), 1955-56.

No papers have survived.

HILL, Air Chief Marshal Sir Roderic Maxwell (1894-1954)

Served European War, 1914-18. Air Officer Commanding, Palestine and Transjordan, 1936-38. Director of Technical Development, Air Ministry and Ministry of Aircraft Production, 1938-40. Director-General of Research and Development,

Aircraft Production, 1940-41. Air Marshal Commanding, Air Defence of Great Britain, 1943-44. Air Officer C.-in-C., Fighter Command, 1944-45. Air Member for Training, 1945-46; for Technical Services, 1946-48.

Papers, including notebooks, publications and photographs (1917-66), can be found at the Royal Air Force Museum. Subject matter includes experimental flying, Farnborough (1920-23).

HINDE, Major-General Hon. Sir (William) Robert Norris (1900-   )

Military career; served War of 1939-45. Military Commander, British Sector, Berlin, 1945-48. Deputy Commissioner, Land Niedersachsen, Hanover, 1949-51. District Commander, Cyrenaica, 1952-53. Deputy Director of Operations, Kenya, 1953-56. Chief Civil Affairs Officer to the Commander, Suez Expedition, 1956-57.

Sir Robert retains few papers relating to his career. Details are not available. Some material concerning Kenya is held in Rhodes House Library, Oxford.

HIRTZEL, Sir Arthur (1870-1937)

Private Secretary to the Secretary of State, India, 1903-09. Permanent Under-Secretary, India, 1924-30.

Some official printed material, and a file of correspondence (1918-22) on the future of German missions, and mission property in India, survives at the India Office Library. The Private Office collection (D 714) at the India Office Library also includes some of Hirtzel's papers.

HOARE, Sir Reginald Hervey (d. 1954)

Minister, Persia, 1931-34; Romania, 1935-41.

Mr J. A. C. Hoare, Hartbridge Manor Farm, Cranbrook, Kent, says that certain letters to and from his father and some press cuttings remain with the family.

HOBART, Major-General Sir Percy Cleghorn Stanley (1885-1957)

Served India; European War in France, Mesopotamia and Palestine; War of 1939-45. Inspector of Royal Tank Corps, 1933-36. Director of Military Training, War Office, 1937-38. Commander, 79th Armoured Division, 1942-45.

A number of Hobart's papers survive in the Liddell Hart Collection. Enquiries should be addressed to the Liddell Hart Centre for Military Archives at King's College, London.

HODGE, Rear-Admiral Hon. Claude Preston Hermon- (1888-1952)

Naval career; served World War I. Naval Assistant Secretary, Committee of Imperial Defence, 1924-28. Deputy Director of Naval Intelligence, 1936-38.

Contact could not be established with surviving members of the Rear-Admiral's family.

HODGSON, Sir Robert Macleod (1874-1956)

Consul, Vladivostok, 1911-19 (and onetime Acting High Commissioner, Siberia). Commercial Counsellor in Russia, 1919-21. Agent to the Soviet Government, 1921-24. Chargé d'Affaires, Moscow, 1924-27. Minister, Albania, 1928-36. Agent in Nationalist Spain, 1937-39 (Chargé d'Affaires, Burgos, 1939).

Lady Hodgson retains no papers which would be of any interest.

HODSOLL, Sir Eric John (1894-1971)

Assistant Secretary (R.A.F.), Committee of Imperial Defence, 1929-35. Assistant Under-Secretary for Air Raid Precautions, Home Office, 1935-37, and Inspector-General, 1938-48. Director-General, Civil Defence Training, 1948-54. Chief Civil Defence Adviser, North Atlantic Treaty Organisation, 1954-61.

A collection of papers survives at Churchill College, Cambridge. The nine sections relate to the various parts of Sir John Hodsoll's career, and the papers are mainly concerned with civil defence. Few papers date from before 1935. Rare copies of numerous printed pamphlets, handbooks and reports are included in the collection, as are Sir John's appointments diaries (1938-54). The material is not all open for research, and enquiries should be addressed to the Archivist at Churchill College.

HODSON, Sir Arnold Wienholt (1881-1944)

Consul, Southern Abyssinia, 1914-23; South West Abyssinia, 1923-26. Governor, Falkland Islands, 1926-30; Sierra Leone, 1930-34; Gold Coast, 1934-41.

Enquiries should be addressed to Messrs Dickinson, Manser & Co., 5 Parkstone Road, Poole, Dorset BH15 2NL, who are in touch with Sir Arnold's sister.

HOGARTH, David George (1862-1927)

Director of Arab Bureau, Cairo, 1916-18.

An important collection of papers survives at the Middle East Centre, St Antony's College, Oxford. The material includes World War I papers and peace settlement records.

HOHLER, Sir Thomas Beaumont (1871-1946)

Minister, Hungary, 1921-24 (High Commissioner, 1920); Chile, 1924-27; Denmark, 1928-33.

Mr G. A. Hohler, Trent Manor, near Sherborne, Dorset, has kept his father's papers. These consist of letters, telegrams and newspaper cuttings bound in 66 volumes and dating from 1898 to 1932; a number of manuscript diaries of approximately the same dates; and an unpublished autobiography. The more unusual aspects of the early papers involve the siege of Port Arthur (1904), Ethiopia under Menelik, and Mexico in revolution.

HOLDERNESS, Sir Thomas William, 1st Bt (1849-1924)

Permanent Under-Secretary, India Office, 1912-19.

Sir Richard Holderness knows of no papers relating to his grandfather's career. Some correspondence may be found in the Hardinge papers as well as in the Austen Chamberlain collection at Birmingham University Library.

HOLE, Edwyn Cecil

Consul, Damascus, 1926-32; Athens, 1932-36; Marrakesh, 1936. Consul-General, Salonika, 1938-41; Smyrna, 1941-45; Nice, 1945-50.

Mr Hole never kept a diary, and his personal papers and records were destroyed or looted on two occasions, at Smyrna in 1922 and at Salonika in 1941. Mr Hole has written a series of memoirs, and his wife has retained many of her personal diaries.

HOLLINGHURST, Air Chief Marshal Sir Leslie Norman (1895-1971)

Served European War, 1914-19. Director of Organisation, 1940; Director-General of Organisation, R.A.F., 1941-43. Air Officer Commanding, No. 38 Group, 1943-44. Air Marshal Commanding Base Air Forces, South East Asia, 1944-45. Air Member for Supply and Organisation, 1945-48; Personnel, 1949-52. Inspector-General, R.A.F., 1948-49.

The Imperial War Museum has a number of reports on operations in Mohmand and Waziristan, and World War II papers including reports on Operations Neptune, Market, Doomsday, Varsity, Amherst and Keystone (1930-45). Other papers are at the Royal Air Force Museum, and they include logbooks, letters, files, lectures, articles, publications and photographs (1915-71). Subject matter includes Shanghai (1927), India and the North West Frontier Province (1930), the Frontier Defence Committee (1931), the Empire Air Training Scheme of Canada (1939-40), and airborne forces (1940-45).

HOLLIS, Sir Alfred Claud (1874-1961)

High Commissioner, Zanzibar, 1924-30. Governor, Trinidad and Tobago, 1930-36. Colonial Representative, Imperial Communications Advisory Committee, 1936-47.

An unpublished autobiography, in 12 volumes, is held at Rhodes House Library, Oxford.

HOLLIS, Sir Leslie Chasemore (1897-1963)

Senior Assistant Secretary, War Cabinet, 1939-46. Chief Staff Officer to Minister of Defence, and Deputy Secretary (Military), Cabinet Office, 1947-49. Company director and author.

Information regarding papers was not forthcoming.

HOLMAN, Sir Adrian (1895-1974)

Minister, Romania, 1947-49 (Political Representative, 1946-47). Ambassador, Cuba, 1950-54 (Minister, 1949-50).

A collection of papers survives with Lady Holman, Bohunt Manor, Liphook, Hampshire GU30 7DL. The collection includes letters to Lady Holman from Berlin at the outbreak of World War II, letters from The Hague before the invasion, letters from Russia where Sir Adrian was with Anthony Eden, and letters dating from World War I. The World War I papers are at the Imperial War Museum.

HOLMES, Sir Maurice Gerald (1885-1964)

Permanent Secretary, Board of Education, 1937-45.

Contact with Lady Holmes could not be established.

HOLT, Lieutenant-Colonel H. B.

Army career.

A typescript diary of Holt's, kept while he was serving as Military Attaché in Addis Ababa (1935-36), is in the care of the National Army Museum.

HOLT, Major-General Sir Maurice Percy Cue (1862-1954)

Served South Africa, 1899-1902; European War, 1914-18.

A typescript diary relating to Holt's service at Ladysmith survives at the Royal Army Medical College.

HOLT, Vice-Admiral Reginald Vesey (1884-1957)

Naval career. Chief of Staff to C.-in-C., The Nore, 1931-33.

A collection of papers survives with Vice-Admiral Holt's widow. The papers, c/o Messrs James Capel & Co., Winchester House, 100 Old Broad Street, London EC2N 1BQ, include letters from Holt to his wife, with some interesting letters relating to the time when he was Rear-Admiral, Yangtse River (1937-39), during the Japanese invasion of China.

HOLT, Sir Vyvyan (1896-1960)

Minister, Korea, 1949-50; El Salvador, 1954-56.

Messrs Yarde & Loader, the solicitors who acted for the executors of Sir Vyvyan Holt's estate, have made enquiries and have found no surviving papers relating to Sir Vyvyan Holt. However, a few photographs of the Middle East and drafts of lectures on Iraq and the Middle East have been deposited in the Middle East Centre, St Antony's College, Oxford.

HONE, Major-General Sir (Herbert) Ralph (1896-   )

Military career and Colonial Service. Secretary-General to Governor-General, Malaya, 1946-48. Deputy Commissioner-General, South East Asia, 1948-49. Governor, North Borneo, 1949-54. Head of Legal Division, Commonwealth Relations Office, 1954-61. Constitutional adviser.

A collection of papers is held at Rhodes House Library, Oxford. The material (1937-72) includes correspondence, reports and memoranda on the administration of Italian colonies in East Africa, on Malaya, North Borneo, Southern Rhodesia, Kenya, the East African Federation and the Bahamas.

HOOD, Rear-Admiral Hon. Horace Lambert Alexander (1870-1916)

Naval career. Naval Secretary to 1st Lord of the Admiralty, 1914-16.

Papers at Churchill College, Cambridge, cover the period 1872-1916. Family papers, also in the care of Churchill College, date from 1782.

HOPKINS, Sir Richard Valentine Nind (1880-1955)

Chairman, Board of Inland Revenue, 1922-27. Permanent Secretary, Treasury, 1942-45.

Mr Alan Hopkins, Great Shefford House, Great Shefford, Newbury, Berks., has a number of personal papers, letters and press cuttings relating to his father. These are of family interest only. A collection of Private Office papers (1914-42) at the Public Record Office (T.175) relates to Hopkins's long career at the Treasury. The 124 volumes include material on home defence policy (1930-34) and colonial and defence policy (1930-35), briefs on Cabinet papers (1930-39), correspondence on tariffs, etc. (1931), papers on general financial policy, on the Budget and the National Debt (1935), and on the Inland Revenue (1935-38).

HORE, Sir Charles Fraser Adair (1874-1950)

Permanent Secretary, Ministry of Pensions, 1935-41; Ministry of Petroleum 1941-42.

Efforts to contact persons mentioned in the Act of Probate proved unsuccessful.

HORNBY, Brigadier-General Edmund Phipps (1857-1947)

Entered Royal Artillery, 1887. Served Bechuanaland, 1884-85; South Africa, 1900; European War, 1914-15. Brigadier-General Commanding 4th Divisional Artillery, 1909-13.

A collection of papers is now in the care of the Royal Artillery Institution.

HORNBY, Admiral Robert Stewart Phipps (1866-1956)

Naval career from 1879; served in Egyptian War, 1882; World War I.

Papers (1901-19) are preserved at the National Maritime Museum. These include letterbooks, notes and memoranda on various aspects of his service, e.g. the visit of the Russian Fleet (1904); the Akbar boundary dispute (1906); gas-propelled torpedoes, etc.; and papers relating to the North American and West Indian Stations.

HORNIMAN, Rear-Admiral Henry (1870-1956)

Naval career from 1887; active service, World War I. Paymaster, Admiralty Controller's Department, 1917-19.

Memoirs and a diary (1914-15) are held on microfilm at the Imperial War Museum.

HORROCKS, Lieutenant-General Sir Brian Gwynne (1895-   )

Served European War, 1914-18; War of 1939-45. G.O. C.-in-C., Western Command, 1946; British Army of the Rhine, 1948.

Sir Brian Horrocks reports that his papers have been reduced to a minimum through constant changes of address, and that he has little he considers of value. His autobiography, *A Full Life* (1960), contains details of his career.

HOUNSELL, Major-General Harold Arthur (1897-1970)

Served European War, 1914-18; War of 1939-45.

The Imperial War Museum holds a collection of Hounsell's official reports relating to the wartime activities of the 37th and 62nd Anti-Aircraft Brigades, which Hounsell commanded, and to Anti-Aircraft Command (1941-51). The collection also contains a very substantial number of letters and photographs, both personal and official.

HOWARD OF PENRITH, 1st B
Sir Esme William Howard (1863-1939)

Consul-General, Hungary, 1908-11. Minister, Switzerland, 1911-13; Sweden, 1913-19. Ambassador, Spain, 1919-24; United States, 1924-30.

The present (2nd) Lord Howard of Penrith, Dean Farm, Coln St Aldwyns, Cirencester, Glos., retains his father's papers which have been roughly sorted. A further collection of papers survives with Lord Howard's brother in Cumberland.

HOWARD, Sir Douglas Frederick (1897-   )

Chargé d'Affaires, Spain, 1946-49. Ambassador, Uruguay, 1949-53. Minister, Holy See, 1953-57.

Sir Douglas Howard has kept no diaries or correspondence relating to his career.

HOWARD, Sir Henry (1843-1921)

Minister, Netherlands and Luxembourg, 1896-1908; Holy See, 1914-16.

Messrs Coutts & Co. knew of no papers and they are no longer in touch with the family.

HOWE, Admiral Hon. Sir Assheton Gore Curzon- (1850-1911)

Naval career from 1863. Assistant Director of Naval Intelligence, 1892. C.-in-C., Mediterranean, 1908-10; Portsmouth, 1910-11.

Papers at the National Maritime Museum cover the years 1895-1911, and include service records, logs, maps, and papers relating to the China Fleet (1903-06), manoeuvres (1906, 1909-10), and personal papers and correspondence (1906-10).

HOWE, Sir Robert George (1893-   )

Minister, Latvia, 1940; Abyssinia, 1942-45. Assistant Under-Secretary, Foreign Office, from 1945. Governor-General, Sudan, 1947-55.

No contact was established.

HOWELL, Sir Evelyn Berkeley (1877-1971)

Military Governor, Baghdad, 1918. Resident, Waziristan, 1924-26; Kashmir, 1927-29. Foreign Secretary, Government of India, 1930-32.

The papers (1896-1970) at the India Office Library consist of correspondence between members of the Howell family in India (1896-1904); Howell's reports as censor of the Indian Mails in France (1914-15); literary papers and reports.

HOWELL, Brigadier-General Philip (1877-1916)

Served Indian Army; European War, 1914-16.

A collection of papers has been given to the Liddell Hart Centre for Military Archives. The papers include correspondence, memoranda, field message books and diaries covering the establishment of a frontier intelligence organisation in India (1904-05). Other papers relate to cavalry organisation and tactics before 1914, the 4th Hussars in Flanders, and the defence of Salonika (1915-16).

HOWICK OF GLENDALE, 1st B
Sir Evelyn Baring (1903-1973)

Governor, Southern Rhodesia, 1942-44; Kenya, 1952-59. High Commissioner, South Africa, and Basutoland, Bechuanaland and Swaziland, 1944-51.

Family papers survive with the present (2nd) Baron Howick, Howick, Alnwick, Northumberland. Mr Charles Douglas-Home, c/o *The Times*, P.O. Box 7, New Printing House Square, Gray's Inn Road, London WC1X 8EZ, is writing a biography of Lord Howick and has care of a number of other papers, notes and letters. These papers are not available for inspection.

HOWORTH, Sir Rupert Beswicke (1880-1964)

Civil Service career. Deputy Secretary, Cabinet Office, 1930-42. Clerk of the Privy Council, 1938-42. Secretary of Commissions to the Lord Chancellor, 1945-48.

The Cabinet Office holds two files covering the Abdication crisis (1936-37). These are closed until 2037.

HUBBACK, Vice-Admiral Sir (Arthur) Gordon Voules (1902-1970)

Naval career. Joint Planning Staff, Cabinet Office, 1944-45. 4th Sea Lord, 1958.

It is believed that no papers survive.

HUBBOCK, Sir John Austen (1878-1968)

Governor of Orissa, 1936-41. Adviser to Secretary of State for India, 1942-47.

Memoirs concerning his career in India have been deposited with the Cambridge South Asia Archive.

HUGESSEN, Sir Hughe Montgomery Knatchbull- (1886-1971)

Minister, Baltic States, 1930-34; Persia, 1934-36. Ambassador, China, 1936-37; Turkey, 1939-44; Belgium (and Minister, Luxembourg), 1944-47.

A good collection of Sir Hughe Knatchbull-Hugessen's papers is now with Mr Richard Langhorne, c/o Rutherford College, The University, Canterbury, Kent. The papers consist of general correspondence and a diary, of which the diary is incomplete and the general correspondence is chiefly of a family nature, though still of some interest. One volume of Private Office correspondence (1936-38) is available at the Public Record Office (F.O. 800/297).

HUGGINS, Sir John (1891-1971)

Head of British Colonies Supply Mission, Washington, 1942-43. Captain-General and Governor-in-Chief, Jamaica, 1943-51.

The Colonial Records Project found that Sir John Huggins had kept no papers.

HUGHAN, Admiral Sir Arthur John Henniker- (1866-1925)

Naval career. Captain, H.M.S. *Ajax*, Grand Fleet, 1914-16. Admiral Superintendent, Devonport Dockyard, 1916-19. M.P. (Con.) Galloway, 1924-25.

None of Sir John Henniker-Hughan's parliamentary papers have survived. However, his daughter, Miss Henniker-Hughan, has deposited in the National Maritime Museum, London SE10, a copy of an autobiographical account of her father's naval career (1881-1919). She has also retained a number of press cuttings relating to his election in 1924 and his obituary notices.

HUME, Andrew Parke (1904-1965)

Indian Civil Service, 1927-47.

The interesting collection (1927-65) at the India Office Library consists of weekly letters written by Hume to his parents in England. There are also his personal and tour diaries, along with newspaper cuttings (1928-65).

HUMPHRYS, Lieutenant-Colonel Sir Francis Henry (1879-1971)

Deputy Foreign Secretary, Government of India, 1921. Minister, Afghanistan, 1922-29. High Commissioner and C.-in-C., Iraq, 1929-32. Ambassador, Iraq, 1932-35.

Mr A. F. W. Humphrys was unable to provide information regarding papers left by his father.

HUNTER, General Sir Archibald (1856-1936)

Military service; Egypt and Sudan, South Africa. Governor, Omdurman, 1899. Commander, Southern Army, India, 1907-09. Governor and C.-in-C., Gibraltar, 1910-13. G.O.C., 13th (Western) Division, 1914. Commander, 3rd Army, 1914. M.P. (Coalition Unionist) Lancaster, 1918-22.

Information regarding papers may be available for Volume III of this Guide.

HUNTINGFIELD, 5th B
Sir William Charles Arcedeckne Vanneck (1883-1969)

M.P. (Con.) Eye, 1923-29. Governor, Victoria, 1934-39.

At the time of writing no information was yet available. Researchers should see Vol. III of this Guide for further details.

HURCOMB, 1st B
Sir Cyril William Hurcomb (1883-1975)

Director of Commercial Services, Shipping, 1915-18. Permanent Secretary, Transport, 1927-37. Chairman, Electricity Commission, 1938-47. Director-General, Shipping, 1939-41; War Transport, 1941-47. Chairman, British Transport Commission, 1947-53.

Lord Hurcomb stated that he had kept no set of private papers.

HURST, Sir Cecil James Barrington (1870-1963)

Legal Adviser, Foreign Office, 1918-29. Judge of the Permanent Court of International Justice, 1929-46.

Sir Cecil's daughter, Miss B. Hurst, Churchcroft, Rusper, Horsham, Sussex, says that the papers of her father which remain with her family refer only to family and estate matters. There is material in the Lothian papers as well as in the Cecil of Chelwood papers at the British Library.

HUTCHINSON, Sir Herbert John (1889-1971)

Under-Secretary, Ministry of Supply, 1941-46. 2nd Secretary, Board of Trade, 1946-47. Secretary, National Coal Board, 1947-51.

Messrs Williams Montague & Piper, solicitors of Brighton, acted in the estate. No information regarding papers was secured.

HUTCHINSON, Sir Walter Francis Hely- (1849-1913)

Lieutenant-Governor, Malta, 1884-89. Governor, Windward Islands, 1889-93; Natal and Zululand, 1893-1901; Cape Province, 1901-10.

Family records survive, and enquiries should be addressed to Mr Henry Hely-Hutchinson, 99 Aldwych, London WC2B 4JS.

HUTCHISON, Lieutenant-General Sir Balfour Oliphant (1889-1967)

Served European War, 1916-18; Mesopotamia; Palestine, 1938-39; War of 1939-45. G.O.C., Sudan and Eritrea, 1942-43. Quartermaster-General, India, 1944-45.

Lady Hutchison (widow), Rendham Court, Saxmundham, Suffolk, says that her husband never kept a diary, and all she has in her care are some letters, several being letters of appointment.

HUTCHISON, Sir John Colville (1890-1965)

Trade Commissioner, Hong Kong, from 1938. Chargé d'Affaires, China (Peking), 1949-51.

Messrs Rootes & Alliott, solicitors of Folkestone, dealt with the estate. It was not possible to contact Sir John's son, Mr J. A. D. Hutchison, C9 Le Clos Salibert, 78860 St Nom la Bretèche, Yvelines, France.

HUTTON, Lieutenant-General Sir Edward Thomas Henry (1848-1923)

Served South Africa, 1881, 1900; Egypt, 1882, 1884-85; Australia, 1893-96, 1901-04. Assistant Adjutant-General, Ireland, 1896-98. Commander, Dominion Militia (Canada), 1898-1900; 3rd Army, 1914-15.

A collection of papers survives at the British Library (Add. MSS. 50078-50114). The material includes royal and special correspondence, family letters, general correspondence (1874-1922), military books, diaries and letter books, literary papers and drafts of unpublished memoirs. Correspondents include the Sovereign's private secretaries, Theodore Roosevelt, A. J. Balfour, Joseph Chamberlain, Alfred Lyttelton, and prominent figures in the Colonial Office, Canada and Australia. The National Library of Australia, Canberra, holds a collection of letters, cuttings and invitations (1893-1906).

ILBERT, Sir Courtenay Peregrine (1841-1924)

Legal Member, Council of Viceroy of India, 1882-86. Clerk of the House of Commons, 1902-21.

The House of Lords Record Office has some twenty-three volumes of engagement diaries (1895-1922) and fifteen volumes of narrative diaries (1896-1926). Papers on India can be found at the India Office Library, and the Asquith MSS and the Bryce papers contain further material.

INCE, Sir Godfrey Herbert (1891-1960)

Permanent Secretary, Minister of Labour and National Service, 1944-56.

It was not possible to contact persons mentioned in the Will and Act of Probate.

INCHCAPE, 1st E of
Sir James Lyle Mackay (1852-1932)

Member, Council of India, 1897-1911. Member of Government committees, and British representative at international conferences, and on special missions, e.g. member, National Economy (Geddes) Committee, 1921-22; Indian Retrenchment Committee, 1922-23.

The present (3rd) Earl of Inchcape, 40 St Mary Axe, London EC3A 8EU, fears that his grandfather's papers are extremely sparse. However, he does have some unsorted materials which may be of interest. The National Library of Scotland has three letters to Curzon (1923-24).

INCHYRA, 1st B
Sir Frederick Robert Hoyer Millar (1900-)

Minister, Washington, 1948. U.K. Permanent Representative, NATO Council, 1952. High Commissioner, Germany, 1953-55. Ambassador, German Federal Republic, 1955-57. Permanent Under-Secretary, Foreign Office, 1957-61.

Lord Inchyra never kept a diary whilst in the Diplomatic Service, and those papers relating to his career which he had on retirement he either destroyed or returned to the Foreign Office.

INGRAM, Edward Maurice Berkeley (1890-1941)

Served Foreign Office and Diplomatic Service. Diplomatic Adviser to Ministry of Economic Warfare, 1939-41.

Messrs E. F. Turner & Sons, solicitors, know of no private papers and could not provide contact with members of the family.

INNES, Alfred Mitchell- (1864-1950)

Minister, Uruguay, 1913-19.

Neither Mr D. I. Mitchell-Innes nor the executors to Mr A. Mitchell-Inne's estate know of any surviving papers. Some 17 letters to Bryce are in the Bryce papers in the Bodleian Library.

INSKIP, Major-General Roland Debenham (1885-1971)

Served European War, 1914-18; India. G.O.C., Ceylon, 1941-42.

The Imperial War Museum holds a series of papers, including letters from Field-Marshal Lord Birdwood and Lord Gort. The central topic of Lord Birdwood's letters (1932-48) is the Indianisation of the Indian Army, and Lord Gort's correspondence (1937-40) covers the Waziristan campaign, the progress of rearmament and the need to reform the Indian Army.

INVERCHAPEL, 1st B
Sir Archibald John Kerr Clark Kerr (1882-1951)

Minister, Central America, 1925-28; Chile, 1928-30; Sweden, 1931-35. Ambassador, Iraq, 1935-38; China, 1938-42; U.S.S.R., 1942-46; United States, 1946-48.

Six volumes of Private Office correspondence (1935-49) are available at the Public Record Office (F.O. 800/298-303). A further collection of unsorted private papers survives in the care of Sir William A. Lewthwaite, Bt, 73 Dovehouse Street, London SW3 6JZ.

IRONSIDE, 1st Vt
Field-Marshal Sir William Edmund Ironside (1880-1959)

Served South Africa, 1899-1902; European War, 1914-19. C.-in-C., British Forces in Russia, 1918-19; North Persia, 1920-21. Commandant, Staff College, Camberley, 1922-26; 2nd Division, Aldershot, 1926-28; Meerut District, India, 1928-31. Quartermaster-General, India, 1933-36. G.O. C.-in-C., Eastern Command, 1936-38. Governor and C.-in-C., Gibraltar, 1938-39. Chief of Imperial General Staff, 1939-40. C.-in-C., Home Forces, 1940.

Six files, representing the various parts of the original typescript and manuscript war diary kept by Ironside during his service in North Persia (1920-21), are available at the National Army Museum. The present (2nd) Lord Ironside has a collection of papers and may be contacted c/o Broomwood Manor, Chignal St James, Chelmsford, Essex. This collection includes private diaries (1918-59), correspondence, articles and lectures, and press cuttings (1937-41). In addition, Lord Ironside has retained a collection of photographs, portraits, recordings and insignia. Unpublished material is not generally made available, though the present Lord Ironside may be consulted on all matters relating to the Field-Marshal. The Imperial War Museum has a number of Ironside's original dispatches and appendices relating to the North Russian campaign (1918-19). These papers are included in the collection of Major A. E. Sturdy. The Liddell Hart Centre for Military Archives has a copy of the duplicated book *A Secret Service Agent in South West Africa* covering Ironside's career from birth to 1904.

IRONSIDE, Sir Henry George Outram Bax- (1859-1929)

Minister, Venezuela, 1902-07; Chile, 1907-09; Switzerland, 1909-10; Bulgaria, 1910-15.

Efforts to trace persons mentioned in the Will and Act of Probate met with no success.

ISLINGTON, 1st B
Sir John Poynder Dickson-Poynder (1866-1936)

M.P. (Con.) Chippenham, 1892-1910. Governor, New Zealand, 1910-12. Under-Secretary of State, Colonies, 1914-15. Parliamentary Under-Secretary, India, 1915-18.

A collection of papers survives in the care of Mr John Grigg. These are not political papers, but mainly letters written by Lord Islington to his wife and other letters to Lady Islington.

ISMAY, 1st B
General Sir Hastings Lionel Ismay (1887-1965)

Served India, Somaliland, etc. Assistant Secretary, Committee of Imperial Defence, 1926-30; Deputy Secretary, 1936-38. Military Secretary to Viceroy of India, 1931-33. Chief of Staff to Minister of Defence (W. S. Churchill), 1940-45. Deputy Secretary (Military), War Cabinet, 1940-45; Additional Secretary (Military), 1945. Chief of Staff to Viceroy of India, 1947. Secretary of State, Commonwealth Relations, 1951-52. Secretary-General, North Atlantic Treaty Organisation, 1952-57.

A collection of papers covering the whole of Ismay's career has been deposited at the Liddell Hart Centre for Military Archives. The papers include personal correspondence and material written for an autobiography. The Cabinet Office has a further collection of personal lecture notes at Staff College, Quetta; papers on the Anglo-French meetings of 1940; notes for Prime Minister's speeches, and on post-war defence organisation; correspondence with Chiefs of Staff, Commanders-in-Chief and Military Representatives (1922-46).

JACKSON, Sir Francis Stanley (1870-1947)

M.P. (Con.) Howdenshire, 1915-26. Financial Secretary, War Office, 1922-23. Chairman, Conservative and Unionist Party, 1923-26. Governor, Bengal, 1927-32.

Lord Allerton, nephew of Sir Francis Jackson, knows of no surviving papers. It has not been possible to trace Jackson's daughter-in-law, Mrs H. S. L. Jackson, who Lord Allerton believed had information concerning Jackson's papers.

JACKSON, Admiral of the Fleet Sir Henry Bradwardine (1855-1929)

Naval career from 1868. Controller of the Navy, 1905-08. Chief of War Staff, 1912-14. 1st Sea Lord, 1915-16.

Jackson's papers as 1st Sea Lord are in the care of the Naval Library, Ministry of Defence.

JACKSON, General Sir Henry Cholmondeley (1879-1972)

Served European War, 1914-18. Director of Military Training, India, 1926-30. Commander, 2nd Division, 1931-35. G.O. C.-in-C., Western Command, 1936-39, 1940.

General Sir H. C. Jackson kept no papers of interest.

JACOB, Lieutenant-General Sir (Edward) Ian Claud (1899-   )

Military career. Military Assistant Secretary, Committee of Imperial Defence, 1938; War Cabinet, 1939-46. Chief Staff Officer to Minister of Defence, and Deputy Secretary (Military) of the Cabinet, 1952. Director-General, British Broadcasting Corporation, 1952-60.

Sir Ian Jacob has in his possession a collection of papers, including diaries and correspondence relating to his service with Sir Winston Churchill.

JAMES, Sir Frederick Seton (1870-1934)

Colonial Service, High Commissioner, Malay States, 1919-20, 1922. Governor, Windward Islands, 1924-30.

A visit to Somerset House brought forward no information useful in tracing members of the family.

JAMES, Admiral Sir William Milbourne (1881-1973)

Naval career; served World War I. Chief of Staff, Atlantic Fleet, 1929-30. Deputy Chief of Naval Staff, 1935-38. C.-in-C., Portsmouth, 1939-42. Chief of Naval Information, 1943-44. M.P. (Con.) Portsmouth North, 1943-45.

According to information received by the Imperial War Museum, the Admiral retained no papers. The original of his World War II diary (used in his published works) has apparently been mislaid.

JAMESON, Brigadier-General Sydney Bellinghame

Military career.

A collection of some 200 letters, mainly written to his wife in the years 1914-20, survives at the National Library of Scotland.

JEFFREY, Sir John (1871-1947)

Secretary, Scottish Board of Health, 1919-28; Department of Health for Scotland, 1929-33. Under-Secretary, Scotland, 1933-37. Chairman, General Board of Control for Scotland, 1939-45.

Mr James S. Jeffrey states that his father left no papers.

JEFFRIES, Sir Charles Joseph (1896-1972)

Assistant Under-Secretary, Colonial Office, 1939-47; Joint Deputy Under-Secretary, 1947-56.

Rhodes House Library, Oxford, has a copy of an unpublished memoir of a visit to West Africa.

JELLICOE, 1st E
Admiral of the Fleet Sir John Rushworth Jellicoe (1859-1935)

Naval career from 1872. Director of Naval Ordnance, 1905-07. Controller of the Navy, 1908-10. Commanded Atlantic Fleet, 1910-11; 2nd Division, Home Fleet, 1911-12. 2nd Sea Lord, 1912-14. Commanded Grand Fleet, 1914-16. 1st Sea Lord, 1916. Chief of Naval Staff, 1917. Governor-General, New Zealand, 1920-24.

A selection of the papers of Earl Jellicoe is available at the British Library (Add. MSS. 48989-49057). This is an important collection in 69 volumes covering all phases of Jellicoe's career. The collection is arranged as follows: (1) correspondence and papers (48989-49037); (2) literary manuscripts (49038-49044); (3) papers relating to the Empire Mission, 1919-20 (49045-49057). The volumes of particular interest include 48990-48992 (correspondence with the Admiralty when Jellicoe was C.-in-C., Grand Fleet), 49006-49009 (letters from important colleagues), 49014, 49027-49028, 49040-49042 (Jutland material), and 49038 (autobiographical notes). Add. MS. 45356 consists of a draft of Jellicoe's *The Grand Fleet, 1914-16*, preceded by notes on the manuscript by Admiral Sir F. C. Dreyer. Letters from Lord Jellicoe to E. E. Bradford (1914-17) are available at the National Maritime Museum.

JENKINS, Sir Evan Meredith (1896-   )

Private Secretary to Viceroy of India and Secretary to Governor-General, 1943-45. Governor, Punjab, 1946-47.

The papers (1947-72) at the India Office Library are not open for inspection.

JENKINS, Sir Thomas Gilmour (1894-   )

Deputy Director-General, War Transport, 1941-46. Permanent Secretary, Control Office for Germany and Austria, 1946-47. Joint Permanent Under-Secretary, Foreign Office, 1947. Permanent Secretary, Transport, 1947-53; Transport and Civil Aviation, 1953-59.

Sir Gilmour Jenkins has kept few papers, but retains certain minutes and drafts of conventions, agreements, etc., from the international shipping conferences over which he presided. These include the conferences on Pollution of the Sea by Oil (1954 and 1962), on Load Lines (1966), and on Safety of Life at Sea (1960).

JERRAM, Sir Cecil Bertrand (1891-1971)

Acting Agent at Burgos and Chargé d'Affaires, Spain, 1939. Minister, Austria, 1948-49. Ambassador, Sweden, 1947-48 (Minister, 1945-47); Chile, 1949-51.

Several beneficiaries are mentioned in the Will. Enquiries may be addressed to Barclays Bank Trust Company, 54 Lombard Street, London EC3.

JERRAM, Admiral Sir (Thomas Henry) Martyn (1858-1933)

Naval career from 1871. C.-in-C., China Station, 1913-15. Commanded 2nd Battle Squadron, 1915-16.

A collection of Jerram's papers is available at the National Maritime Museum. This includes material covering much of his active career, and comprises logs, diaries and private accounts; photograph albums dating from 1872; a cuttings album, commissions, certificates, etc., relating to his naval service, and correspondence; papers relating to his work as Vice-Consul at Mapondas, Portuguese East Africa (1891); papers concerning the China Station (1912-15); and papers concerning his Grand Fleet service (1916-17).

JEUDWINE, Lieutenant-General Sir Hugh Sandham (1862-1942)

Served European War, 1914-18. Chief of General Staff, British Army of the Rhine, 1919. Commander, 5th Division, Ireland, 1919-22. Director-General, Territorial Army, 1923-27.

A collection of papers at the Imperial War Museum includes a diary of the Boer War, in which Jeudwine served as a Major in the Royal Artillery, and papers and correspondence relating to Jeudwine's command of the 55th Division in World War I. The most important part of the collection relates to Irish affairs in the period 1920-22. These papers include correspondence with Sir Henry Wilson and Winston Churchill, and an unpublished history of the 5th Division in Ireland. Additional material is to be found in the Lancashire Record Office.

JOHNSTONE, Hon. Sir Alan Vanden-Bempde (1858-1932)

Minister, Denmark, 1905-10; Netherlands, 1910-17.

Lords Derwent, Blakenham and Listowel have each stated that they hold no papers relating to Sir Alan Johnstone, or his son Harcourt Johnstone. The solicitors, Messrs Turner Peacock, know of no papers. A few letters may be found in the Hardinge papers.

JOHNSTONE, Vice-Admiral Charles (1843-1927)

Naval career.

Papers in the care of the National Maritime Museum cover most of Johnstone's career, chiefly in the nineteenth century, and include a run of diaries and other material.

JONES, Air Marshal Sir Robert Owen (1901-1972)

Royal Air Force career from 1924. Served British Air Commission, Washington, 1941-43; Ministry of Aircraft Production, 1943-46; Technical Services (Plans), Air Ministry, 1946-47. Air Officer Commanding, No. 24 Group, Technical Training Command, 1947, 1949-52. Controller of Engineering and Equipment, Air Ministry, 1952-56.

Sir Owen informed the Liddell Hart Centre for Military Archives that he had no papers of interest.

JONES, Sir (William John) Andrew (1889-1971)

Colonial Service. Chief Secretary to Resident Minister, West Africa, 1942-45. Head of British Food Mission, Canada, 1946-53.

Rhodes House Library, Oxford, has a number of memoranda and notes, mainly relating to the Gold Coast and Togoland (1934, 1937, 1947).

JORDAN, Sir John Newell (1852-1925)

Minister, Korea, 1901-06 (Consul-General, 1896-98, Chargé d'Affaires, 1898-1901). Minister, China, 1906-20.

A collection of private correspondence (1901-12), mainly with the Foreign Office, together with two registers of correspondence, are available at the Public Record Office (F.O. 350/1-16).

JORDAN, Stanley Rupert (1894-   )

Minister, Saudi Arabia, 1943-45.

No contact could be established.

KEELING, Edward Allis (1885-   )

Minister, Venezuela, 1932-36. Consul-General, Tangier, 1936-39.

Mr Keeling states that he has no papers, apart from some private papers of no consequence.

KEKEWICH, Sir George William (1841-1921)

Secretary, Board of Education, 1900-03. M.P. (Lib.) Exeter, 1906-10.

At the B.L.P.E.S. there is a guardbook containing letters to Sir George and press cuttings of his speeches, etc., on his retirement from the Board of Education and during his subsequent political career.

KELL, Major-General Sir Vernon George Waldegrave (1873-1942)

Served European War, 1914-18; War Office (M.I.5, etc.).

Mrs S. M. Simpson, Spring House, Walhampton Hill, Lymington, Hants., has an unpublished biography of her grandfather, Sir Vernon Kell, written by her grandmother. She also has three of her grandfather's diaries, dated 1939, 1940 and 1941, together with photographs and memorabilia. Certain other papers survive with another of Sir Vernon's granddaughters, Mrs R. S. Frost, Fyfield House, Barrows Road, Cheddar, Somerset.

KELLY, Sir David Victor (1891-1959)

Minister, Switzerland, 1940-42. Ambassador, Argentine Republic, 1942-46; Turkey, 1946-49; U.S.S.R., 1949-51.

Lady Kelly, 27 Carlyle Square, London SW3, retains a fair-sized collection of press cuttings relating to the career of her late husband.

KELLY, Admiral of the Fleet Sir John Donald (1871-1936)

Naval career from 1884; active service in World War I. 4th Sea Lord, 1924-27. C.-in-C., Atlantic Fleet, 1931-32; Home Fleet, 1932-33; Portsmouth, 1934-36.

A collection of Kelly's papers at the National Maritime Museum covers much of his career, though some of the material is rather sparse. Of particular interest are papers relating to Kelly's period as Captain of the light cruiser H.M.S. *Dublin*, during World War I; as Military Commander at Chanak (1922-23); and papers concerning the Invergordon Mutiny and its aftermath (1931).

KELLY, Admiral Sir (William Archibald) Howard (1873-1952)

Naval career from 1886. Naval Attaché, Paris, 1911-14. Served World War I. Admiralty Representative, League of Nations, 1927-29. C.-in-C., China Station, 1931-33. British Naval Representative, Turkey, 1940-44.

A collection of papers at the National Maritime Museum includes various drafts of his autobiography; service records, particularly relating to the British Adriatic Force (1917-19), Greece (1919-21), his various posts (1923-30), China (1931-33), and Turkey (1940-44); personal diaries (1899-1910); and press cuttings and articles (1926-49).

KEMPE, Sir John Arrow (1846-1928)

Comptroller and Auditor-General, 1904-11.

A collection of papers (1866-1909) at Duke University, Durham, North Carolina, includes some 100 letters (1874-79) from Sir Stafford Northcote, to whom Kempe acted as secretary. A later series of letters (1906-09) gives details of government financial matters, and correspondents include T. G. Bowles, M.P., and Sir Robert Williams, M.P.

KENNARD, Sir Howard William (1878-1955)

Minister, Yugoslavia, 1925-29; Sweden, 1929-31; Switzerland, 1931-35. Ambassador, Poland, 1935-41.

Mr A. N. Kennard, 19 Park Place Villas, London W2, has a few of his father's private papers, but the diary volumes covering the years which Sir H. W. Kennard spent in the diplomatic service appear to be missing.

KENNEDY, Admiral Francis William (1862-1939)

Naval career. Commanded H.M.S. *Indomitable*, 1912-16, and served at Dardanelles, Dogger Bank, Jutland, etc.

The material at the Liddell Hart Centre for Military Archives includes Kennedy's papers as Captain of H.M.S. *Indomitable* (1914-15), chiefly relating to actions against the German battleships *Goeben* and *Breslau* in August 1914. Other papers relate to naval bombardments in the Dardanelles (November 1914), the sinking of the *Blücher* (January 1915) and the sinking of the *Indomitable* at the Battle of Jutland (May 1916).

KENNEDY, Sir (Henry Charles) Donald Cleveland Mackenzie-(1889-1965)

Colonial Service, Northern Rhodesia and Tanganyika. Governor, Nyasaland, 1939-42; Mauritius, 1942-49. Chief Political Liaison Officer, East Africa Force, 1939-40.

The Oxford Colonial Records Project believe that papers survive with Sir Donald's son, John Mackenzie-Kennedy, in Mauritius. It has not been possible to contact him. Lady Mackenzie-Kennedy has no papers and says that her husband destroyed many documents.

KENNEDY, Sir Robert John (1851-1936)

Minister, Montenegro, 1893-1906; Uruguay, 1906-13.

Efforts to contact the executors and their heirs proved unsuccessful. Sir Robert's son-in-law was Sir Herbert Hall Hall (1879-1964), also of the Foreign Office.

KEPPEL, Admiral Sir Colin Richard (1862-1947)

Naval career from 1870s. Rear-Admiral in Atlantic Fleet, 1909-10.

Research enquiries should be directed to Keppel's grandson, Mr Henry Hely-Hutchinson, 99 Aldwych, London WC2B 4JS.

KEPPEL, Sir George Roos- (1866-1921)

Chief Commissioner and Agent to the Governor-General, North West Frontier Province, 1908-19.

A collection of correspondence (1902-19) is deposited at the India Office Library.

KEPPEL, Admiral of the Fleet Hon. Sir Henry (1809-1908)

Naval career.

Personal papers and diaries (1824-1900) are available at the National Maritime Museum. Further enquiries should be addressed to Mr Henry Hely-Hutchinson, 99 Aldwych, London WC2B 4JS.

KERMODE, Rev. Sir Derwent William (1898-1960)

Ambassador, Indonesia, 1950-53; Czechoslovakia, 1953-55.

Lady Kermode states that her late husband kept very few papers of any sort and no diaries or cuttings.

KERR, Admiral Mark Edward Frederic (1864-1944)

C.-in-C., Greek Navy, 1913-15; Adriatic Squadron, 1916-17. Deputy Chief of Air Staff, 1918.

Miss Rosemary Kerr states that her father's papers were all sorted by Mrs M. Kerr, O.B.E. (his widow). Relevant papers were sent to the Admiralty, and no papers now survive with the family.

KERR, Admiral of the Fleet Lord Walter Talbot (1839-1927)

1st Lord of the Admiralty, 1899-1904.

The Lothian family papers at the Scottish Record Office appear to contain no papers of relevance. No other papers were located.

KEYES, 1st B
Admiral of the Fleet Sir Roger John Brownlow Keyes, 1st Bt (1872-1945)

Naval career. C.-in-C., Mediterranean, 1925-28; Portsmouth, 1929-31. Special Liaison Officer to the King of the Belgians, 1940. Director of Combined Operations, 1940-41. M.P. (Con.) Portsmouth North, 1934-43.

Lord Keyes's papers are deposited in the Library of Churchill College, Cambridge. The collection has been arranged into the following main groups: Personal, Naval Career, Political Career, General. The Personal papers date from the 1890s and include correspondence between Keyes and his wife, and appointments diaries. The Naval papers again date from the 1890s, and cover all Keyes's major interests and activities, with papers on submarine construction; his active service during World War I, including correspondence concerning the Dardanelles Expedition and papers relating to the Zeebrugge and Ostend operations; his naval career during the inter-war years; and the Fleet Air Arm. The Political papers include constituency material (1934-42); copies of speeches made by Keyes; a considerable amount of correspondence; newspaper cuttings; and papers relating to Keyes's activities during World War II. These are supplemented by wide-ranging material in the General files. Many of these papers are not open to general inspection and application to see any of them should be made beforehand to the Archivist, Churchill College, Cambridge.

KEYES, Brigadier-General Sir Terence Humphrey (1877-1939)

Indian Political Service, 1903-33. Member, British Military Mission, South Russia, 1917-20.

A collection of correspondence and papers (1904-39) at the India Office Library includes material relating to Keyes's service in Persia, Baluchistan and South Russia; as envoy in Nepal in 1928 and as Resident in Hyderabad (1930-33). The collection also includes correspondence (1897-1902) with Sir Arthur Henry McMahon.

KIDSTON, George Jardine (1873-1954)

Minister, Finland, 1920-21.

Mrs Patricia Kidston, Breach Farm, Dummer, Basingstoke, Hants., states that practically none of her father-in-law's papers have been kept. However, she does have his diary written during a trip into Mongolia (1904).

KIGGELL, Lieutenant-General Sir Launcelot Edward (1862-1954)

Served South Africa, 1899-1902; Staff College. Director of Staff Duties, War Office, 1909-13. Director of Home Defence, 1914-15. Chief of General Staff, British Armies in France, 1915-18. G.O.C. and Lieutenant-Governor, Guernsey, 1918-20.

The papers have been deposited at the Liddell Hart Centre for Military Archives. Among this material is Kiggell's correspondence with Chiefs of the General Staff Sir William Robertson and Sir Henry Wilson, and with Field-Marshal Earl Haig (1909-18).

KILBRACKEN, 1st B
Sir John Arthur Godley (1847-1932)

Private Secretary to W. E. Gladstone, 1872-74, 1880-82. Commissioner of Inland Revenue, 1882-83. Permanent Under-Secretary, India, 1883-1909.

The political and literary correspondence of Lord Kilbracken, including correspondence with W. E. Gladstone and letters from Lord Rosebery, Lord Morley and Lord F. C. Cavendish, is held at the British Library (Add. MSS. 44900-44902). Papers relating to Kilbracken's service at the India Office can be found in the India Office Library. The correspondence includes letter books (1883-1909), letters from Secretaries of State for India, from Permanent Under-Secretary Sir Louis Mallet (1885), from Viceroys of India and from their Private Secretaries, and letters from members of the Viceroy's Council and provincial governors. A further series of files and papers relate to particular matters, e.g. legislative councils (1888) and the Calcutta Corporation (1897).

KILLEARN, 1st B
Sir Miles Wedderburn Lampson (1880-1964)

Minister, China, 1926-33. High Commissioner, Egypt and Sudan, 1934-36. Ambassador, Egypt, and High Commissioner, Sudan, 1936-46. Special Commissioner, South East Asia, 1946-48.

A collection of diaries and papers, covering most of Killearn's career, is to be placed in the library of St Antony's College, Oxford. For the Egyptian papers, enquiries should be addressed to the Private Papers Secretary at the Middle East Centre.

KINDERSLEY, 1st B
Sir Robert Molesworth Kindersley (1871-1954)

Company director; merchant banker. President, National Savings Committee, 1920-46. Director, Bank of England, 1914-46. Senior British Representative, Dawes Committee, 1922. Member of Bankers' Committee on German Finance, 1921-25.

The present (2nd) Lord Kindersley states that few of his father's papers have been kept.

KING, Sir Alexander Freeman (1851-1942)

Secretary, Post Office, 1911-14.

King's solicitors have no relevant records and they are no longer in contact with members of the King family.

KING, Sir Geoffrey Stuart (1894-)

Secretary, National Assistance Board, 1944-48. Deputy Secretary, National Insurance, 1949-57. Permanent Secretary, Pensions and National Insurance, 1953-55.

Sir G. S. King stated that he never kept a diary and retained no papers relating to official matters.

KING, Sir Norman (1880-1963)

Consular Service from 1907. Chargé d'Affaires, Mexico, 1925. Consul-General, Barcelona, 1926-38; Marseilles, 1938-40.

Lady King, 27 Abbey Street, Faversham, Kent, has a collection of her husband's papers. This includes a typescript diary (including photographs) relating to King's service in East Africa (1914-16), material relating to his service in Spain, miscellaneous pocket diaries, and a certain amount of correspondence, much of it congratulatory or of a formal nature. Other papers, including a diary of his work in Mexico, were destroyed by Sir Norman before his death.

KINNEAR, Sir Walter Samuel (1872-1953)

Controller of Insurance Department, Health, 1919-36; Deputy Chairman, National Health Joint Committee, 1920-38.

Sir Walter's daughter, Mrs T. H. C. Amies, knows of no private papers which have survived.

KIRBY, Major-General Stanley Woodburn (1895-1968)

Served European War, 1914-18; Singapore, 1923-26; Staff College, War Office, and Imperial Defence College, India. Deputy Chief of General Staff, India, 1942-43. Director of Civil Affairs, War Office, 1943-44. Deputy Chief of Staff, Control Commission for Germany, 1945. Military historian.

The papers at the Liddell Hart Centre for Military Archives are not available for inspection.

KIRKBRIDE, Sir Alec Seath (1897-   )

British Resident, Transjordan, 1939. Minister, Jordan, 1946-51. Ambassador, Libya, 1954 (Minister, 1951-54).

It is believed that Sir Alec has kept no papers.

KIRKE, General Sir Walter Meryn St George (1877-1949)

Military career from 1896. Served Waziristan Campaign, 1901-02; European War, 1914-18. Deputy Director of Military Operations, 1918-22. Head of Naval, Military and Air Force Mission to Finland, 1924-25. Deputy Chief of General Staff, India, 1926-29. Commander, 5th Division and Catterick Area, 1929-31. G.O.C.-in-C., Western Command, 1933-36. Director-General, Territorial Army, 1936-39. Inspector-General, Home Defences, 1939. C.-in-C., Home Forces, 1939-40.

Certain papers are retained by the Intelligence Corps Museum. These consist of reminiscences on Lt.-Gen. Sir George MacDonogh; papers on the history of Intelligence; notes on World War I; lectures dated 1924; instructions for reports (India); published material; and other papers.

KIRKMAN, Major-General John Mather (1898-1964)

Served European War, 1917-18; War of 1939-45. Deputy Director of Military Intelligence, 1942. Chief of Staff, Palestine, 1947; Far East Land Forces, 1948-50. Chief of Intelligence Division, Germany, 1950-54.

General Sir Sidney Kirkman states that his brother left no papers.

KIRKMAN, General Sir Sidney Chevalier (1895-   )

Served European War, 1914-18; War of 1939-45. G.O. C.-in-C., Southern Command, 1945. Deputy Chief of Imperial General Staff, 1945-47. Quartermaster-General, 1947-50. Special Financial Representative, Germany, 1951-52. Director-General, Civil Defence, 1954-60.

The General has bequeathed his diaries and certain other papers to the Liddell Hart Centre for Military Archives.

KIRKPATRICK, Sir Ivone Augustine (1897-1964)

Head of Chancery, Berlin, 1933-38. Director of Foreign Division, Ministry of Information, 1940. Controller (European Services), British Broadcasting Corporation, 1941. Deputy Commissioner (Civil), Control Commission, Germany (British Element), 1944. Assistant Under-Secretary, Foreign Office, from 1945, and Deputy Under-Secretary, 1948; Permanent Under-Secretary (German Section), 1949. United Kingdom High Commissioner, Germany, 1950-53. Permanent Under-Secretary, Foreign Office, 1953-57.

Lady Kirkpatrick, c/o Messrs Collyer-Bristow & Co., 4 Bedford Row, London WC1 4DF, states that her husband did not keep a diary, but Lady Kirkpatrick has a few letters and press cuttings, particularly relating to his work in Germany. These papers are at present in store and not available for inspection.

KISCH, Sir Cecil (1884-1961)

Private Secretary, Secretary of State, India, 1917-23. Secretary, Financial Department, India Office, 1921-33; Under-Secretary, 1933-43, and Deputy Under-Secretary, India, 1943-46. Director-General, Petroleum Department, 1939-42.

Sir Cecil's son, Mr J. M. Kisch, C.M.G., Hatchford Corner, Cobham, Surrey KT11 1LW, has retained a certain number of unsorted papers, newspaper cuttings, letters and copies of published articles and letters to *The Times*. One box of correspondence and papers (1920-35) has been deposited with other family papers at the India Office Library.

KITCHENER OF KHARTOUM, 1st E
Field-Marshal Sir Horatio Herbert Kitchener (1850-1916)

Commander, Dongola Expeditionary Force, 1896; Khartoum Expedition, 1898. Chief of Staff, South Africa, 1899-1900. C.-in-C., South Africa, 1900-02; India, 1902-09. Agent and Consul-General, Egypt, 1911-14. Secretary of State for War, 1914-16.

A collection of Kitchener's papers has been deposited in the Public Record Office (P.R.O. 30/57). The papers relate to the period up to 1914, the World War, and personal and estate matters; there is also a series of papers collected by Sir George Arthur for his biography of Kitchener. The collection is supplemented by a small Private Office series (1914-16), again at the Public Record Office (W.O. 159), and by the papers at the India Office Library among the Birdwood Collection. The British Library holds a collection of correspondence (Add. MSS. 52276-78), mostly between Kitchener and Lt.-Col. R. J. Marker, his aide-de-camp in India, Details of all these papers are given in Hazlehurst and Woodland, op. cit., pp.85-6.

KNOLLYS, 1st Vt
Sir Francis Knollys (1837-1924)

Private Secretary to King Edward VII, 1901-10; King George V, 1910-13.

A collection of papers survives in the Royal Archives, Windsor. Family papers (1736-1931) and the Knollys-Wallenford correspondence are in the Hampshire Record Office. Knollys' letters to Lord Rendel can be found at the National Library of Wales, and other Knollys correspondence is contained in numerous other collections.

KNOX, Sir Geoffrey George (1884-1958)

Chairman, Saar Governing Commission, 1932-35. Minister, Hungary, 1935-39. Ambassador, Brazil, 1939-41.

Sir G. G. Knox died in Tobago, without heirs. The executor and solicitors were not traced.

KNOX, General Sir Harry Hugh Sidney (1873-1971)

Served India; European War, 1914-19. Director of Military Training, War Office, 1926-30. Commander, 3rd Division, 1930-32. Adjutant-General, 1935-37.

The General's daughter, Lady Nye, has no papers, and it is understood that General Knox kept none.

KNOX, Sir Ralph Henry (1836-1913)

Permanent Under-Secretary, War Office, 1897-1901.

A visit to Somerset House brought forward no information useful in tracing the family and executors.

LAGDEN, Sir Godfrey Yeatman (1851-1934)

Colonial Service. Resident Commissioner, Basutoland, 1893-1901. Commissioner for Native Affairs, Transvaal, 1901-07.

Rhodes House Library, Oxford, has 67 volumes (1877-1934) of Lagden's diary, and a collection of correspondence and papers, mainly relating to Basutoland and Swaziland (1883-1934). There is also a supplementary collection of correspondence, notes and miscellaneous papers.

LAITHWAITE, Sir (John) Gilbert (1894-   )

Private Secretary to Viceroy of India, 1936-43. Assistant Under-Secretary, India Office, 1943. Under-Secretary (Civil), War Cabinet, 1944-45. Deputy Under-Secretary, Burma, 1945-47; India, 1947; Commonwealth Relations, 1948-49. Ambassador, Eire, 1950-51 (U.K. Representative, 1949-50). High Commissioner, Pakistan, 1951-54. Permanent Under-Secretary, Commonwealth Relations, 1955-59.

Correspondence, papers and photographs (1912-69) are deposited at the India Office Library. The collection covers Sir Gilbert's entire career and includes his official and private correspondence from 1927-1968. Included in the collection are Commonwealth tour diaries (1955-59) and overseas tour diaries (1960-69). Also included are Irish papers from the period 1949-51. These papers are not as yet open for inspection. The Imperial War Museum holds Sir Gilbert Laithwaite's correspondence (1916-19) with his family and Oxford contemporaries, relating to the impact of the World War, and a personal account of the great retreat of March 1918.

LAMB, Sir John (1871-1952)

Under-Secretary, Scotland, 1926-33.

Messrs Will & Philip, solicitors, state that, according to an informed source, Sir John left neither diaries nor letters.

LAMB, Sir Lionel Henry (1900-   )

China Consular Service, Minister, China (Nanking), 1947-49. Chargé d'Affaires, China (Peking), 1951-53. Ambassador, Switzerland, 1953-58.

Sir Lionel Lamb states that he has retained no papers. He had, during twenty-five years' service in China, collected a considerable amount of papers, press cuttings, photographs, and copies and English translations of Chinese legislation from 1928-1941. However, all these were destroyed in a fire in Nanking in 1947.

LAMINGTON, 2nd B
Charles Wallace Alexander Napier Cochrane Baillie (1860-1940)

M.P. (Con.) St Pancras North, 1886-90. Governor, Queensland, 1895-1901; Bombay, 1903-07.

The India Office Library holds an assortment of letters (1904-07) to Lamington from politicians, including Lords Morley, Minto, Kitchener and Ampthill, and a microfilm of two letter books (with indexes) kept by Lamington in the years 1903-07. The originals are now at Duke University, Durham, North Carolina.

LAMPLOUGH, Major-General Charles Robert Wharram (1896-)

Military career, Royal Marines. Served European War, 1914-18; War of 1939-45. Staff of Supreme Allied Commander, South East Asia Command, 1943-46. Major-General Commanding Plymouth Group, Royal Marines, 1946-49.

Major-General Lamplough has agreed to place any papers of interest which he has in the Royal Marines Museum.

LANE, Major-General Sir Charles Reginald Cambridge (1890-1964)

Military career. Served with Indian Expeditionary Force in France, 1914-18; Egypt and Palestine, 1918-19; India from 1924. Deputy Principal Administrative Officer, Supreme Allied Command, South East Asia, 1943-44. Representative in India of Supreme Allied Commander, South East Asia, 1944-46.

Papers which survive in the care of Lady Lane have been promised to the Imperial War Museum.

LANG, Sir John Gerald (1896-)

Civil Service career. Permanent Secretary, Admiralty, 1947-61. Principal Adviser on Sport to the Government, 1964-71; Deputy Chairman, Sports Council, 1965-71.

Sir John has kept no papers, diaries or press cuttings relating to his career. However, he does retain a few memoranda about the Admiralty.

LANGLEY, Sir Walter Louis Frederick Goltz (1855-1918)

Assistant Under-Secretary, Foreign Office, 1907-18.

A collection of Private Office correspondence (1886-1918) survives at the Public Record Office (F.O. 800/29-31). Members of the family could not be traced.

LASCELLES, Sir Daniel William (1902-1967)

Chargé d'Affaires, Athens, 1946 and 1947. Ambassador, Ethiopia, 1949-51 (Minister, 1948-49); Afghanistan, 1953-57; Japan, 1957-59.

Miss P. D. Lascelles states that her brother destroyed all his papers before his death.

LASCELLES, Sir Frank Cavendish (1841-1920)

Minister, Romania, 1886; Persia, 1891. Ambassador, Russia, 1894; Germany, 1895-1908.

There is a collection of Private Office correspondence (1874-1908) at the Public Record Office (F.O. 800/6-20). Other relevant papers may survive in the family archive at Harewood House, Leeds, home of the Earl of Harewood. Details are not available.

LATHBURY, General Sir Gerald William (1906-   )

Military career. Served World War II and in Palestine, 1945-46. G.O.C., 16th Airborne Division, 1948-51. C.-in-C., East Africa, 1955-57. Director-General of Military Training, War Office, 1957-60. G.O.C.-in-C., Eastern Command, 1960-61. Quartermaster-General to the Forces, 1961-65. Governor of Gibraltar, 1964-69.

The General's Arnhem diary, describing how Lathbury, who was a temporary Brigadier, was captured by the Germans and escaped, is preserved in the Airborne Forces Museum. A photocopy is available at the Imperial War Museum.

LATTER, Major-General John Cecil (1896-1972)

Military career. Served World War I; Diplomatic Service, 1919-21. Deputy Military Secretary, War Office, 1940-43. Deputy Director, Territorial Army and Army Cadet Force, 1945-47.

Latter's World War I papers are preserved at the Imperial War Museum. These comprise a record of his experiences in France and Italy (mainly 1917-18). Major-General Latter informed King's College that he had kept no further papers.

LAWRANCE, Major Sir Arthur Salisbury (1880-1965)

Colonial Service. Governor, Somaliland, 1935-39. British Red Cross Representative, Lisbon, 1941-42. Intelligence Officer, Home Guard, 1943-45.

Mrs Pamela Donovan (niece) knows of no papers.

LAWRENCE, General Hon. Sir Herbert Alexander (1861-1943)

Military career. South Africa, 1899-1902; Dardanelles, 1915; Egypt, 1916. Chief of Staff, British Armies in France, 1918. Member, Royal Commission on Coal Industry, 1925.

The National Library of Scotland has a collection of papers, including 5 folders relating to campaigns in 1918.

LAWRENCE, Thomas Edward (1888-1935)*

Served in Arabia, 1914-18. Attached to Staff of General Sir F. Wingate, Hejaz Expeditionary Force, 1917; served on General Allenby's Staff, 1918; on British Delegation to Peace Conference, 1919. Adviser on Arab Affairs, Colonial Office, 1921-22. Author of *The Seven Pillars of Wisdom* (1926, 1935), etc.

Various collections of T. E. Lawrence's papers survive. The British Library has, *inter alia*, Lawrence's pocket diaries (Add. MS. 45938 AB). A small collection of letters is preserved at the Bodleian Library, Oxford. Another collection is held by the Library of the University of Texas, including correspondence; a sketch book; B. H. Liddell Hart's papers relating to a biography of Lawrence; a photographic collection relating to his Arab campaign; and notes and manuscripts of certain of his works. A collection of 250 letters is preserved in the Library of Harvard University. The Imperial War Museum has a Lawrence of Arabia collection, the fruits of research that produced the biography by P. Knightley and C. Simpson, *The Secret Lives of T. E. Lawrence* (1969). The collection contains the typescript of the book,

*Changed name by Deed Poll to SHAW, 1927.

including an unpublished chapter, numerous photocopies of official and other documents, copies of letters from Lawrence and those concerned with his activities in the Arab revolt and in the subsequent history of the Middle East, and relevant newscuttings from publications of the past fifty years. The National Library of Scotland has certain papers for 1918.

LAWRENCE, Sir Walter Roper, 1st Bt (1857-1940)

Private Secretary to Lord Curzon, 1898-1903. Member of Council of India, 1907-09.

The papers at the India Office Library cover the whole of Lawrence's career (c. 1880-1939), and include diaries, correspondence and literary papers. Important parts of the collection relate to the period as Commissioner to Lord Kitchener for Indian sick and wounded, and the period as Curzon's Private Secretary.

LAYTON, 1st B
Sir Walter Thomas Layton (1884-1966)

Member, Munitions Council, World War I. Director of Economic and Financial Section, League of Nations. Financial Adviser, Indian Statutory Commission, 1929-30. Editor, *The Economist*, 1922-38. Served Ministry of Supply and Ministry of Production, World War II. Leader of Liberal Party, House of Lords, 1952-55. Director, Reuters Ltd., 1945-53.

A substantial quantity of papers, including fragments of an unpublished autobiography, survive in the care of the present (2nd) Lord Layton, 45 Westleigh Avenue, Putney, London SW15.

LAYTON, Admiral Sir Geoffrey (1884-1964)

Naval career. Served World War I. Director of Personal Services, 1936-38. Commanded Battle Cruiser Squadron, 1938. Commanded 1st Battle Squadron and 2nd-in-Command, Home Fleet, 1939-40. C.-in-C., China, 1940-42; Ceylon, 1942-45; Portsmouth, 1945-47.

Correspondence and papers (1939-45) are retained at the British Library. These are 'reserved' for fifty years.

LEAKE, Vice-Admiral Francis Martin- (1869-1928)

Served European War, 1914-18. Commanded H.M.S. *Pathfinder*, 1914; *Achilles*, 1915-17. Chief of Staff to Admiral Commanding, Queenstown, 1918-19.

The collection of papers at the Hertfordshire Record Office consists of 192 letters and one album for the period 1900-18. The Record Office also holds papers of Lieutenant-Colonel Arthur Martin-Leake (1900-18), and other members of the family.

LECHE, Sir John Hurleston (1889-1960)

Diplomatic Service. Chargé d'Affaires, Spanish Republic, 1937-38. Minister and Consul-General, Central America, 1939-45. Ambassador, Chile, 1945-49.

No contact was established with the surviving members of the family.

LEE, Sir Frank Godbould (1903-1971)

Civil Service career. Permanent Secretary, Board of Trade, 1951-59; Ministry of Food, 1959-61; Treasury (Joint), 1960-62.

The Public Record Office (class B.T. 91) includes four files relating to the work of Sir Frank Lee and Sir J. Woods at the Board of Trade.

LEE, Sir Henry Austin (1847-1918)

Commercial Attaché, France, Belgium and Switzerland.

Correspondence and diaries (1914-16) of Madeleine, wife of Sir Henry, are available at the British Library (Add. MSS. 46766-75).

LEE, Sir Kenneth, 1st Bt (1879-1967)

Member, Advisory Committee to Department of Overseas Trade (Development and Intelligence), 1918-25; also several other Government Committees and Missions. Director-General and Secretary, Ministry of Information, 1939-40. Director-General, Raw Materials Controls, Ministry of Supply, 1942-45.

Messrs March, Pearson & Skelton, solicitors, suggested that Sir Kenneth's sister, Vivienne Lady Cawley, Berrington Hall, Leominster, Herefordshire, might be able to help. It has not proved possible to contact Lady Cawley.

LEECH, Sir Stephen (1864-1925)

Minister, Cuba, 1909-19; Haiti and Dominican Republic, 1913-19.

Messrs William Sturges & Co., solicitors, wrote to the only known surviving members of Sir Stephen Leech's family, who replied that they do not have any papers. William Sturges, who was one of Sir Stephen's executors, was instructed in the Will to receive all private MSS. in the estate. The Will states: 'I express the desire that he will deliver such of them as he may determine to my sister Ethel Hyde Parker or my nephew John Cyril Leech and destroy or otherwise dispose of the remainder as he may in his discretion deem advisable.'

LEEDS, 12th D of
Francis D'Arcy Godolphin Osborne (1884-1964)

Minister, Washington, 1931-35; Holy See, 1936-47.

A diary kept whilst 'captive' Minister in the Vatican is in the care of Sir Robert McEwen, Bt, Marchmont, Greenlaw, Berwickshire.

LEEPER, Sir Reginald Wildig Allen (1888-1968)

Assistant Under-Secretary, Foreign Office, 1940-43. Ambassador, Greece, 1943-46; Argentina, 1946-48.

Lady Leeper, Southward, Rambledown Lane, West Chiltington, Sussex, has a number of papers relating to her late husband. The material includes diaries of a visit to Poland (1920); a trip down the Russo-Polish frontier, Volhynia and Galicia (1924); and the periods May to December 1923 in Poland and 1940, 1941 and 1942 whilst working on enemy propaganda. There is also a memorandum regarding Litvinov's departure for Russia (1919) and a report of an interview with him (1933); letters from Cairo and Greece (1943-45); and papers relating to war-time propaganda work at Woburn. A long series of letters written by Sir Reginald and his brother Allen Leeper to their father, from about 1908 to 1934, are in the possession of the Leepers' half-sister in Melbourne, Australia. Enquiries may be directed to Lady Leeper.

LEESE, Lieutenant-General Sir Oliver William Hargreaves, 3rd Bt (1894-   )

Military career. Served World War I. Deputy Chief of the General Staff, British Expeditionary Force, 1940. Commanded Guards Armoured Division, 1941; XXX Corps, 1942. Commander, 8th Army, 1944. C.-in-C., Allied Land Forces, South East Asia, 1944-45. G.O. C.-in-C., Eastern Command, 1945-46.

The General has kept some papers, mainly of a personal nature. They will probably be given in due course to the Imperial War Museum.

LEGGETT, Henry Aufrere (1874-1950)

Director of Establishments, Ministry of Health, 1924-37; Chief General Inspector, 1934-37.

Miss C. G. M. Leggett knows of no papers left by her father.

LE HUNTE, Sir George Ruthven (1852-1925)

Colonial Service, Western Pacific and West Indies. Lieutenant-Governor, British New Guinea, 1898-1903. Governor, South Australia, 1903-08; Trinidad and Tobago, 1908-15.

The Will and Act of Probate gave no details helpful in tracing the heirs.

LE ROUGETEL, Sir John Helier (1894-1975)

Ambassador, Iran, 1946-50; Belgium, 1950-51. High Commissioner, South Africa, 1951-55.

Sir John Le Rougetel kept no diary or papers which might be of public interest.

LETHEM, Sir Gordon James (1886-1962)

Governor, Seychelles, 1933-35; Leeward Islands, 1936-41; British Guiana, 1941-46.

Rhodes House Library, Oxford, has a collection of correspondence, reports, papers, etc., relating to Lethem's service in Nigeria, the Leeward Islands and British Guiana (1914-46). The collection amounts to some 22 boxes of papers.

LEVER, Sir (Samuel) Hardman, 1st Bt (1869-1947)

Served Ministry of Munitions and Treasury.

A collection of Private Office papers survives in the Public Record Office (T.172 and T.186). A number of files (T.172), dated 1917 to 1920, relate to Lever's appointment as Assistant Commissioner for Finance in the United States, and a further collection of papers (T. 186) covers the period 1919-22, when Lever was Treasury Representative at the Ministry of Transport. This interesting material includes Railway Advisory Committee and Road Improvement Fund papers; papers on the establishment of the Ministry of Transport; and papers on bridges, canals, docks, rivers, London traffic, the Channel Tunnel, unemployment relief, motor tax, and transport in Ireland.

LIDDELL, Lieutenant-General Sir Clive Gerard (1883-1956)

Military career. Adjutant-General, 1937-39. Governor, Gibraltar, 1939-41. Inspector-General for Training, 1941-42.

Mrs J. W. Crundall, Lower Leigh, West Street, Mayfield, Sussex, has three books of press cuttings relating to her father.

LIESCHING, Sir Percivale (1895-   )

Service in Colonial Office and High Commissions in Canada, South Africa and Australia. 2nd Secretary, Board of Trade, 1942-46. Permanent Secretary, Ministry of Food, 1946-48. Permanent Under-Secretary, Commonwealth Relations Office, 1949-55. High Commissioner in South Africa, and for Basutoland, Bechuanaland and Swaziland, 1955-58.

Sir Percivale states that he has kept no papers, press cuttings or diary relating to his service under the Crown.

LIMPUS, Admiral Sir Arthur Henry (1863-1931)

Naval career from 1876; served Suakin, 1884-89; South Africa. Naval Adviser to Turkish Government, 1912-14. Admiral Superintendent, Malta, 1914-16; Senior Naval Officer, Malta, 1915-16. President, Shell Committee at the Admiralty, 1917.

A substantial collection of papers is preserved at the National Maritime Museum. It consists of personal correspondence and official papers, and covers all the major aspects of Limpus's career, including the naval mission to Turkey (1912-14).

LINDLEY, Sir Francis Oswald (1872-1950)

Commissioner and Consul-General, Russia, 1918-19; High Commissioner and Minister, Austria, 1919-20; Minister, Greece, 1922-23; Norway, 1923-29. Ambassador, Portugal, 1929-31; Japan, 1931-34.

A certain number of papers, in particular a diary kept whilst in Russia during World War I, is retained by Sir Francis's grandson, Sir Robert McEwen, Bt., Marchmont, Greenlaw, Berwickshire.

LINDSAY, Major-General George Mackintosh (1880-1956)

Served South Africa, 1900-02; European War, 1914-18. Inspector, Royal Tank Corps, War Office, 1925-29. Member, Mechanical Warfare Board, 1926-29. Service in Egypt and India. Commissioner of British Red Cross, etc., North West Europe, 1944-46.

A collection of papers survives in the Royal Armoured Corps Tank Museum.

LINDSAY, Sir Ronald Charles (1877-1945)

Financial Under-Secretary, Egyptian Government, 1913-19. Minister, Paris, 1920-21. Under-Secretary, Foreign Office, 1921-24. Ambassador, Turkey, 1925-26 (British Representative, Constantinople, 1924-25); Germany, 1926-28; United States, 1930-39. Permanent Under-Secretary, Foreign Office, 1928-30.

No private papers are known to have survived. Mr C. P. Lindsay, Sir Ronald's nephew, states that his uncle had no children and there was no obvious member of the family to whom papers might have been passed. Some relevant correspondence survives in the Lothian and Hardinge papers.

LINDSELL, Lieutenant-General Sir Wilfrid Gordon (1884-1973)

Military career; served World War I. Deputy Military Secretary, War Office, 1935-36. Commander, Royal Artillery, 4th Division, 1937-38. Quartermaster-General of British Expeditionary Force, 1939-40. Lieutenant-General in Middle East, 1942-43. Principal Administrative Officer to the Indian Command, 1943-45.

A collection of papers is in the care of the Liddell Hart Centre for Military Archives. The papers include memoranda and notes accumulated by Lindsell when he was Quartermaster-General of the British Expeditionary Force (1939-40), dealing particularly with the withdrawal to Dunkirk. There are also notes on the maintenance of the 8th Army and the supporting Royal Air Force (1943); memoranda, correspondence and lectures, mainly on India as a base for operations in the Far East (1944-45); and post-war lectures and newspaper articles on war administration and the Suez Canal question.

LINLITHGOW, 1st M of
Sir John Adrian Louis Hope, Earl of Hopetoun (1860-1908)

Governor, Victoria, 1889-95. Paymaster-General, 1895-98. Governor-General, Australia, 1900-02. Secretary for Scotland, 1905.

Most of the papers which survive relate to the period in Australia, and they are described by Hazlehurst and Woodland, op. cit., p.77.

LINLITHGOW, 2nd M of
Victor Alexander John Hope (1887-1952)

Civil Lord of the Admiralty, 1922-24. Viceroy and Governor-General of India, 1936-43.

Correspondence and papers of the Marquess of Linlithgow as Viceroy are deposited at the India Office Library. A handlist gives details of correspondence and telegrams with the Secretary of State, with provincial governors, and with other officials in India and Great Britain, and also Linlithgow's speeches and his private and personal files. Other items in the collection include maps and records of Parliamentary debates (Hansard). The Hopetoun Family Trust papers remain with the present Marquess of Linlithgow.

LITHGOW, Sir James, 1st Bt (1883-1952)

Director of Shipbuilding Production, Admiralty, 1917. Controller of Merchant Shipbuilding and Repairs, and Member of the Board of Admiralty, 1940-46.

A considerable amount of material survives with Sir William Lithgow, Bt, c/o Kingston Shipbuilding Yard, Port Glasgow, Renfrewshire PA14 5DR. Much of this is of little importance to the researcher, and the papers remain largely un-catalogued. The collection includes letters from Sir James Lithgow criticising the war management whilst at the Front in World War I, and papers relating to the various aspects of his career in industry and government service.

LITTLE, Admiral Sir Charles James Colebrooke (1882-1973)

Naval career; specialised in submarine branch. Commanded H.M.S. *Fearless* and Grand Fleet Submarine Flotilla, 1916-18. Director of Trade Division, Naval Staff, 1920-22. Director, Royal Naval Staff College, 1927-30. Rear-Admiral, Submarines, 1931-32. Deputy Chief of Naval Staff, 1932-35. C.-in-C., China Station, 1936-38. Chief of Naval Personnel, 1938-41. C.-in-C., Portsmouth, 1942-45.

According to information supplied to the Imperial War Museum, no papers survive.

LITTLE, Sir Rudolf Alexander (1895-   )

Director-General, Post Office, 1949-55.

Sir Alexander Little has retained no records or papers.

LIVERPOOL, 2nd E of
Arthur William de Brito Savile (1870-1941)

Governor-General and C.-in-C. (Governor, 1912-17), New Zealand, 1917-20.

The present (5th) Earl of Liverpool, The Grange Farm, Oakham, Leics. LE15 8BN, has a diary written by the 2nd Earl while he was Governor-General of New Zealand. This records brief details of his day-to-day movements. There are no further papers.

LLOYD, 1st B
Sir George Ambrose Lloyd (1879-1941)

M.P. (Con.) Staffordshire West, 1910-18; Eastbourne, 1924-25. Governor, Bombay, 1918-23. High Commissioner, Egypt and Sudan, 1925-29. Secretary of State for the Colonies, and Leader of the House of Lords, 1940-41.

Most of Lloyd's papers are housed at Churchill College, Cambridge. The collection includes personal and literary papers, and records relating to the various aspects of Lloyd's career in politics and public service. Hazlehurst and Woodland, op. cit., pp.92-3, provide further details.

LLOYD, Lieutenant-General Sir Francis (1853-1926)

Military career. Commanded 1st Guards Brigade, 1904-08; Welsh Division, Territorial Forces, 1909-13; London District, 1913-19. Food Commissioner for London and Home Counties, 1919-20.

A collection of papers is preserved in Essex Record Office. The material, including letters, relates to the Egyptian and South African campaigns, and to the 1914-18 war.

LLOYD, Air Chief Marshal Sir Hugh Pughe (1895-   )

Served European War, 1914-18; War of 1939-45. Air Officer Commanding, Malta, 1941-42. Commander, Allied Coastal Air Forces, Mediterranean, 1943-44; Commonwealth Bomber Force, Okinawa, 1944-45. C.-in-C., Air Command Far East, 1947-49. Air Officer C.-in-C., Bomber Command, 1950-53.

It is understood that certain unspecified papers are retained.

LLOYD, Sir Thomas Ingram Kynaston (1896-1968)

Colonial Office service. Secretary, Palestine Commission, 1929-30; West India Royal Commission, 1938-39. Permanent Under-Secretary, Colonial Office, 1947-56.

Lady Lloyd states that her late husband's private diaries and letters have been destroyed.

LOCH, 2nd B
Major-General Edward Douglas Loch (1873-1942)

Army career from 1893. Served Sudan, 1898; South Africa, 1900-02; World War I, 1914-18. Lord-in-Waiting, 1913-14.

A collection of papers (1886-1917), mainly relating to Loch's service in the Sudan, in the Boer War as a divisional signalling officer, and in the European War, has been given to the National Army Museum. World War I papers are preserved at the Imperial War Museum. The outstanding item is Loch's diary for the period 13 August to 6 November 1914, which is a good personal account of the landing in France, the retreat from Mons and the advance to the Aisne. Other papers of the Loch family have been sent by the present Lord Loch to the Scottish Record Office.

LOCKHART, Sir James Haldane Stewart (1858-1937)

Colonial Service. Commissioner, Wei Hai Wei, 1902-21.

A collection of papers is held at the National Library of Scotland. The material includes correspondence, notes, newspaper and magazine cuttings, photographs and printed papers relating to Stewart Lockhart's long career in Hong Kong and China. Apart from the political affairs of China, Hong Kong and Wei Hai Wei, and conditions there, the papers deal with Stewart Lockhart's literary interests. Much of the material is in the Chinese language. Much of the correspondence is with Sir Reginald F. Johnston (1874-1938).

LOCKHART, Sir Robert Hamilton Bruce- (1887-1970)

Head of Special Mission, Russia, 1918; Commercial Secretary, Czechoslovakia, 1919-22. Political Intelligence Department, Foreign Office, 1939-40; Representative to Provisional Czechoslovak Government, London, 1940-41; Deputy Under-Secretary of State, Foreign Office, and Director-General, Political Warfare Executive, 1941-45. Journalist and author.

The diaries and journals of Sir Robert Bruce-Lockhart in the possession of the Beaverbrook Foundation are not available for inspection. Other letters and papers remain with Mr Robin Bruce-Lockhart of Brookside, Ditchling, Sussex. The National Library of Scotland has a MS copy (1932) of *Memoirs of a British Agent*.

LOCKSPEISER, Sir Ben (1891-)

Head of Air Defence Department, Royal Aircraft Establishment, Farnborough, 1937-39. Director-General (formerly Director) of Scientific Research, Ministry of Aircraft Production, 1945. Chief Scientist, Ministry of Supply, 1946-49. Secretary, Committee of Privy Council for Scientific and Industrial Research, 1949-56.

Sir Ben Lockspeiser has retained only a few papers, mainly copies of his lectures and addresses, and a collection of press cuttings and photographs of personal interest.

LOGAN, Sir William Marston (1889-1968)

Colonial Service. Acting Governor, Northern Rhodesia, 1938 and 1941. Governor, Seychelles, 1942-47.

Rhodes House Library holds a copy of 'Colonial Springtime' an unpublished memoir of Logan's colonial career in Kenya, Northern Rhodesia and the Seychelles (1913-47).

LOMAX, Sir John Garnett (1896-)

Commercial Agent, Jerusalem, 1938-40; Commercial Counsellor, Madrid, 1940; Ankara, 1943-46. Minister, Buenos Aires, 1946-49. Ambassador, Bolivia, 1949-56.

Sir John Lomax has in his care certain memoirs, notes and copies of articles which he has had published.

LOMBE, Rear-Admiral Sir Edward Malcolm Evans- (1901-1974)

Naval career. Naval Assistant to 3rd Sea Lord, 1939-42. Commanding Officer, H.M.S. *Glasgow*, 1942-43. Director of Gunnery Division, Admiralty, 1943-44. Chief of Staff, Eastern Fleet, 1944; Pacific Fleet, 1944-46. Deputy Chief of Naval Staff, 1950-53. Commander, Allied Naval Forces in Northern Europe, 1953-55.

Certain papers are retained in the Naval Library, Ministry of Defence.

LONGMORE, Air Chief Marshal Sir Arthur Murray (1885-1970)

Served European War, 1914-19. Air Officer Commanding Inland Area, 1933-34; Coastal Command, 1934-36. Commandant, Imperial Defence College, 1936-38. Air Office C.-in-C., Training Command, 1939; R.A.F. Middle East, 1940-41. Member of Air Mission, Australia and New Zealand, 1939. Inspector-General, R.A.F., 1941.

The Royal Air Force Museum has photocopies of personal papers (1911-70), mainly relating to Longmore's career in the Royal Naval Air Service and the R.A.F. Part of the material covers Middle East affairs (1940-41).

LORAINE, Rear-Admiral Sir Lambton, 11th Bt (1838-1917)

Naval career in nineteenth century.

Diaries and papers (1871-1913) are preserved at the National Maritime Museum.

LORAINE, Sir Percy Lyham, 12th Bt (1880-1961)

High Commissioner, Egypt and Sudan, 1929-33. Ambassador, Turkey, 1933-39; Italy, 1939-40.

Many of the papers are held by the executor, Mr C. A. Sherman, Messrs Dawson & Co., 2 New Square, Lincoln's Inn, London WC2. Eleven volumes of press cuttings (1929-39) are available at the Middle East Centre, St Antony's College, Oxford, and a typescript diary (Aug.-Sep. 1929) is at the Bodleian Library.

LOTHIAN, 11th M of
Philip Henry Kerr (1882-1940)

Chancellor of Duchy of Lancaster, 1931; Parliamentary Under-Secretary, India, 1931-32. Secretary to Prime Minister, 1916-21. Ambassador, United States, 1939-40. Journalist; editor, *Round Table*, 1910-16.

Correspondence and papers are available at the Scottish Record Office. Details are given in Hazlehurst and Woodland, op. cit., pp.84-5. Private Office papers (1939-40) will be made available at the Public Record Office.

LOTHIAN, Sir Arthur Cunningham (1887-1962)

Resident, Jaipur, 1929-31, 1933-34. Special Representative of the Viceroy for Federation discussions with the Indian States, 1935-37. Resident for Rajputana and Chief Commissioner, Ajmer-Merwara, 1937-42; Resident, Hyderabad, 1942-46.

Correspondence and papers at the India Office Library cover varied aspects of Sir Arthur's long connection with the Indian States, and extend to the period of his retirement.

LOWTHER, Sir Gerard Augustus, 1st Bt (1858-1916)

Minister, Chile, 1901-04; Morocco, 1904-08. Ambassador, Turkey, 1908-13.

Press cuttings books are retained by Mrs J. H. G. Black, West Monkton House, Taunton, Somerset. Some correspondence (1908-13) is available at the Public Record Office (F.O. 800/193) and there is further material in the Hardinge papers.

LOYD, Sir Francis Alfred (1916-   )

Colonial Service, Kenya. Commissioner, Swaziland, 1964-68.

The Colonial Records Project found that Sir Francis has kept many papers relating to his career in Kenya and Swaziland, including a number of safari diaries and intelligence reports from the Kenya-Ethiopia border in 1941-42; papers relating to the Kenya-Ethiopia boundary commission (1947); personal papers and some confidential letters and minutes of meetings, etc., concerning Nyanza province (1959-61); the Kenya constitutional conference (1962); the handing over of the country at independence, and other subjects.

LUCAS, Sir Charles Prestwood (1853-1931)

Assistant Under-Secretary, Colonial Office, from 1897. Head of Dominions Department, 1907-11.

Members of the family could not be traced. The Librarian of All Souls College, Oxford, where Lucas was a Fellow, knows of no papers. Some correspondence, however, can be located in the Gell papers (N.R.A. List 5438).

LUCE, Admiral Sir (John) David (1906-1971)

Naval career. Served World War II. Deputy Director, Plans Division, Admiralty, 1948-51. Director of Royal Naval Staff College, 1953-54. Naval Secretary to 1st Lord of the Admiralty, 1954-56. C.-in-C., Far Eastern Station, 1960-62; British Forces in Far East, 1962-63. 1st Sea Lord and Chief of Naval Staff, 1963-66.

According to information supplied to the Imperial War Museum, the Admiral retained no papers.

LUGARD, 1st B
Sir Frederick Dealtry Lugard (1858-1945)

Military and Colonial Service. High Commissioner, Northern Nigeria, 1900-06. Governor, Hong Kong, 1907-12; Northern Nigeria and Southern Nigeria, 1914-19. British Member, League of Nations Mandates Commission, 1922-36.

Rhodes House Library, Oxford, has a collection of correspondence, notebooks, official reports, photographs and maps, relating mainly to service in Burma, Hong Kong and Africa (1858-1919).

LUKE, Sir Harry Charles (1884-1969)

Colonial and Naval Service, British Chief Commissioner, Georgia, Armenia and Azerbaijan, 1920. Chief Secretary, Palestine, 1928-30. Lieutenant-Governor, Malta, 1930-38. Governor, Fiji, and High Commissioner, Western Pacific, 1938-42. Author.

A collection of diaries and papers kept by Sir Harry Luke (1903-59) can be found at the Middle East Centre, St Antony's College, Oxford. These relate mainly to service during World War I, and in Cyprus and Palestine. Correspondence as

Governor of Malta is kept at Rhodes House Library. The material includes letters exchanged with Secretaries of State, former Governors of Malta, and Church dignatories.

LUND, Lieutenant-General Sir Otto Marling (1891-1956)

Military career; commissioned in Royal Artillery, 1911; served World War I. Assistant Military Secretary, Eastern Command, 1923-24. Military Assistant to Chief of Imperial General Staff, 1934-36. Deputy Director of Operations, War Office, Sept. 1939. Major-General, Royal Artillery, Home Forces, 1940-44. Director of Royal Artillery, 1944-46. G.O.C.-in-C., Anti-Aircraft Command, 1946-48.

Mr A. M. Lund, 16 St Martin's Le Grand, London EC1, has a collection of his father's papers, including diaries of campaigns in North Russia and the North West Frontier, and a lot of photographs.

LYALL, Sir Alfred Comyn (1835-1911)

Secretary, Government of India, Home Department, 1873-74; Foreign Department, 1878-80. Lieutenant-Governor, North West Provinces, 1882-87. Member, Council of India, 1888-1903.

The India Office Library holds a collection of papers and correspondence (1842-1914) of Sir Alfred Comyn Lyall, Sir James Broadwood Lyall (1838-1916) and J. E. Lyall (1811-45), all of whom spent their careers in India. The papers of Sir A. C. Lyall include official and private correspondence, diaries, and drafts of articles and books.

LYDFORD, Air Marshal Sir Harold Thomas (1898-   )

Director of Organisation, Air Ministry, 1941. Member of R.A.F. Delegation, Washington, 1942-44. Air Officer Commanding, No. 28 Group, 1944; British Forces in Aden, 1945-48; No. 18 Group, Coastal Command, 1950-52. Air Officer C.-in-C., Home Command, 1952-56.

The Imperial War Museum has, on microfilm, a collection of official and semi-official correspondence, mainly covering the period in Aden. There are also other miscellaneous papers and photographs. These papers are subject to the Thirty Year Rule.

LYNE, Major-General Lewis Owen (1899-1970)

Military career. Commanded 9th Battalion, Lancashire Fusiliers, 1940; 169th Infantry Brigade in Iraq, North Africa, Italy, 1942-44. Commanded 59th Division, 50th (Northumbrian) Division, and 7th Armoured Division in North West Europe. Military Governor, British Zone, Berlin, 1945. Director of Staff Duties, War Office.

The Major-General's papers have been donated to the Imperial War Museum. The collection contains a variety of writings, photographs and published material relating to Lyne's appointments during World War II. An unpublished auto-biography is of particular importance. In this he describes his career in the Army from 1937 and his experience as the first British Military Governor in Berlin after the war.

LYTTELTON, General Sir Neville Gerald (1845-1931)

Military career. Commanded forces in South Africa, 1902-04. Chief of General Staff and 1st Military Member of Army Council, 1904-08. G.O. C.-in-C., Ireland, 1908-12.

A collection of letters, mostly written by Lyttelton to his brother-in-law Major-General Hon. Reginald Talbot during the Boer War (1899-1901), survives at the Liddell Hart Centre for Military Archives. The bulk of Lyttelton's papers are housed in the Library of Westfield College, London. This collection consists chiefly of letters written to or by Sir Neville and his wife. About a third of these are letters written by them to each other (1883-1926), the most important of which were written during the South African War. In addition there are letters to and from members of his own and his wife's family, chiefly of a domestic nature but also containing letters of public relevance. The balance is similar in the main part of the collection, which consists of correspondence between Lady Lyttelton, relatives and friends. Many of these were people of public note.

LYTTON, 2nd E of
Victor Alexander George Robert Lytton (1876-1947)

Civil Lord of the Admiralty 1916, 1919-20. Parliamentary Secretary (Additional) to the Admiralty, 1916-19. Under-Secretary of State for India, 1920-22. Governor of Bengal, 1922-27; Viceroy and Acting Governor-General of India, 10 Apr.-9 Aug. 1925. Chairman, League of Nations Mission to Manchuria, 1932.

Lady Hermione Cobbold, Lake House, Knebworth, Herts., daughter of the 2nd Earl of Lytton, has a large unlisted collection of her father's papers. The principal subjects covered include: women's suffrage, League of Nations, Palestine, education, town and country planning (particularly garden suburbs), and the National Theatre. In addition, the papers relating to Lytton's Indian career have been deposited in the India Office Library. The collection includes correspondence with the Viceroy (1922-27), with the Secretary of State (1921-27) and with King George V (1922-26). Other correspondence in India include Sir George Lloyd, Lord Willingdon and Sir Evan Cotton, and in England Lord Curzon, E. S. Montagu, Sir F. W. Duke and Vt Winterton. A separate series of correspondence relates to the period when Lytton was Acting Viceroy. There are other files of papers on particular subjects, e.g. constitutional reform, terrorism in Bengal (1926) and Tibetan affairs, and a collection of printed papers, pamphlets and official reports.

MACARTNEY, Dr Carlile Aylmer (1895-   )

Consular official. Served Intelligence Department, League of Nations Union, 1928-36; Research Department, Foreign Office, 1939-46. Historian and author.

Some papers relating to his studies of Eastern Europe are deposited at St Antony's College, Oxford. The collection is extensive and includes typed notes and drafts as well as printed material.

McCALL, Admiral Sir Henry William Urquhart (1895-   )

Naval career. Served World War I. Naval Attaché, Buenos Aires, 1938-40. Commanded H.M.S. *Dido*, 1940-42; Chief of Staff to Head of British Admiralty Delegation, Washington, 1943. Commanded H.M.S. *Howe*, 1944-46. Senior British Naval Officer, Middle East, 1946-48. Flag Officer, Destroyers, Mediterranean Fleet, 1949-50. Vice-Admiral Commanding Reserve Fleet, 1950-53.

Certain papers are preserved at the Imperial War Museum.

McCLINTOCK, Admiral Sir Francis Leopold (1819-1907)

Naval career from 1831. Served in four Arctic voyages. C.-in-C., North American and West Indian Stations, 1879-82.

Papers are preserved at the National Maritime Museum, and consist of logs, journals, notebooks, and family correspondence (1830-1900). Much of the material, however, is for the period before *c*. 1875.

McCLOUGHRY, Air Vice-Marshal Edgar James Kingston- (1896-1972)

Served European War, 1914-18. Air Officer Commanding, No. 44 Group, 1942; No. 18 Group, 1947; No. 38 Group, 1950. Head Planner, Air Operations, Allied Expeditionary Air Force, 1943-44 (Overlord). Air Member, C.-in-C., India Reorganisation Committee of Armed Forces, 1945-46. Senior Air Staff Officer, R.A.F. India, 1946; Fighter Command, 1948-50. Chief Air Defence Officer, Ministry of Defence, 1951-53.

A collection of papers (12 boxes) can be found at the Imperial War Museum. Miscellaneous papers relate to service with No. 44 Group, and to the period 1944-45, and there is an Indian diary for the years 1929-33. Daily operations reports (1944) and Intelligence summaries cover work with the A.E.A.F. Other papers include reports, addresses, personal material, copies and drafts of books, articles and lectures, and correspondence relating to historical writings. Some of the material relates to service with Air Chief Marshal Sir Frederick William Bowhill.

McCORMICK, Sir William Symington (1859-1930)

Chairman, University Grants Committee, 1919-30; Advisory Council on Scientific and Industrial Research.

Information available at Somerset House was not helpful in tracing members of the family.

McCRACKEN, Lieutenant-General Sir Frederick William Nicholas (1859-1949)

Army career. Commanded 7th Infantry Brigade, 1912-14; 15th Scottish Division, 1915; Army Corps, 1917-18. C.-in-C., Scottish Command, 1918-19.

A number of diaries covering most of McCracken's career (1882-1922) are in the care of the Berkshire Record Office (N.R.A. List 1284).

McCREERY, General Sir Richard Loudon (1898-1967)

Military career. Served World Wars I and II. Chief of General Staff, Middle East, 1942. Commanded 8th Army in Italy, 1944-45. G.O.C.-in-C., British Occupation Forces in Austria, 1945-46; British Army of the Rhine, 1946-48.

Lady McCreery, Stowell Hill, Templecombe, Somerset, has a collection of papers relating to her late husband. A biography by Major-General J. M. Strawson has been privately published.

MACDONALD, Sir Claude Maxwell (1852-1915)

Minister, China, 1896-1900. Ambassador, Japan, 1900-12.

Information available at Somerset House was not sufficient to trace Sir Claude's papers. A few relevant letters are available in the Hardinge papers.

MACDONALD, Major-General Sir Hector Archibald (1853-1903)

Army career from 1870. Served in Afghan War, 1879-80; Sudan, 1890s; India, 1899; South Africa, 1899-1901. Commanded in Ceylon, 1902-03.

Photocopies of documents relating to Macdonald and the controversy surrounding his court martial and death are available at the National Army Museum. Two dispatch copy books, South Africa and India, July 1900-April 1901, survive in the Scottish United Services Museum.

MACDONALD, Malcolm John (1901-)

M.P. (Lab.) Bassetlaw, 1929-31; (National Lab.) 1931-35; (National) Ross and Cromarty, 1936-45. Parliamentary Under-Secretary, Dominions Office, 1931-35. Secretary of State, Dominion Affairs, 1935-38 and 1938-39; Colonies, 1935 and 1938-40. Minister of Health, 1940-41. High Commissioner, Canada, 1941-46; India, 1955-60; Kenya, 1964-65. Governor-General, Malayan Union and Singapore, 1946; Malaya, Singapore and British Borneo, 1946-48; Kenya (Governor, 1963), 1963-64. British Commissioner-General, South East Asia, 1948-55. British Special Representative in Africa, 1966-69.

Mr MacDonald's papers are not available. Details are given in Hazlehurst and Woodland, op. cit., p.97.

MACDONNELL OF SWINFORD, 1st B
Sir Antony Patrick MacDonnell (1844-1925)

Indian Civil Service. Member of Council of Viceroy of India, 1893-95, 1902. Lieutenant-Governor, North West Province, and Chief Commissioner of Oudh, 1895-1901. Under-Secretary, Ireland, 1902-08. Member of Irish Convention, 1917-18.

A collection of papers is held at the Bodleian Library (MSS. Eng. Hist. a 11-12). There are four main series of papers, with a further assortment of family letters, formal papers and newspaper cuttings. The main collection consists of a large general correspondence; press cuttings; speeches and photographs; papers relating to India; a series on Ireland (c. 1902-20); and letters (1893-1930) to Lady MacDonnell.

MACDONELL, Sir Hugh Guion (1832-1904)

Minister, Brazil, 1885-88; Denmark, 1888-93; Portugal, 1893-1902.

No papers were located.

McDONNELL, Hon. Sir Schomberg Kerr (1861-1915)

Principal Private Secretary to Prime Minister, 1888-1902. Secretary, Office of Works, 1902-12.

A number of interesting papers are held in the care of the Earl of Antrim, Glenarm Castle, Glenarm, Ballymena, Co. Antrim, Northern Ireland.

MACDONOGH, Lieutenant-General Sir George Mark Watson (1865-1942)

Military career from 1884. Director of Military Intelligence, 1916-18. Adjutant-General to the Forces, 1918-22.

Eight files of papers (1916-18) can be found at the Public Record Office (W.O.106/1510-17). Messrs Charles Russell & Co., solicitors of London who acted in the estate, know of no further papers.

MACDOUGALL, Major-General Alastair Ian (1888-1972)

Military career; served World Wars I and II. Commanded Royal Scots Greys, 1928-32; 6th (Midland) Cavalry Brigade, Territorial Army, 1932-34. General Staff, War Office, 1936-39. Area Commander, 1939. District Commander, 1944.

A microfilm of Macdougall's diaries for World Wars I and II is available at the Imperial War Museum.

MACFARLANE, Lieutenant-General Sir (Frank) Noel Mason- (1889-1953)

Military career. Served South Africa; India; World War I. Military Attaché at Budapest, Vienna and Berne, 1931-34; Copenhagen and Berlin, 1937-39. Director of Military Intelligence with British Expeditionary Force, 1939-40. Head of British Military Mission to Moscow, 1942-44. Governor and C.-in-C., Gibraltar, 1942-44. Chief Commissioner, Allied Control Commission for Italy, 1944. M.P. (Lab.) Paddington North, 1945-46.

The Imperial War Museum has a collection of papers. These include diaries kept during service in Mesopotamia and France with the Royal Field Artillery (1915-18); diaries/engagement books for the years 1943, 1944 and 1946; papers kept as Governor of Gibraltar and concerning the appointment as Deputy President of the Allied Control Commission in Italy (1944); a number of letters, mainly dating from the period in Italy; and a collection of miscellaneous papers, press cuttings and drafts of articles (arranged roughly by subject matter) written by Mason-Macfarlane after World War II.

MACGILLIVRAY, Sir Donald Charles (1906-1966)

Colonial Service. Under-Secretary, Palestine, 1946-47. Liaison Officer, United Nations Special Committee, 1947. High Commissioner, Malayan Federation, 1954-58.

Papers at the Middle East Centre, St Antony's College, Oxford include engagement books (1938-45) with some personal papers (1942-49), and papers on the Arab rebellion (1938), the British withdrawal from Palestine (1947-48), and the internationalisation of Jerusalem (1947). A good collection of photographs and press cuttings relating to MacGillivray was gathered by M. G. Power and is to be placed in Rhodes House Library. It appears that papers relating to other aspects of MacGillivray's career have not survived.

MACGREGOR, Sir Evan (1842-1926)

Permanent Secretary, Admiralty, 1884-1907.

Colonel Sir Gregor MacGregor of MacGregor, Bt, 4 Bloomsbury Court, High Holborn, London WC1, states that the family papers and correspondence in his possession include some material relating to Sir Evan MacGregor. The bulk of Sir Evan's papers has not been located.

McHARDY, Major-General Alexander Anderson (1868-1958)

Career in Royal Artillery from 1888. Served North West Frontier, India; South Africa; World War I. Controller of Surplus Stores and Salvage, War Office, 1919-22. Director of Movements and Quarterings, War Office, 1923-27. Major-General in charge of Administration, Southern Command, 1927-30. Colonel Commandant, Royal Artillery, 1934-38. Air Raid Precautions Sub-Controller, 1939-45.

Certain papers relating to McHardy's career are available at the Royal Artillery Institution.

MACHTIG, Sir Eric Gustav (1889-1973)

Permanent Under-Secretary, Dominions Office, later Commonwealth Relations, 1940-48.

The trustees to the estate of Sir Eric Machtig, Messrs Halsey Lightly and Hemsley, in amalgamation with Garrard Wolfe & Co., 1-2 Mill Lane, Guildford, Surrey GU1 3XX, know of certain papers, including correspondence, which survive in private hands.

MACK, Sir William Henry Bradshaw (1894-1974)

Assistant Under-Secretary, Foreign Office. Deputy Commissioner (Civil), Allied Commission for Austria, 1944. U.K. Political Representative in Austria and Political Adviser, 1945; Minister, Austria, 1947-48. Ambassador, Iraq, 1948-51; Argentine Republic, 1951-54.

Sir Henry stated that he had no letters, diaries or papers which would be of any interest.

MACKERETH, Sir Gilbert (1893-1962)

Consul-General, Addis Ababa, 1940. Political Adviser to C.-in-C., and Consul-General, Batavia, 1946-47. Ambassador, Colombia, 1947-53.

Sir Gilbert kept no papers connected with his career.

MACKINDER, Sir Halford John (1861-1947)

M.P. (Lib. Un.; later Con.) Glasgow Camlachie (Jan.) 1910-22. High Commissioner, South Russia, 1919-20. Geographer. Director, London School of Economics.

The various records relating to Sir Halford Mackinder are described in *Sir Halford Mackinder, 1861-1947: Some New Perspectives* by Brian W. Blouet (School of Geography, University of Oxford. Research Paper 13). The School of Geography at Oxford holds the principal collection of Mackinder papers known to survive. This material includes autobiographical fragments, maps, photographs, pamphlets, etc. and papers relating to the first ascent of Mount Kenya (1899). The Kenya diaries are at the Rhodes House Library, Oxford and Mackinder's correspondence concerning the Russian intervention are at the Public Record Office (FO 800/251). Professor Blouet provides details of other papers.

McLEAN, Lieutenant-General Sir Kenneth Graeme (1896-   )

Served War of 1939-45. Assistant Secretary, Committee of Imperial Defence, from 1938. Military Secretary to Secretary for War, 1949-57.

One or two papers only (1943) are held in the Imperial War Museum. Sir Kenneth has no further papers.

MACLEAR, Admiral John Pearse (1838-1907)

Naval career from 1851. Served with Survey Service, 1870s and 1880s.

Papers are retained at the National Maritime Museum, and relate to Maclear's naval career in the nineteenth century. The papers consist of eleven volumes of journals, out-letter books and work books, relating to his service in Survey Ships (1872-87).

MACLEAY, Sir (James William) Ronald (1870-1943)

Diplomatic Service. Minister, Argentine, 1919-22; China, 1922-26; Czechoslovakia, 1927-29. Ambassador, Argentine, 1930-33.

Messrs Lawrence, Graham & Co., solicitors, believe that the late Lady Macleay disposed of all private papers, diaries, etc., soon after her husband's death.

MACLEISH, Commander A. A. F.

Naval career, with active service during World War I.

A collection of diaries and letters, covering the period 1914-15, and particularly relating to the Gallipoli campaign, is preserved at Churchill College, Cambridge.

MACLEOD, Sir James MacIver (1866-1944)

Vice-Consul, later Consul, Fez, 1907-17. Consul-General, Chile, 1919-23; Tunis, 1923-30.

The collection at the Public Record Office (P.R.O. 30/26/85) includes correspondence with Sir Ernest Satow, and notes of persons and subjects concerned with Morocco (1895-1929, 1937).

MACLEOD OF MACLEOD, Sir Reginald (1847-1935)

Registrar-General for England and Wales, 1900-02. Permanent Under-Secretary, Scotland, 1902-08.

Mrs Joan Wolrige-Gordon, Sir Reginald's granddaughter, states that family papers are held in Dunvegan Castle, Isle of Skye. Enquiries may be directed to N.R.A. (Scotland).

McLEOD, General Sir Roderick William (1905-   )

Military career. Commanded Special Air Services Brigade, 1944-45. Director of Military Operations, India, 1945-46; London, 1951-54. G.O.C., 6th Armoured Division, 1955-56. Deputy Chief of Defence Staff, 1957-60. Commander, British Forces in Hong Kong, 1960-61. G.O. C.-in-C., Eastern Command, 1962-64.

A collection of papers has been placed in the care of the Special Air Services Regimental Headquarters.

MACMAHON, James (1865-1954)

Under-Secretary to Lord-Lieutenant, Ireland, 1918-22.

No papers were located.

MACMICHAEL, Sir Harold Alfred (1882-1969)

Sudan political service. Governor, Tanganyika, 1933-37. High Commissioner, Palestine and Transjordan, 1938-44. Special Representative, Malaya, 1945.

A large collection of papers is held in the Library of Durham University, and copies of relevant material can be found at Rhodes House Library and the Middle East Centre, St Antony's College, Oxford. The papers and correspondence relate to service in the Sudan, Tanganyika, Palestine, Malaya and Malta (1946). Volumes of press cuttings have also been copied by the Middle East Centre.

MACMILLAN OF MACMILLAN, General Sir Gordon Holmes Alexander (1897-   )

Military career. Served in France, 1916-18. General Staff Officer 2, War Office and Eastern Command, 1937-40; General Staff Officer 1, 1940-41. Commands, 1940-45. G.O.C., Palestine, 1947-48. G.O.C.-in-C., Scottish Command, and Governor of Edinburgh Castle, 1949-52. Governor and C.-in-C., Gibraltar, 1952-55.

A microfilm of papers relating to MacMillan's service in North Africa, Sicily and Palestine (1941-47) is available at the Imperial War Museum.

MACMUNN, Lieutenant-General Sir George Fletcher (1869-1952)

Military career from 1888. Served in Burma, India, South Africa; European War, 1914-18. C.-in-C., Mesopotamia, 1919-20. Quartermaster-General, India, 1920-24.

Mr P. A. Williams, D.S.C., the Warden of Sackville College, East Grinstead, and the sole executor to Lady MacMunn's estate, knows of no papers.

MACNAB, Brigadier Sir Geoffrey Alex Colin (1899-   )

Military career. Military Attaché, Prague and Bucharest, 1938-40; Rome, 1947-49; Paris, 1949-54. Served War of 1939-45. Western Desert, Greece, Crete; Military Mission to Hungary, 1945. Director of Military Intelligence, Middle East, 1945-47. Secretary, Government Hospitality Fund, 1957-68.

Sir Geoffrey has always kept diaries and has a number of photobooks with press cuttings, together with papers and letters for the period 1938-68.

McNAIR, 1st B
Sir Arnold Duncan McNair (1885-1975)

Secretary, Advisory Board of Coal Controller, 1917-19; Coal Industry (Sankey) Commission, 1919. Chairman, Committee on Supply and Training of Teachers, 1942-44; Palestine Jewish Education Commission, 1945. British Member, Permanent Court of Arbitration, The Hague, 1945-65. President, International Court of Justice, 1952-55; European Court of Human Rights, 1959-65.

Lord McNair stated that he had no diaries and few press cuttings, and that it had been his practice to destroy as many papers as possible.

MACONACHIE, Sir Richard Roy (1885-1962)

Indian Civil Service. Minister, Afghanistan, 1930-35. Controller (Home Division), British Broadcasting Corporation, 1941-45.

Lady Maconachie was unable to provide any information regarding papers.

MACPHERSON, Sir John Stuart (1898-1971)

Colonial Service. Chief Secretary, Palestine, 1939-43. Head, British Colonies Supply Mission, Washington, and Member of Anglo-American Caribbean Commission, 1943-45. Governor-General (Governor, 1948-54), Nigeria, 1954-55. Permanent Under-Secretary, Colonial Office, 1956-59.

It is understood that Sir J. S. Macpherson did keep some papers. However, this information was not confirmed by the executors.

MACREADY, General Sir (Cecil Frederick) Nevil, 1st Bt (1862-1946)

Military career: Egypt; South Africa, 1899-1902; European War, 1914-16. Director of Personal Services, 1910-14. Adjutant-General, British Expeditionary Force, 1914-16. Adjutant-General to the Forces, 1916-18. Commissioner of Metropolitan Police, 1918-20. G.O. C.-in-C., Ireland, 1920-22.

It is understood that General Macready destroyed his papers after completing his autobiography *Annals of an Active Life* (1924). Relevant correspondence is available in the Asquith and Lloyd George papers.

MACREADY, Lieutenant-General Sir Gordon Nevil, 2nd Bt (1891-1956)

Military career. Served World War I. Assistant Adjutant and Quartermaster-General, Supreme War Council, Versailles, 1918-19. Assistant Secretary, Committee of Imperial Defence, 1926-32. Deputy Director of Staff Duties, War Office, 1936-38. Assistant Chief of Imperial General Staff, 1940-42. Chief of British Army Staff at Washington, 1942. Regional Commissioner for Lower Saxony, 1946-47. Economic Adviser to U.K. High Commissioner in Germany, 1949-51.

Most of the General's papers were lost at sea on the *Empress of Britain*. Some later papers may survive with the family, and enquiries should be addressed to Sir Nevil Macready, Bt, Flat 4, 61 Rutland Gate, London SW7.

MADDEN, Admiral Sir Alexander Cumming Gordon (1895-1964)

Naval career, War of 1939-45. Deputy Controller of the Navy and Director of Naval Equipment, 1946-48. Flag Officer Commanding 5th Cruiser Squadron and Flag Officer 2nd-in-Command, Far East Station, 1948-50. Lord Commissioner of the Admiralty, 2nd Sea Lord and Chief of Naval Personnel, 1950-53. C.-in-C., Plymouth, 1953-55.

Major J. C. P. Madden, O.B.E., T.D., has none of his brother's papers.

MADDEN, Archibald Maclean (1864-1928)

Consular Service. Consul, Casablanca, 1907-14; Bilbao, from 1914. Served Foreign Office, 1923-25.

A collection of family papers, scrapbooks, photographs, press cuttings and letters includes some material on Moroccan affairs. A. M. Madden was a central figure in the Agadir incident.

MADDEN, Admiral of the Fleet Sir Charles Edward, 1st Bt (1862-1935)

Naval career. 4th Sea Lord, 1910-11. Commanded 3rd and 2nd Cruiser Squadrons in Home Fleet, 1912-14. Chief of Staff to C.-in-C., Grand Fleet, 1914-16; 2nd-in-Command, Grand Fleet, 1917-19. C.-in-C., Atlantic Fleet, 1919-22. 1st Sea Lord and Chief of Naval Staff, 1927-30.

Nineteen volumes of diaries, covering Madden's service with the Grand Fleet during World War I, are preserved in the National Maritime Museum.

MAGOWAN, Sir John Hall (1893-1951)

Consul, Mainz (Saar and Bavaria), 1924-29. Chargé d'Affaires and Consul, Haiti, 1929-31. Commercial Secretary and then Counsellor, Washington, 1931-34; Berlin, 1935-37 and 1937-39. Minister, Commercial Adviser, Washington, 1942-48. Ambassador, Venezuela, 1948-51.

Mr J. I. Magowan understands that his brother lost all his personal belongings, including papers, when he left Berlin in haste in 1939. No surviving private papers of more than family interest are known to either Mr J. I. Magowan or Mr W. A. Magowan, Sir John's son.

MAHON, General Sir Bryan Thomas (1862-1930)

Military career, India; Egypt and Sudan; South Africa. Commander, Salonika, 1915-16. C.-in-C., Ireland, 1916-18. Senator, Irish Free State, from 1922.

Mrs P. I. Pease (niece) was unable to help the survey. No other member of the family was located.

MALCOLM, Sir Dougal Orme (1877-1955)

Private Secretary to Lord Selborne (South Africa), 1905-10; Lord Grey (Canada), 1910-11. Chairman, Committee on Education and Industry (Board of Trade and Ministry of Labour), 1926-28. Director, British South Africa Company (President, 1937).

Two volumes of correspondence (1903-13) between Malcolm and the 5th Earl of Onslow can be found at All Souls College, Oxford. A few papers only, concerning South African affairs (1906), are held in Rhodes House Library. There is extensive correspondence in the P. L. Gell papers (see NRA List 5438).

MALCOLM, Major-General Sir Neill (1869-1953)

Military career. Served India, South Africa, etc; World War I; British Military Mission, Berlin, 1919-21. G.O.C., Malaya, 1921-24. High Commissioner for German Refugees, 1936-38.

Papers preserved in the Library of St Antony's College, Oxford, relate to Sir Neill's period with the Allied Commission in the Rhineland (c. 1919). The material includes MSS. and typescript copies of a diary kept from April to August and September to December 1919, and from March to September 1920; press cuttings, account books, examples of German propaganda, typescript articles, etc.; papers relating to the Peace Conference; semi-official correspondence (c. 1919); reports on the situation in Germany, etc. Also included is certain correspondence (e.g. of the period 1935-37). Rhodes House Library, Oxford, has two volumes of a diary relating to the Uganda Mutiny (1897-99).

MALKIN, Sir (Herbert) William (1883-1945)

Legal Adviser, Foreign Office, 1929-45.

Sir William did not keep a diary and retained no private papers.

MALLABY, Sir (Howard) George Charles (1902-   )

Served Military Secretariat, War Cabinet, 1942-45. Assistant Secretary, Ministry of Defence, 1946-48. Secretary-General, Brussels Treaty Defence Organisation, 1948-50. Under-Secretary, Cabinet Office, 1950-54. Secretary, War Council and Council of Ministers, Kenya, 1954. Deputy Secretary, University Grants Committee, 1955-57. High Commissioner, New Zealand, 1957-59. 1st Civil Service Commissioner, 1959-64.

Sir George has retained no papers relating to his career.

MALLESON, Major-General Sir (J.) Wilfred (1866-1946)

Indian Army from 1904. Served General Staff. Inspector-General of Communications, British East Africa, 1914-15; Commander, 1915-16. Served Special Mission, Belgian Congo, 1915. Head of Military Mission, Turkestan, 1918-20.

Lt.-Cdr. Vivian Malleson, Thorne Lodge, Thorne, Yeovil, Somerset, states that most of his father's papers were destroyed.

MALLET, Sir Bernard (1859-1932)

Commissioner of Inland Revenue, 1897-1909. Registrar-General, 1909-20.

A collection of papers survives with Mr Philip Mallet, c/o Foreign and Commonwealth Office, London SW1. The material relates to aspects of Sir Bernard's career, and includes papers on the incidence of taxation and calculation of the national income (1899-1906); the National Registration of 1915 and the subsequent maintenance of the Register; staffing of government offices (1917-19); the General Register Office (1914-17); and population estimates (1917-19). There is also a diary (1894-1906) and a number of printed pamphlets. A second series of records consists of the papers of Sir Bernard's wife, Marie Constance Mallet, mostly relating to her appointments as Maid of Honour and Extra Woman of the Bedchamber to Queen Victoria (1897-1900).

MALLET, Sir Claude Coventry (1860-1941)

Chargé d'Affaires, Lima, 1894; Quito, 1894-95; Bogotá, 1902-03. Minister, Panama and Costa Rica, 1908-19; Argentine Republic, 1919-20, 1922; Uruguay, 1919-25.

A substantial collection of papers concerning the career of Sir Claude Mallet exists in the possession of his daughter, Mrs Dita Mallet, of Mallet Court, Curry Mallet, near Taunton, Somerset. The collection is contained in several large trunks at present unsorted. An unpublished incomplete biography of Sir Claude Mallet (partly reminiscences written by Sir Claude, partly details written by the daughter) is also in the possession of Mrs Dita Mallet.

MALLET, Sir Louis du Pan (1864-1936)

Private Secretary, Sir Edward Grey, 1905-07. Assistant Under-Secretary, Foreign Office, 1907-13. Ambassador, Turkey, 1913-14.

A few papers held by Mr Philip Mallet, c/o Foreign and Commonwealth Office, relate mainly to Sir Louis's period as Ambassador at Constantinople (1913-14). These include copies of Foreign Office telegrams (1913-14) and of correspondence with Sir Edward Grey and Sir Arthur Nicolson; also official letters from various public figures. Among other materials are diary notes and notes of conversations (1916-19), notes taken at the Paris Peace Conference, letters (1914-32) from Sir Walter Tyrrell and an assortment of private correspondence, printed matter and official papers.

MALLET, Sir Victor Alexander Louis (1893-1969)

Minister, Stockholm, 1940-45. Ambassador, Spain, 1945-46; Italy, 1947-53.

A collection of papers is retained by Sir Victor's son, Mr Philip Mallet, c/o Foreign and Commonwealth Office. The records include some correspondence; papers relating to Tehran (1933-35) and to Sweden; notes for speeches; press cuttings and unpublished memoirs.

MALTBY, Air Vice-Marshal Sir Paul Copeland (1892-1971)

Served India, 1911-14, 1919-24; European War. Royal Flying Corps. Air Officer Commanding, R.A.F. Mediterranean, 1935-38; No. 24 (Training) Group, 1938-40; No. 71 (A.C.) Group, 1940-41; R.A.F. Java, 1942. Sergeant-at-Arms, House of Lords, 1946-62.

The R.A.F. Museum has a collection of records, including diaries, log books, letters, files and reports (1914-62). The material relates mainly to service in France (1914-18), Malaya and the Netherlands East Indies (1941-42); and to prisoners of war in the Far East (1942-45).

MANCE, Brigadier-General Sir H. Osborne (1875-1966)

Director of Railways, Light Railways and Roads, War Office, 1916-20. Transport-ation Adviser to British Delegation, Paris, 1919-20. Director of Canals, Ministry of War Transport, 1941-44. Technical Adviser to Ottoman Bank, 1924-62.

Certain papers preserved at the Middle East Centre, St Antony's College, Oxford, relate to the Ottoman Bank's dealings throughout the Middle East, and concern railways, trade agreements, oil, mines, etc. (1911-60). At the Public Record Office a collection (P.R.O. 30/66) relates to his Army career; to his subsequent advisory work for the British Government on communications; and to his service on League of Nations committees and conventions dealing with transport problems (1899-1924).

MANSERGH, Vice-Admiral Sir (Cecil) Aubrey Lawson (1898-   )

Naval career. Served World War I. Commanded H.M.N.Z.S. *Achilles*, 1942; H.M.N.Z.S. *Leander*, 1943. Commodore 1st Class, Admiralty, 1944-46. Vice-Controller of Navy and Director of Naval Equipment, 1948-50. Commanded 2nd Cruiser Squadron, 1950-52. President, Royal Naval College, 1952-54.

A collection of papers is preserved at the Imperial War Museum.

MANSERGH, General Sir (Eric Carden) Robert (1900-1970)

Military career. C.-in-C., Allied Forces, Netherlands East Indies, 1946. Military Secretary, 1948-49. Deputy C.-in-C. and C.-in-C., Allied Forces Northern Europe, 1951-53. C.-in-C., U.K. Land Forces, 1956-59.

Books and pamphlets have been given to the Royal Artillery Museum, Woolwich. The General kept no diaries or letters.

MARCHANT, William Sydney (1894-1953)

Colonial Service, East Africa. Resident Commissioner, British Solomon Islands, 1939-43. Chief Native Commissioner, Kenya, 1943-47. Labour Adviser to Overseas Food Corporation, 1947-50.

There is a collection of papers, press cuttings, etc., at Rhodes House Library. These relate to service in the Solomon Islands (1942-43), military administration in Tripolitania and the Solomon Islands (1941-43), and service in Kenya (1925, 1946-47).

MARKER, Lieutenant-Colonel Raymond John (d. 1914)

Army career; active service in Ceylon, South Africa, and World War I. A.D.C. to Lord Curzon, Viceroy of India, 1898-1900. Military Secretary to Lord Kitchener, 1902-14.

Correspondence and documents relating to Marker are available at the National Army Museum. The collection largely consists of letters written to his sister, Gertie. A collection at the British Library (Add. MSS. 52276-52278) consists largely of correspondence between Kitchener and Marker, together with related material and general correspondence (1898-1912).

MARKHAM, Admiral Sir Albert Hastings (1841-1918)

Naval career from 1856. 2nd-in-Command, Mediterranean Squadron, 1892-94. C.-in-C., The Nore, 1901-04.

A collection of papers is preserved at the National Maritime Museum. It consists of 22 volumes and loose papers, and includes personal correspondence from family, colleagues and superiors; and official and private papers, particularly relating to his Polar expeditions. Certain Admiralty papers are also available at the Public Record Office (Adm. 205).

MARKHAM, Sir Henry Vaughan (1897-1946)

Civil Service career. Permanent Secretary, Admiralty, 1940-46.

Rev. Canon J. V. Markham, Three Elms, Bossingham, Canterbury, Kent, states that he has very few of his late brother's papers. The surviving material consists of letters of congratulation and condolence, and obituary notices.

MARLING, Sir Charles Murray (1862-1933)

Consular and Diplomatic Service. Minister, Persia, 1915-19; Denmark, 1919-21; Netherlands, 1921-26. British Delegate (and President), Plebiscite Commission, Schleswig, 1920.

Sir John Marling, Bt, Woodcray Manor Farm, Wokingham, Berks., states that he has in his care a number of papers relating to his father. There is a little correspondence in the Hardinge papers at Cambridge University Library.

MARRACK, Rear-Admiral Hugh Richard (1888-1972)

Naval career. Submarine service, with commands during World War I. Commanded Portland Submarine Flotilla, 1929-31; China Submarine Flotilla, 1931-33; H.M.S. *Carlisle*, 1934-37. Commodore in charge and Superintendent, Sheerness, 1939-43. Commodore Superintendent, Gibraltar, 1943-45.

The Imperial War Museum has certain papers relating to Marrack's career. These relate to the Shanghai incident (1932); a visit to Tristan da Cunha in 1937; and to submarines.

MARSH, Sir Edward Howard (1872-1953)

Private Secretary to W. S. Churchill, 1917-22, and 1924-29; to the Duke of Devonshire, 1922-24; to J. H. Thomas, 1924 and 1929-36; and to Malcolm MacDonald 1936-37.

There are over 5000 letters to Marsh, from poets, novelists, writers and artists, and from theatrical, musical, political and social personalities, in the Berg Collection at New York Public Library.

MARSHALL, Lieutenant-General Sir William Raine (1865-1939)

Military career. Served India, South Africa, World War I. G.O.C.-in-C. Mesopotamia Expeditionary Force, 1917-19; Southern Command, India, 1919-23.

164

A collection of Marshall's letters to his brother (1915-19), whilst he was holding commands at Gallipoli, Salonika and in Mesopotamia, is housed in the Liddell Hart Centre for Military Archives.

MARTEL, Lieutenant-General Sir Giffard Le Quesne (1889-1958)

Military career. Served India, South Africa, World War I. G.O.C.-in-C., Meso-Office, 1936-38; Deputy Director, 1938-39. Command of Royal Armoured Corps, 1940. Head of Military Mission at Moscow, 1943.
A large collection of correspondence and papers (1914-58) is held at the Imperial War Museum. Other papers survive among the Liddell Hart collection at the Liddell Hart Centre for Military Archives.

MARTIN, Sir John Miller (1904-   )

Home and Colonial Civil Service. Secretary, Palestine Royal Commission, 1936. Private (later Principal Private Secretary) to Prime Minister Winston Churchill, 1940-45. Assistant (later Deputy) Under Secretary, Colonial Office, 1945-65.

Sir John has retained a collection of papers, mainly consisting of letters home written in the 1930s. The material has been promised to Churchill College, Cambridge.

MARWOOD, Sir William Francis (1863-1935)

Permanent Secretary, Board of Trade, 1916-19; Ministry of Transport, 1921-23.

Information available at Somerset House was not helpful in tracing the papers.

MASON, Vice-Admiral Sir Frank Trowbridge (1900-   )

Naval career. Chief Gunnery Engineer Officer and Deputy Director of Naval Ordnance, 1947-48. Engineer-in-Chief of the Fleet, 1953-57.

According to information at the Imperial War Museum, Sir Frank has no war papers but retains an amount of personal correspondence.

MASON, Sir Paul (1904-   )

Minister, Bulgaria, 1949-51. Assistant Under-Secretary, Foreign Office, 1951-54. Ambassador, Netherlands, 1954-60. British Representative, North Atlantic Council, 1960-62; United Nations Disarmament Conference, Geneva, 1962-64.

Sir Paul Mason states that he kept no diary, copies of letters, or papers relating to his official career.

MASSINGBERD, Field-Marshal Sir Archibald Armar Montgomery- (1871-1947)

Military career. Served South Africa; World War I. Deputy Chief of General Staff, India, 1920-22. G.O.C.-in-C., Southern Command, 1928-31. Adjutant-General to the Forces, 1931-33. Chief of Imperial General Staff, 1933-36.

A collection of papers (1891-1944) and an unpublished autobiography have been deposited with the Liddell Hart Centre for Military Archives.

MAUDE, Sir (Evelyn) John (1883-1963)

Permanent Secretary, Ministry of Health, 1940-45. Deputy Chairman, Local Government Boundary Commission, from 1945.

Mr E. W. Maude states that his father kept no diary or correspondence, and that there are no private papers relating to Sir John Maude's career.

MAUDE, Lieutenant-General Sir (Frederick) Stanley (1864-1917)

Military career from 1884. Served Sudan; South Africa, 1899-1901; European War, 1914-18. Private Secretary to Secretary of State for War, 1905. Chief of General Staff, 5th Division, 1912-14. Commander, 33rd Division, 1915; 13th Division; Tigris Army Corps, 1916. C.-in-C., Mesopotamia, 1916.

It has not been possible to contact members of the family.

MAURICE, Major-General Sir Frederick (Barton) (1871-1951)

Army career from 1892; Served South Africa. Director of Military Operations, Imperial General Staff, 1915-18. Principal, Working Men's College, 1922-23; Queen Mary College, University of London, 1933-44.

The Liddell Hart Centre for Military Archives has a collection of correspondence and papers, including some relating to the Maurice case and the debate in the Commons (May 1918). The collection also includes papers of Maurice's father, Major-General Sir John Frederick Maurice, and a few early family papers. *The Maurice Case* edited by Nancy Maurice and based on the papers was published in 1972.

MAXSE, General Sir Frederick Ivor (1862-1958)

Military career, Sudan, 1897-99; South Africa, 1899-1900; European War, 1914-18. Inspector-General of Training, British Armies in France, 1918-19. G.O. C.-in-C., Northern Command, 1919-23.

The General's private papers are deposited, under seal for fifty years, in the West Sussex Record Office. Files of papers relating to World War I are preserved at the Imperial War Museum. These consist of official and private notes, documents, photographs and published works relating to Maxse's career (1901-19). The subject matter includes training and manoeuvres, operations in Belgium and France, and with the Army of Occupation on the Rhine.

MAXWELL, Sir Alexander (1880-1963)

Chairman of Prison Commission, England and Wales, 1928-32. Permanent Under-Secretary, Home Office, 1938-48.

The Rev. R. R. Maxwell, 24 Tyler Hill Road, Blean, Canterbury, Kent CT2 9HT, states that his father left no diaries and few press cuttings. However, there are in the Rev. Maxwell's care some private papers relating to lectures given by Sir Alexander Maxwell on penal reform, the work of the Home Office and kindred subjects.

MAXWELL, Brigadier Laurence Edward Lockhart (1901-1973)

Army career, with service in India (Indian Cavalry, 1921-40; 1st Indian Armoured Division, 1940-41).

Five volumes of a manuscript journal (1920-41), covering Maxwell's service in India, are available at the National Army Museum. In addition to recording his own sports and activities he also comments on political and military developments of the time.

MAXWELL, Brigadier-General Laurence Lockhart (1869-1954)

Army career, with service in India (2nd Bengal Lancers, 1894-1918), South African War and World War I.

Letters and papers relating to Maxwell's service in the 2nd Bengal Lancers, covering his service in Waziristan, South Africa, and during World War I, are in the care of the National Army Museum.

MAXWELL, Sir (William) George (1871-1959)

Magisterial and judicial service, Malayan States and Straits Settlements. Chief Secretary, Federated Malay States, 1920-26.

Rhodes House Library, Oxford, has a collection of correspondence and memoranda regarding the introduction in the Federated Malay States of a policy of decentralisation (1958-59); also a variety of cuttings, many from Malayan newspapers, and other papers. A collection of papers, relating mainly to the period after Sir George's retirement and to the subject of Malayan independence, is held with the records of the British Association of Malaya in the Royal Commonwealth Society Library.

MAY, Sir Francis Henry (1860-1922)

Governor, Fiji (High Commissioner, Western Pacific), 1910-12; Hong Kong, 1912-19.

Rhodes House Library has some correspondence, mainly with Sir Charles Eliot in connection with the appointment of a Vice-Chancellor to Hong Kong University in 1918, and with Sir Claud Severn who was acting Governor of Hong Kong in 1919.

MAY, Admiral of the Fleet Sir William Henry (1849-1930)

Naval career from 1863. Served Arctic Expedition, 1875-76. Naval Attaché, Europe, 1891-93. Director of Naval Ordnance and Torpedoes, 1901. Controller of the Navy, 1901-05. C.-in-C., Atlantic, 1905-07. 2nd Sea Lord, 1907-09. Commanded Home Fleet, 1909-11. C.-in-C., Plymouth, 1911-13.

A collection of material is preserved at the National Maritime Museum, and covers much of May's career. The material includes ships' logs (1873-90); photographs and charts; papers relating to Arctic expeditions (1875-76); papers relating to Admiralty policy (1903-09); tactical reports (1908-13); and material relating to the Dardanelles Commission (1917). Other relevant correspondence is in the Corbett papers.

MAY, Lieutenant-Colonel Sir William Rupert (1893-1962)

Indian Political Department. Resident, Waziristan, 1940-41; Persian Gulf, 1941-42, 1946-53. Served Baluchistan, 1942-46.

The Middle East Centre at St Antony's College, Oxford, has a collection of papers relating to the affairs of the Persian Gulf, the North West Frontier and Baluchistan (1920-53). The collection includes a series of May's personal diaries (1916-36, 1954, 1956); detailed notes on events in Mesopotamia in 1917-20; correspondence with Sir Arnold Wilson; a note on a tour of the Trucial States (1942); and copies of May's articles.

MAYBURY, Brigadier-General Sir Henry Percy (1864-1943)

Military career. Director-General of Roads, Ministry of Transport, 1919-28. Consulting Engineer and Adviser to Minister of Transport, 1928-32.

Mrs P. F. Maybury, Summer Court, Strandway, Felpham, Sussex, Sir Henry Maybury's daughter-in-law, has several large boxes of press cuttings and other literature relating to Sir Henry Maybury.

MAYERS, Norman (1895-   )

Levant Consular Service. Minister, El Salvador, 1945-48. Consul-General, São Paulo, 1948-51. Ambassador, Ecuador, 1951-55.

Mr Mayers has retained some correspondence, cuttings and scrapbooks. These have been promised to St Antony's College, Oxford.

MEIKLEJOHN, Sir Roderick Sinclair (1876-1962)

Private Secretary to Sir E. Hamilton, 1903-04; to the Duke of Devonshire, 1904-05; to H. H. Asquith, 1905-11. Deputy Controller of Supply Services, Treasury. 1st Civil Service Commissioner, 1928-39.

Major N. J. Stewart-Meiklejohn, Sir Roderick's nephew, knows of no papers. Neither he nor Sir Roderick's solicitors are in touch with the executors of the estate. It was not possible to trace these executors.

MELLISS, Major-General C. J. (1862-1936)

Army career.

A collection of papers is available at the National Army Museum. This includes some correspondence and printed material, and notes on various campaigns, e.g. East Africa (March-July 1896); Ashanti War (1899); an expedition with the Somaliland Field Force (Nov. 1902-May 1903); and the Kut campaign (1915).

MESSERVY, General Sir Frank Walter (1893-1974)

Military career. Served World War I. G.O.C.-in-C., Malaya Command, 1945; Northern Command, India, 1946-47. C.-in-C., Pakistan, 1947.

Papers survive at the Liddell Hart Centre for Military Archives. The collection includes miscellaneous publications and narratives produced by units, Ministry of Information and the Indian War Department, relating to SEAC and CMF in World War II.

MESTON, 1st B
James Scorgie Meston (1865-1943)

Financial Secretary, Government of India, 1906-12. Lieutenant-Governor, United Provinces of Agra and Oudh, 1912-18.

A collection of papers (1906-36) can be found at the India Office Library. The collection includes correspondence with the Viceroy (1916-17), correspondence as Lieutenant-Governor, and files of correspondence with (*inter alia*) Sir Guy Fleetwood Wilson, Lionel Curtis and P. H. Kerr (Lord Lothian). Subject files relate to currency problems; work in the United Provinces; India's services during the war; and Indian constitutional reforms after 1917. There are also printed volumes of speeches and proceedings of the Council of the Lieutenant-Governor of the United Provinces. Additional material may be found in the Hardinge papers at Cambridge University Library.

METHUEN, 3rd B
Field-Marshal Paul Sanford Methuen (1845-1932)

Military career from 1864. Military Attaché, Berlin, 1877-81. Served Ireland, Egypt, South Africa. C.-in-C., Eastern Command, 1903-08. G.O. C.-in-C., South Africa, 1908-09. Governor, Natal, 1909-15; Malta, 1915-19.

A collection of papers survives in the care of the Hon. A. J. Methuen, Corsham Court, Wilts. SN13 0BZ. The material is not open for inspection.

MEUX, Admiral of the Fleet Hon. Sir Hedworth (1856-1929)

Naval career from 1870. C.-in-C., China Station, 1908-10; Portsmouth, 1912-16. M.P. (Con.) Portsmouth, 1916-18.

The Lambton family archives (at the Lambton Estate Office, Lambton Park, Chester-le-Street, Co. Durham) have a few papers only relating to Meux. These consist of a few letters written by Meux to his brother, the 3rd Earl of Durham.

MEYRICK, Admiral Sir Sidney Julius (1879-1973)

Naval career from 1893. Served World War I. Director of Training and Staff Duties, Admiralty, 1926-27. Naval Secretary to 1st Lord of the Admiralty, 1932-34. Commanded 2nd Cruiser Squadron, 1934-36. C.-in-C., America and West Indies Station, 1937-40.

It is believed that no papers have survived.

MICHELL, Sir Robert Carminowe (1876-1956)

Consular and Diplomatic Service. Chargé d'Affaires and Consul-General, Ecuador, 1921-26. Minister, Bolivia, 1926-30; Uruguay, 1930-33. Ambassador, Chile, 1933-37.

A collection of papers relating to Sir R. C. Michell survives in the care of Mr J. F. Michell, Pembroke Lodge, Hindhead, Surrey.

MIDDLETON, Sir John (1870-1954)

Colonial Service. Governor, Falkland Islands, 1920-27; Gambia, 1927-28; Newfoundland, 1928-32.

Messrs Lindsays, solicitors and executors to Sir John's estate, have been in touch with his sister and last surviving relative. No private papers are known to survive.

MILES, Admiral Sir Geoffrey John Audley (1890-)

Naval career. Served with submarines and destroyers, World War I. Head of Military Mission to Moscow, 1941-43. Flag Officer Commanding Western Mediterranean, 1944-45. C.-in-C., Royal Indian Navy, 1946-47.

It is understood that the Admiral has decided to bequeath his papers to the National Maritime Museum. Details are not available.

MILES, Lieutenant-General Sir Herbert Scott Gould (1850-1926)

Director of Recruiting and Organisation, 1904. Quartermaster-General to the Forces, 1908-12. Governor and C.-in-C., Gibraltar 1913-18.

A representative of Messrs Devonshire & Co., solicitors, remembers dealing with Lady Miles's estate but knows of no papers.

MILFORD HAVEN, 1st M of
Admiral of the Fleet Louis Alexander Mountbatten,
Prince Louis of Battenberg (1854-1921)

Naval career from 1868. Director of Naval Intelligence, 1902-05. Commanded 2nd

Cruiser Squadron, 1905-07. C.-in-C., Atlantic Fleet, 1908-10. Commanded 3rd and 4th Divisions, Home Fleet, 1911. 2nd Sea Lord, 1911-12. 1st Sea Lord, 1912-14.

The papers of the 1st Marquess of Milford Haven are the property of the Broadlands Archives Trust, Broadlands, Romsey, Hants. A microfilm of the papers is preserved at the Imperial War Museum. Although the papers cover his entire naval career, the bulk of the collection relates to his work as 2nd Sea Lord and 1st Sea Lord, and to his resignation from this post in 1914.

MILLER, Vice-Admiral Charles Blois (1867-1926)

Naval career from 1880. Active service in World War I, including Battle of Jutland.

Certain papers are retained at the National Maritime Museum, including logs (1882-1903).

MILLER, Rear Admiral Hugh (1880-1972)

Naval career. Served World Wars I and II. Secretary to Admiral of the Fleet Lord Wemyss.

A microfilm of an important collection of papers covering Miller's naval service (1898-1945), including his unpublished memoirs and a diary for 1914-15, is available at the Imperial War Museum.

MILNE, 1st B
Field-Marshal Sir George Francis Milne (1866-1948)

Army career from 1884. Served Sudan; South Africa; World War I. Commanded British Salonika Force and Army of Black Sea. G.O. C.-in-C., Eastern Command, 1923-26. Chief of Imperial General Staff, 1926-33.

Papers survive in the care of the present (2nd) Lord Milne, 33 Lonsdale Road, Barnes, London SW13. They mainly include documents concerning the Macedonian theatre in World War I and secret correspondence on general subjects whilst he was C.I.G.S.

MILNE, Admiral Sir (Archibald) Berkeley, 2nd Bt (1855-1938)

Naval career from 1869. Commanded 2nd Division, Home Fleet, 1908-10. C.-in-C., Mediterranean, 1912-14.

A collection of papers relating to Milne's career is available at the National Maritime Museum. It includes journals and log books relating to his work from c. 1870-1914; copies of telegrams from the Admiralty (July-Aug. 1914); a diary of events; press cuttings; and miscellaneous personal papers (mainly pre-1914) and a collection of personal letters (1914-33).

MILNE, Sir David (1896-1972)

Permanent Under-Secretary, Scottish Office, 1946-59.

Mr C. D. Milne, A.R.I.B.A., 4 Murrayfield Gardens, Edinburgh EH12 6DF, states that his father, Sir David, left few private papers which would be of historical interest. Such papers as remain are of a personal nature and are not available for any purpose.

MILNER, 1st Vt
Sir Alfred Milner (1854-1925)

Chairman, Board of Inland Revenue, 1892-97. Governor, Cape Colony, 1897-1907; Transvaal and Orange Free State, 1901-05. High Commissioner, South Africa, 1897-1905. Minister without Portfolio, 1916-18. Secretary of State for War, 1918-19; Colonies, 1919-21.

The bulk of Milner's papers were bequeathed to New College, Oxford, and are housed in the Bodleian Library, Oxford. Further papers are deposited in the Public Record Office (P.R.O. 30/30, F.O. 848). Details of these collections can be found in Hazlehurst and Woodland, op. cit., pp.104-6. Five letters written by Lord Milner to his A.D.C., Captain F. J. Henley (1914), are available in the National Army Museum.

MILVERTON, 1st B
Sir Arthur Frederick Richards (1885-   )

Malayan Civil Service, Governor, North Borneo, 1930-33; Gambia, 1933-36; Fiji (and High Commissioner, Western Pacific), 1936-38; Jamaica (Captain-General), 1938-43; Nigeria, 1943-47.

A tape recording and transcript of an interview given by Lord Milverton in 1969, relating to his career in colonial administration, are held in Rhodes House Library. Lord Milverton has kept no papers.

MILWARD, Major-General Sir Clement Arthur (1877-1951)

Military career. Served India; European War, 1914-18; Mesopotamia. Brigade Commander, Khyber Pass, 1927-30. Commander, Lucknow District, 1934-38.

A collection of papers and diaries can be found at the National Army Museum.

MINTO, 4th E of
Gilbert John Murray Kynynmond Elliot (1847-1914)

Governor-General, Canada, 1898-1904. Viceroy of India, 1905-10.

A large collection of papers survives at the National Library of Scotland. The material has been listed in some detail, and copies of much of the collection are available in the Public Archives of Canada. The main series of papers consists of royal correspondence, speeches made in Canada, semi-official letters and private letters (Canada), particular subject files and memoranda of conversations.

MITCHELL, Admiral Francis Herbert (1876-1946)

Naval career from 1889. Served World War I (Gallipoli, etc.; Egypt). Rear-Admiral in 2nd Battle Squadron, Atlantic Fleet, 1925-26. Admiral Superintendent, Malta Dockyard, 1928-31.

Copies of letters written by Mitchell to his wife and mother during the Dardanelles campaign and after (1915-18) are available at the British Library (Add. MSS. 52537).

MITCHELL, Major-General Sir Philip Euen (1890-1964)

Colonial Service. Political Adviser to General Sir Archibald Wavell, 1941. British Plenipotentiary in Ethiopia and Chief Political Officer to G.O. C.-in-C., East Africa, 1942. Governor, Fiji (High Commissioner, Western Pacific), 1942-44; Kenya, 1944-52.

Rhodes House Library has a 24-volume collection of diaries (1927-44, 1953-59) relating to service in Tanganyika (1927-34), Uganda and the Western Pacific.

MOBERLY, Sir Walter Hamilton (1881-1974)

Vice-Chancellor, Manchester University, 1926-34. Chairman, University Grants Committee, 1935-49.

Certain family papers, including a very few relating to Sir Walter, have been placed in the Bodleian Library, Oxford.

MOLESWORTH, Lieutenant-General George Noble (1890-1968)

Army career. Director of Military Operations and Intelligence, India, 1936-38. Deputy Chief of General Staff, Army Headquarters, India, 1941-42. Secretary of Military Department, India Office, 1943-44.

A collection of Molesworth's papers is deposited in the National Army Museum. The material includes scrapbooks compiled by Molesworth, reports and correspondence, chiefly relating to the war in the Far East (early 1940s). Some of the material relates to Field-Marshal Auchinleck.

MONCKTON OF BRENCHLEY, 1st Vt
Sir Walter Turner Monckton (1891-1965)

Director-General, Press and Censorship Bureau, 1939-40; Ministry of Information, 1940-41; British Propaganda and Information Services, Cairo, 1941-42. Solicitor-General, 1945. United Kingdom delegate, Allied Reparation Committee, Moscow, 1945. M.P. (Con.) Bristol West, 1951-57. Minister of Labour and National Service, 1951-55; Minister of Defence, 1955-56. Paymaster-General, 1956-57.

Papers are held at the Bodleian Library.

MONCRIEFF, Sir Colin Campbell Scott- (1836-1916)

Under-Secretary, Scottish Office, 1892-1902.

Mr John R. Ingram, 39 Murrayfield Road, Edinburgh EH12 6EU, a great-grandnephew of Sir Colin, knows of no papers left by Sir Colin, but he has in his possession a *Life of Sir Colin Scott-Moncrieff*, by Mary Albright Hollings, privately printed in 1917. The Project's letter of enquiry to Messrs Scott-Moncrieff & Trail, solicitors of Edinburgh, founded by Sir Colin's brother, was passed on to Mr Ingram. No other member of the family was contacted.

MONEY, Major-General Sir Arthur Wigram (1866-1951)

Military career: Royal Artillery from 1885. Served India, South Africa, etc., and with Egyptian Expeditionary Force, 1915-19.

A collection of papers remains in the care of the Major-General's son, Mr J. H. Money, 65 Charters Close, London SE19.

MONKBRETTON, 2nd B
John William Dodson (1869-1933)

Diplomatic Service. Principal Private Secretary to Colonial Secretary, 1900-03.

A large collection of family papers is housed at the Bodleian Library, Oxford. The material relating to the 2nd Baron includes diaries (1904-30); private correspondence (1887-1918) with family, friends and colleagues, including Joseph

Chamberlain and Lord Morley; diplomatic service papers (1894-99) relating to periods in Paris, Constantinople and the Middle East; miscellaneous correspondence (1893-1930); Foreign Office and Colonial Office correspondence (1895-1904); papers relating to South Africa (1896-1902) and the war there; papers relating to Joseph Chamberlain's South African tour (1902-03); papers on tariff reform (1902-08); several files on colonial affairs; London County Council papers (1924-32); and miscellaneous personal papers and scrapbooks.

MONRO, General Sir Charles Carmichael, 1st Bt (1860-1929)

C.-in-C., India, 1916-20. Governor and C.-in-C., Gibraltar, 1923-28.

The collection at the India Office Library comprises letters, papers, newspaper cuttings, scrapbooks and photographs, dating from *c.* 1900 to 1946. The correspondence is mainly concerned with the military situation in 1917, and the other material includes cuttings relating to Monro's marriage and death, and scrapbooks compiled by Lady Monro.

Certain other documents are available at the National Army Museum. These include bound MS. notebooks, 'things to be done' (1917 and 1918); and a bound scrapbook concerning an appeal for Red Cross funds run by Lady Monro (1917).

MONSON, Sir Edmund John, 1st Bt (1834-1909)

Ambassador, Belgium, 1892; Austria, 1893-96; France, 1896-1904.

A large collection of Monson papers is held at the Lincolnshire Archives Office. Most of the material relating to Sir Edmund John Monson, Bt, is early family correspondence, covering periods spent in Hungary and Uruguay during the nineteenth century. More recent family papers are believed to survive with the present (11th) Baron Monson, The Manor House, South Carlton, near Lincoln.

MONSON, Sir Edmund St John Debonnaire John, 3rd Bt (1883-1969)

Minister, Colombia, 1926-29; Mexico, 1929-34; Baltic States, 1935-37; Sweden, 1938-39.

Messrs Boxall & Boxall, solicitors, 3 South Square, Gray's Inn, London WC1R 5HX, state that their former client left in the custody of his bank a great mass of private correspondence.

MONTAGU OF BEAULIEU, 2nd B
Brigadier-General Hon. John Walter Edward Douglas-Scott-Montagu (1866-1929)

M.P. (Con.) New Forest, 1892-1905. Attained rank of Brigadier-General, World War I. Adviser on Mechanical Transport Services to Government of India, 1915-19.

The Liddell Hart Centre for Military Archives has a collection of correspondence, speeches and memoranda, relating to air policy in World War I, and photographs and notes on India and mechanical transport (1916-21).

MONTEATH, Sir David Taylor (1887-1961)

Assistant Secretary, India Office, 1931-37. Secretary, Burma Round Table Conference, 1931. Assistant Under-Secretary, Burma, 1937-41. Permanent Under-Secretary, India and Burma, 1941-47; Burma, 1947.

A Private Office collection (D. 714) at the India Office Library includes some material relating to Monteath. Lady Monteath retains none of her late husband's papers, apart from a few personal letters written on the occasion of an official visit to Burma in 1937.

MONTGOMERY OF ALAMEIN, 1st Vt
Field-Marshal Sir Bernard Law Montgomery (1887-)

Military career. Served World Wars I and II. Commanded 8th Army, 1942-44 (North Africa, Sicily, Italy). C.-in-C., British Group of Armies and Allied Armies, North France, 1944. C.-in-C., British Army on the Rhine, and British Member of Allied Control Commission, Germany, 1945-46. Chief of the Imperial General Staff, 1946-48. Chairman of Western European Commanders-in-Chief Committee, 1948-51. Deputy Supreme Allied Commander, Europe, 1951-58.

Viscount Montgomery of Alamein has kept his private papers, but these are not available for inspection. Plans for future preservation are not known.

MONTGOMERY, Sir (Charles) Hubert (1876-1942)

Foreign Office and Diplomatic Service. Assistant Private Secretary to Prime Minister, Sir H. Campbell-Bannerman, 1908. Deputy Under-Secretary, Foreign Office, from 1930. Minister, Netherlands, 1933-38.

Messrs Walker Martineau & Co., solicitors, 10-11 Gray's Inn Square, London WC1R 5JL, are no longer in touch with members of the family. A little relevant material is available in the Plunkett and Hardinge papers.

MOORE, Admiral Sir Arthur (1847-1934)

Naval career from 1860. Member of Australian Defence Committee, 1890-91. Sea Lord, 1898-1901. C.-in-C., Cape of Good Hope and West Coast of Africa, 1901-04. 2nd-in-Command, Channel Fleet, 1904-05. C.-in-C., China, 1906-08; Portsmouth, 1911-12.

A small collection of material, including a copy of a privately published book, and papers relating to Moore's service in the China Station (1906-08), are held by the National Maritime Museum. Additional material is to be found in Liverpool Public Library.

MOORE, Sir Henry Monck-Mason (1887-1964)

Colonial Service. Served European War, 1914-18. Governor, Sierra Leone, 1934-37; Kenya, 1939-44; Ceylon, 1944-48 (Governor-General, 1948-49). Assistant (later Deputy) Under-Secretary, Colonial Office, 1937-39.

Lady Moore, 409 Grosvenor Square, Rondebosch, Cape Town, South Africa, states that she has given to the Oxford Colonial Records Project a collection of papers, including letters written by her late husband and diaries which she herself wrote. These papers are not generally open for inspection.

MOORE, Admiral Sir Henry Ruthven (1886-)

Naval career from 1902. Naval Assistant Secretary to Committee of Imperial Defence, 1921-24. Assistant Secretary, British Delegation to Washington Disarmament Conference, 1921-22, and at Geneva, 1927. Deputy Director (later Director), Plans Division, Admiralty, 1930-33. Chief of Staff to C.-in-C., Portsmouth, 1938-39. Rear-Admiral Commanding 3rd Cruiser Squadron, 1939-40. Assistant Chief of Naval Staff (Trade), 1940-41. Vice Chief of Naval Staff, 1941-43. C.-in-C., Home Fleet, 1944-45. Head of British Naval Mission, Washington, 1945-48. C.-in-C., The Nore, 1948-50.   The Admiral has retained many of his papers.

MORANT, Sir Robert Laurie (1863-1920)

Permanent Secretary, Board of Education, 1903-11. Chairman, Insurance Commission, 1912-19. 1st Secretary, Ministry of Health, 1919-20.

Information derived from Somerset House was not helpful in tracing the family. A little relevant material is available in the Marvin collection (N.R.A. List 12562) and in the Lloyd George papers.

MORGAN, Admiral Sir Vaughan (1891-1969)

Naval career. Served World War I. Flag Lieutenant to Sir Roger Keyes, 1918, and Earl Jellicoe, 1919. 2nd Naval Member, Navy Board, New Zealand, 1934-36. Commanded 5th Destroyer Flotilla, 1937-39. Chief Staff Officer, Dover, 1939-41. Captain of H.M.S. *Revenge*, 1941. Director of Signal Division, Admiralty, 1943-45. Admiral-Superintendent, H.M. Dockyard, Portsmouth, 1945-49.

Certain papers are in the care of the Imperial War Museum. These include a diary, with a large number of photographs, kept during Morgan's Empire Mission of 1919-20; papers relating to the evacuation from Dunkirk; and public and private writings on naval and other matters.

MORGAN, General Sir William Duthie (1891-)

Military career. Served World War I; Waziristan, 1922-23. Military Attaché, Budapest, 1929-31. Served in France, 1939-40. Chief of General Staff, Home Forces, 1942-43. G.O. C.-in-C., Southern Command, 1944. Chief of Staff to Supreme Allied Commander, Mediterranean, 1945. Supreme Allied Commander, Mediterranean, 1945-47. Commander, British Army Staff, Washington, 1947-50.

Five essays written by Sir William Morgan are preserved at the Imperial War Museum. These record, *inter alia*, his personal contacts with Viscount Alanbrooke and Earl Alexander of Tunis, and describe the retreat from Dunkirk in 1940. Morgan also comments on relations between Churchill and commanders in the field.

MORRIS, Thomas Joseph (1876-1953)

Minister, Cuba, 1925-31; Bolivia, 1934-37. Consul-General, Strasbourg, 1931-34.

It has not yet been possible to contact Mrs Morris, or other members of the family.

MORTON, Major Sir Desmond John Falkiner (1891-1971)

Principal Assistant Secretary, Ministry of Economic Warfare, 1939. Personal Assistant to Prime Minister, 1940-46. United Kingdom delegate, Inter-Allied Reparation Agency.

A collection of Sir Desmond's papers is to be lodged in the Public Record Office. Details are not available.

MOUNSEY, Sir George Augustus (1879-1966)

Diplomatic Service. Assistant Under-Secretary, Foreign Office, 1929-39. Secretary, Ministry of Economic Warfare, 1939-40.

A collection of papers has survived in private hands. The material consists mainly of diaries, interspersed with letters and press cuttings, for the years 1914-19, when Mounsey was First Secretary at the Rome embassy. It is hoped to place the papers in a suitable repository and enquiries may be directed to the N.R.A.

MOUNTBATTEN OF BURMA, 1st E

Admiral of the Fleet Louis Francis Albert Victor Nicholas Mountbatten (1900-   )

Naval career from 1913. Commanded H.M.S. *Kelly*, and 5th Destroyer Flotilla, 1939-41; H.M.S. *Illustrious*, 1941. Adviser on Combined Operations, 1941-42. Supreme Allied Commander, South East Asia, 1943-46. Viceroy of India, Mar.-Aug. 1947. Governor-General, India, 1947-48. Flag-Officer Commanding 1st Cruiser Squadron, Mediterranean Fleet, 1948-49. 4th Sea Lord, 1950-52. C.-in-C., Mediterranean, and Allied Forces, Mediterranean, 1952-54. 1st Sea Lord, 1955-59. Chief of U.K. Defence Staff and Chairman of Chiefs of Staff Committee, 1959-65.

The papers are owned by the Broadlands Archives Trust, Broadlands, Romsey, Hants. Enquiries should be addressed to the Archivist.

MOWATT, Sir Francis (1837-1919)

Permanent Secretary, Treasury, 1894-1903.

There was no trace of persons mentioned in the Will. Some correspondence may be found in the Balfour papers. (Hazlehurst and Woodland, *op. cit.* pp. 9-11).

MUDIE, Sir Robert Francis (1890-   )

Secretary, Round Table Conference, 1930-31. Governor, Sind, 1946-47; West Punjab, 1947-49. Head, (British) Economic Mission to Yugoslavia, 1951-54.

The papers (1927-48) at the India Office Library cover many aspects of Sir R. F. Mudie's career. The material includes correspondence, notes, official circulars, and printed papers and reports. Subjects covered include debt legislation (1930s), the Cabinet Delegation (1945), the affairs of West Punjab and the establishment of Pakistan. Principal correspondents include Lord Mountbatten, M. A. Jinnah and Sir Maurice Hallett.

MÜLLER, Sir William Grenfell Max- (1867-1945)

Foreign Office and Diplomatic Service. Minister, Poland, 1920-28.

A considerable volume of documents covering the career of Sir W. G. Max-Müller survives with his son, Mr J. H. Max-Müller, 3 Whitehall Court, Flat 151, London SW1A 2EP. The papers consist of diaries, and correspondence between Sir William, his father and mother, and his wife. In addition, there is correspondence with various politicians and officials.

MURRAY, General Sir Archibald James (1860-1945)

Military career from 1879. Director of Military Training, 1907-12. Inspector of Infantry, 1912-14. Chief of Imperial General Staff, 1915. G.O.C. 1st Class, Egypt, 1916-17. G.O. C.-in-C., Aldershot, 1917-19.

Three volumes of correspondence (1916-17) between Murray and General Sir William Robertson, Chief of the Imperial General Staff, are preserved at the British Library (Add. MSS. 52461-52463). Four folders (1914-18) can be found in the Public Record Office (W.O. 79/69-72).

Some papers remain with the General's grandson, Major A. R. Murray, 1 Horseshoe Cottages, Greywell, Basingstoke, Hants. These concern the South African War; Murray's dismissal in January 1915; and his Egyptian Command (1916). There is a volume of correspondence with Robertson (1916-17) and four, very sparsely annotated, War Office diaries.

MURRAY, Sir (George) Evelyn Pemberton (1880-1947)

Secretary, Post Office, 1914-34. Chairman, Board of Customs and Excise, 1934-40.

Certain papers may survive with the Hon. Simon Maxwell, 85 Dovehouse Street, London SW3.

MURRAY, Sir George Herbert (1849-1936)

Private Secretary to Prime Ministers W. E. Gladstone and Lord Rosebery. Chairman, Board of Inland Revenue, 1897-99. Secretary, Post Office, 1899-1903. Permanent Secretary, Treasury, 1903-11.

The Hon. Simon Maxwell, 85 Dovehouse Street, London SW3, has a dispatch box and a collection of letters which belonged to Sir G. H. Murray. The material was collected together by Mrs Irene Roberts, his grandmother, who was Sir George's daughter and Sir Evelyn Murray's sister. A letter book, relating to appointments and including letters from W. E. Gladstone and H. H. Asquith, survives with the Hon. Mrs A. Campbell-Preston, Blair Castle, Blair Atholl, Perthshire. Additional material may be found in the Asquith papers (at the Bodleian Library) and in the Rendel MSS at the National Library of Wales.

MURRAY, John (1883-1937)

Foreign Office and Egyptian Civil Service. Minister, Mexico, 1935-37.

Information available at Somerset House was not helpful in tracing members of the family, or other executors.

MURRAY, Sir Oswyn Alexander Ruthven (1873-1936)

Permanent Secretary, Admiralty, 1917-36.

Mr M. P. Murray states that a collection of his father's papers has survived. They are in the care of his sister, Mrs Priscilla Bergne, Annery Cottage, Wonersh, Guildford, Surrey, and they were used by his mother for her biography *The Making of a Civil Servant* (1940). The papers include letters from various people to Lady Murray giving recollections of Murray's work and career, and there are one or two rough drafts of memoranda, including one on proposals of the May Committee for economies in the naval estimates. The unfinished manuscript of a book by Sir O. A. R. Murray on Admiralty history and administration can be found at the National Maritime Museum.

NALDER, Major-General Reginald Francis Heaton (1895-   )

Military service, European War, 1914-18; India; War Office; War of 1939-45. Chief Signal Officer, Allied Armies in Italy, 1943-45, and Allied Forces Headquarters, 1945. Signal Officer-in-Chief, India, 1946-47.

Major-General Nalder has given all papers which he considered might have some historical interest to the Royal Signals Museum, School of Signals, Blandford Camp, Dorset.

NAPIER, Hon Sir Albert Edward Alexander (1881-1973)

Clerk of the Crown in Chancery and Permanent Secretary to the Lord Chancellor, 1944-54.

Lady Napier has found no papers relating to her late husband's career which she thinks would be of any national interest. Her late husband did not keep a diary. Further papers, now in the Lord Chancellor's Office, will be transferred to the Public Record Office.

NAPIER, Brigadier Arthur F. S. (1890-1971)

Military career. Served European War, 1914-18. Member of Ordnance Board, 1938. Military Adviser, Ministry of Supply, from 1940.

The Imperial War Museum has Napier's diaries covering service in France (1914-15), and as Military Adviser to the Minister of Supply (1940-45). There are also some inter-war diaries and photographs covering service in India.

NATHAN, Lieutenant-Colonel Sir Matthew (1862-1939)

Secretary, Colonial Defence Committee, 1895-1900. Governor, Gold Coast, 1900-03; Hong Kong, 1903-07; Natal, 1907-09; Queensland, 1920-26. Secretary, Post Office, 1909-11. Chairman, Board of Inland Revenue, 1911-14. Under-Secretary to Lord-Lieutenant of Ireland, 1914-16. Secretary, Ministry of Pensions, 1916-19. Chairman, Special Grants Committee, 1919.

A large collection of papers has survived. The material is mainly arranged chronologically in sections, according to stages in Nathan's career. Those papers relating to colonial affairs are kept at Rhodes House Library, and the others are in the Bodleian Library, Oxford. In the three general series there are diaries for the years 1881-1939; notebooks (1876-1939); and private correspondence (1868-1939). The rest of the collection consists of letters, notes and papers relating to the Royal Engineers' School, Chatham (1880-84); the Sudan Expedition (1884-85); the Lushai Expedition (1889-94); the Royal Engineers (1894-95); the Colonial Defence Committee (1896-98); Sierra Leone, Gold Coast, Hong Kong and Natal (1899-1909); the Post Office (1909-11); the Pacific Cable Board (1910-15); the Board of Inland Revenue (1911-14); the Royal Commission on the Civil Service (1912); the Committee on Crown Employment (1912-13); the Committee on Civil Employment of Ex-Soldiers (1914-19); Ireland; London defences (1916); pensions (1916-19); the Special Grants Committee (1917-20); Queensland (1920-25); the Committee on Geophysical Surveys (1927-28); Ceylon Constitutional Committee (1927-28); the Civil Research Committee and the Great Barrier Reef Expedition (1925-28); the City of Westminster Health Society (1921-30); the Irrigation Research Committee (1928-30); and further miscellaneous subjects.

NATION, Brigadier-General John James Henry (1874-1946)

Military career, from 1895. Served World War I. Assistant Adjutant-General, War Office, 1921-27. Military Attaché, Rome, 1927-31. M.P. (Con.) Hull East, 1931-35. Member of Overseas Settlement Board, 1936-37. Zone Commander, Home Guard, 1940-42.

A small collection of papers has been placed in the care of the Imperial War Museum. The material includes a minute from Sir Douglas Haig to the Adjutant-General concerning the best date for opening the Somme offensive (1916).

NEAME, Lieutenant-General Sir Philip (1888-   )

Military career from 1908. Served European War, 1914-18; India. Deputy Chief of General Staff, British Expeditionary Force, France, 1939-40. Commander 4th Indian Division, Western Desert, 1940. G.O.C., Palestine, Transjordan, Cyprus,

1940. G.O.C.-in-C. and Military Governor, Cyrenaica, 1941. Lieutenant-Governor and C.-in-C., Guernsey, 1945-53.

Sir Philip has kept no papers, but his autobiography *Playing with Strife* was published in 1947.

NEEDHAM, Major-General Henry (1876-1965)

Military career. Served World War I. Military Attaché, Brussels, 1922-26; Paris, 1927-31. Commander, Bombay, 1931-35. Chief of Mission to Belgian Army, 1939-40.

The General's daughter, Miss L. M. Needham, 86 Swan Court, London SW3, has a number of scrapbooks, particularly relating to the Archangel expedition.

NELSON, Sir Frank (1883-1966)

M.P. (Con.) Stroud, 1924-31. Vice-Consul, Basle, 1939. Chief of Special Operations Executive, 1940-42. Air Commodore, Air Intelligence, Washington and Germany, 1942-46.

Lady Nelson, 20 Norham Gardens, Oxford, states that most of her late husband's papers were destroyed, and that only a few items remain with her. These include a few photographs and press cuttings relating to Sir Frank's parliamentary career and some letters concerning his appointments at Basle and to S.O.E. There is nothing of a confidential nature.

NEVILLE, Major-General Sir Robert Arthur Ross (1896-   )

Military service, European War, 1914-18; War of 1939-45. Assistant Director of Naval Intelligence, Admiralty. Served Combined Operations, and in Mediterranean. Governor and C.-in-C., Bahamas, 1950-53.

Sir Robert has a fairly detailed record of his time in the Services. This relates mainly to personal matters. Papers of historical interest will be passed in due course to the Royal Marines Museum.

NEWALL, 1st B
Marshal of the Royal Air Force Sir Cyril Louis Norton Newall (1886-1963)

Served European War, 1914-19. Director of Operations and Intelligence and Deputy Chief of Air Staff, 1926-31. Air Officer Commanding, Wessex Bombing Area, 1931; R.A.F. Middle East, 1931-34. Air Member for Supply and Organisation, 1935-37. Chief of Air Staff, 1937-40. Governor General and C.-in-C., New Zealand, 1941-46.

A collection of papers is held at the Royal Air Force Museum. The papers consist of a series of correspondence, reports, photographs and awards for the period 1918-56, and a few further letters (1940-49).

NEWMAN, Sir George (1870-1948)

Chief Medical Officer, Ministry of Health, 1919-35; and Board of Education, 1907-35. Chairman, Health of Munition Workers Committee. Member, Central Control Board (Liquor Traffic), 1915-19; Inter-Departmental Committees on Play-grounds, Reformatories, Tuberculosis, Medical Research, etc.

Papers have survived in three places. The important Newman diaries (1907-46) and letters can be found at the Library of the Ministry of Health. A small collection dealing mostly with the later part of Newman's life is at the Wellcome Historical Medical Library, and papers of a mainly personal nature are held at the Hereford Record Office. These last papers include a few letters, newspaper cuttings, notes compiled for a proposed autobiography, and notes for a proposed biography.

NEWSAM, Sir Frank Aubrey (1893-1964)

Permanent Under-Secretary, Home Office, 1948-57.

Messrs Lloyds Bank (Trustee) have no information regarding papers and have lost contact with members of the family.

NEWTON, Sir Basil Cochrane (1889-1965)

Minister, Czechoslovakia, 1937-39. Ambassador, Iraq, 1939-41. Served Foreign Office, 1942-46.

Major-General T. C. Newton has no papers relating to his late brother.

NEWTON, Major-General Thomas Cochrane (1885-)

Served Indian Army; European War, 1914-18. Commandant, School of Anti-Aircraft Defence, 1935-39.

Major-General Newton has few papers, apart from a number of letters to his wife from India in the late 1920s and 1930s.

NEYLAN, Sir Daniel (1866-1943)

Permanent Secretary, Ministry of Munitions, 1920-21. Joint Secretary, Disposal and Liquidation Commission, and Secretary, Surplus Stores, etc., Liquidation Department, Treasury.

Mrs Mary G. Neylan has a box of her father-in-law's papers. These remain unsorted. Enquiries may be directed to Mrs Neylan's solicitors, McKenna & Co., 12 Whitehall, London SW1A 2DZ.

NICHOLS, Sir Philip Bouverie Bowyer (1894-1962)

Ambassador, Czechoslovakia, 1942-47; Netherlands, 1948-51.

Mr Francis Nichols, of Lawford Hall, Manningtree, Essex, has retained certain unopened boxes, believed to contain material relating to his father's service in Czechoslovakia and Holland.

NICHOLSON, 1st B
Field-Marshal Lord William Gustavus Nicholson (1845-1918)

Military career. Afghan War, 1878-80; Egypt, 1882; Burma, 1886-87. Adjutant-General, India, 1898-99. Military Secretary to C.-in-C., South Africa, 1899-1900. Director-General of Mobilisation and Military Intelligence, War Office, 1901-04. Military Attaché, Japanese Army, 1904-05. Quartermaster-General, 1905-07. Chief of Imperial General Staff, 1908-12.

Messrs Pollock & Co., who were solicitors to Lady Nicholson, know of no papers. Members of the family could not be traced. A useful collection of correspondence with Professor Spenser Wilkinson is in the Army Museums Ogilby Trust.

NICHOLSON, General Sir Cameron Gordon Graham (1898-   )

Military career. Served World War I. Commands during World War II. Director of Artillery, War Office, 1946. G.O.C.-in-C., West Africa, 1948-51; Western Command, 1951-53. C.-in-C., Middle East Land Forces, 1953. Adjutant-General to the Forces, 1953-56.

Certain personal accounts written by the General are available on microfilm at the Imperial War Museum. They include an account of Villeselve (1918, the last successful cavalry charge); the operations of 'Sickle Force' in the Andalsnes episode of 1940, and of the 'Nick Force' (Feb. 1943); and the link-up between the 8th and 1st Armies for the final battle of Tunis (May 1943).

NICHOLSON, Sir Walter Frederic (1876-1946)

Secretary, Air Ministry, 1920-31.

Information in the Will and Act of Probate was not helpful in tracing members of the family.

NICOLSON, Hon. Sir Harold George (1886-1968)

Foreign Office and Diplomatic Service, 1919-29. M.P. (Nat. Lab.) Leicester West, 1935-45. Parliamentary Secretary, Ministry of Information, 1940-41. Journalist and author.

The diaries (1930-64) are held in the Library at Balliol College, Oxford. Volumes for the post-1945 period are closed until 1980. Copyright belongs to William Collins (Publishers), and a search fee is charged to consult the diaries. Letters to V. Sackville-West (his wife) and other personal papers are held at Sissinghurst Castle, Kent. Application to view these papers should be made to Mr Nigel Nicolson at that address.

NIEMEYER, Sir Otto Ernst (1883-1971)

Assistant Secretary, Treasury, from 1919. Controller of Finance, 1922-27. Member of Financial Committee, League of Nations, 1922-37. Banker. Director, Bank of England.

A collection of papers can be found in the Treasury Private Office Class (T. 176) at the Public Record Office. Two indexed volumes of papers relate to monetary policy (1920-29) and the Bank Rate (1923-30), and the material includes correspondence with Sir George Schuster in the Sudan (1922-27), and notes on reparation. Other volumes deal with Allied debts, taxation, the gold standard, imperial economic conferences, financial agreement with the Irish Free State, and the Royal Commission on Indian Currency (1925-27).

NOBLE, Sir Andrew Napier, 2nd Bt (1904-   )

Assistant Under-Secretary, Foreign Office, 1949. Minister, Finland, 1951-54. Ambassador, Poland, 1954-56; Mexico, 1956-60; Netherlands, 1960-64.

Sir Andrew Noble retains papers of family interest only.

NOBLE, Admiral Sir Percy Lockhart Harnam (1880-1955)

Naval career from 1894. Served Grand Fleet, 1914-19. Director of Operations Division, Admiralty Naval Staff, 1928-30. Director of Naval Equipment, 1931-32.

Commander 2nd Cruiser Squadron, 1932-34. 4th Sea Lord, 1935-37. C.-in-C., China Station, 1938-40; Western Approaches, 1941-42. Head of British Naval Delegation, Washington, 1942-44.

Cdr. Rt Hon. Sir Allan Noble, Sir Percy's son, believes that his father left no papers.

NOEL, Admiral of the Fleet Sir Gerard Henry Uctred (1845-1918)

Naval career. Commanded Home Fleet, and Admiral Superintendent, Naval Reserves, 1900-03. C.-in-C., China Station, 1904-06; The Nore, 1907-08. Admiral of the Fleet, 1908-15.

A collection of papers is available at the National Maritime Museum, which includes letters received by Noel (from his family, colleagues and superiors); a few routine service papers; diaries, with brief entries (1880-1918); and copies of pamphlets and lectures written by him on various specialist subjects.

NORMAN, 1st B
Sir Montagu Collet Norman (1871-1950)

Governor, Bank of England, 1920-44.

Lady Norman, Aubrey Lodge, Aubrey Road, London W8, retains a collection of her late husband's papers, including personal letters and diaries, printed material and papers relating to the biographies written about Lord Norman. The Bank of England still holds Lord Norman's diaries as Governor, and Mr Mark Norman of Moor Place, Much Hadham, Herts., has some diaries of the South African War, scrapbooks, press cuttings, and household accounts. All these papers are closed, except for serious research with the consent of Lady Norman or Mr Mark Norman.

NORMAN, Brigadier-General Claude Lumsden (1876-1967)

Military career. Served North West Frontier, 1897-98; East Africa, 1903-04; World War I.

The Imperial War Museum has in its care Norman's diaries (1896-1918), mainly covering service in India and Mesopotamia.

NORMANBROOK, 1st B
Sir Norman Craven Brook (1902-1967)

Deputy Secretary (Civil), War Cabinet, 1942. Permanent Secretary, Ministry of Reconstruction, 1943-45. Additional Secretary, Cabinet, 1945-46; Secretary, 1947-62. Joint Secretary, Treasury, and Head of Home Civil Service, 1956-62.

Lord Normanbrook's surviving papers are held at the Bodleian Library, Oxford. The papers include drafts of speeches, invitations, luncheon engagements, etc., but the purely political material is sparse. The papers are closed until 1997.

NORRIE, 1st B
Lieutenant-General Sir (Charles) Willoughby Moke Norrie (1893-   )

Military career. Served World War I. Brigade Major, Infantry and Tank Brigades. G.O.C., 1st Armoured Division, 1940. Formed and commanded XXX Corps (Middle East), 1941-42. Commanded Royal Armoured Corps, 1943. Governor, South Australia, 1944-52. Governor-General and C.-in-C., New Zealand, 1952-57.

Lord Norrie has retained certain material, including six thick volumes of press cuttings relating to his work in South Australia and New Zealand.

NORRIS, Vice-Admiral Sir Charles Fred Wivell (1900-   )

Naval career. Commanded H.M.S. *Aberdeen*, 1936-39; H.M.S. *Bellona*, 1943-45; H.M.S. *Dryad* (Navigation and Directional School), 1945-46. Director of Naval Training and Deputy Chief of Naval Personnel, 1950-52. Flag Officer (Flotilla), Mediterranean, 1953-54. C.-in-C., East Indies Station, 1954-56. Director, British Productivity Council, 1957-65.

The Vice-Admiral has kept a certain number of papers. These are expected to remain with the family.

NORRIS, Admiral David Thomas (1875-1937)

Naval career from 1889. Served World War I. Commodore, 2nd Class, in command Persian Gulf, and British Naval Forces on Caspian Sea, 1918-19. In charge of British Naval Mission to Persia, 1920-21. Director, Trade Division, Naval Staff, 1922-24. Captain, H.M.S. *Valiant*, 1924. Rear-Admiral in 1st Battle Squadron, Mediterranean Fleet, 1926-27.

Certain papers are preserved at the National Maritime Museum. These chiefly cover the World War I period, though some date from 1892, and include letters, notes, and copies of reports as well as photographs. Many of the papers relate to Norris's service in the Caspian Sea area.

NORTH, Admiral Sir Dudley Burton Napier (1881-1961)

Naval career. Served World War I (commanding H.M.S. *New Zealand* at battles of Dogger Bank and Jutland). Director of Operations Division, Naval Staff, 1930-32. Chief of Staff, Home Fleet, 1932-33. Commanded H.M. Yachts, 1934-39. Admiral Commanding North Atlantic Station, 1939-40. Flag Officer-in-Charge, Great Yarmouth, 1942-45.

A collection of papers is preserved at Churchill College, Cambridge, and includes material for North's early career, as well as correspondence with prominent naval figures for the period up to, during and after World War II.

NORTHCOTE, 1st B
Sir Henry Stafford Northcote, 1st Bt (1846-1911)

M.P. (Con.) Exeter, 1880-99. Financial Secretary, War Office, 1885-86. Governor, Bombay, 1899-1903. Governor-General, Australia, 1903-08.

The Rt Hon. The Earl of Iddesleigh, Shillands House, Upton Pyne Hill, Exeter EX5 5EB, has a certain amount of unsorted papers from his great-uncle, Lord Northcote. One volume of papers (1904-08), including letters from Lord Elgin, A. J. Balfour and Joseph Chamberlain, is held in the Public Record Office (P.R.O. 30/56).

NORTHCOTE, Sir Geoffry Alexander Stafford (1881-1948)

Colonial Service. Governor, British Guiana, 1935-36; Hong Kong, 1937-41.

No collection of personal papers was located.

NORTHEY, Major-General Sir Edward (1868-1953)

Military career. Served India Frontier, 1891-92, South Africa, 1899-1902; European War, 1914-18; Governor, Kenya, and High Commissioner, Zanzibar, 1918-22.

Lt.-Col. E. G. V. Northey, of Brooke House, Norton, Malmesbury, Wilts., has in his possession a small but interesting collection of material relating to his father's career as Commander of the Nyasa-Rhodesian force during World War I. The material includes diaries, memoranda and correspondence on military operations. No papers appear to have survived for the period after 1918. The material is to be placed in the Imperial War Museum. Papers relating to the constitutional situation in Kenya are in the Coryndon collection at Rhodes House Library, Oxford.

NORTON, Sir Clifford John (1891-   )

Political Officer, Damascus, Deraa, and Haifa, 1919-20. Minister, Switzerland, 1942-46. Ambassador, Greece, 1946-51.

Sir Clifford Norton states that he has retained no papers that could be of interest to this project.

NORWICH, 1st Vt
Alfred Duff Cooper (1890-1954)

M.P. (Con.) Oldham, 1924-29; Westminster St George's, 1931-45. Financial Secretary, War Office, 1928-29, 1931-34; Treasury, 1934-35. Secretary of State for War, 1935-37. First Lord of the Admiralty, 1937-38. Minister of Information, 1940-41. Chancellor, Duchy of Lancaster, 1941-43. Representative, French Committee of National Liberation, 1943-44. Ambassador, France, 1944-47.

The papers are held by Sir Rupert Hart-Davis and are not available for inspection. A short description is given in Hazlehurst and Woodland, op. cit., p.41.

NOSWORTHY, Sir Richard Lysis (1855-1966)

Minister, Bolivia, 1931-34. Commercial Counsellor, Rome, 1934-40; Rio de Janeiro, 1942-44. Minister (Commercial), Rome, 1944-46.

Mr T. Nosworthy, Brackengarth, Lealholm, Whitby, Yorks., says that none of his uncle's private papers are available.

NOVAR, 1st Vt
Sir Ronald Crauford Munro-Ferguson (1860-1934)

M.P. (Lib.) Ross and Cromarty, 1884-85; Leith Burghs, 1886-1914. Governor-General, Australia, 1914-20. Secretary of State for Scotland, 1922-24.

Papers relating to Munro-Ferguson's service in Australia are held at the National Library of Australia; and other material is at the Australian War Memorial (Canberra) and with the National Register of Archives (Scotland). Details are given by Hazlehurst and Woodland, op. cit., pp.52-3.

NYE, Lieutenant-General Sir Archibald Edward (1895-1967)

Director of Staff Duties, 1940. Vice Chief of Imperial General Staff, 1941-46. Governor, Madras, 1946-48. High Commissioner, India, 1948-52; Canada, 1952-56.

Lady Nye states that her late husband left no papers.

O'BRIEN, Lieutenant-Colonel Sir Charles Richard Mackey (1859-1935)

Military career. Served South Africa, 1899-1902. Governor, Seychelles, 1912-18; Barbados, 1918-25. Special Commissioner, Sierra Leone, 1926.

Rhodes House Library has, on microfilm, copies of letters and a diary for the period 1900-02. The material relates to the Boer War, and to O'Brien's work with the Military Tribunal at Johannesburg (1900-01) and the Johannesburg civil police (1901-02). There is also a collection of photographs and cuttings.

O'CONNOR, General Sir Richard Nugent (1889-)

Military career. Served European War, 1914-18; War of 1939-45. Military Governor, Jerusalem, 1938-39. Corps Commander, Western Desert, 1940-41; France, 1944. G.O. C.-in-C., Eastern Command, India, 1945; North Western Army, India, 1945-46. Adjutant-General to the Forces, 1946-47.

Sir Richard's papers are to be placed in the Liddell Hart Centre for Military Archives. These include memoirs and material relating to his service as Military Governor of Jerusalem (1938-39); service in the Western Desert (1940-41); and there is a narrative about escape from an Italian prisoner-of-war camp.

O'CONOR, Sir Nicholas Roderick (1843-1908)

Minister, China, 1892-95. Ambassador, Russia, 1895-98; Ottoman Empire, 1898-1908.

The research undertaken was insufficient to locate any papers, although some material for 1906-08 may be found in the Hardinge MSS at Cambridge University Library.

O'DOWDA, Lieutenant-General Sir James Wilton (1871-1961)

Military career. India; World War I. Commander, Baluchistan District, India, 1927-31.

Miscellaneous papers are with the archives of the Royal West Kent Regiment, at the Kent Archives Office. The material includes private war diaries (1914-19).

OGDEN, Sir Alwyne George Neville (1889-)

China Consular Service. Consul-General, Tientsin, 1941; Kunming, 1942-45; Shanghai, 1945-48.

Sir Alwyne Ogden has retained a number of papers, memoirs, letters and diaries relating to his career. Sir Alwyne is using this material for an autobiography.

OGLANDER, Brigadier-General Cecil Faber Aspinall- (1878-1959)

Served South Africa, 1901-02; European War, 1914-18. General Staff, India, and at War Office, 1909-14. Chief General Staff Officer at Gallipoli, 1915.

Family papers can be found in the Isle of Wight Record Office. The General's daughter, Miss M. Aspinall-Oglander, states that she has no further papers.

O'GRADY, Sir James (1866-1934)

M.P. (Lab.) Leeds East, 1906-18; Leeds South-East, 1918-24. Special Envoy to Russia, 1917, and to meet Soviet envoy at Copenhagen, Nov. 1919. Governor, Tasmania, 1924-30; Falkland Islands, 1931-34.

Messrs Corsellis & Berney, the London solicitors who acted in the estate, were unable to supply any relevant information. It was not possible to contact members of the family. For details of O'Grady's career, see Bellamy, J., and Saville, J., *Dictionary of Labour Biography*, Vol. II pp. 286-9.

OLIPHANT, Sir Lancelot (1881-1965)

Foreign Office and Diplomatic Service. Deputy Under-Secretary, Foreign Office, 1936-39. Ambassador, Belgium (Minister, Luxembourg), 1939-40, 1941-44.

A collection of correspondence (1921-28) can be found in the Private Office series (F.O. 800/252-4) at the Public Record Office. This covers the period when Oliphant was a Counsellor at the Foreign Office, mainly in the Eastern Department. Rt. Hon. the Viscount Churchill, 6 Cumberland Mansions, George Street, London W.1, has such personal papers as were left by his step-father. These include some volumes of press cuttings relating to 1940 and after, a few personal letters and the manuscript of the book *An Ambassador in Bonds* covering the period of his imprisonment in Germany, 1940-41.

OLIVER, Admiral Sir Geoffrey Nigel (1898-)

Naval career from 1915. Served during World War I. Commanded H.M.S. *Hermione*, 1940-42. Senior Officer, Inshore Squadron, North Africa, 1942-43. British Assault Force Commander, Salerno, 1943. Commander, 21st Aircraft Carrier Squadron, 1944-45. Sea Lord and Assistant Chief of Naval Staff, 1947-48. C.-in-C., East Indies Station, 1950-52; The Nore, 1953-55.

The Admiral has retained a few papers only.

OLIVER, Admiral of the Fleet Sir Henry Francis (1865-1965)

Naval career from 1878. Director of Intelligence, Admiralty War Staff, 1913-14. Acting Vice-Admiral and Deputy Chief of Admiralty War Staff, 1914-17. Sea Lord and Deputy Chief of Naval Staff, 1917-18. Commanded 1st Battle Cruiser Squadron, 1918; Home Fleet, 1919; Reserve Fleet, 1919-20. 2nd Sea Lord, 1920-24. C.-in-C., Atlantic Fleet, 1924-27.

Papers available at the National Maritime Museum include material (correspondence, notes, etc.) covering many of the main events of Oliver's career, particularly during World War I. Of particular value is a typescript memoir and a diary (1925-27), kept while he was C.-in-C., Atlantic Fleet.

OLIVER, Vice-Admiral Robert Don (1895-)

Naval career, with commands in World War II. Assistant Chief of Naval Staff (Weapons), 1945-46. Deputy Chief of Naval Staff, 1946-47. Flag Officer Commanding 5th Cruiser Squadron, 1947-48.

The Vice-Admiral has retained papers relating both to his own career and to that of his uncle, Admiral of the Fleet Sir Henry Oliver (see above). It is his intention to send the bulk of these papers to the National Maritime Museum, to join those of Sir Henry Oliver already there, when he has completed his 'recollections'.

OLIVIER, 1st B
Sir Sydney Olivier (1859-1943)

Colonial Service and Home Civil Service. Governor, Jamaica, 1907-13. Permanent Secretary, Board of Agriculture and Fisheries, 1913-17. Assistant Comptroller and Auditor of the Exchequer from 1917. Secretary of State for India, 1924.

Hazlehurst and Woodland, op. cit., p.112, give details of the papers in private hands at present not available for research.

O'MALLEY, Sir Owen St Clair (1887-1974)

Served Foreign Office, 1911-37. Minister, Mexico, 1937-38; Hungary, 1939-41. Chargé d'Affaires, Spain (St Jean de Luz), 1938-39. Ambassador, Poland, 1942-45; Portugal, 1945-47.

Mr S. L. Scarlett-Smith, 2 Akenside Road, London NW3, Sir Owen's executor, has a large collection of unsorted papers relating to Sir Owen O'Malley's career. Correspondence and papers connected with the early period in Peking (1925-27) are held in the library of St Antony's College, Oxford. The main collection of papers is to be placed in due course in the archives centre at Churchill College, Cambridge.

OMMANEY, Sir Montagu Frederick (1842-1925)

Crown Agent for the Colonies, 1897-1900. Permanent Under-Secretary, Colonial Office, 1900-07.

A small collection of papers is held in the Library of Duke University, Durham, North Carolina. The papers concern Ommaney's career as Crown Agent and in the Colonial Office, under Joseph Chamberlain, Arthur Lyttelton and Lord Elgin. Rhodes House Library, Oxford, has some correspondence of Ommaney with Sir G. J. Bower, relating in part to events in South Africa (1895-1906).

ORDE, Sir Charles William (1884-)

Minister, Baltic States, 1938-40. Ambassador, Chile, 1940-45.

Sir Charles has retained no records or other papers of any interest.

O'REILLY, William Edmund (1873-1934)

Foreign Office and Diplomatic Service. Acting High Commissioner, Vladivostock, 1919. Minister, Bolivia, 1919-24; Guatemala, 1924-26; Albania, 1926; Venezuela, 1926-32.

Messrs Stephenson Harwood & Tatham, solicitors, Saddlers Hall, Gutter Lane, Cheapside, London EC2V 6BS, dealt with the estates of both Mr and Mrs O'Reilly. They have only a few formal documents regarding Mr O'Reilly's appointments and know of no further papers.

OTTLEY, Rear-Admiral Sir Charles Langdale (1858-1932)

Naval career. Director of Naval Intelligence, 1905-07. Secretary, Committee of Imperial Defence, 1907-11.

Mr A. J. Ottley knows of no papers relating to his father. Mr F. B. Ottley, Sir Charles's nephew, states that his daughter in New Zealand has some press cuttings relating to the family.

OVERTON, Sir Arnold Edersheim (1893-)

Served Board of Trade. Permanent Secretary, Board of Trade, 1941-45; Ministry of Civil Aviation, 1947-53. Head of British Middle East Office, Cairo, 1945-47. Member, Board of British European Airways, 1953-63.

Sir Arnold Overton states that he has no private papers which would add significantly to the official records.

OVEY, Sir Esmond (1879-1963)

Diplomatic Service. Minister, Mexico, 1925-29. Ambassador, Soviet Union, 1929-33; Belgium, 1934-37; Argentine Republic (and Minister, Paraguay), 1937-42.

Mr and Mrs D. Woodrow, c/o Messrs. Hedges & Mercer, 16 Market Place, Wallingford, Berks. OX10 0AE, son-in-law and daughter of Sir Esmond Ovey, have in their care a collection of papers.

PACKARD, Lieutenant-General Sir (Charles) Douglas (1903-   )

Military service, War of 1939-45, in Middle East and Italy. Chief of Staff, Allied Commission for Austria (British Element), 1945-46. Director of Military Intelligence, 1948-49. Commander, British Military Mission in Greece, 1949-51. Chief of Staff, Middle East Land Forces, 1951-53. Vice-Quartermaster-General, 1953-56. Military Adviser, West African Governments, 1956-58.

Lt.-Gen. Sir Douglas Packard has kept no papers.

PAGET, General Sir Arthur Henry Fitzroy (1851-1928)

Military career from 1869. Officer Commanding in Ireland, 1911-17.

The British Library has a collection of papers (Add. MSS. 51245-50), including correspondence with royalty and nobility and general correspondence (1880-1919).

PAGET, Sir Ralph Spencer (1864-1940)

Minister, Serbia, 1910-13; Denmark, 1916-18. Assistant Under-Secretary, Foreign Office, 1913-16. Ambassador, Brazil, 1918-20.

The Paget papers at the British Library (Add. MSS. 51252-9) include royal correspondence; correspondence with successive Foreign Secretaries (1906-18); correspondence with Lord Hardinge (1916-18); Foreign Office correspondence (1916-18); general correspondence (1894-1921); and a letter book (1901-07).

PAKENHAM, Hon. Sir Francis John (1832-1905)

Diplomatic Service. Minister, Chile, 1878-85; Argentine and Paraguay, 1885-96; Sweden and Norway, 1896-1902.

The Longford family papers are in the hands of the Hon. Thomas Pakenham, 32 Ladbroke Grove, London W11. The collection includes no papers relating to Hon. Sir F. J. Pakenham.

PALAIRET, Sir Michael (1882-1956)

Minister, Romania, 1929-35; Sweden, 1935-37; Austria, 1937-38; Greece, 1939-42. Ambassador, Greece, 1942-43. Assistant Under-Secretary, Foreign Office, 1943-45.

It has not been possible to contact Lady Palairet.

PALLISER, Admiral Sir Arthur Francis Eric (d. 1956)

Naval career. Chief of Staff to C.-in-C., China, 1936-38; and to C.-in-C., Eastern Fleet, 1941-42. Served H.M.S. *Excellent*, 1938-40; H.M.S. *Malaya*, 1940-41; New

Delhi, 1942-43; 1st Cruiser Squadron, 1943-44. 4th Sea Lord and Chief of Supplies and Transport, 1944-46. C.-in-C., East Indies Station, 1946-48.

Lady Palliser, 33 South Terrace, London SW7, states that her husband did not keep a diary, and that she has few of his papers.

PALMER, Sir William (1883-1964)

Principal Industrial Adviser, Board of Trade, 1944-46.

Lady Palmer states that she has none of her late husband's papers.

PARHAM, Admiral Sir Frederick Robertson (1901-   )

Naval career. Commands in World War II (H.M.S. *Belfast*, 1942-44), and after (H.M.S. *Vanguard*, 1947-49). Deputy Chief of Naval Personnel, 1949-51. Flag Officer (Flotillas) and 2nd-in-Command, Mediterranean, 1951-52. 4th Sea Lord and Chief of Supplies and Transport, 1954-55. C.-in-C., The Nore, 1955-58.

According to information supplied to the Imperial War Museum, no papers survive.

PARKER, Sir Harold (1895-   )

Civil Service career. Permanent Secretary, Ministry of Pensions, 1946-48; Ministry of Defence, 1948-56.

Sir Harold has kept no papers, apart from one or two letters of thanks and a number of photographs.

PARKINSON, Sir (Arthur Charles) Cosmo (1884-1967)

Permanent Under-Secretary, Colonial Office, 1937-40; Dominions Office, 1940. Special service, Colonies, from 1942.

Messrs Coutts & Co., who acted as executors to the estate, were unable to provide any information helpful in tracing papers.

PARRY, Admiral Sir (William) Edward (1893-1972)

Naval career from 1905. Active service in World War I. Commanded Anti-Submarine Establishment (H.M.S. *Osprey*), 1936-37; H.M.S. *Achilles*, 1939. 1st Naval Member of New Zealand Naval Board, 1940-42. Commanded H.M.S. *Renown*, 1943. Naval Commander Force 'L' in Invasion of France, 1944. Deputy Head of Naval Division, Control Commission for Germany, Berlin, 1945-46. Director of Naval Intelligence, 1946-48. C.-in-C., Indian Navy, 1948-51.

An important and substantial collection of papers relating to Parry's career has been donated to the Imperial War Museum. The papers, consisting mainly of personal diaries, letters and photograph albums, cover Admiral Parry's service in the Mediterranean and the North Sea during World War I, and all the important appointments which he held from 1939 to 1945. The material includes a useful account of the River Plate action, at which Parry commanded H.M.S. *Achilles*.

PARSONS, Major-General Sir Arthur Edward Broadbent (1884-1966)

Agent to the Governor-General, Baluchistan, 1936-39. Acting Governor, North West Frontier Province, 1939.

Correspondence, memoranda, reports and notes (1882-1963) are deposited at the India Office Library. The material relates mainly to North West Frontier tribes and Frontier policy.

PARSONS, Lieutenant-General Sir Lawrence Worthington (1850-1923)

Military career. Served South Africa, 1899-1900. Inspector-General of Artillery, India, 1903-06. Commanded 6th Division, Cork, 1906-09; 16th (Irish) Division, 1914-15. Colonel Commandant, Royal Artillery, 1917.

A collection of papers is preserved at the Royal Artillery Institute.

PATERSON, Sir (Alexander) Swinton (1893-   )

Minister, Dominican Republic, 1935-43. Inspector-General, Consular Establishments, 1945-50; Senior Inspector, Foreign Service Establishments, 1950-54.

Sir Swinton Paterson has retained no papers which would be of any use to this project.

PATON, George Pearson (1882-   )

Vice-Consul, High Commission in Siberia, 1918-19; Vladivostok, 1921-28. Commercial Counsellor, Moscow, 1930-37. Consul-General, Istanbul, 1937-42. Director, Intelligence Division, Far Eastern Bureau, Ministry of Information (New Delhi), 1943-46.

Mr Paton is engaged in writing his memoirs, but has retained very few papers relating to his career.

PAUNCEFOTE, 1st B
Sir Julian Pauncefote (1828-1902)

Permanent Under-Secretary, Foreign Office, from 1882. Ambassador, United States (Minister, 1889-93), 1893-1902.

A large quantity of his personal and official papers was destroyed by his widow after his death. Details of papers in other collections may be found at the National Register of Archives.

PAYNE, Sir Henry Arthur (1873-1931)

2nd Secretary, Board of Trade, 1919-29. Adviser to Department of Commerce, Egypt.

It was not possible to trace persons mentioned in the Will and Act of Probate.

PEACHEY, Captain Allan Thomas George Cumberland (1896-1967)

Naval career from 1914. Active service in various stations, with commands during World War II. Commodore, Palestine and Levant, 1947-48.

An interesting collection of papers is available in the National Maritime Museum, and includes material on World Wars I and II, Palestine (e.g. Peachey's signals as Commodore in Palestine), Suez and NATO.

PEAKE, Sir Charles Brinsley Pemberton (1897-1958)

Head, Foreign Office News Department, and Chief Press Officer, Ministry of Information, 1939. Personal Assistant to Lord Halifax, 1941. Representative to French National Committee, 1942-44. Consul-General, Tangier, 1945-46. Ambassador, Yugoslavia, 1946-51; Greece, 1951-57.

Some papers survive with Mr John S. Peake, Durnford House, Eton College, Windsor SL4 6DS. They comprise a diary covering the period when Sir Charles

Peake was with Lord Halifax in Washington in 1941; a diary — with gaps — covering the period 1946-50; a diary for the years 1954-57; and correspondence with Lord Halifax (1944-58).

PEAKE, Colonel Frederick Gerard (1886-1970)

Military career. Served World War I. Inspector-General of Gendarmerie, Transjordan, 1921, and Director of Public Security from 1923. Raised Arab Legion, 1922.

A microfilm of autobiographical material and official and private papers relating to Peake's command of the Arab Legion (1922-38) is housed at the Imperial War Museum. Notes on Peake's work for the Arab Legion are available at the Middle East Centre, St Antony's College, Oxford.

PEAT, Sir Harry William Henry (1878-1959)

Financial Secretary, Ministry of Food, 1917-20, 1939-46. Member of several government committees. Chartered accountant.

Messrs Peat, Marwick, Mitchell & Co., solicitors who acted for Sir H. W. H. Peat, know of no papers. A collection of material will be included in the Private Office series (M.A.F. 129) at the Public Record Office.

PEDLER, Sir Frederick Johnson (1908-)

Colonial Service. Secretary to Lord Hailey in Africa, 1939 and 1940. Chief British Economic Representative, Dakar, 1942.

The Oxford Colonial Records Project found that Sir Frederick has kept a collection of diaries, letters and official papers, mainly relating to African affairs. A tape recording and transcript of an interview, together with an unpublished statement (1944) about war-time economic problems in French West Africa, are held in Rhodes House Library.

PEEL, Sir Arthur Robert (1861-1952)

Minister, Siam, 1909-15; Brazil, 1915-20; Bulgaria, 1920-21.

The Viscount Gage, Sir Arthur's nephew, knows of no surviving papers, nor of anyone who might have further information.

PEEL, Robert Francis (1874-1924)

M.P. (Con.) Woodbridge, Jan. 1910-20. Governor and C.-in-C., St Helena, 1920-24.

Major C. R. Peel, The Hill, Weare Gifford, North Devon, son of Colonel R. F. Peel, has a collection of press cuttings dealing primarily with his father's election campaigns (1906-18).

PEEL, Sir William (1875-1945)

Malayan Civil Service. Governor, Hong Kong, 1930-35.

A series of notes covering Sir William's career in Malaya, Singapore and Hong Kong is housed in Rhodes House Library.

PEIRSE, Air Chief Marshal Sir Richard Edmund Charles (1892-1970)

Served European War, 1914-18. Air Officer Commanding, Palestine and Transjordan, 1933-36. Deputy Chief of Air Staff, 1937-40. Vice Chief of Air Staff, 1940.

Air Officer C.-in-C., Bomber Command, 1940-42; India, 1942-43. Allied Air C.-in-C., South East Asia Command, 1943-44.

Records at the R.A.F. Museum include diaries, letters, press cuttings, files, photographs and published works (1913-65). Subjects include service in the Adriatic (1918), Palestine (1936) and South East Asia (1943-44).

PELHAM, Sir (Edward) Henry (1876-1949)

Civil Service career. Permanent Secretary, Board of Education, 1931-37.

Mrs I. J. Hayne, Sir Henry's daughter, states that she and members of her family know of no papers.

PELHAM, Sir (George) Clinton (1898-)

Trade Commissioner and Commercial Secretary, South China, from 1933. Served Madagascar, Baghdad, Madrid. Ambassador, Saudi Arabia, 1952-55; Czechoslovakia, 1955-57.

Sir Clinton Pelham states that he has kept no private papers relating to his career.

PENNEY, Major-General Sir (William) Ronald Campbell (1896-1964)

Military career. Served World War I; India, 1921-26, 1935-36; War Office, 1929-30; and World War II. Worked for Ministry of Supply, 1946-49, and for Foreign Office, 1953-57.

The collection at the Liddell Hart Centre for Military Archives includes papers on Shanghai (1932); the Middle East, North Africa and Sicily (1941-43); Anzio (1944); and South East Asia Command (1945).

PENTLAND, 1st B
John Sinclair (1860-1925)

M.P. (Lib.) Dunbartonshire, 1892-95; Forfarshire, 1897-1909. Secretary of State for Scotland, 1905-12. Governor, Madras, 1912-19.

Hazlehurst and Woodland, op. cit., p.133, were unable to find the papers used by Marjorie, Lady Pentland, widow of the 1st Baron, for the biography *The Right Honourable John Sinclair, Lord Pentland, G.C.S.I.: A Memoir* (1928).

PERCIVAL, Lieutenant-General Arthur Ernest (1887-1966)

Military career. Brigadier, General Staff, I Corps, British Expeditionary Force, 1939-40. G.O.C., 43rd (Wessex) Division, 1940. Assistant Chief of Imperial General Staff, 1940. G.O.C., 44th (Home Counties) Division, 1940-41; Malaya, 1941-42.

The Imperial War Museum has a large collection of documents, letters, maps and photographs covering the whole of Percival's military career from 1914. There is a substantial post-war correspondence relating to the Malayan campaign. Some of these papers are under restriction.

PEROWNE, Sir John Victor Thomas Woolrych Tait (1897-1951)

Foreign Office and Diplomatic Service. Minister, Holy See, 1947-51.

It was not possible to contact Lady Perowne.

PERTH, 16th E of
Sir James Eric Drummond (1876-1951)

Private Secretary, Prime Minister, 1912-15, and Foreign Secretary, 1915-19. Secretary-General, League of Nations, 1919-33. Ambassador, Italy, 1933-39. Chief Adviser on Foreign Publicity, Information, 1939-40.

The Private Office papers at the Public Record Office include correspondence of Sir Eric Drummond (1915-18) (F.O. 800/329, 383-5). All of Lord Perth's papers relating to the League of Nations were given by him to the League and were deposited in Geneva, but upon threat of a German invasion of Switzerland many records were burnt. Some remain in the League archives. Lord Perth did not keep a diary, but certain family letters remain in the family. These are not available for inspection.

PETERSON, Sir Maurice Drummond (1889-1952)

Acting High Commissioner, Egypt, 1934. Minister, Bulgaria, 1936-38. Ambassador, Iraq, 1938-39; Spain, 1939-40; Turkey, 1944-46; Soviet Union, 1946-49. Controller of Overseas Publicity, Information, 1940-41.

Lady Peterson has retained no papers. Some correspondence with Lord Robert Cecil (1932-43) is in the Cecil of Chelwood collection at the British Library (Add. MSS 51091).

PHILBY, Harry St John Bridger (1885-1960)

Indian Civil Service. Political Officer, Middle East Forces, Mesopotamia, from Nov. 1915. Served British Political Mission to Central Arabia, 1917-18. Adviser to Ministry of Interior, Mesopotamia, 1920-21. Chief Political Representative, Transjordan, 1921-24. Traveller and businessman in Arabia.

A substantial and important collection of papers relating to Middle Eastern affairs has been placed in the Middle East Centre, St Antony's College, Oxford. The material relates to the various stages in Philby's career, and consists of diaries (fragments), notes, memoranda, drafts of articles and books, and correspondence often with persons prominent in Middle Eastern affairs. Other papers relate to Philby's concern with politics in Britain, to his unpublished books and to his business interests.

PHILLIMORE, Admiral Sir Richard Fortescue (1864-1940)

Naval career. Served World War I. Commanded 1st Battle Cruiser Squadron, 1916-18, later Flying Squadron; Reserve Fleet, 1920-22. C.-in-C. Plymouth Station, 1923-26.
The Imperial War Museum has a collection of papers covering Phillimore's naval career from 1914, with special reference to the naval mission to Russia in 1915-16.

PHILLIPS, Sir Frederick (1884-1943)

Under-Secretary, Treasury, from 1932; and Joint 2nd Secretary. Treasury Representative, United States, 1940-43.

A collection of papers (1922-40) can be found in the Treasury Private Office class (T.177) at the Public Record Office. The material, which extends to 52 pieces, includes papers on estimates and national expenditure (1922-26); the World Economic and Financial Conference (1932-33); dollar depreciation (1933); international monetary policy; and budget matters. There are also a large number of miscellaneous papers.

PHILLIPS, Sir Thomas Williams (1883-1966)

Permanent Secretary, Ministry of Labour, 1935-44; Ministry of National Insurance, 1944-48. Chairman, Central Land Board and War Damage Commission, 1949-59.

Miss C. M. Phillips, Cross House, St Clears, Carmarthen SA33 4ED, has only a very small number of papers relating to her father. There are a few letters, usually letters of congratulation, written by people of interest; some press cuttings and photographs.

PHIPPS, Sir Edmund Bampfylde (1869-1947)

General Secretary, Ministry of Munitions, 1916-17. Principal Assistant Secretary, Elementary Education, 1912-26. Deputy Secretary, Board of Education, 1926-29.

Mr John Phipps, 26 Astell Street, London SW3 3RU, states that his father sorted out and destroyed many of his personal papers before he died. Those which survive are with Mr Phipps, and the papers are mainly of family and social interest. They include a short autobiographical summary; a photograph album-cum-scrapbook covering Sir Edmund's early career; a bound copy of a weekly school magazine; a scrapbook covering later years, and including obituaries and articles written by Sir Edmund; records kept whilst tutor to the Duke of Connaught's children (1890s); a few letters from friends and contemporaries, including Lord Alfred Douglas, and letters from Winston Churchill and Lloyd George in connection with Sir Edmund's knighthood; also a number of letters of condolence, written after Sir Edmund's death.

PHIPPS, Sir Edmund Constantine Henry (1840-1911)

Diplomatic Service from 1858. Minister, Paris, 1893; Brazil, 1894-1900; Belgium, 1900-11.

Captain Roskill, who arranged the placing of Sir Eric Phipps's papers at Churchill College, knows of no papers.

PHIPPS, Sir Eric Clare Edmund (1875-1945)

Minister, Paris, 1922-28; Austria, 1928-33. Ambassador, Germany, 1933-37; France, 1937-39.

A large collection of papers can be found at Churchill College, Cambridge. The papers cover Phipps's career from the early 1920s. There is one series of copies of telegrams, dispatches, and correspondence with Secretaries of State for Foreign Affairs from Lord Curzon to Halifax. Further series of letters cover royal correspondence (1925-39), extensive correspondence with numerous members of the Foreign Office, and a general collection of correspondence with politicians, senior members of various government departments, society personalities and foreign ambassadors. Other papers are arranged by subject or period, and the files include papers of the Paris embassy and of the Berlin embassy, and material concerning the Hague Reparations Conferences of 1929 and 1930. The collection is completed with series of speeches, honours and appointments, and the correspondence of Lady Phipps.

PIKE, Major-General Sir William Watson (1860-1941)

Army career from 1882. Director of Medical Services, 1st Army, British Expeditionary Force, 1914-17. Special Commissions, East Africa, 1917-18; India, 1918-19.

Certain papers are now housed in the Royal Artillery Institution.

PILE, General Sir Frederick Alfred, 2nd Bt (1884-)

Military career. Served World War I. Assistant Director of Mechanisation, War Office, 1928-32. Commander, Canal Brigade, Egypt, 1932-36; 1st Anti-Aircraft Division, Territorial Army, 1937-39. G.O.C.-in-C., Anti-Aircraft Command, 1939-45. Director-General, Ministry of Works, 1945.

It is understood that the General has retained a number of papers.

PINSENT, Gerald Hume Saverie (1888-)

Served Treasury and Board of Trade; British Food Mission, Ottawa, 1942 and 1943. Financial Adviser, Berlin Embassy, 1932-39; Washington Embassy, 1939-41.

Mr Pinsent has kept no private papers.

PIRIE, Air Chief Marshal Sir George Clark (1896-)

Served European War, 1914-18. Air Attaché, Washington, 1937-40. Director-General of Organisation, Air Ministry, 1943-45. Allied Air C.-in-C., South East Asia, 1946-47. Inspector-General, R.A.F., 1948. Air Member for Supply and Organisation. 1948-50. Head of Air Force Staff, British Joint Services Mission to United States, 1950-51.

It is understood that there are no papers.

PLATT, General Sir William (1885-)

Military career. Served World War I. Commanded 7th Infantry Brigade, 1934-38. Commandant, Sudan Defence Force, 1938-41, G.O.C.-in-C., East African Command, 1941-45.

The Imperial War Museum has one bound volume entitled 'The Campaign against Italian East Africa, 1940-41', and the text of three lectures given at Cambridge in 1951. The Museum also has a collection of slides, photographs and printed material. The Liddell Hart Centre for Military Archives also has copies of the lectures on the campaign in East Africa. Other material may be found in the papers of Colonel F. O. Cave at the Imperial War Museum.

PLAYFAIR, Air Marshal Sir Patrick Henry Lyon (1889-1974)

Royal Field Artillery, Royal Flying Corps and R.A.F. career, from 1910. Air Officer Commanding in Chief, India, 1940-42.

The Imperial War Museum has a collection of papers which includes a scrapbook containing letters and photographs; files relating to the Advanced Air Strike Force, France, 1939-40; copies of early R.F.C. photographs; and a copy of Playfair's unpublished memoirs.

PLUMER OF MESSINES, 1st Vt
Sir Herbert Charles Onslow Plumer (1857-1932)

Military career. Quartermaster-General and Member of Army Council, 1904-05. G.O.C., Northern Command, 1911-14. Commanded 5th Army Corps, 1915, and 2nd Army, British Expeditionary Force, France, 1915-17, 1918; Army of the Rhine, 1918-19. G.O.C., Italian Expeditionary Force, 1917-18. Governor, Malta, 1919-24. High Commissioner, Palestine, 1925-28.

Since the writing of the biography *Plumer of Messines* by General Sir Charles Harington (1939), the papers, which included letters written to Lady Plumer over many years, have been totally mislaid.

PLUNKET, 5th B
William Lee Plunket (1864-1920)

Private Secretary to Lords Lieutenant of Ireland, 1900-04. Governor, New Zealand, 1904-10.

Efforts to contact the family were unsuccessful.

PLUNKETT, Hon. Sir Francis Richard (1835-1907)

Diplomatic service from 1855. Minister, Japan, 1883-87; Sweden, 1888-93; Belgium, 1893-1900. Ambassador, Austria-Hungary, 1900-05.

No information was secured.

POLLOCK, James Huey Hamill (1893-   )

Colonial Service. Chief Civil Adviser to G.O.C., British Troops in Palestine, 1948. Member, Senate of Northern Ireland, 1954-57.

A collection of family papers at the Northern Ireland Public Record Office (D 1581) includes Pollock's correspondence as Administrative Officer in Nigeria (1923), Assistant Secretary to the Nigerian Secretariat in Lagos (1927), District Commissioner in Haifa (1939) and Jerusalem (1944-48), and as Chief Adviser (1948).

POLLOCK, Sir William H. Montagu- (1903-   )

Minister, Syria, 1950-52. Ambassador, Syria, 1952-53; Peru, 1953-58; Switzerland, 1958-60; Denmark, 1960-62.

Sir William has retained no papers.

PONSONBY, Major-General Sir John (1866-1952)

Military career. Africa, and European War, 1914-18. Commander, 2nd Guards Brigade, 1915-17; 40th Division, 1917-18; 5th Division, 1919. G.O.C., Madras District, 1922-26.

Certain papers (1917-18) are at the National Army Museum.

POPHAM, Air Chief Marshal Sir Henry Robert Moore Brooke- (1878-1953)

Director of Research, Air Ministry, 1919-21. Commandant, Royal Air Force Staff College, 1921-26; Imperial Defence College, 1931-33. Air Officer Commanding, Fighting Area Air Defence of Great Britain, 1926-28; Iraq Command, 1928-30. Air Officer C.-in-C., Air Defence of Great Britain, 1933-35; Middle East, 1935-36. Inspector-General, Royal Air Force, 1935. Governor and C.-in-C., Kenya, 1937-39. C.-in-C., Far East, 1940-41.

Some papers are held at the Liddell Hart Centre for Military Archives. The material includes files relating to air defence in Great Britain and the Inspectorate-General of the Royal Air Force (1934-35). Other papers relate to Brooke-Popham's career in Iraq and the Middle East, the Far East, and his work with the Empire Air Training Scheme (1939-40) and the Air Training Corps (1942-47). A further collection of papers covering the period in Kenya is housed at Rhodes House Library, Oxford.

PORTAL OF HUNGERFORD, 1st Vt
Marshal of the Royal Air Force Sir Charles Frederick Algernon Portal (1893-1971)

Served European War, 1914-18. Air Member for Personnel, 1939-40. Air Officer C.-in-C., Bomber Command, 1940. Chief of Air Staff, 1940-45. Controller, Atomic Energy, Ministry of Supply, 1946-51.

Christ Church, Oxford, has copies of correspondence between Portal and Winston Churchill during World War II. Other private and personal letters remain with the Viscountess Portal, West Ashling House, Chichester, Sussex.

PORTER, Surgeon-Admiral Sir James (d. 1935)

Naval career from 1877. Served in various campaigns, including World War I. Director-General, Medical Department, Royal Navy, 1908-13.

A collection of papers is preserved at the National Maritime Museum. This includes family papers (dating from the 1840s) and Porter's correspondence as Fleet Surgeon in South Africa (1899-1901); a box file of correspondence (1901-13); and material relating to Porter's war service (letters and signals from Gallipoli, 1915; papers on hospital trains, 1914-17; and relating to National Service, 1917-19).

POUND, Admiral of the Fleet Sir (Alfred) Dudley Pickman Rogers (1877-1943)

Naval career, with service in World War I (commanded H.M.S. *Colossus* at Battle of Jutland). Director of Plans Division, Admiralty, 1922-25. Assistant Chief of Naval Staff, 1927-29. 2nd Sea Lord and Chief of Naval Personnel, 1932-35. C.-in-C., Mediterranean, 1936-39. 1st Sea Lord and Chief of Naval Staff, 1939-43.

According to information supplied to the National Register of Archives (Scotland) by his son, Sir Dudley left no papers.

POWER, Admiral of the Fleet Sir Arthur John (1889-1960)

Naval career. Commanded Gunnery School, Portsmouth, 1935-37; H.M.S. *Ark Royal*, 1938-40. Assistant Chief of Naval Staff, 1940-42. C.-in-C., East Indies Station, 1945. 2nd Sea Lord and Chief of Naval Personnel, 1946-48. C.-in-C., Mediterranean Station, 1949-50; Portsmouth, 1950-52; and Naval C.-in-C., Home (designate), 1951-52. Allied C.-in-C., Channel and North Sea Command, 1952.

A collection of papers (1905-50) is available at the British Library (Add. MSS. 56093-8).

POWER, Admiral Sir Manley Laurence (1904-   )

Naval career. Served World War II. 5th Sea Lord and Deputy Chief of Naval Staff, 1957-59. C.-in-C., Portsmouth, Allied C.-in-C., Channel, and C.-in-C., Home Station (Designate), 1959-61.

Two folders of papers on Operations 'Torch' and 'Husky' (1942-43) are preserved at the Imperial War Museum.

POWLETT, Vice-Admiral Sir Peveril Barton Reibey Wallop William (1898-   )

Naval career. Served at Gallipoli and Jutland, World War I. Commands. Director of Manning, 1939-40. Chief of Staff Force 'H', 1941-42. Captain of Fleet, Home

Fleet, 1944-45. Naval Secretary to 1st Lord of the Admiralty, 1948-50. C.-in-C., South Atlantic, 1952-54. Governor, Southern Rhodesia, 1954-59.

The Vice-Admiral states that he has a collection of diaries, press cuttings, etc., relating to his early naval service and to periods spent in South Africa (1952-55) and Rhodesia (1955-60).

POWNALL, Lieutenant-General Sir Henry Royds (1887-1961)

Military career. Served India, European War of 1914-18, etc. Military Assistant Secretary, Committee of Imperial Defence, 1933-38. Director of Military Operations and Intelligence, War Office, 1938-39. Chief of General Staff, British Expeditionary Force, 1939-40. Inspector-General of Home Guard, 1940. Commanded British Troops in Northern Ireland, 1940-41. Vice Chief of Imperial General Staff, 1941. C.-in-C., Far East, Dec. 1941-Jan. 1942, Persia—Iraq, 1943. G.O.C., Ceylon, 1942-43. Chief of Staff to Supreme Allied Commander, South East Asia, 1943-44.

A collection of papers is to be placed in due course with the Liddell Hart Centre for Military Archives. The material includes diaries (1933-45), documents arising from Churchill's war memoirs and the official war histories, and miscellaneous documents. The papers are owned by Mr J. W. Pownall Gray, M.B.E., The Manor, Abbotts Ann, Andover, Hants.

PRATT, Sir John Thomas (1876-1970)

China Consular Service from 1898. Foreign Office and Diplomatic Service. Head of Far East Section, Ministry of Information, 1939-41.

Lady Pratt, Hollyoak, Nairdwood Lane, Great Missenden, Bucks. HP16 0QQ, states that most of her late husband's papers were destroyed by bombing in 1940. However, there remains with her a crate of unsorted papers.

PRESTON, Admiral Sir Lionel George (1875-1971)

Naval career. Served World War I. Commanded Grand Fleet Mine-Sweeping Flotilla, 1914-17. Director of Mine-Sweeping Division, Admiralty, 1917-19. Various commands, 1919-30. 4th Sea Lord and Chief of Supplies and Transport, 1930-32. Commandant, Imperial Defence College, 1933-34. Director, Small Vessels Pool, 1940-45.

According to information supplied to the Imperial War Museum, the Admiral retained no papers.

PRESTON, Sir Thomas Hildebrand, 6th Bt (1886-)

Consular and Diplomatic Service. Minister, Lithuania. Resident Representative, Middle East, Intergovernmental Committee on Refugees, 1947.

It was not possible to make contact with Sir Thomas Preston.

PREVOST, Sir Augustus, 1st Bt (1837-1913)

Director, Bank of England, Governor, 1901-03.

Messrs Janson Cobb Pearson & Co., solicitors, know of no private papers kept by Sir Augustus Prevost. Sir Augustus's daughter was married to the late Mr Halsey Janson, a partner in the firm.

PRICE, Sir (Charles) Roy (1893-   )

Served Colonial Office and Dominions Office; London Naval Conference, 1930; Disarmament Conference, 1932-34; League of Nations Assembly, 1928, 1932-34, 1939. Joint Secretary, Oversea Settlement Board, 1937-39. Deputy High Commissioner, South Africa, 1940-42; Australia, 1948-49. High Commissioner, New Zealand, 1949-53.

Sir Roy Price has kept a number of letters from prominent personalities, which might be of interest, and a collection of press cuttings.

PRIDHAM, Vice-Admiral Sir (Arthur) Francis (1886-   )

Naval career from 1901. Served World War I; active commands during 1930s. Flag Officer, Humber Area, 1939-40. President of the Ordnance Board, 1941-45.

A copy of Pridham's unpublished autobiography is housed at Churchill College, Cambridge.

PRIMROSE, Sir Henry William (1846-1923)

Private Secretary to Viceroy of India, 1880-84; and to W. E. Gladstone, 1886. Permanent Secretary, Office of Works, 1886-95. Chairman, Board of Customs, 1895-99; Board of Inland Revenue, 1899-1907.

A good collection of papers is at Duke University, Durham, North Carolina. The papers (1864-1942) consist of political and family correspondence, and include some 50 items on the work of the Committee on Irish Finance (1911-12), and other material on Gladstone's 1886 administration, the formation of the 1892 Cabinet, Irish Home Rule, the Church in Wales, the international conference on the question of sugar bounties (1901), and the civil loyalty of Catholic converts (1873). Correspondents include W. E. Gladstone and the 1st Marquess of Ripon.

PROBYN, General Sir Dighton Macnaghten (1833-1924)

Entered Army, 1849. Served India, China, etc. Keeper of the Privy Purse and Extra Equerry to King Edward VII, 1901-10.

Photostat copies of documents relating to Sir Dighton Probyn have been given on loan to the National Army Museum.

PROCTOR, Surgeon Rear-Admiral Richard Louis Gibbon (1900-1969)

Entered Naval Medical Service, 1924. Naval Medical Officer of Health at various bases, 1941-51. Deputy Medical Director-General, 1955-58.

A collection of papers (1941-57) is preserved at the Imperial War Museum. This includes diaries (1944-57) and Proctor's annual reports as Naval Health Officer, Rosyth (1941-43), Levant and Eastern Mediterranean (1944-45), The Nore (1946-50).

PROTHERO, Admiral Reginald Charles (1849-1927)

Naval career from 1863. Served South Africa, 1900.

A collection of papers is preserved at the National Maritime Museum.

PURSEY, Commander Harry (1891-   )

Naval career from 1907. Served ten years on lower deck in World War I and thereafter until 1936. Journalist and lecturer. M.P. (Lab.) Hull East, 1945-70.

Commander Pursey has retained a substantial collection of papers relating to both his naval and political activities. The personal papers he hopes to retain for biographical purposes. In addition to these papers, Commander Pursey has accumulated a large collection of material relating to general naval matters and particularly relating to conditions of service on the 'lower deck'. This collection Commander Pursey intends to use for a study of the subject. The printed documents which Commander Pursey received during his years as an M.P. are deposited in Hull University Library.

PYMAN, General Sir Harold English (1908-1971)

Military career. Served World War II (Western Desert, Normandy, etc.). Chief of Staff, G.H.Q., Middle East Land Forces, 1946-49. Director-General, Fighting Vehicles, Ministry of Supply, 1951-53. Director of Weapons and Development, War Office, 1955-56. Deputy Chief of Imperial General Staff, 1958-61. C.-in-C., Allied Forces, Northern Europe, 1961-63.

A collection of Pyman's papers (1929-64) is now housed at the Liddell Hart Centre for Military Archives.

RADCLIFFE, 1st Vt
Sir Cyril John Radcliffe (1899-   )

Director-General, Ministry of Information, 1941-45. Chairman of numerous government committees and commissions, e.g. Royal Commission on the Taxation of Profits and Income, 1952-55.

Viscount Radcliffe states that he has always destroyed private papers at the end of each period of employment in public service.

RADCLIFFE, Brigadier-General Sir Charles Delmé- (1864-1937)

Served India, 1884-90, etc. British Commissioner for Delimitation of Anglo-German Uganda Boundary, 1902-04. Military Attaché, Rome, 1906-11. Chief of British Military Mission, General Headquarters, Italian Army, 1915-19; Klagenfurt, Austria, 1919-20.

Certain papers have survived. Mr Peter Delmé-Radcliffe, Pond House, Aldbourne, Wilts., has papers relating to his uncle's activities on the Italian front during the World War and in Uganda (1901-04). Other material on the Greco-Turkish War is with the Red Cross, and Marlborough College, Wilts., has some papers on Delmé-Radcliffe's work in Austria relating to the attempted recovery of Habsburg property from the successor states.

RADCLIFFE, General Sir Percy Pollexfen de Blaquiere (1874-1934)

Military career, serving in France during European War, 1914-18. Director of Military Operations, War Office, 1918-22. G.O.C., 48th (South Midland) Division, Territorial Army, 1923-26; 4th Division, 1926-27; Scottish Command, 1930-33. G.O. C.-in-C., Southern Command, 1933-34.

According to information given to the Liddell Hart Centre for Military Archives, the General's papers were destroyed in a fire.

RAIKES, Arthur Stewart (1856-1925)

Diplomatic Service. Minister, Chile, 1904-07.

Sir Victor Raikes states that he has no information regarding papers left by his great-uncle, A. S. Raikes.

RAMSAY, Admiral Hon. Sir Alexander Robert Maule (1881-1972)

Naval career. Served World War I (Dardanelles, 1914-15, etc.). Commodore, Royal Naval Barracks, Portsmouth, 1929-31. C.-in-C., East Indies, 1936-38. 5th Sea Lord and Chief of Naval Air Service, 1938-39.

According to information obtained by the Imperial War Museum, the Admiral retained no papers.

RAMSAY, Sir George Dalhousie (1828-1920)

Civil Service career. Director of Army Clothing, 1863-93.

Papers (c. 1835-93) are deposited in the British Library (Add. MSS 46446-50).

RAMSAY, Sir Malcolm Graham (1871-1946)

Private Secretary to Prime Minister, A. J. Balfour, 1902-05. Treasury Service. Chairman, National Whitley Council for Civil Service, 1919-21. Comptroller and Auditor-General, 1921-31.

Certain papers at the Exchequer and Audit Department may be passed to the Public Record Office.

RAMSAY, Hon. Sir Patrick William Maule (1879-1962)

Minister, Greece, 1929-33; Hungary, 1933-35; Denmark, 1935-39.

Mr D. P. M. Ramsay, Diego de Leon 41, Madrid, Spain, son of the Hon. Sir P. W. M. Ramsay, was unable to assist in the survey. Details of surviving papers are not available.

RANCE, Major-General Sir Hubert Elvin (1898-1974)

Military career. Served European War, 1914-18; War of 1939-45. Director of Technical Training, War Office, 1942-43. General Staff, Western Command, 1943-45. Director of Civil Affairs, Burma, 1945-46. Governor, Burma, 1946-1948; Trinidad and Tobago, 1950-55.

No information is available.

RANDALL, Sir Alec Walter George (1892-   )

Minister, Denmark, 1945-47; Ambassador, 1947-52. Alternate Delegate, U.N. Assembly and Economic and Social Council, New York and Geneva, 1953-57.

Sir Alec Randall has no diaries or other private records. However, he retains a collection of press cuttings and is engaged in writing his autobiography.

RANFURLY, 5th E of
Uchter John Mark Knox (1856-1933)

Lord-in-Waiting, 1895-97. Governor, New Zealand, 1897-1904.

The present (6th) Earl of Ranfurly, 26 Fenchurch Street, London EC3M 3DR, has papers relating to his grandfather, including diaries, press cuttings and dispatches. These date mainly from the period spent in New Zealand.

RANKEILLOUR, 2nd B
Sir Arthur Oswald James Hope (1897-1958)

Served European War, 1914-18; Turkey, 1922-23. M.P. (Con.) Nuneaton, 1924-29; Birmingham Aston, 1931-39. Junior Lord of the Treasury, 1935-37. Vice-Chamberlain of H.M. Household, 1937. Treasurer of H.M. Household, 1937-39. Governor of Madras, 1940-46.

It is believed that no papers have survived.

RAPP, Sir Thomas Cecil (1893-   )

Consul-General, Zagreb, 1939-41; Tabriz, 1943-44; Salonika, 1944-45. Head of British Economic Mission to Greece, 1946-47. Ambassador, Mexico, 1947-50. Head of Middle East Office, Cairo, 1950-53.

Sir Thomas Rapp has retained no papers, but a copy of his unpublished memoirs is deposited at the Middle East Centre, St Antony's College, Oxford. The material covers various periods of service in the Middle East, and in Bulgaria (1931-32), the Soviet Union, Yugoslavia, Azerbaijan and Mexico.

RAW, Brigadier Cecil Whitfield (1900-1969)

Service in Royal Artillery, A.D.C. (Additional) to the Queen, 1951-61.

A box of material relating to Raw's career is available at the Royal Artillery Institution.

RAWLINS, Evelyn Charles Donaldson (1884-1971)

Consular official, and Commercial Secretary. Commercial Counsellor, Vienna, 1932-34; Berlin, 1934-37. Minister, Bolivia, 1937-40.

Mr R. E. D. Rawlins, Lyndene, Ballakilpheric, Colby, Isle of Man, has no papers of importance concerning his father except for one or two letters written to him by fairly prominent people. The manuscript of an unpublished autobiography, which the late Mr Rawlins produced, appears to have been lost.

RAWLINS, Colonel Stuart William Hughes (1880-1927)

Military career from 1898. Served South African War and World War I. Chief of Staff to Artillery Adviser to G.H.Q., 1916-18. Director of Artillery, War Office, 1924-27. Commanded Royal Artillery, 2nd Division, Aldershot, 1927.

A trunk of papers relating to Rawlins's work and including a typescript history of the Royal Artillery is available at the Royal Artillery Institution.

RAWLINSON, 1st B
General Sir Henry Seymour Rawlinson, 2nd Bt (1864-1925)

Military career from 1884. Service in India, South Africa and during World War I. Commander of Forces, IV Corps and 4th Army; North Russia, 1919. C.-in-C., India, 1920-25.

The National Army Museum has a collection of letters, written by Rawlinson in the 1880s during his service in India. Most of these are addressed to his parents, and many relate to the social, sporting and regimental life of a young officer in India. Others relate to his period as A.D.C. to the C.-in-C., India, Sir Frederick Roberts (1886-89), and include accounts of military manoeuvres, operations in Burma, etc. A further collection at the National Army Museum includes journals, diaries, sketchbooks, photograph albums and papers (1864-1925).

Diaries and papers relating to Rawlinson's work during World War I are available at Churchill College, Cambridge. Correspondence (1920-24) between Rawlinson and the Earl of Derby, and relating to Rawlinson's work as C.-in-C., India, is preserved at the India Office Library. The Imperial War Museum has a number of 4th Army papers (1916-18), and a further assortment of papers is in the Royal Armoured Corps Tank Museum.

READING, 1st M of
Sir Rufus Daniel Isaacs (1860-1935)

M.P. (Lib.) Reading, 1904-13. Solicitor-General, 1910. Attorney-General, 1910-13. Lord Chief Justice, 1913-21. Ambassador, United States, 1918-19. Viceroy of India, 1921-26. Secretary of State, Foreign Affairs, 1931.

Apart from a few personal papers which remain with the present Marquess of Reading and the Foreign Office Private Office correspondence (1918-19 and 1931) at the Public Record Office (F.O. 800/222-6), a large collection of Reading's papers is available at the India Office Library. The material comprises Reading's official Indian papers, including printed correspondence and copies of speeches, and his personal letters (c. 1910-35), correspondence with leading politicians and political papers. Further details are given by Hazlehurst and Woodland, op. cit., pp.80-1.

REDCLIFFE-MAUD, Baron
Sir John (Primatt Redcliffe) Maud (1906-   )

2nd Secretary, Ministry of Food, 1941-44; Secretary Ministry of Reconstruction, 1944-45; Office of Lord President of the Council, 1945. Permanent Secretary, Ministry of Education, 1945-52; Ministry of Fuel and Power, 1952-58. Ambassador, South Africa, 1961-63 (High Commissioner, 1959-61) and High Commissioner, Basutoland, Bechuanaland and Swaziland, 1959-63. British delegate at several international conferences, and chairman of various government committees and commissions, e.g. Royal Commission on Local Government in England, 1966-69.

Lord Redcliffe-Maud has a collection of unsorted papers. These relate to various periods and events, in particular to service at the Ministry of Food (1939-43); to the Hot Springs Conference on Food and Agriculture (1943) and the first Council Meeting of United Nations Relief and Rehabilitation Administration, Atlantic City (1943); the office of the Minister of Reconstruction (1943-45); the Ministry of Education (1945-52); UNESCO conferences (1946-52); the Ministry of Fuel and Power, and the Ministry of Power (1952-58); and also to South African affairs (1959-63). One box of papers of Sir Francis Hill relating to the Redcliffe-Maud Commission is at Nottingham University Library. Access is restricted.

REDMAN, Lieutenant-General Sir Harold (1899-   )

Commissioned into Royal Artillery, 1917. Served in France and Germany, 1918; Waziristan, 1923-24, etc.; War Cabinet Secretariat, 1939-40. Commands, 1940-43. Secretary, Combined Chiefs of Staff Committee, 1943-44. Deputy Commander, French Forces of the Interior, Aug.-Sept. 1944. Head of British Military Mission (France), 1945-46. Director of Military Operations, War Office, 1948-51. Deputy

Supreme Allied Commander, Europe, 1951-52. Vice-Chief of Imperial General Staff, 1952-55. Governor and C.-in-C., Gibraltar, 1955-58.

According to information received by the Liddell Hart Centre for Military Archives, Sir Harold Redman deliberately refrained from collecting papers.

REES, Thomas Ifor (1890-)

Consular service. Acted as Chargé d'Affaires, Venezuela, Nicaragua, Cuba, Mexico. Ambassador, Bolivia (Minister, 1944-47), 1947-49.

Mr Rees has retained no papers of a political nature.

REES, Major-General Thomas Wynford (1898-1959)

Military career. Served World War I; India, 1920, 1922-24, 1936-37. Commander, 10th Indian Division, Iraq and North Africa, 1942; 19th Indian Division, Burma, 1944-45; 4th Indian Division, 1945-47; Punjab Boundary Force, Aug.-Sept. 1947. Head of Military Emergency Staff to Emergency Committee of the Cabinet, Delhi, Sept.-Dec. 1947.

A collection of the Major-General's papers is preserved in the Library of the University of Sussex.

REES, Admiral William Stokes (1853-1929)

Naval career from 1866, with active service mainly in the nineteenth century.

Papers are available at the National Maritime Museum and include logs (1868-73); letter books (1898-1901); and material relating to various expeditions and incidents, e.g. Ashanti expedition (1895-96), Benin expedition (1897) and the deposition of the Sultan of Zanzibar (1896).

REID, Sir George Thomas (1881-1966)

Secretary, Trade Boards, 1912-19; Industrial Court, 1919-23. Permanent Secretary, National Assistance Board, 1938-44. Director of Welfare Division, United Nations Relief and Rehabilitation Administration (Europe), 1944-45.

Lady Reid, 21 Rugby Road, Worthing, Sussex, states that most of her late husband's papers were destroyed. Lady Reid has only a few letters and press cuttings, relating to her husband's work with the Worthing and District Council of Social Service.

REID, Sir Robert Niel (1883-1964)

Governor, Assam, 1937-42. Acting Governor, Bengal, 1938 and 1939. China Relations Officer, Calcutta, 1942-43.

The collection (1918-63) at the India Office Library includes correspondence with 5th Baron Brabourne, 2nd Marquess of Linlithgow, Sir Henry Joseph Twynam and Sir John Ackroyd Woodhead (b. 1881). Other papers consist of notes and memoirs prepared by Reid, copies of his speeches, drafts of his articles and some press cuttings (1941-43).

REILLY, Lieutenant-Colonel Sir Bernard Rawdon (1882-1966)

Indian Political Department. Chief Commissioner, Aden, 1932-37; Governor, 1937-40. Envoy, Yemen, 1933-34; Ethiopia, 1944. Head of War Office Working Party, ex-Italian Colonies in Africa, 1946-47.

The Oxford Colonial Records Project found that Sir B. R. Reilly had kept no papers.

RENDEL, Sir George William (1889-   )

Minister, Bulgaria, 1938-41. Minister and later Ambassador, Yugoslav Government in London, 1941-43. U.K. Representative, European Committee of U.N.R.R.A., 1944-47. Ambassador, Belgium, 1947-50 (Minister, Luxembourg, 1947-49).

Sir George Rendel kept very few records, apart from an engagement diary which he retains. In addition to his published memoirs, Sir George has deposited at the Middle East Centre, St Antony's College, Oxford, a collection of notes on Saudi Arabia in the 1930s and on Middle Eastern affairs with which he was concerned. Some files of letters and comments about his book, as well as copies of one or two lectures, remain with Sir George.

RENISON, Sir Patrick Muir (1911-1965)

Colonial Secretary, Trinidad and Tobago, 1948-52. Governor, British Honduras, 1952-55; British Guiana, 1955-59; Kenya, 1959-62.

A collection of speeches, correspondence and memoranda, relating to service in the West Indies and Kenya, can be found at Rhodes House Library.

RENNELL OF RODD, 1st B
Sir James Rennell Rodd (1858-1941)

M.P. (Con.) St Marylebone, 1928-32. Minister, Sweden, 1904-08. Ambassador, Italy, 1908-19. Delegate, League of Nations, 1921 and 1923.

The present (2nd) Lord Rennell of Rodd, The Rodd, near Presteigne, Powys, has retained his father's papers. They comprise two large deed boxes full of official, semi-official and personal correspondence, going back to about 1890, together with two large volumes of press cuttings and most of Lord Rennell's diaries. These records are roughly sorted but not calendared, and are to be deposited at the Bodleian Library, Oxford.

RENNELL OF RODD, 2nd B
Major-General Francis James Rennell Rodd (1895-   )

Served World War I. Diplomatic Service, 1919-24. Major-General, Civil Affairs Administration, Middle East, East Africa, and Italy; World War II.

A collection of papers may be found in the Library of Nuffield College, Oxford. The papers include confidential reports relating to the British military administration in Malaya (1945-46), Eritrea (1945), the Dodecanese Islands (1945), and Tripolitania (1945); the finance and accounts of the Civil Affairs Branch, Middle East Forces (1944) and of relief work in Somalia (1943); agriculture in Somalia (1943); a survey of Madagascar (1942-43); also Foreign Office confidential papers (1886); and personal correspondence (1943).

RENNIE, Sir Ernest Amelius (1868-1935)

Diplomatic Service. Chargé d'Affaires, Chile, 1906-08. Minister, Peru, 1913-19; Finland, 1921-30. British Commissioner and President, Inter-Allied Plebiscite Commission, East Prussia, 1919-20.

Messrs Eland Hore Patersons, the solicitors who acted for Rennie, have no information regarding papers or surviving members of the family. According to Sir

Ernest's will, family letters were left to his brother, John Assheton Rennie, a marine engineer.

RENNIE, Sir Gilbert McCall (1895-   ).

Colonial Service, Ceylon, Gold Coast, Kenya. Governor, Northern Rhodesia, 1948-54. High Commissioner, Federation of Rhodesia and Nyasaland, 1954-61.

Rhodes House Library has a collection of miscellaneous memoranda as an administrative officer in Ceylon (1920-37), including staff standing orders, papers on salaries and notes on official records. Sir Gilbert retains in his care a number of papers relating to Rhodesia.

RENTON, Brigadier (Hon. Major General) James Malcolm Leslie (1898-1972)

Military career. Head of British Military Mission to Iraq Army and Inspector General, 1944-48.

The Middle East Centre at St Antony's College, Oxford, has a number of Renton's papers relating to Iraq, the Iraq Army (lecture, 1948), the Iraq Levies (1927), and the British Military Mission to the Iraqi Army (1944-48).

REPINGTON, Lieutenant-Colonel Charles A'Court (1858-1925)

Entered Army, 1878. Served Afghanistan, Burma, Sudan, South Africa. Military Attaché, Brussels and The Hague, 1899-1902. Military correspondent and writer.

It has not proved possible to trace Repington's papers, apart from a large box of unsorted material in the *Times* archive. The papers include correspondence with Moberly Bell and Geoffrey Dawson for the period 1904-20.

REY, Lieutenant-Colonel Sir Charles Fernand (1877-1968)

Served Board of Trade; Ministry of Munitions; Ministry of National Service, and Ministry of Labour (World War I). Chief British Representative, Inter-Allied Commission for Food Supply to Germany, 1919. Served Unemployment Grants Committee, 1927-29. Resident Commissioner, Bechuanaland, 1930-37.

The papers in the library of Rhodes House, Oxford, fall into four main groups: personal and biographical papers for the period 1899-1964; material relating to Abyssinia; papers about Bechuanaland; and papers accumulated during retirement in South Africa.

RICARDO, Sir Harry Ralph (1885-1974)

Consulting engineer. Consultant to Mechanical Warfare Department, 1916; to Air Ministry on aero-engines, 1918.

The main collection of Ricardo's papers (1918-55) is at Churchill College, Cambridge. Photocopies of the drawing office catalogue of Ricardo and Co. Engineers (1927) Ltd, giving a summary of all tank and other diesel engines designed by Ricardo and his associates, are available at the Imperial War Museum.

RICHARDS, Sir Edmund Charles (1889-1955)

Colonial Service. Resident Commissioner, Basutoland, 1935-42. Governor, Nyasaland, 1942-48.

Rhodes House Library has a number of press cuttings about Basutoland (1938-40), and a copy of Richards's farewell address as Governor of Nyasaland (1947).

RICHARDS, Sir Henry Erle (1861-1922)

British Counsel, Samoan arbitration, 1903; Venezuela Arbitration, 1903. Legal member, Viceroy of India's Council, 1904-09. Legal adviser, India Office, 1911-21. Chichele Professor of International Law, Oxford.

At the India Office Library there are papers relating to Erle Richard's appointment to the Viceroy's Council, a collection of correspondence (1904-08) with colleagues in India and other correspondence with colleagues in England and with Indians, and an assortment of personal and family letters. The collection also includes notes and journals of tours, caricature and sundry photographs, and newspaper cuttings albums. Papers of Lady Richards are also at the India Office Library.

RICHMOND, Admiral Sir Herbert W. (1871-1946)

Naval career, with Commands 1909-12. Assistant Director of Operations, Admiralty, 1913-15. Liaison Officer with Italian Fleet, 1915. Director of Staff Duties and Training, 1918. President of the Royal Naval War College, Greenwich, 1920-23. C.-in-C., East Indies Squadron, 1924-25. Commandant of the Imperial Defence College, 1927-28. Naval historian. Master of Downing College, 1936-46.

A collection of papers is available at the National Maritime Museum. This includes private diaries, 15 vols. (1886-1920); press cuttings, with comments (1928-45); log books, commonplace books, and correspondence on naval matters, notes and drafts for lectures and papers, etc.

RICHMOND, Vice-Admiral Sir Maxwell (1900-   )

Naval career from 1918. Commands from 1936, and during World War II. Assistant Chief of Supplies, Admiralty, 1946-48. Naval Liaison Officer, Wellington, New Zealand, 1948-50. Senior Naval Officer, Northern Ireland, 1951. Deputy Chief of Naval Personnel (Training), 1952-55. Flag Officer (Air), Mediterranean, and Flag Officer, 2nd-in-Command, Mediterranean Fleet, 1955-56.

A microfilm of Sir Maxwell Richmond's papers is available at the Imperial War Museum.

RIDDELL, Sir Walter Robert Buchanan-, 12th Bt (1879-1934)

Chairman, University Grants Committee, 1930-34.

Family papers are deposited with the Northumberland Record Office. Some letters of the 12th Bt remain with Sir John Buchanan-Riddell at Hepple, Morpeth, Northumberland.

RIDGEWAY, Sir Joseph West (1844-1930)

Under-Secretary, India, 1880-84; Ireland, 1887-92. Special Envoy, Morocco, 1892-93. Governor, Isle of Man, 1893-95; Ceylon, 1896-1903.

Papers survive relating mainly to the Afghan Boundary Commission, the Indian section of which was commanded by Ridgeway, and to the period when he was

Under-Secretary for Ireland. Political correspondents include A. J. Balfour, Lords Roberts, Dufferin, Rosebery and Curzon, and Louis Botha and de Wet. The material is in the care of Mrs V. Tollemache, Devenish House, Sunningdale, Berks.

RISLEY, Sir Herbert Hope (1851-1911)

Census Commissioner, Bengal, 1899-1902. Financial Secretary, Government of India, 1898; Home Secretary, 1902-09; Secretary, Judicial and Public Department, 1910-11.

The papers (1893-1911) at the India Office Library include private and official correspondence, lecture notes, draft and printed articles, together with reports and circulars on the 1901 Census of Bengal and the Ethnographical Survey of India.

RITCHIE, General Sir Neil Methuen (1897-   )

Military career. Served World War I in France, Mesopotamia, Palestine. Deputy Chief of Staff, Middle East, 1941. Commander of 8th Army, Libya, 1941. Commanded 52nd Lowland Division, 1942-43; XII Corps, British Liberation Army, 1944-45. G.O.C.-in-C., Scottish Command, 1945-47. C.-in-C., Far East Land Forces, 1947-49. Commander, British Army Staff, Washington, and Military Member of Joint Services Mission, 1950-51.

The General's papers covering service in the Middle East in 1941 and early 1942 were destroyed by enemy action. Other papers are presently still in Sir Neil Ritchie's care.

RITCHIE, Sir Richard Thackeray (1854-1912)

Political Secretary, Indian Government, 1902-10. Permanent Under-Secretary, India Office, 1910-12.

No papers were located. The widow and son mentioned in the Letters of Administration could not be traced. Political correspondence (1895-97, 1909-13), with Lord Welby concerning the Commission on Indian expenditure and committee on Indian military service, can be found in the Welby collection at the Lincolnshire Archives Office.

ROBB, Air Chief Marshal Sir James Milne (d. 1968)

Served European War, 1914-18. Air Officer Commanding, No. 2 Bomber Group, 1940; No. 15 Coastal Group, 1941; R.A.F. North West Africa, 1943-44. Chief of Staff (Air) to General Eisenhower, 1944-45. Air Officer C.-in-C., R.A.F. Fighter Command, 1945-47. Vice Chief of Air Staff, 1947-48. C.-in-C., Air Forces Western Europe, 1948-51. Inspector-General, R.A.F., 1951.

The R.A.F. Museum has a collection of papers including log books, diaries, files, letters, photographs, map lectures and published material (1914-63). Subjects include service in France (1914-18), Iraq (1924-25), the Royal Navy (1930-36), the Central Flying School (1936-40); the Empire Air Training Scheme, Canada (1938-39); Air Operations (1940-44), Combined Operations (1942), Fighter Command (1945-47), the Air Staff (1947-48), and Air Forces Western Europe (1948-51).

ROBERTS OF KANDAHAR, 1st E
Field-Marshal Sir Frederick Sleigh Roberts (1832-1914)

C.-in-C., Madras, 1881-85; India, 1885-93. Commander of Forces in Ireland, 1895-99. C.-in-C., South Africa, 1899-1900; British Army, 1901-04.

A collection of Roberts's papers is preserved at the National Army Museum. This consists of nine boxes, and includes correspondence, mainly incoming and official; papers labelled 'official military, South Africa', and including some 16 volumes of letter books, home and overseas correspondence (1899-1900); operational telegrams, proclamations and reports; 22 volumes of official military correspondence, comprising letter books and telegrams (1901-14); a box of speeches, books, press cuttings, etc. (1878-1941); and 20 volumes of news cuttings and scrapbooks (1870-1914).

At the India Office Library are printed minutes and notes (1883-93) relating to Roberts's service in India. The British Library has certain material consisting of a small amount of correspondence (Add. MSS. 45102, 45680, 45807, 45918).

At the Public Record Office (W.O. 105) there are some 40 boxes, relating to operations in South Africa (1899-1902), and including dispatches, telegrams and reports exchanged between Roberts and officials.

The Transvaal Archives Depot, Pretoria, South Africa (the South Africa Government Archives) has a collection of papers (1899-1900), and the Library of Duke University, Durham, North Carolina, has a small collection of correspondence, chiefly addressed to journalists and writers, and covering the years 1881-1910 (some 55 items).

ROBERTS, General Sir Ouvry Lindfield (1898-)

Military career, Royal Engineers. Served War of 1939-45. G.O.C., Northern Ireland District, 1948-49. G.O. C.-in-C., Southern Command, 1949-52. Quartermaster-General, 1952-55.

General Roberts has kept a number of records relating to his career.

ROBERTS, Sir Walter St Clair Howland (1893-)

Head of Western Europe Department, 1936-39, and Prisoner of War Department, Foreign Office, 1941-45. Ambassador, Peru, 1945-48. Minister, Romania, 1949-51; Holy See, 1951-53.

No private papers likely to be of value to the historian have been retained by Sir Walter Roberts.

ROBERTSHAW, Vice-Admiral Sir Ballin Illingworth (1902-1971)

Naval career. Commander, H.M.S. *Cleopatra*, 1944-46; H.M.S. *Implacable*, 1952. Served Staff of C.-in-C., Mediterranean, 1942-43. Naval Assistant to 2nd Sea Lord, 1949-51. Chief of Staff to C.-in-C., Portsmouth, 1953-55. Chief of Allied Staff, Mediterranean, 1955-58.

The Imperial War Museum has a diary kept as a Commander on the 1939 staff mission to Russia, and other miscellaneous papers.

ROBERTSON OF OAKRIDGE, 1st B
General Sir Brian Hubert Robertson, 1st Bt (1896-1974)

Chief Administrative Officer to C.-in-C., Italy, 1944-45. C.-in-C. and Military Governor, Germany, 1947-49; U.K. High Commissioner, 1949-50. C.-in-C., Middle East Land Forces, 1950-53.

The present (2nd) Lord Robertson of Oakridge, 259 Dover House Road, London SW15 5BZ, states that a collection of his father's papers has survived. The collection will be placed in due course in the Liddell Hart Centre for Military Archives.

ROBERTSON, Sir James Wilson (1899-   )

Sudan Political Service. Governor-General, Nigeria, 1955-60.

Rhodes House Library has the transcript of two interviews, concerning Sudan and Nigeria, and a memorandum (1957) on the Nigerian constitution. Other papers will be placed in the Sudan Archive, Durham University.

ROBERTSON, Field-Marshal Sir William Robert, 1st Bt (1860-1933)

Military career. Served South African War (Intelligence). Assistant Director of Military Operations, 1901-07. Brigadier-General, General Staff, Aldershot, 1907-10. Director of Military Training, 1913-14. Chief of General Staff, British Expeditionary Force, 1915. Chief of Imperial General Staff, 1915-18. G.O. C.-in-C., Eastern Command, 1918. C.-in-C., British Army on the Rhine, 1919-20.

The papers at the Liddell Hart Centre for Military Archives cover Robertson's military career from 1898 onwards, and include personal and semi-official correspondence kept whilst Chief of the Imperial General Staff (1916-18). Three volumes of papers (1916-17) can be found at the Public Record Office.

ROBINSON, Sir (Frederick) Percival (1887-1949)

Civil Service career. Financial Secretary, Sudan Government, 1926-30. Member, (Indian) Federal Finance Committee, 1932. Financial Secretary, King George VI, 1937-41. Secretary, War Damage Commission, 1941-43. Permanent Secretary, Ministry of Works, 1943-46.

Information given in the Will and Act of Probate was not helpful in tracing the family.

ROBINSON, Sir William Arthur (1874-1950)

Permanent Secretary, Air Ministry, 1917-20. Secretary, Ministry of Health, 1920-35. Chairman of Supply Board, Committee of Imperial Defence, 1935. Secretary, Ministry of Supply, 1939-40.

Information available at Somerset House was not helpful in tracing members of the family.

RODGER, Sir John Pickersgill (1851-1910)

British Resident, Pahang, 1888-96; Selangor, 1896-1902; Perak, 1902-03. Governor, Gold Coast, 1903-10.

Papers covering Rodger's career are available in the National Library of Wales. They relate to the history of the Rodger family and of the Hadlow Castle estate; letters of introduction during his world tour (1880) etc.; papers (1886-94) relating to work as a colonial official in South East Asia; papers (1904-10) relating to the Gold Coast, including estimates, addresses; and papers on tariffs, civil service, railway construction, sanitary regulations, agriculture as well as personalia and press cuttings. Rhodes House Library, Oxford, has a series of miscellaneous extracts from notes, by Rodger, Sir Hugh Clifford *et al.*, about territorial rights and land ownership, etc., in the Gold Coast.

RONALD, Sir Nigel Bruce (1894-1973)

Private Secretary to successive Foreign Secretaries, 1929-34. Ambassador, Portugal, 1947-54.

Sir Nigel Ronald stated that he had no papers likely to be of interest to the historian.

ROSKILL, Captain Stephen Wentworth (1903-)

Naval career, 1917-48. Commanded H.M.S. *Warspite*, 1939. Served on Naval Staff, 1939-41. Commander, H.M.N.Z.S. *Leander*, 1941-44. Deputy Director of Naval Intelligence, 1946-48. Cabinet Office, Official Naval Historian, 1949-60. Fellow of Churchill College, Cambridge, from 1961.

Captain Roskill's papers are preserved at Churchill College, Cambridge. The material consists of correspondence and papers about World War II and a fairly large collection of family papers and correspondence. Other papers, including letters and documents concerning Captain Roskill's historical work, will be housed in Churchill College in due course.

ROSS, Sir Frederick William Leith- (1887-1968)

Private Secretary to Prime Minister, H. H. Asquith, 1911-13. British Representative, Reparation Commission Finance Board, 1920-25, and several international conferences, etc. Chief Economic Adviser, British Government, 1932-46. Head of British Financial Mission to China, 1935-36. Director-General, Ministry of Economic Warfare, 1939-42. Chairman, Inter-Allied Post-War Requirements Committee, 1942-43; European Committee of Council, United Nations Relief and Rehabilitation Administration, 1944-45. Governor, National Bank of Egypt, 1946-51.

A collection of papers survives in the Treasury Private Office, Class T.188 at the Public Record Office. The material includes papers relating to service as British Representative on the Finance Board of the Reparation Commission, 1920-25; Deputy Controller of Finance at the Treasury, 1925-32; Chief Economic Adviser, 1932-46; Director General, Ministry of Economic Welfare, 1939-42; and as a member of various international conferences and organisations dealing with financial and economic matters.

ROSS, Sir James Stirling (1877-1961)

Served War Office, from 1900. Deputy Secretary and (later) 1st Deputy Under-Secretary, Air Ministry, 1934-38. Air Ministry Representative, South Africa and Southern Rhodesia, 1940-43. Served Air Ministry Secretariat and Planning Executive, 1944-46. Chairman, Selection Board, Allied Control Commission (Germany), 1946. Served Ministry of Health, 1946-49.

A collection of material (1917-45) at the Public Record Office (AIR 19) includes papers of Sir James Ross, some of which relate to the Czech crisis of 1938.

ROUNDELL, Christopher Foulis (1876-1958)

Chief General Inspector, Ministry of Health, 1935-41.

Mr C. W. Roundell states that correspondence and papers relating to his father have not survived.

ROWAN, Sir (Thomas) Leslie (1908-1972)

Civil Service career. Assistant and later Principal Private Secretary to Prime Minister, Winston Churchill, 1941-45, and Clement Attlee, 1945-47. Permanent Secretary, Ministry for Economic Affairs, 1947. 2nd Secretary, Treasury, 1947-49, 1951-58. Economic Minister, Washington Embassy, 1949-51.

A collection of papers survives in the care of Lady Rowan, 16 The Vale, Chelsea, London SW3. This includes personal correspondence (mainly with Lady Rowan); albums containing letters, photographs and press cuttings; appointment diaries; notes, reports, a few Treasury papers, and drafts of speeches and articles. The papers are largely unsorted, and the correspondence is not open for inspection.

ROWCROFT, Major-General Sir (Eric) Bertram (1891-1963)

Military career. European War, 1914-18; Palestine, 1936; War Office. Director of Mechanical Engineering, War Office, 1942-46.

Papers (1942-46) survive in the Corps Museum, Royal Electrical and Mechanical Engineers (Moat House, Arborfield, Reading RG2 9LN).

ROWLAND, Sir John (1877-1941)

Private Secretary to President of the Board of Trade, 1905-08; and to the Chancellor of the Exchequer, David Lloyd George, 1908-12. Chairman, Welsh Board of Health.

Mr R. J. Rowland states that he has no papers relating to his father. Some 35 letters (1936-40) are in the Lloyd George papers now at the House of Lords Record Office.

ROWLANDS, Sir Archibald (1892-1953)

War Office career. Financial Adviser (Military), Indian Government, 1937-39. Deputy Under-Secretary, Air Ministry, 1939-40. Permanent Secretary, Ministry of Aircraft Production, 1940-43. Member of Beaverbrook-Harriman Mission to Moscow, 1941. Adviser on War Administration to Viceroy of India, 1943. Finance Member, Viceroy's Council, 1945-46. Permanent Secretary, Ministry of Supply, 1946-53. Economic Adviser to Governor-General of Pakistan, 1947. Member of Economic Planning Board, 1947-53.

Messrs Nicholas Williams & Co., solicitors, state that the late Lady Rowlands's sister, Mrs Sanby Thomas, has no papers in her possession and that when Lady Rowlands moved from England in 1969 all papers were cleared.

RUCKER, Sir Arthur Nevil (1895-   )

Principal Private Secretary to Prime Minister, 1939-40. Secretary, Minister of State's Office, Cairo, 1941-43. Deputy Secretary, Health, from 1943. Deputy Director-General, International Refugee Organisation, 1948. Deputy Agent-General, United Nations, Korean Reconstruction Agency, 1951.

Sir Arthur Rucker has not kept a diary and retained no papers from the various offices in which he served. Sir Arthur says that nothing among his private papers appears likely to be of interest to the historian.

RUGBY, 1st B
Sir John Loader Maffey (1877-1969)

Private Secretary to Viceroy of India, 1916-20. Chief Commissioner, North West Frontier Province, India, 1921-24. Governor-General, Sudan, 1926-33. Permanent Under-Secretary, Colonies, 1933-37. Representative in Eire, 1939-49.

Lady Aitken, 47 Phillimore Gardens, London W8, retains a large collection of papers amassed by her father and mother. A biography is being prepared by Sir

Ronald Wingate who has sorted the earlier papers and taken copies of many of them. The papers consist of letters, together with books of photographs and press cuttings.

RUMBOLD, Sir Horace, 8th Bt (1829-1913)

Minister, Chile, 1872-78; Switzerland, 1878-79; Argentina, 1879-81; Sweden and Norway, 1881-84; Greece, 1884-88; Netherlands, 1888-96. Ambassador, Austria-Hungary, 1896-1900.

A substantial collection of papers remains with Sir Anthony Rumbold, Bt, Hatch House, Tisbury, Wilts.

RUMBOLD, Sir Horace George Montagu, 9th Bt (1869-1941)

Minister, Switzerland, 1916-19; Poland, 1919-20. High Commissioner and Ambassador, Turkey, 1920-24. Ambassador, Spain, 1924-28; Germany, 1928-33.

A large collection of papers has been deposited at the Bodleian Library, Oxford. The papers include diaries, letters, copies of official dispatches and memoranda.

RUNCIMAN, 1st Vt
Walter Runciman (1870-1949)

M.P. (Lib.) Oldham, 1899-1900; Dewsbury, 1902-18; Swansea West, 1924-29; (Lib.Nat.) St Ives, 1931-37. Parliamentary Secretary, Local Government Board, 1905-07. Financial Secretary, Treasury, 1907-08. President, Board of Education, 1908-11; Board of Agriculture and Fisheries, 1911-14; Board of Trade, 1914-16, 1931-37. Lord President of the Council, 1938-39. Special Envoy to Czechoslovakia, 1938.

A collection of Runciman's papers is held in the Library of the University of Newcastle-upon-Tyne. The material includes Cabinet papers, notes made by Runciman, press cuttings, and political papers relating to elections, party and constituency matters and current affairs. Private Office papers relating to the mission to Czechoslovakia are available at the Public Record Office (F.O. 800/304-8). Further details are given by Hazlehurst and Woodland op. cit., pp.124-5.

RUNDLE, General Sir (Henry Macleod) Leslie (1856-1934)

Military career. Served Zulu War, 1879; Boer War, 1882; Nile Expedition, 1884-85; Sudan; South African War, 1900-02. General Officer Commanding in Chief, Northern Command, 1905-07. Governor, Malta, 1909-15.

The Sudan Archive, University of Durham, has one box of papers, including letters from Lord Kitchener.

RUSHBROOKE, Vice-Admiral Edmund Gerard Noel (1892-1972)

Naval career. Served World War I (destroyers). Chief of Intelligence Staff, China Station, 1937. Commanded H.M.S. *Guardian*, 1939; H.M.S. *Argus*, 1940; H.M.S. *Eagle*, 1941. Director of Naval Intelligence, 1942-46.

Papers relating to his naval career (1911-68) are in the care of the Imperial War Museum.

RUSHCLIFFE, 1st B
Sir Henry Bucknall Betterton, 1st Bt (1872-1949)

M.P. (Con.) Rushcliffe, 1918-34. Parliamentary Secretary, Ministry of Labour, 1923-24, 1924-29. Minister of Labour, 1931-34. Chairman, Unemployment Assistance Board, 1934-41.

Hazlehurst and Woodland, op. cit., p.16, located no papers.

RUSSELL, Sir Claud Frederick William (1871-1959)

Minister, Abyssinia, 1920-25; Switzerland, 1928-31. Ambassador, Portugal, 1931-35.

Mr Martin Russell, 6 Austin Friars, London EC2P 2HU, states that Lady Russell may have in storage a collection of documents and letters, some of which relate to the career of her late husband. Such papers would not be available for study.

RUSSELL, Hon. Sir Odo William Theophilus Villiers (1870-1951)

Diplomatic Service. Private Secretary to Foreign Secretary, Sir Edward Grey. Diplomatic Secretary to Foreign Secretary, 1915-19. Minister, Switzerland, 1919-22; Holy See, 1922-28; Netherlands, 1928-33.

No papers have been located.

RYAN, Sir Andrew (1876-1949)

Consular and diplomatic official, Turkey, 1897-1914, 1918-24. Consul-General, Rabat, 1924-30. Minister, Saudi Arabia, 1930-36; Albania, 1936-39.

Correspondence and papers (1881-1929) are available at the Public Record Office (F.O. 800/240). Some other material, including photographs, is to be deposited by the family with the Middle East Centre, St Antony's College, Oxford.

SACKVILLE, 4th B
Major-General Charles John Sackville-West (1870-1962)

Military career. British Representative, Supreme War Council, Versailles, 1918-19. Military Attaché, Paris, 1920-24.

It is understood from the present (6th) Lord Sackville that no papers survive relating to the 4th Baron.

SALMOND, Marshal of the Royal Air Force Sir John Maitland (1881-1968)

Served South Africa, 1901-02; European War, 1914-18; War of 1939-45. Air Officer Commanding, Inland Area, 1920-22; British Forces in Iraq, 1922-24. Air Officer Commanding in Chief, Air Defence of Great Britain, 1925-29. Air Member for Personnel, 1929-30. Chief of Air Staff, 1930-33.

A small collection has been deposited at the Royal Air Force Museum. The papers (1914-43) consist of a diary (1923), correspondence, files, notebooks and other manuscripts (1915-64). Subjects include Iraq and India (1921-24), and the Australia and New Zealand Air Forces Mission, 1928.

SALMOND, Air Chief Marshal Sir William Geoffrey Hanson (1878-1933)

Served South Africa, 1899-1902; China, 1900; European War, 1914-18. Director General, Supply and Research, Air Ministry, 1922. Air Member Supply and Research, Air Council, 1922-27. Air Officer Commanding, R.A.F. India, 1927-31. Air Officer Commanding in Chief, Air Defence of Great Britain, 1931-33. Chief of Air Staff, 1933.

The Royal Air Force Museum knows of no papers.

SALOWAY, Sir Reginald Harry (1905-1959)

Indian and Colonial Civil Service. Director-General, Indian Resettlement and Employment, 1946. Chief Secretary and Minister of Defence and External Affairs, Gold Coast, 1951-54. Controller of Operations, Colonial Development Corporation, from 1955.

Rhodes House Library has a collection of letters received (1953-54), press cuttings and photographs, and the diary of Lady Saloway (1948).

SAMUEL, 1st Vt
Sir Herbert Louis Samuel (1870-1963)

M.P. (Lib.) Cleveland, 1902-18; Darwen, 1929-35. Parliamentary Under-Secretary, Home Office, 1905-09. Chancellor of the Duchy of Lancaster, 1909-10. Postmaster-General, 1910-14, 1915-16. President, Local Government Board, 1914-15. Secretary of State for Home Affairs, 1916, 1931-32. High Commissioner, Palestine, 1920-25.

Hazlehurst and Woodland, op. cit., pp.126-7, describe the papers which are located in the House of Lords Record Office, the Israel State Archives and with the Samuel family.

SANDARS, John Satterfield (1853-1934)

Private Secretary to A. J. Balfour, 1892-1905.

The papers at the Bodleian Library, Oxford, consist of correspondence and memoranda, mainly dating to the period 1902-05 when A. J. Balfour was Prime Minister. This important collection is described in Hazlehurst and Woodland, op. cit., p. 11.

SANDERS, Air Chief Marshal Sir Arthur Penrose Martyn (1898-1974)

Served European War, 1916-18; War of 1939-45. Air Office C.-in-C., British Air Forces of Occupation, Germany, 1947-48. Vice Chief of Air Staff, 1948-50. Deputy Chief of Air Staff, 1950-52. C.-in-C., Middle East Air Force, 1952-53.

The Imperial War Museum found that the Air Chief Marshal had no papers.

SANDERSON, 1st B
Sir Thomas Henry Sanderson (1841-1923)

Permanent Under-Secretary, Foreign Office, 1894-1906.

Two volumes of correspondence (1860-1922) covering Sanderson's long career in the Foreign Office are available at the Public Record Office (F.O. 800/1-2). Other material is known to survive among the papers of the late Dame Lillian Penson presently at Bedford College, London. Details of this collection, which is important and wide-ranging, are not available. Some correspondence with Lord Rendel is in the National Library of Wales.

SANDERSON OF AYOT, 1st B
Basil Sanderson (1894-1971)

Military service, European War, 1914-18. President, International Shipping Federation, 1934-51. Director of Shipping in Port, Ministry of Shipping, 1939-41. Head
of Port and Transport Control, Ministry of War Transport, 1941-45.

Churchill College, Cambridge, has a collection of Sanderson's papers, including
memoirs of war service (1914-17).

SANDERSON, Sir Percy (1842-1919)

Consul-General, Romania, 1882-94 (Consul, 1876-82); New York, 1894-1907.

A collection of Private Office correspondence (1876-1908) survives at the Public
Record Office (F.O. 800/21).

SANDFORD, Sir Folliott Herbert (1906-   )

Served Air Ministry from 1930. Secretary, Office of Resident Minister, West Africa,
1942-44. Assistant, later Deputy Under-Secretary, Air Ministry, 1944-58. Registrar,
University of Oxford, 1958-72.

Rhodes House Library has a diary for the years 1942-44, and a number of notes
and photographs relating to West Africa. Sir F. H. Sandford retains in his care a
further collection of unsorted papers, relating mainly to Oxford.

SANSOM, Sir George Bailey (1883-1965)

Served in Admiralty and Intelligence Directorate of War Office, 1914-18.
Commercial Counsellor, Tokyo, 1924-40. Civilian Member of Far Eastern War
Council, 1941-42. Minister, Washington, 1942-47. British Member, Allied Far
Eastern Commission, 1946-47. Professor, 1947-53 and Director, East Asian In-
stitute, Columbia University, 1949-53.

Two boxes of correspondence and papers are housed at St Antony's College,
Oxford.

SARGENT, Sir Orme (1884-1962)

Permanent Under-Secretary, Foreign Office, 1946-49.

Mr J. H. Loch, Palace West, Much Hadham, Herts., has kept nearly all the papers
that were in Sir Orme Sargent's possession when he died. The material consists of
personal papers, such as letters from friends, letters of congratulation and family
letters, together with a series of personal and engagement diaries. None of the
papers appear to relate directly to Sir Orme Sargent's career in public service. The
collection is not available for study. However, a collection of Private Office
correspondence (1926-48) is available at the Public Record Office (F.O.
800/272-9).

SATOW, Sir Ernest Mason (1843-1929)

Minister-Resident, Siam, 1885-88 (Consul-General, 1884); Uruguay, 1888-93.
Minister, Morocco, 1893-95; Japan, 1895-1900; China, 1900-06.

A large collection of papers has been deposited at the Public Record Office (P.R.O.
30/33). The correspondence, letter books, diaries and other papers fill 23 boxes and
cover the years 1856-1927.

SAUNDBY, Air Marshal Sir Robert Henry Magnus Spencer (1896-1971)

Royal Flying Corps and Royal Air Force career from 1915. Director of Organisational Requirements, Air Ministry, 1938-39. Assistant Chief of Air Staff, 1940. Senior Air Staff Officer, Bomber Command, 1941-42. Deputy Air Officer C.-in-C., Bomber Command, 1943-45.

A collection of papers, including log books, letters, manuscripts, photographs and published material (1914-71), is held at the Royal Air Force Museum. Subject matter includes service in France (1914-18), the Middle East (1923-26), and official histories (1948-51).

SAVORY, Lieutenant-General Sir Reginald Arthur (1894-)

Commissioned in 1914; served World War I, etc. Commanded 11th Indian Infantry Brigade, 1940-41. G.O.C., Eritrea, 1941. Commanded 23rd Indian Division, 1942-43. Director of Infantry, India, 1943-45. G.O.C., Persia and Iraq, 1945-46. Adjutant-General, India, 1946-47.

Lt.-Gen. Sir R. A. Savory has a collection of private letters and other papers (1914-49). The material consists of letters written to his parents and his wife, and also many official and semi-official papers.

SAWBRIDGE, Henry Raywood (1907-)

Consul-General, Yokohama, 1949-50. Chargé d'Affaires, Korea, 1950. Consul-General, Geneva, 1953-60. Counsellor, Foreign Office, 1960-64.

Mr Sawbridge says he has retained no private papers relating to his Foreign Service career.

SAYER, Vice-Admiral Sir Guy Bourchier (1903-)

Naval career. Served World War II. Vice-Controller of the Navy and Director of Naval Equipment, 1953-56. Flag Officer, Home Fleet Training Squadron, 1956-57; Commanding Reserve Fleet, 1958-59.

The Imperial War Museum has a small collection of miscellaneous World War II papers and Suez Crisis records (1939-56).

SCARBROUGH, 11th E of
Lawrence Roper Lumley (1896-1969)

M.P. (Con.) Kingston-upon-Hull East, 1922-29; York, 1931-37. Governor, Bombay, 1937-43. Parliamentary Under-Secretary, India and Burma, 1945. Lord Chamberlain, 1952-63.

The present (12th) Earl of Scarbrough, Sandbeck Park, Rotherham, Yorks., has a large and comprehensive collection of documents and press cuttings relating to his father's career. The papers are largely unsorted, but they include a private diary and material concerning the Governorship of Bombay, and the period as Lord Chamberlain. These papers are not available for inspection. A further collection of papers connected with Scarbrough's office as Grand Master of the Freemasons is held in the Library at Freemasons' Hall.

SCHOFIELD, Vice-Admiral Brian Betham (1895-)

Naval career. Served World War I. Naval Attaché, The Hague and Brussels, 1939-40. Commanded H.M.S. *King George V*, 1945-46.

A collection of the Vice-Admiral's papers is to be bequeathed to the Imperial War Museum. The Museum has Schofield's midshipman's journals (1913-15).

SCHRIEBER, Lieutenant-General Sir Edmond Charles Avon (1890-1972)

Military career. Served European War, 1914-18. G.O.C.-in-C., Western Command, 1942-44; South Eastern Command, 1944. Governor and C.-in-C., Malta, 1944-46.

In 1965 Sir Edmond reported to the Liddell Hart Centre for Military Archives that he had found no papers of interest.

SCHUSTER, 1st B
Sir Claud Schuster (1869-1956)

Civil Service career. Clerk of the Crown in Chancery, and Permanent Secretary to Lord Chancellor, 1915-44. Director of Legal Division, Allied Control Commission, Austria (British Element), 1944-46.

The Hon. Mrs E. A. Turner, The Grange, North Cadbury, Yeovil, Somerset, states that she has in store a certain number of her father's letters, which might be of interest. Some of Lord Schuster's papers were destroyed, and others survive with his granddaughter, Mrs Jenny Hughes, Old Wardow House, Tisbury, Wilts. These consist of letters exchanged between Lord Schuster and Sir George Schuster, while the latter was Financial Secretary to the Viceroy of India; and Lord Schuster's correspondence over some twenty years on the subject of reform of the administration of justice; a variety of articles, drafts and the texts of lectures relating to legal reform, literary criticism and mountaineering. Letters between Schuster and Lord Birkenhead concerning Sir Roger Casement have not survived in the family's care. Some other papers, at present in the Lord Chancellor's Office, will eventually be transferred to the Public Record Office.

SCHUSTER, Sir George Ernest (1881-   )

Military service in European War, 1914-18; North Russia, 1919. Financial Secretary, Sudan, 1922-27. Economic and Financial Adviser, Colonial Office, 1927-28. Finance Member, Viceroy of India's Council, 1928-34. Chairman, Joint Committee, Anglo-Argentine Meat Trade, 1935-38. M.P. (Lib. Nat.) Walsall, 1938-45. Member of various government committees.

Sir George Schuster has a good deal of correspondence relating to experiences during different periods, for example in North Russia (1918-19); on investigations in Northern Europe for the League of Nations (1921-22); in the Sudan (1922-28); on the East African Commission (1928); in India (1928-34); and in the House of Commons, etc.

SCOBIE, Lieutenant-General Sir Ronald MacKenzie (1893-1969)

Assistant Adjutant-General, War Office, 1938-39. Deputy Director of Mobilisation, 1939-40. G.O.C., 70th Division, Tobruk, 1941; Malta, 1942; Greece, 1944-46.

A collection of papers is to be placed in the Imperial War Museum.

SCOTT, Vice-Admiral Albert Charles (1872-1969)

Naval career. Served World War I. Commanded H.M.S. *Blonde*, 1914-16; H.M.S. *Dublin* from 1916 (present at Jutland, etc.).

The Vice-Admiral's 1914-16 diaries are preserved at the Imperial War Museum.

SCOTT, Sir Charles Stewart (1838-1924)

Minister, Switzerland from 1888; Denmark 1893-98. Ambassador, Russia, 1898-1904.

Seventeen volumes of Sir Charles Scott's correspondence and papers have been deposited in the British Library (Add. MSS. 52294-52310). The collection consists of general, family and royal correspondence; correspondence with successive Foreign Secretaries (1866-1904) and with Lord Sanderson of the Foreign Office (1867-1904); letter books (1899-1904); a diary (1900 and 1907); autobiographical notes, and some miscellaneous papers.

SCOTT, Hon. Sir Ernest Stowell (1872-1953)

Minister, Uruguay, 1925-30.

The Hon. Lady Scott, The Manor House, Bradford Peverell, Dorchester, Dorset, has kept a collection of unsorted papers relating to her late husband's career.

SCOTT, Sir Harold Richard (1887-1969)

Served Home Office, from 1911; Foreign Trade Department, 1916-18; Ministry of Labour, etc. Chairman, Commissioners of Prisons for England and Wales, 1932-39. Permanent Secretary, Ministry of Home Security, 1942-43; Ministry of Aircraft Production, 1943-45. Commissioner of Metropolitan Police, 1945-53.

No contact was established with members of the family. Mr F. C. Golledge (brother-in-law) is believed to live in Castle Cary, Somerset.

SCOTT, Sir (James) George (1851-1935)

Colonial service, Burma, Siam and Indo-China. Chargé d'affaires, Siam, 1893-94. British Commissioner, Burma-China Boundary Commission, 1898-1900. Superintendent and Political Officer, Southern Shan States, 1902-10. Author.

Two volumes of scrapbooks, covering the period 1888-97, are deposited in Duke University. The material includes official correspondence, notes, drawings, etc., and relates to service at Bangkok (1893-94) and on the Mekong Commission (1894-95).

SCOTT, Sir Oswald Arthur (1893-1960)

Minister, Finland, 1947-51. Ambassador, Peru, 1951-53.

Lady Scott states that her late husband retained no papers of official interest.

SCOTT, Sir (Robert) Russell (1877-1960)

Civil Service career. Permanent Under-Secretary, Home Office, 1932-38.

Mrs Anne Monro states that her late uncle kept few papers relating to his service in government departments. None of these papers have survived.

SCRIVENER, Sir Patrick Stratford (1897-1966)

Minister, Syria, 1947. Deputy Special Commissioner, later Deputy Commissioner-General (Foreign Affairs), South East Asia, 1947-49. Minister, subsequently Ambassador, Switzerland, 1949-53.

The Middle East Centre at St Antony's College, Oxford, found that there were no papers.

SCRIVENOR, Sir Thomas Vaisey (1908-)

Colonial Service, Tanganyika, Palestine, Malta and Nigeria. Deputy High Commissioner, Basutoland, Bechuanaland and Swaziland, 1953-60.

Rhodes House Library has a number of papers, including diaries (1930s); correspondence and police reports (1937-38); the record of an interview with General Montgomery in Haifa (12 Jan. 1939); and the tape and transcript of an interview given to the Colonial Records Project.

SELBORNE, 2nd E of
William Waldegrave Palmer, Vt Wolmer (1859-1942)

M.P. (Lib.) Hampshire East, 1885-86; (Lib. U.) 1886-92; Edinburgh West, 1892-95. Parliamentary Under-Secretary, Colonial Office, 1895-1900. 1st Lord of the Admiralty, 1900-05. High Commissioner, South Africa, 1905-10. President, Board of Agriculture and Fisheries, 1915-16.

Hazlehurst and Woodland, op. cit., pp.114-15, describe the papers in the Bodleian Library and in the Hampshire Record Office.

SELBY, Sir Walford Harmood Montague (1881-1965)

1st Secretary, Cairo, 1919-22. Principal Private Secretary to the Foreign Secretary, 1924-32. Minister, Austria, 1933-37. Ambassador, Portugal, 1937-40.

Mr R. W. Selby, C.M.G., c/o Lloyds Bank Ltd, 16 St James's Street, London SW1, has retained his father's papers. They are at present unsorted and unavailable for study. Some correspondence with Lord Robert Cecil is available at the British Library (Add. MSS. 51090).

SELF, Sir (Albert) Henry (1890-)

Civil Service career. Air Ministry, from 1919; Deputy Under-Secretary, from 1937. Director-General, British Air Commission, Washington, 1940-41. Permanent Secretary, Ministry of Production, 1942-43. Deputy for Minister of Production, Combined Production and Resources Board, Washington, 1943-45. Deputy Chairman, British Supply Council, Washington, 1945. U.K. Member, Combined Raw Materials Board, 1944-45. Permanent Secretary, Ministry of Civil Aviation, 1946-47. Deputy Chairman, later Chairman, British (later Central) Electricity Authority (later Electricity Council), from 1947).

Sir Henry states that when he retired he returned official papers to the departments concerned. His personal papers are not available.

SETON, Sir Malcolm Cotter-Cariston (1872-1940)

Secretary, Judicial and Public Department, India Office, 1911; Assistant Under-Secretary, 1919, and Deputy Under-Secretary, India Office, 1924-33.

A collection of papers and printed material has been deposited at the India Office Library. Among the mass of correspondence are letters from 1st Earl of Halifax, Sir Claude Hamilton Archer Hill (1866-1934), and Sir William Sinclair Morris (1873-1945). The collection includes a few letters on South Africa (1914), on Seton's visit to India in 1917, and papers on the protection of wildlife in India. Other material consists of Seton's typed articles, programmes and photographs, postcards, books and pamphlets.

SEVERN, Sir Claud (1869-1933)

Foreign Office and Colonial Service, Malaya. Colonial Secretary, Hong Kong, 1912-26.

Rhodes House Library has a collection of Severn's papers, including letters home (1894, 1899 and 1911), miscellaneous correspondence (1913-29), documents relating to the Chinese land tax and tariff duties (1896), and Lady Severn's letters home (1921-25).

SEYMOUR, Admiral of the Fleet Sir Edward Hobart (1840-1929)

Naval career from 1852. Service in China, Egypt, etc. C.-in-C., China Station, 1898-1901; Devonport, 1903-05.

A journal of a voyage to the Arctic (1867) together with a journal and correspondence concerning the Crimean War are in the National Library of Scotland. His diaries for the period 1861-1879 are deposited in McGill University Library, Canada.

SEYMOUR, Sir Horace James (1885-   )

Minister, Persia, 1936-39. Assistant Under-Secretary, Foreign Office, 1939-42. Ambassador, China, 1942-46.

Sir Horace Seymour states that he has kept no papers of interest.

SEYMOUR, Richard Sturgis (1875-1959)

Minister, Siam, 1919-24; Bolivia, 1924-26.

Mr G. F. Seymour (son) knows of no papers.

SHACKLETON, Sir David James (1863-1938)

M.P. (Lab.) Clitheroe, 1902-10 (Dec.). President, Trades Union Congress, 1908 and 1909; etc. National Health Insurance Commissioner, 1911-16. Permanent Secretary, Ministry of Labour, 1916-21. Chief Labour Adviser, Ministry of Labour, 1921-25.

David E. Martin, in the *Dictionary of Labour Biography* II, pp. 335-9, mentions no papers or surviving relations. However, he did make use of archival materials at Transport House.

SHAW, Sir John Valentine Wistar (1894-   )

Military and Colonial Service. Chief Secretary, Palestine, 1943-46. Governor and C.-in-C., Trinidad and Tobago, 1947-50.

Sir John states that he gave certain memoranda, press cuttings and photographs to the Oxford Colonial Records Project. No further papers survive with him.

SHEEPSHANKS, Sir Thomas Herbert (1895-1964)

Civil Service career; Ministry of Health; Home Office. Deputy Secretary, Ministry of Home Security, 1942; Ministry of National Insurance, 1944-45. Under-Secretary, Treasury, 1945-46. Permanent Secretary, Town and Country Planning, 1946-51; Ministry of Housing and Local Government, 1951-55.

It has not proved possible to contact Lady Sheepshanks, 29 Belgrave Manor, Brooklyn Road, Woking, Surrey.

SHEPHERD, Sir Edward Henry Gerald (1886-1967)

Consul-General, Liberia, 1921-23. Consul, Fernando Po, 1922-23; Le Havre, 1924-25; Riga, 1926-28; New York, 1929-37. Consul-General, Danzig, 1938-39; Amsterdam, 1939-40. Minister, Iceland, 1943-47.

Lady Shepherd, White House, 17th Avenue, RR1, Richmond Hill, Ontario, Canada, retains only a few of her late husband's papers, none of which she believes to be of much public interest.

SHEPHERD, Sir Francis Michie (1893-1962)

Minister, Haiti, 1932-37. Acting Consul-General, Barcelona, March-May 1938. Consul, Dresden, 1938-39. Acting Consul-General, Danzig, July-Aug. 1939. Consul-General, Reykjavik, 1940-42. British Political Representative, Finland, 1944-47. Consul-General, Netherlands East Indies, 1947-49. Ambassador, Iran, 1950-52; Poland, 1952-54.

Efforts to contact persons mentioned in the Will and Act of Probate proved unsuccessful.

SHONE, Sir Terence Allen (1894-1965)

Chargé d'Affaires, Yugoslavia, 1937, 1938 and 1939. Minister, Cairo, 1940-44. Minister, Syria and Lebanon, 1944-46. High Commissioner, India, 1946. Deputy Permanent Representative, United Nations, 1948-51.

Some papers have been deposited at the Middle East Centre, St Antony's College, Oxford, These papers include an account by Prince Paul (1941) of events leading to Yugoslavia's accession to the Axis; a report on the Levant States in 1945, e.g. events in Damascus; and notes by Lady Shone.

SHUCKBURGH, Sir John Evelyn (1877-1953)

Civil Service career, India Office and Colonial Office. Deputy Under-Secretary, Colonial Office, 1931-42. Served Cabinet Office (Historical Section), 1942-48.

Sir Evelyn Shuckburgh states that his father left no papers. Some correspondence with Sir Arnold Wilson is available at the British Library (Add. MSS. 52456) covering the period 1918-20.

SILLITOE, Sir Percy Joseph (1888-1962)

Colonial Service, Tanganyika. Police Service, Chief Constable, Glasgow, 1931-43; Kent, 1943-46, etc. Director-General, Security Service, 1946-53.

An autobiography, *Cloak Without Dagger*, appeared in 1955, and W. H. Allen's *Sir Percy Sillitoe* (1975) mentions diaries and papers in private hands.

SIMPSON, General Sir Frank Ernest Wallace (1899-   )

Commissioned in Royal Engineers, 1916; served World Wars I and II. Vice Chief of the Imperial General Staff, 1946-48. G.O. C.-in-C., Western Command, 1948-51. Chief Royal Engineer, 1966-67.

Any papers which come to light will be placed in the Liddell Hart Centre for Military Archives.

SIMSON, Brigadier Ivan (1890-1971)

Military career. Chief Engineer in Malaya, 1941-42.

Typescript copies of Simson's book *Singapore, Too Little, Too Late* (1970) and the original draft on the Malayan campaign (1941-42) are deposited at the Liddell Hart Centre for Military Archives.

SINCLAIR OF CLEEVE, 1st B
Sir Robert John Sinclair (1893-   )

Deputy Director of Munitions Inspection, 1917-19. Director-General of Army Requirements, 1939-42. Chief Executive, Ministry of Production, 1943; and at Board of Trade until 1945.

According to information supplied to the Liddell Hart Centre for Military Archives by Lord Sinclair of Cleeve, he returned all his papers to the departments in which he worked. Any further private papers found will be passed to the Liddell Hart Centre for Military Archives.

SINKER, Sir (Algernon) Paul (1905-1975)

Academic career. Civil Servant, Admiralty and Treasury, from 1940. 1st Civil Service Commissioner, 1951-54. Director-General, British Council, 1954-68.

Sir Paul Sinker felt that he had kept no papers which would be of public interest.

SKEEN, General Sir Andrew (1873-1935)

Military career, North West Frontier, India, 1897-98; China, 1900; East Africa, 1902-04; European War, 1914-17; Afghanistan, Waziristan and India. G.O.C.-in-C., Southern Command, India, 1923-24. Chief of General Staff, India, 1924-28.

Brigadier A. Skeen, I.C.D., O.B.E., 19 Granta Road, Vainona, P. O. Borrowdale, Salisbury, Rhodesia, has a few of his father's papers, but the bulk of them have been placed in the Royal Military College Museum, Sandhurst.

SKRINE, Sir Clarmont Percival (1888-1974)

Political Agent, Quetta, 1921; Sibi, Baluchistan, 1929-31; Kalat and Chagai, 1932-35. Consul-General, Chinese Turkestan, 1922-24; Meshed, 1942-46; Consul, Seistan and Kain, 1927-29. Resident, Madras States, 1936-39; Punjab States, 1939-41. Counsellor for Indian Affairs, Tehran, 1946-48.

The papers (1912-52) at the India Office Library are not available for inspection. The collection consists of weekly letters which Skrine sent home to his parents, some personal and private correspondence, semi-official papers, official diaries, and notes and articles by Skrine. There are also the letters from Skrine's mother from 1936 to 1940, and a number of personal items. Much of the material relates to the affairs of Persia.

SLADE, Admiral Sir Edmond John Warne (1859-1928)

Naval career from 1872. C.-in-C., East Indies, 1909-12.

A microfilm of papers (still preserved in private hands) is available at the National Maritime Museum, and includes a diary (1903-14) and other material relating to the Admiral's career.

SLATER, Sir (Alexander) Ransford (1874-1940)

Colonial Service. Governor, Sierra Leone, 1922-27; Gold Coast, 1927-32. Captain General and Governor in Chief, Jamaica, 1932-34.

There was no success in tracing the family and solicitors mentioned in the Will and Act of Probate.

SLATIN, Baron Rudolf Carl [Slatin Pasha] (1857-1932)

Colonial service, Sudan. Inspector General, Sudan, 1900-14.

The Sudan Archive at Durham University has a collection of papers. These include correspondence, from 1888 onwards, with persons in Austria-Hungary and Britain, etc.; formal documents; diaries (1896-1932, with gaps); personal papers; press cuttings; drafts and notes for his book *Fire and Sword in the Sudan;* and other papers.

SLAYTER, Admiral Sir William Rudolph (1896-1971)

Naval career. Chief of Staff, Home Fleet, 1943. British Naval Representative, United Nations Military Staff Committee, 1947. C.-in-C., East Indies, 1952-54.

The Imperial War Museum found that there were no private papers.

SLESSOR, Marshal of the Royal Air Force Sir John Cotesworth (1897-)

Served European War, 1915-18; War of 1939-45. Director of Plans, Air Ministry, 1937-41. Air Representative, Anglo-French Conversations, 1939, and Anglo-American (A.B.C.) Staff Conversations, 1941. C.-in-C., R.A.F. Mediterranean and Middle East, 1944-45. Air Member for Personnel, 1945-47. Commandant, Imperial Defence College, 1948-49. Chief of Air Staff, 1950-52.

Sir John Slessor has a large mass of papers, letters and press cuttings. These will in time be placed in the Royal Air Force Museum.

SLIM, 1st Vt
Field-Marshal Sir William Joseph Slim (1891-1970)

Served in Sudan, Eritrea, Burma, during World War II, with commands of 1st Burma Corps, 15th Indian Corps, 14th Army. C.-in-C., Allied Land Forces, South East Asia, 1945-46. Chief of Imperial General Staff, 1948-52. Governor-General and C.-in-C., Australia, 1953-60.

Papers left by Viscount Slim are with his official biographer, Mr Ronald Lewin. Enquiries should be directed to the present (2nd) Viscount Slim, 5 Grosvenor Gardens, London SW1.

SMITH, Lieutenant-General Sir Arthur Henry (1890-)

Chief of General Staff, Middle East, 1940. G.O.C., London District, 1942-44. G.O.C.-in-C., Persia and Iraq Command, 1944-45; Eastern Command, India, 1945-46. Chief of General Staff, India, 1946. Deputy C.-in-C., India, 1947. Commander, British Forces in India and Pakistan, Nov. 1947.

It is understood that there are no papers.

SMITH, Sir Bryan Evers Sharwood- (1899-)

Colonial administrator (Nigeria 1927-57). Governor, Northern Nigeria, 1954-57.

Tapes and transcripts of service in Nigeria are deposited in Rhodes House Library, Oxford.

SMITH, Charles Howard (1888-1942)

Assistant Under-Secretary, Foreign Office, 1933-39. Minister, Copenhagen, Oct. 1939-Apr. 1940. Minister, Reykjavik, 1940-42.

Efforts to contact Mr Smith's executors proved unsuccessful.

SMITH, Vice-Admiral Sir (Edward Michael) Connolly Abel- (1899-)

Naval career. Served World Wars I and II. Naval Attaché, Washington, 1944-46. Vice-Controller (Air), Chief of Naval Air Equipment and Chief Naval Representative, Ministry of Supply, 1950.

According to information supplied to the Imperial War Museum, the Vice-Admiral kept no papers.

SMITH, Sir Henry Wilson (1904-)

Civil Service career; Treasury. Permanent Secretary, Ministry of Defence, 1947-48. Additional 2nd Secretary, Treasury, 1948-51.

Sir Henry states that he has kept no diary or collection of press cuttings, and that on the termination of any particular appointment he has returned all relevant papers to the appropriate government or company archive.

SMITH, Sir Hubert Llewellyn (1864-1945)

Permanent Secretary, Board of Trade, 1907-19. General Secretary, Ministry of Munitions, 1915. Chief Economic Adviser to H.M. Government, 1919-27. British delegate, Member of Commission, etc., on numerous occasions.

A collection of papers has survived with the family. The papers relate mainly to the period after 1914, but the collection includes a small fragment of autobiography on his early life; a dozen letters to his family (1885-93) on his life at Toynbee Hall and his work for the National Association for the Promotion of Technical Education; printed copies of lectures; and a few letters, e.g. to W. S. Churchill relating to House of Lords reform (1908). For the war-time period there is a diary of a visit to France, and memoranda on the Belgian Congo, Egyptian cotton, and future British trade policy. Post-war papers include letters to Lady Llewellyn Smith from the Peace Conference and from the League of Nations in the 1920s; also minutes of the proceedings of the British Institute of Industrial Art, with papers and correspondence relating to it. Enquiries should be addressed to Messrs. A. & H. Llewellyn Smith, 1 Ockley Road, Streatham, London SW16.

SMITH, Sir James Edward Masterton- (1878-1938)

Assistant Secretary, War Office and Air Ministry, 1919-20. Joint Permanent Secretary, Ministry of Labour, 1920-21. Permanent Under-Secretary, Colonial Office, 1921-24.

Papers accumulated by Masterton-Smith, who served in the Private Office of the 1st Lord of the Admiralty (1911-17), and in the Ministry of Munitions (1917-18), are available at the Public Record Office (Cab. 1).

SMITH, Sir James Robert Dunlop- (1858-1921)

Private Secretary to the Viceroy, 1905-10, and Political A.D.C. to the Secretary of State for India, 1910-21.

The collection at the India Office Library consists of the private and official letters and papers (1855-1923) of Dunlop-Smith and his father-in-law, Charles Umpherston Aitchison (1832-96) of the Indian Civil Service. In addition to members of the family, correspondents include Lord and Lady Minto, Lord Morley and Lord Kitchener. Dunlop-Smith's private diary and journals cover much of the period 1883-84 and 1905-12.

SMITH, Sir Laurence Barton Grafftey- (1892-   )

Levant Consular Service, 1914-51. Consul-General, Albania, 1939-40. Minister, Saudi Arabia, 1945-47. High Commissioner, Pakistan, 1947-51.

The material at the Middle East Centre, St Antony's College, Oxford, relates to Grafftey-Smith's four years at Karachi (1947-51) and his period as British delegate on the Governor-General's Commission in Khartoum (1953-56).

SMITH, Montague Bentley Talbot Paske- (d. 1946)

Minister, Colombia, 1936-41.

No members of the family were traced, and the firm of solicitors mentioned in the Will and Act of Probate is no longer in business.

SMITH, Sir Reginald Hugh Dorman- (1899-   )

M.P. (Con.) Petersfield, 1935-41. Minister of Agriculture and Fisheries, 1939-40. Governor, Burma, 1941-46.

Sir Reginald has kept no papers, apart from those deposited at the India Office Library. This material relates to the Governorship of Burma, and is not at present open for inspection. Full details are given in Hazlehurst and Woodland, op. cit., p.135.

SNOW, Lieutenant-General Sir Thomas D'Oyly (1858-1940)

Army career from 1879. Commands during World War I; Western Command, 1918-19.

A collection of papers survives with the family. This includes an account of the desert campaign (1884-85); letters, and a diary covering the early stages of the war in France up to June 1915. Enquiries should be addressed to the Rt. Rev. George D'Oyly Snow, Meadow Cottage, Corfe Castle, Wareham, Dorset. An account of the Cambrai action of 1917 is available at the Lancashire Record Office (see NRA report 16608(49)).

SNOW, Thomas Maitland (1890-   )

Minister, Cuba, 1935-37; Finland, 1937-40; Colombia, 1941-44 (Ambassador, 1944-45); Switzerland, 1946-49.

Mr Snow has retained some of his papers, but these are not as yet available for study.

SOMERVILLE, Admiral of the Fleet Sir James Fownes (1882-1949)

Naval career from 1898. Served World War I (Dardanelles, etc.). Director of the Signal Department, Admiralty, 1925-27. Naval Instructor, Imperial Defence College, 1929-31. Director of Personal Services, Admiralty, 1934-36. Commanded Destroyer Flotillas, Mediterranean Fleet, 1936-38. C.-in-C., East Indies, 1938-39;

Eastern Fleet, 1942-44. Head of British Admiralty Delegation, Washington, 1944-45.

Papers preserved at Churchill College, Cambridge, include diaries (1910-49); correspondence (1927-44); and various official papers. There is a useful collection of correspondence in the Cummingham papers at the British Library (Ad. MSS. 52563-64).

SORLEY, Air Marshal Sir Ralph Squire (1898-1974)

Served European War, 1914-18. Assistant Chief of Air Staff (Technical Requirements), 1941. Controller of Research and Development, Ministry of Aircraft Production, 1943-45. Member of Air Council, and Aircraft Supply Council. Air Officer C.-in-C., Technical Training Command, 1945-48.

The Imperial War Museum has two unpublished reports, on Technical Training Command (1945-47) and the long-range world record flight (1933).

SOULBURY, 1st Vt
Sir Herwald Ramsbotham (1887-1971)

M.P. (Con.) Lancaster, 1929-41. Parliamentary Secretary, Board of Education, 1931-35; Ministry of Agriculture and Fisheries, 1935-36. Minister of Pensions, 1936-39. 1st Commissioner of Works, 1939-40. President of the Board of Education, 1940-41. Chairman, National Assistance Board, 1941-48; Burnham Committees, 1942-49. Governor-General, Ceylon, 1949-54.

Hazlehurst and Woodland, op. cit., p.120, found only a small collection of papers, owned by Lord Soulbury's son, Hon. Sir Peter Ramsbotham, K.C.M.G., c/o Foreign and Commonwealth Office, London SW1.

SOUTHBOROUGH, 1st B
Sir Francis John Stephens Hopwood (1860-1947)

Civil Service career, Board of Trade. Permanent Secretary, Board of Trade, 1901-07. Permanent Under-Secretary, Colonial Office, 1907-11. A Civil Lord of the Admiralty, 1912-17. Chairman, Grand Committee on War Trade, World War I. Secretary, Irish Convention, 1917-18; etc.

The papers, in the possession of the present (3rd) Baron Southborough, Bingham's Melcombe, Dorset, fill four tin boxes and three dispatch cases. Most of the surviving papers consist of personal letters dating from the 1890s to 1947, and a wide range of Lord Southborough's activities are covered. Important correspondents include Sir Arthur Bigge, later Lord Stamfordham, private secretary to King George V. There are early family letters (1890s), and other papers concerning work with A. J. Mundella at the Board of Trade and concerning service in the Railway Department. A long series of letters from Lords Elgin and Crewe covers the period at the Colonial Office, and there are important letters from Viscount Gladstone and Louis Botha on South Africa. Correspondence with Churchill and Fisher on naval matters, for the period before and after the outbreak of war in August 1914, has survived. Few papers remain concerning Southborough's mission to Scandinavia (1917) to investigate Austrian peace feelers, but a good deal of correspondence, etc., relates to the Irish Convention and the Committee to study Indian franchise reform (1918-19). The remaining correspondence covers Southborough's business interests, his investigations into shell shock and the situation of ex-servicemen in the Civil Service. There are also a number of appointment diaries.

SPEAIGHT, Richard Langford (1906-   )

Head of Information Policy Department, Foreign Office, 1948-50. Ambassador, Burma, 1950-53. Assistant Under-Secretary, Foreign Office, 1953-56. Minister, Bulgaria, 1956-58. Director of East-West Contacts, Foreign Office, 1960-66.

Mr Speaight retains few papers, apart from some diaries kept whilst Director of East-West Contacts at the Foreign Office (1960-66), concerned with the negotiation of cultural agreements with the Soviet Union and Eastern Europe. These papers are not open for inspection.

SPEARS, Major-General Sir Edward Louis, 1st Bt (1886-1974)

Served World War I. Head of British Military Mission, Paris, 1917-20. M.P. (Nat. Lib.) Loughborough, 1922-24; (Con.) Carlisle, 1931-45. Head of British Mission to General de Gaulle, June 1940. Head of Mission to Syria and Lebanon, July 1941. First Minister to Syria and Lebanon, 1942-44.

The bulk of the Spears papers, including the political material, is held at Churchill College, Cambridge. Papers on Middle Eastern affairs are at the Middle East Centre, St Antony's College, Oxford and the Liddell Hart Centre for Military Archives has the World War I papers.

SPEED, Sir Eric Bourne Bentinck (1895-1971)

Civil Service career. Private Secretary to Prime Minister, Stanley Baldwin, 1936-37.

Lady Speed states that she has none of her late husband's papers.

SPENDER, Lieutenant-Colonel Sir Wilfrid Bliss (1876-1960)

Military service, World War I. Permanent Secretary, Ministry of Finance, and Head of the Northern Ireland Civil Service, 1925-44.

The papers at the Northern Ireland Public Record Office include diaries (1934-44), and some 500 papers relating to Sir Wilfrid's career (1912-44). Lady Spender's own diaries are also included in the collection. Many of Sir Wilfrid's papers relate to his involvement with the Ulster Volunteer Force, and to his compulsory retirement from the Army in 1913. The others cover his later career. Correspondents include Lord Craigavon, Lord Carson and General Gough.

SPERLING, Sir Rowland Arthur Charles (1874-1965)

Minister, Switzerland, 1924-27; Bulgaria, 1928-29; Finland, 1930-35.

Mrs P. M. Sperling, Wissett Lodge, Harbury, Leamington Spa, Warwicks., CV33 9EY, has a collection of her father-in-law's letters and press cuttings that might be of interest. The papers are unsorted, and include some personal material.

SPRING-RICE, Sir Cecil Arthur (1859-1918)

Minister, Persia, 1906-08; Sweden, 1908-12. Ambassador, United States, 1912-18.

A collection of papers (c. 1885-1918) is held at Churchill College, Cambridge. Some 14 boxes of material include correspondence with members of Spring-Rice's family and his friends, and papers relating to social life. Important correspondents include Lord Curzon, and Sir Valentine Chirol (1852-1929). Private Office correspondence (1903-18) is available at the Public Record Office (F.O. 800/241-2).

STANLEY, Sir George Frederick (1872-1938)

M.P. (Con.) Preston, 1910-22; Willesden East, 1924-29. Comptroller, H.M. Household, 1919. Financial Secretary, War Office, 1921-22. Parliamentary Under-Secretary, Home Office, 1922-23. Parliamentary Secretary, Ministry of Pensions, 1924-29. Governor, Madras, 1929-34.

Surviving papers are in the care of Sir G. F. Stanley's daughter, Lady Buchanan, St Anne's Manor, Sutton Bonington, Loughborough, Leics. These include two personal and confidential diaries concerning his experiences in World War I, and as Governor of Madras; and press cuttings kept during his time in India.

STANLEY, Sir Herbert James (1872-1955)

Colonial Service, etc. Imperial Secretary, South Africa, 1918-24. Governor and C.-in-C., Northern Rhodesia, 1924-27; Ceylon, 1927-31; Southern Rhodesia, 1935-42. High Commissioner, South Africa, 1931-35.

Rhodes House Library has a collection of correspondence and memoranda (1910-41), mainly relating to Southern Rhodesia.

STEEL, Sir Christopher Eden (1903-1973)

Political Officer, SHAEF, 1945. Political Adviser to C.-in-C., Germany, 1947. Minister, Washington, 1950-53. Permanent Representative, North Atlantic Council, 1953-57. Ambassador, German Federal Republic, 1957-63.

Lady Steel, Southrop Lodge, Lechlade, Glos. GL7 3NU, retains a number of letters relating to her late husband. The papers are unsorted, but it is understood that they are mainly of family interest.

STEEL, Air Chief Marshal Sir John Miles (1877-1965)

Served European War, 1914-18. Deputy Chief of Air Staff, 1919-26. Air Officer Commanding, Wessex Bombing Area, 1926-31; R.A.F. India, 1931-35; Reserve Command, 1939-40. Air Officer C.-in-C., Air Defence of Great Britain, 1935-36; Bomber Command, 1936-37. Controller-General of Economy, Air Ministry, 1941-45.

The Royal Air Force Museum knows of no papers.

STEELE, General Sir James Stuart (1894-)

Served in France and Belgium 1915-17. North West Frontier, 1919-20. Commanded in Palestine, 1939. Assistant Adjutant-General, War Office, 1939. Brigade Commander, 1939-41. Divisional Commander, Deputy Chief and Chief of General Staff, Middle East, 1942-43. Director of Staff Duties, War Office, 1943-45. C.-in-C. and High Commissioner, Austria, 1945-47. Adjutant-General to the Forces, 1947-50.

According to information supplied to the Liddell Hart Centre for Military Archives, the General has retained no papers.

STEPHENS, General Sir Reginald Byng (1869-1955)

Served Nile Expedition, 1898; South Africa, 1899-1902; European War, 1914-18. Director-General, Territorial Army, 1927-31.

The Imperial War Museum has a small collection, including the texts of lectures, narratives, diaries, manuscripts, official orders, etc., relating to service on the Western Front (1914-18).

STEPHENSON, Sir Hugh Lansdown (1871-1941)

Indian Civil Service from 1895. Governor of Bihar and Orissa, 1927-32; Burma, 1932-36.

A collection of papers has been given to the Cambridge South Asian Archive. The collection includes personal correspondence (1932-35); speeches (1926-36); engagement diaries (1927-36); and newspaper cuttings.

STEPTOE, Harry Nathaniel (1892-1942)

Served in China Consular Service, 1920s and 1930s. Minister, El Salvador, 1948-49.

The Executor and Trustee Department of Lloyd's Bank Ltd, who acted in the estate, were unable to supply any information which could lead to the whereabouts of Steptoe's papers.

STERN, Lieutenant-Colonel Sir Albert (1878-1966)

Secretary, Landship Committee, Admiralty, 1915. Chairman, Tank Committee, Director of Tank Supply Department, and Director-General, Mechanical Warfare Department, 1916. Chairman, Special Vehicle Development Committee, 1939-43.

Some papers relating to the development of the armoured fighting vehicle during the World Wars have been deposited at the Liddell Hart Centre for Military Archives.

STEVENS, Air Marshal Sir Alick Charles (1898-   )

Royal Naval Air Services from 1916, and Royal Air Force. Served World War II. Air Officer Commanding, Gibraltar, 1944-45; No. 47 Group, 1945; No. 4 Group, Transport Command, 1946; No. 22 Group, Technical Training Command, 1946-48; British Forces, Aden, 1948-50. A.O.C.-in-C., Coastal Command, 1951-53; Eastern Atlantic Area, 1952-53. Allied Maritime Air C.-in-C., Channel and Southern North Sea, Channel Command, 1952-53.

The Air Marshal states that he has no papers which could be of any historical value.

STEVENS, Vice-Admiral Sir John Felgate (1900-   )

Naval career from 1918. Served World War II. Director of Plans, Admiralty, 1946-47. Commanded H.M.S. *Implacable*, 1948-49. Director of Naval Training, 1949-50. Flag Officer, Home Fleet Training Squadron, 1952-53. C.-in-C., America and West Indies Station, and Deputy Supreme Allied Commander, Atlantic, 1953-55.

Vice-Admiral Sir John Stevens has kept very few private papers. Five personal diaries of day-to-day events on board ship during World War II are extant.

STEVENS, Sir Roger Bentham (1906-   )

Consular and Diplomatic Service. Assistant Under-Secretary, Foreign Office, 1948-51. Ambassador, Sweden, 1951-54; Persia, 1954-58. Deputy Under-Secretary, Foreign Office, 1958-63. Adviser to First Secretary of State on Central Africa, 1962.

Sir Roger Stevens retains few papers which would be of interest to the historian. However, he has kept a diary for the period 1961-62 covering certain Middle Eastern and African affairs, some notes about his mission to the Central African Federation (1961-62), copies of talks about the Middle East (1959-62) and one in personal recollection of Dag Hammarskjöld.

STEVENSON, Sir Ralph Clarmont Skrine (1895-)

Minister, Spain (Barcelona), 1938-39; Uruguay, 1941-43. Ambassador, Yugoslavia, 1943-46; China, 1946-50; Egypt, 1950-55.

Sir Ralph Stevenson has retained a number of scrapbooks covering his career, together with a mass of papers dealing with the missions of which he was head, texts of speeches and lectures, and correspondence. The papers may eventually be deposited in the Manx Museum, Douglas, Isle of Man.

STEWART, Major-General Sir James Marshall (1861-1943)

Army career from 1881. Served Burma, North West Frontier, and in East Africa during World War I.

The National Army Museum has a collection of documents relating to the East African campaign, including correspondence with General Smuts regarding Stewart's dismissal. Also included are the official reports on operations of the 1st Division between 5 and 16 March 1916.

STEWART, Sir Louis (1870-1949)

Indian Civil Service and Judicature.

A large collection of papers is held in the Bodleian Library. The material includes correspondence and papers relating to the Indian Empire Society; correspondence and papers of the Indian Services Pensioners' Association; material concerning Sir Michael Francis O'Dwyer's memorial fund committee; correspondence and papers relating to Stewart's legal work; and miscellaneous papers.

STEWART, Sir (Percy) Malcolm, 1st Bt (1872-1951)

Commissioner for Special Areas (England and Wales), 1934-36.

Sir Ronald Stewart, Bt, Maulden Grange, Beds., states that he has his father's papers in his possession. Details are not available.

STEWART, Sir Samuel Findlater (1879-1960)

Permanent Under-Secretary, India, 1930-42.

The Private Office collection (D.714) at the India Office Library includes some of Stewart's papers, and there is some additional material at the India Office Library.

STEWART, Sir Thomas Alexander (1888-1964)

Commercial Secretary, Government of India, from 1934. Governor, Bihar, 1939-43.

The India Office Library holds a microfilm of Stewart's speeches (1939-43).

STIRLING, Sir Charles Norman (1901-)

Consul-General, Tangier, 1949-51. Ambassador, Chile, 1951-54; Portugal, 1955-60.

Sir Charles Stirling states that he kept no personal records while in the public service.

STOCKLEY, Gerald Ernest (1900-)

Acting Consul-General, Kunming, 1939; Kweilin, 1943-44. Consul-General, Hankow, 1946-48. Minister, Honduras, 1950-54. Consul-General, Naples, 1954-59.

Mr Stockley says he has retained no diaries and almost no private papers relating to his career.

STONE, Brigadier-General Percy Vere Powys

Military career. South Africa, 1902; Northern Nigeria, 1905-10; European War, 1914-18.

One folder of papers (1915-18) can be found at the Royal Norfolk Regimental Museum.

STONEHAVEN, 1st Vt
Sir John Lawrence Baird, 2nd Bt (1874-1941)

M.P. (Con.) Rugby, 1910-22; Ayr Burghs, 1922-25. Parliamentary Under-Secretary, Air, 1916-19; Home Affairs, 1919-22. Parliamentary Secretary, Munitions, 1919. Minister of Transport and 1st Commissioner of Works, 1922-24. Governor-General, Australia, 1925-30.

The papers, which are mostly held at the National Library of Australia, are described by Hazlehurst and Woodland, op. cit., pp.7-8.

STOPFORD, Robert Jemmett (1895-)

Served European War, 1914-18. Banking career, 1921-28. Member of Runciman Mission, 1938. Liaison Officer for Refugees with Czech Government, 1938-39. Served World War II, Washington Embassy and War Office.

An important collection of papers relating to the Runciman Mission to Czecho-slovakia (1938) and the establishment and administration of the Czech Refugee Trust Fund (1938-39) can be found at the Imperial War Museum. There are also papers relating to the 1946 Trieste Boundary Commission and the administration of Trieste (1946-49).

STORRS, Sir Ronald (1881-1955)

Served Egyptian Government. Military Governor, Jerusalem, 1917-20. Civil Governor, Jerusalem and Judaea, 1920-26. Governor and C.-in-C., Cyprus, 1926-32; Northern Rhodesia, 1932-34.

A number of papers are held in the library of Pembroke College, Cambridge. Others remain with Lady Storrs. Details are not available, and access to the papers is not freely permitted. Enquiries should be addressed to the Librarian at Pembroke College.

STRADBROKE, 3rd E of
George Edward John Mowbray Rous, Vt Dunwich (1862-1947)

Governor, Victoria, 1920-26. Parliamentary Secretary, Ministry of Agriculture and Fisheries, 1928-29.

The Stradbroke family papers are deposited in the Ipswich and East Suffolk Record Office. These include some papers relating to the career of the 3rd Earl as Governor of Victoria, Parliamentary Secretary at the Ministry of Agriculture, Territorial officer and agriculturalist. Diaries of the 3rd Earl cover the years 1928-47, and also preserved are diaries of foreign tours made by the Earl (1890, 1906, 1912, 1924). The permission of the present Earl of Stradbroke may be needed for access to these papers.

STRANG, 1st B
Sir William Strang (1893-   )

Diplomatic Service, 1919-53. Assistant Under-Secretary, Foreign Office, 1939-43. U.K. Representative, European Advisory Commission, 1943-45. Political Adviser to C.-in-C., Germany, 1945-47. Permanent Under-Secretary, Foreign Office (German Section), 1947-49; Foreign Office, 1949-53. Chairman, Royal Institute of International Affairs, 1958-65.

Lord Strang has deposited a small collection of letters at St Antony's College, Oxford. These were written to Sir Owen O'Malley by Lord Strang in the 1920s when he was serving in the Foreign Office Far Eastern Department. Other papers of personal and college interest are held in the library of University College, London, and Lord Strang plans to leave all the other papers which he retains to that same college. A Private Office collection (1938 and 1939-43) in three files will in time be made available at the Public Record Office.

STRATTON, Lieutenant-General Sir William Henry (1903-   )

Military career. Served World War II. Chief of Staff, British Army on the Rhine, 1947-49. Commandant, Joint Services Staff College, 1949-52. Commander, British Army Staff, and Military Member, British Joint Services Mission, Washington, 1952-53. Commander, 42nd (Lancs.) Infantry Division (Territorial Army), 1953-55. Commander, British Forces, Hong Kong, 1955-57. Vice-Chief of the Imperial General Staff, 1957-60. Inspector-General of Civil Defence, Home Office, 1960-62.

The Imperial War Museum has a set of papers relating to exercise 'Bumper', held in Britain as an anti-invasion exercise in 1941, and 'Victor', also in 1941. There is also a training memorandum on infantry and tank co-operation.

STREET, Sir Arthur William (1892-1951)

Permanent Under-Secretary, Air Ministry, 1939-45. Permanent Secretary, Control Office for Germany and Austria, 1945-46. Deputy Chairman, National Coal Board, 1946-51.

No information was secured. Messrs Digby & Co., solicitors of London, acted in the estate.

STRICKLAND, 1st B
Sir Gerald Strickland (1861-1940)

Governor, Leeward Islands, 1902-04; Tasmania, 1904-09; Western Australia, 1909-13; Norfolk Island, 1913-14; New South Wales, 1914-17. M.P. (Con.) Lancaster, 1924-28.

It has not been possible to contact Lord Strickland's surviving family. Correspondence and papers (1930-32) concerning Malta are in the Luke papers at Rhodes House Library.

STROMMENGER, Sir Ernest John (1873-1967)

Civil Service career. Deputy Secretary, Ministry of Health, 1930-32. Under-Secretary, Treasury, 1932-34. Deputy Chairman, Unemployment Assistance Board, 1934-37.

Mr P. J. Strommenger, 147 Almners Road, Lyne, Chertsey, Surrey, has only a very few documents relating to his father. These are letters of appointment, newspaper cuttings, etc.

STRONG, Major-General Sir Kenneth William Dobson (1900-)

Head of Intelligence, Home Forces, 1942; and of General Eisenhower's Intelligence Staff, 1943-45. Director-General, Political Intelligence Department, Foreign Office, 1945-47. Director, Joint Intelligence Bureau, Ministry of Defence, 1948-64. Director-General of Intelligence, Ministry of Defence, 1964-66.

The surviving papers may be placed in the Liddell Hart Centre for Military Archives.

STRONGE, Sir Francis William (1856-1924)

Minister, Colombia, 1906-11; Mexico, 1911-13; Chile, 1913-19.

Neither Sir C. N. L. Stronge, Bt (great-nephew) nor Miss J. Stronge (niece) were able to suggest where papers may have survived.

STUART, Major-General Sir Andrew Mitchell (1861-1936)

Military career from 1879. Director of Works, British Armies in France, 1914-19. Director of Works and Buildings, Air Ministry, 1919-24.

The Liddell Hart Centre for Military Archives has a collection of correspondence and papers relating to the Sudan-Nile campaign and notebooks and diaries of the period 1914-19 when Stuart was director of works in France.

STUART, General Sir John Theodosius Burnett- (1875-1958)

Military career. Served South Africa, 1899-1902. Director of Organisation, New Zealand Military Forces, 1910-12. Served World War I. G.O.C., Madras, 1920-22; British Troops in Egypt, 1931-34. Director of Military Operations and Intelligence, War Office, 1922-26. G.O. C.-in-C., Southern Command, 1934-38.

Mr J. G. S. Burnett-Stuart, Critchie House, Stuartfield, Aberdeenshire, has certain papers of his grandfather's, relating to New Zealand forces (1910-12); to the Moplah rebellion (1921); and to training conferences in the 1930s. There are also various papers on Army mechanisation (1931-37), and correspondence on British defence policy (1936-37). A copy of the General's unpublished memoirs is held by Mrs Evelyn Arthur, Woolstaston House, Church Stretton, Salop.

STUBBS, Sir (Reginald) Edward (1876-1947)

Colonial Service. Governor, Hong Kong, 1919-25; Jamaica, 1926-32; Cyprus, 1932-33; Ceylon, 1933-37.

Information available at Somerset House was insufficient to trace the papers.

STURGIS, Sir Mark Beresford Russell Grant- (1884-1949)

Private Secretary to Prime Minister, H. H. Asquith, 1908-10. Special Commissioner of Income Tax, from 1910. Joint Assistant Under-Secretary, Ireland, 1920-22. Assistant Under-Secretary, Irish Services, 1922-24.

In the Public Record Office (P.R.O. 30/59) there are five volumes of a diary kept in the years 1920-22.

SULLIVAN, Bernard Ponsonby (1891-1958)

Consul-General, Boston, 1944-47. Minister, Costa Rica, 1948-51.

It proved impossible to trace Sullivan's widow or heirs. Messrs Eastleys, solicitors in the estate, were unable to supply any relevant information.

SULLIVAN, Sir William John (1895-1971)

Diplomatic career. Commercial Secretary and Counsellor, Berne, 1941-45. British Political Adviser, Trieste, 1945-50. Minister, Romania, 1951-54. Ambassador, Mexico, 1954-56.

Mr L. F. Sullivan (son) says that most family papers were destroyed in Madrid during the Spanish Civil War; and there was a further loss during the blitz. On his death Sir William left no relevant papers.

SUTTON, Air Marshal Sir Bertine Entwisle (1886-1946)

Served European War, 1914-19. Air Officer Commanding, No. 22 Group, 1936-39; No. 23 Group, 1939-40; No. 24 Group, 1940. Air Member for Personnel, 1942-45.

There is one folder of papers (1916-19) at the Public Record Office.

SUTTON, Brigadier George William (1893-1971)

Military career. Served European War, 1914-18. Commanded 125th Infantry Brigade, 1938-40. General Staff Officer (H.G.), Canadian Corps and Sussex and Surrey District, 1941-44.

The Imperial War Museum has a collection of letters and diaries covering service in Egypt, Gallipoli and France (1914-18); a diary kept when in command of the 125th Infantry Brigade in France, at Dunkirk (1940); and Home Guard official papers for the Sussex and Surrey area (1941-44).

SWAN, Major-General William Travers (1861-1949)

Military career. Served North West Frontier, India, South Africa, and European War. Assistant Director of Medical Service, 1914-18.

The papers of the Major-General have been donated to the Imperial War Museum. They include his diaries (1912-20) and the whole of his voluminous World War I correspondence.

SWAYNE, Brigadier-General Sir Eric John Eagles (1863-1929)

Indian Army. Commissioner and Consul-General, Somaliland, 1902-06. Governor, British Honduras, 1906-13.

Rhodes House Library has a collection of correspondence, memoranda and other papers (1902-14) relating to Somaliland and British Honduras.

SWAYNE, Lieutenant-General Sir John George des Réaux (1890-1964)

Served France and Belgium, 1914-18. Military Assistant to Chief of Imperial General Staff, 1931-33. Head of British Military Mission to French G.H.Q., 1939-40. G.O.C., 4th Division, 1940-42. Chief of General Staff, Home Forces, 1942. G.O. C.-in-C., South Eastern Command, 1942-44. Chief of General Staff, India, 1944-46.

The Liddell Hart Centre for Military Archives has been informed that no papers survive.

SWETTENHAM, Sir Frank Athelstane (1850-1946)

British Resident, Selangor, 1882; Perak, 1889-95; Resident-General, Federated Malay States, 1896-1901; Governor and C.-in-C., Straits Settlements, 1901-04.

The material held at the National Archives of Malaysia, which includes journals and correspondence, is described at the National Register of Archives (List 7154).

SWINTON, Major-General Sir Ernest Dunlop (1868-1951)

Army career from ˙888. Assistant Secretary, War Cabinet, during World War I. Controller of Information, Department of Civil Aviation. Originated the Tanks and raised the Heavy Section, Machine Gun Corps, 1916. Chichele Professor of Military History, Oxford, 1925-39.

The Liddell Hart Centre for Military Archives holds certain papers relating to Swinton's libel action with H. G. Wells, together with copies of his Oxford inaugural lecture and other publications. Other papers can be found at the Royal Armoured Corps Tank Museum.

SYDENHAM, 1st B
Sir George Sydenham Clarke (1848-1933)

Military career, Royal Engineers. Secretary, Colonial Defence Committee, War Office, 1885-92. Member of Committee on War Office Reorganisation, 1900-01. Governor, Victoria, 1901-04. Member of War Office Reconstitution Committee, 1904. Secretary, Committee of Imperial Defence, 1904-07. Governor, Bombay, 1907-13.

The papers in the British Library (Add. MSS. 50831-41) include correspondence with Sir Valentine Chirol, and documents acquired as Secretary to the Committee of Imperial Defence. Bound volumes of articles, papers etc. are held at the Royal Engineers Depot, Woolwich.

SYFRET, Admiral Sir (Edward) Neville (1889-1972)

Naval career from 1904. Served World War I. Naval Secretary to 1st Lord of the Admiralty, 1939-41. Commanded Force 'H' Sea Command, 1941-43. Vice-Chief of Naval Staff, 1943-45. C.-in-C., Home Fleet, 1945-48.

According to information obtained from Sir Neville by the Imperial War Museum, he retained no papers.

SYKES, Major-General Sir Frederick Hugh (1877-1954)

Deputy Director, War Office, 1917. Chief of the Air Staff, 1918-19. Controller-General, Civil Aviation, 1919-22. M.P. (Con.) Sheffield Hallam, 1922-28; Nottingham Central, 1940-45. Governor, Bombay, 1928-33.

The India Office Library holds a collection of papers and scrapbooks (1919-50). The correspondence (1928-33) includes letters to and from the Viceroy (both Lords Irwin and Willingdon), and successive Secretaries of State for India. The twelve scrapbooks deal with India and also with Sykes's Parliamentary career. The Royal Air Force Museum has three volumes of Sykes papers (1901-19), comprising personal letters, certificates, copies of official reports, minutes, etc. Press cuttings are held by the Museum on loan.

SYKES, Sir Mark, 6th Bt (1879-1919)

M.P. (Con.) Hull Central, 1911-19. Adviser to the Foreign Office on Middle Eastern policy during World War I.

Sir Mark Sykes's son has given a substantial collection of papers to the East Riding of Yorkshire County Record Office. The material includes pre-war correspondence and papers, e.g. appointment diaries, personal financial records, military material, political papers relating to Sir Mark's County Council and Parliamentary work, and to his service as a military attaché and to his travels in the Ottoman Empire (1897-1918); war-time correspondence (1914-19); Middle Eastern papers (1915-19), including material relating to the Sykes-Picot Agreement; military material (1914-15); and draft speeches. Dr Roger Adelson of St Antony's College, Oxford, is at present preparing a biography of Sir Mark, and these papers are not yet available for research purposes.

A microfilm of Sir Mark's papers relating to the Middle East (1915-19) is held by the Middle East Centre, St Antony's College, Oxford. The microfilm includes material on the Arab revolt (1915-16), the Sykes-Picot Agreement (1916-17), the liberation of Baghdad (1917), the Asia Minor Agreements, Zionism and the Palestine Settlement (1917-19).

One volume of papers relating to Sir Mark is available at the Public Record Office (F.O. 800/208).

SYKES, Brigadier-General Sir Percy Molesworth (1867-1945)

Military and Consular Service in Persia.

The papers are at the Middle East Centre, St Antony's College, Oxford. The material on British interests in Persia (1893-1919) includes reports of a secret Military Intelligence mission across Turkestan (1892); political dispatches to the Foreign Secretary on events in Persia (1899-1900), etc.; the South Persian rifles (1916-18); and the Russian bombardment of the Meshed Shrine (1912).

SYMONDS, Sir Aubrey Vere (1874-1931)

Civil Service career. Permanent Secretary, Board of Education, 1925-31.

Only Sir Aubrey's wife is mentioned in the Will and Act of Probate. No papers are known to survive.

SZLUMPER, Major-General Gilbert Savil (1884-1969)

Secretary to the Railway Executive Committee and Senior Railway Transport Officer to the British Army, 1914-19. Director-General of Transportation and Movements, War Office, 1939-40. Railway Control Officer, Ministry of Transport, 1940-41. Director-General of Supply Services, Ministry of Supply, 1942-45.

Miscellaneous papers are available at the Imperial War Museum and cover *inter alia* Szlumper's career in the organisation of rail transport during World War II. Among the material is a personal diary (1939-45), on microfilm.

TAIT, Admiral Sir (William Eric) Campbell (1886-1946)

Naval career. Served World War I, with commands thereafter. Deputy Director of Naval Intelligence, 1932-33. Commanded H.M.S. *Shropshire*, 1934-37. Director of Personal Services, 1941. C.-in-C., South Atlantic Station, 1942-44. Governor, Southern Rhodesia, 1945-46.

Certain papers of the Admiral's, covering mainly his naval career, are available at the National Maritime Museum. The material includes logs (1903-05); photograph albums (1908-14); letters of proceedings (1929-30); papers on foreign warships and naval personnel (1930); and papers relating to Naval Intelligence work (1934).

TAYLOR, Sir John William (1895-1974)

Minister (Commercial), Cairo, 1946-48; Washington, 1948-50. Ambassador, Mexico, 1950-54.

Sir John Taylor had no papers of value to the historian.

TEDDER, 1st B
Marshal of the Royal Air Force Sir Arthur William Tedder (1890-1967)

Served European War, 1914-18. Air Officer Commanding, R.A.F. Far East, 1936-38. Director-General, Research and Development, Air Ministry, 1938-40. Air Officer C.-in-C., Middle East, 1941-43. Air C.-in-C., Mediterranean Air Command, 1943. Deputy Supreme Commander, Allied Forces, 1943-45. Chief of Air Staff, 1946-50.

A collection of papers is held at the Royal Air Force Museum. The three series of material consist of a log book (1922-35), notebook (1916) and Staff College lectures; further Staff College lectures (1923-31); and a diary (1943-44).

TEGART, Sir Charles Augustus (1881-1946)

Indian Police, and adviser on police in Palestine, 1937. Member, Council of India, 1932-36. Served Ministry of Food from 1942.

A collection of papers, private correspondence and diaries on Palestine policy and security matters (1937-39) and some material on the Peel and Woodhead Commissions have been deposited at the Middle East Centre, St Antony's College, Oxford. The papers contain material on police activity and liaison with the Army, and include C.I.D. news bulletins and detailed statistics. Material on service in India is with the Cambridge South Asian Archive.

TEICHMAN, Sir Eric (1884-1944)

China Consular Service. Chinese Secretary, H.M. Legation in Peking, 1922-36.

Efforts to contact persons mentioned in the Will and Act of Probate proved unavailing.

TEMPLER, Field-Marshal Sir Gerald Walter Robert (1898-)

Military career, Royal Irish Fusiliers from 1916. Commands during World War II. Director of Military Government, 21 Army Group, 1945-46. Director of Military Intelligence, War Office, 1946-48. Vice-Chief of the Imperial General Staff, 1948-50. G.O. C.-in-C., Eastern Command, 1950-52. High Commissioner and Director of Operations, Federation of Malaya, 1952-54. Chief of the Imperial General Staff, 1955-58.

Sir Gerald has a large collection of papers, mainly relating to Malaya, He intends that these should be placed in the National Army Museum. Certain correspondence (1952-53), as High Commissioner in Malaya, has been placed in Rhodes House Library.

TEMPLEWOOD, 1st Vt
Sir Samuel John Gurney Hoare, 2nd Bt (1880-1959)

M.P. (Con.) Chelsea, 1910-44. Secretary of State, Air, 1922-24, 1924-29, 1940; India, 1931-35; Foreign Affairs, 1935; Home Affairs, 1937-39. 1st Lord of the Admiralty,

1936-37. Lord Privy Seal and Member of the War Cabinet, 1939-40. Ambassador, Spain, 1940-44.

Templewood's papers have been deposited in the Cambridge University Library, whilst a collection of his Indian papers is held at the India Office Library and a volume of Templewood's Foreign Office correspondence (1935) is available at the Public Record Office (F.O. 800/295). Further details are given by Hazlehurst and Woodland, op. cit., pp. 75-6.

TENNANT, Admiral Sir William George (1890-1963)

Naval career from 1905. Served World Wars I and II. Flag Officer, Levant and Eastern Mediterranean, 1944-46. C.-in-C., America and West Indies Station, 1946-49.

A collection of papers is preserved at the National Maritime Museum. This includes Tennant's midshipman's logs and journals of his war service up to 1919; letters relating to long cruises on H.M.S. *Renown,* in the form of a journal; papers relating to H.M.S. *Renown,* of which he had command until her loss in December 1940; some material on cruiser tactics, on the Mulberry Harbours, etc.; papers relating to his American command (1946-49); and miscellaneous prepared papers on, for example, Jutland, the lessons of World War II, and notes for his talks to ships' companies. But there are gaps in the material: for example, there is little on Tennant's work at Dunkirk or covering his period in the Levant.

TENNYSON, 2nd B
Sir Hallam Tennyson (1852-1928)

Governor, South Australia, 1899-1902. Governor-General, Australia, 1902-04.

A collection of papers (1895-1924) including personal diaries of considerable interest is held at the National Library of Australia.

THESIGER, Admiral Sir Bertram Sackville (1875-1966)

Naval career from 1887. Served World War I (Jutland). Admiral Superintendent, Portsmouth Dockyard, 1925-27. C.-in-C., East Indies Station, 1927-29. Flag Officer in Charge, Falmouth, 1942-44.

A collection of papers is housed at the National Maritime Museum. It includes personal journals (1875-1944, 6 vols.); logs; reports and telegrams relating to Central America (1909-10); albums kept whilst on service; memoirs and notes; and papers covering Thesiger's various postings and interests.

THESIGER, Captain Hon. Wilfred Gilbert (1871-1920)

Consular and Diplomatic Services, 1897-1920. Minister, Abyssinia, 1909-19. General Staff, War Office, 1914-18.

Mr W. P. Thesiger, C.B.E., D.S.O., 15 Shelley Court, Tite Street, London SW3 retains the large number of family letters written by his father during his foreign service appointments and his military career. There exists also a considerable number of semi-official letters written from 1915-18 to Rowland Sperling at the Foreign Office. All these letters are sorted and boxed. Mr Thesiger also has xerox copies of his father's official dispatches (1909-19). These papers are to be deposited at the Middle East Centre, St Antony's College, Oxford.

THOMAS, Sir Charles John (1874-1943)

Permanent Secretary, Ministry of Agriculture and Fisheries, 1927-36. Served Reparations Commission, from 1919; Compensation (Ireland) Commission, 1922-25; etc.

The Will and Letters of Administration give no details helpful in tracing papers.

THOMAS, Admiral Sir Hugh Evan- (1862-1928)

Naval career from 1875. Rear-Admiral, 1st Battle Squadron, 1913-14. Commanded 5th Battle Squadron, Battle of Jutland, 1916. C.-in-C., The Nore, 1921-24.

A collection of papers is deposited in the British Library (Add. MSS. 52504-6 and 53738). This includes correspondence and papers of Sir Hugh Evan-Thomas, chiefly regarding his naval career (1876-1927); correspondence, mostly from Sir Hugh to his brother-in-law and the latter's wife (1914-26); biographical notes and press cuttings.

THOMAS, Sir (Thomas) Shenton Whitelegge (1879-1962)

Colonial Service. Governor, Nyasaland, 1929-32; Gold Coast, 1932-34; Straits Settlements (and High Commissioner, Malay States), 1934-42.

An unpublished document, 'Malaya's War Effort, 1940-42', by Sir Shenton Thomas exists in the British Association of Malaya collection at the Royal Commonwealth Society library.

THOMPSON, Sir John Perronet (1873-1935)

Political Secretary, Government of India, 1922-27. Chief Commissioner of Delhi, 1928-32.

The collection at the India Office Library consists of a series of diaries (1897-1932); boxes of letters arranged alphabetically by correspondent; press cuttings and printed material; the text and notes for Thompson's speeches; photographs; and an assortment of papers relating to the organisation called the Union of Britain and India (1933-35).

THORNE, General Sir (Augustus Francis) Andrew Nicol (1885-1970)

Military career; commands during World War I. Assistant Military Attaché, Washington, 1919-20. Military Assistant to Chief of the Imperial General Staff, 1925-26. Military Attaché, Berlin, 1932-35. Commander, 48th Division, British Expeditionary Force, 1939-40; XII Corps (Kent), 1940-41. G.O. C.-in-C., Scottish Command, 1941-45. C.-in-C., Allied Land Forces, Norway; and Head of SHAEF Mission to Norway, 1945. Worked for Norwegian Ministry of Defence, 1950-51.

The Imperial War Museum has a small number of papers collected for the compilation of an article on the Battle of Gheluvelt. No further private papers are known to survive.

THRING, Sir Arthur Theodore (1860-1932)

1st Parliamentary Counsel, 1903-17. Clerk of the Parliaments, 1917-30.

Rear-Admiral G. A. Thring, Alford House, Castle Cary, Somerset, states that there are few papers relating to his father. Those which survive, mostly press cuttings, are stuck into a family photograph album.

THURSFIELD, Rear-Admiral Henry George (1882-1963)

Naval career. Served World War I. Assistant Director of Naval Staff College, 1920. Commanded ships in Mediterranean, 1922-24, 1930-32. Director of Tactical Division, Admiralty Naval Staff, 1928. Naval Correspondent of *The Times*, 1936-52; and editor of *Brassey's Annual*, 1936-63.

Certain papers are available at the National Maritime Museum, and include a collection of lecture notebooks, standing orders and loose papers (*c.* 1902-26); together with logs, midshipman's journals and certain personal papers.

THURSTAN, Edward William Paget (1880-1947)

Chargé d'Affaires, Mexico, 1917-18 (Consul-General, 1915-17). Acting Consul-General, Algiers, 1919-20. Consul-General, Cologne, 1920-24; Rotterdam, 1924-27; Genoa, 1927-35; Milan, 1935-37.

Mr J. D. B. P. Thurstan, Swanbourne House School, Swanbourne, Milton Keynes, Bucks. MK17 0HZ, possesses those of his father's papers which are extant. They include documents relating to Mexico in the period 1915-17, and fragments of an unpublished autobiography.

TILLEY, Sir John Anthony Cecil (1869-1952)

Ambassador, Brazil, 1921-25; Japan, 1926-31.

Efforts to contact a member of the family proved unsuccessful.

TIZARD, Sir Henry Thomas (1885-1959)

Academic career. Permanent Secretary, Department of Scientific and Industrial Research, 1927-29. Member, Council of Minister of Aircraft Production; Air Council, 1941-43. Chairman, Advisory Council on Scientific Policy and Defence Research Policy Committee, 1946-52.

The papers of Sir Henry Tizard are deposited in the Imperial War Museum. Application to view the collection should be made to the Keeper of the Department of Documents. Access will only be granted after the written permission of Professor J. P. M. Tizard and Dr Noble Frankland has been obtained.

TOMKINSON, Vice-Admiral Wilfred (1877-1971)

Naval career. Served China War. 1900; World War I. Chief of Staff to C.-in-C., Mediterranean, 1927. Assistant Chief of Naval Staff, 1929-31. Commanded Battle Cruiser Squadron, 1931-32. Flag Officer in Charge, Bristol Channel, 1940-42.

Diaries (1914-17) and other related papers are preserved at the Imperial War Museum. Other papers, including correspondence, are housed at Churchill College, Cambridge.

TOMLINSON, Sir George John Frederick (1876-1963)

Colonial Service. Assistant Under-Secretary, Colonial Office, 1930-39.

Rhodes House Library has a series of letters, written by Tomlinson to his mother (1900-24), relating to Tanganyika and Nigeria; and notes and photographs on his East African tour (1934).

TOMLINSON, Major-General Sir Percy Stanley (1884-1951)

Military career. Director of Medical Services, Middle East Forces, 1940-43; 21 Army Group, 1943-44.

The Royal Army Medical Corps Museum has one box file of World War II papers.

TOWER, Sir Reginald Thomas (1860-1939)

Minister, Siam, 1901-03; Munich, 1903-06; Mexico, 1906-10; Argentine, 1910-19; Paraguay, 1911-19. Temporary Administrator and High Commissioner of the League of Nations at Danzig, 1919-20.

Miss Winifred Tower (niece), Memories, Chequer Lane, Ash, Canterbury, Kent, reports that Sir Reginald kept fairly full notes of his diplomatic career, which are now deposited in the Foreign Office Library. Three volumes of notes about the Argentine are preserved at the University of London Library. Miss Tower has retained a few personal records, including letters of appointment, a few letters from Peking in 1901 and notes of talks on his diplomatic service which he gave during his retirement.

TOWNLEY, Sir Walter Beaupré Keppel (1863-1945)

Diplomatic career. Secretary of Legation, 1901, and Chargé d'Affaires, Peking, 1902-03. Minister, Argentine and Paraguay, 1906-10; Romania, 1910-12; Persia, 1912-15; Netherlands, 1917-19.

Mr. Charles Townley (nephew) knew of no surviving papers. Efforts to contact other members of Townley's family proved unavailing. A few letters can be found in the Hardinge collection at Cambridge University Library.

TOWNSHEND, Major-General Sir Charles Vere Ferrers (1861-1924)

Entered Royal Marines, 1881. Served Sudan; South Africa; European War, 1914-18. M.P. (Ind.) The Wrekin, 1920-22.

A collection of press cuttings has been placed in the care of Mr P. Liddle, Department of Education, Sunderland Polytechnic. The main collection of papers and diaries, however, remains with Lt.-Col. A. J. Barker, 53 Beechwood Court, Queens Road, Harrogate, North Yorks. HG2 0HG. The material which is owned by Townshend's daughter, the Countess Audrey de Borchgrave Townshend, includes diaries, photograph albums, some letters and various other documents. The papers will be placed in due course in an appropriate library or record office.

TOYNBEE, Arnold Joseph (1889-   )

Historian and writer. Member, Foreign Office Political Intelligence Department, 1918; British Delegation to the Paris Peace Conference, 1919. Director, Foreign Research and Press Service, Royal Institute of International Affairs, 1939-43. Director, Foreign Office Research Department, 1943-46.

Professor Toynbee has a number of unpublished papers, diaries, letters and press cuttings, which are in the process of being sorted. For further details, researchers should write to the Director of the Royal Institute of International Affairs, Chatham House, 10 St James's Square, London SW1Y 4LE.

TRENCHARD, 1st Vt
Marshal of the Royal Air Force Sir Hugh Montague Trenchard
(1873-1956)

Served South Africa, 1899-1902; European War, 1914-18. Chief of Air Staff, 1918 and 1919-29. Commissioner of Metropolitan Police, 1931-35.

A collection of correspondence (1919-25) and documents on Trenchard's awards and commissions (1891-1951) are held at the Royal Air Force Museum. The present (2nd) Viscount Trenchard, Abdale House, North Mymms, Hatfield, Herts AL9 7T, has a further extensive collection of private papers and correspondence covering Trenchard's early career, his service in the Army and the Royal Flying Corps, his work as Chief of the Air Staff and Commissioner of the Metropolitan Police, and his subsequent activities during and after the First World War. The collection has been catalogued.

TREVELYAN, Baron
Sir Humphrey Trevelyan (1905-   )

Career in Indian Civil Service from 1929; in Foreign (later Diplomatic) Service from 1947. Chargé d'Affaires, Peking, 1953-55. Ambassador, Egypt, 1955-56; Iraq, 1958-61. Under-Secretary, United Nations, 1958. Deputy Under-Secretary, Foreign Office, 1962. Ambassador, Soviet Union, 1962-65. High Commissioner, South Arabia, 1967.

Lord Trevelyan has kept a number of personal letters and press cuttings, the latter in family scrapbooks.

TRIBE, Sir Frank Newton (1893-1958)

Civil Service career, Ministry of Labour. Secretary to Commissioner for Special Areas (England and Wales), 1934-38. Permanent Secretary, Ministry of Production, 1942; Ministry of Fuel and Power, 1942-45; Ministry of Aircraft Production, 1945; Ministry of Food, 1945-46.

Dr C. R. Tribe, 19 Hyland Grove, Westbury-on-Trym, Bristol BS9 3NR, has a collection of his father's papers, at present unsorted and in store. Details are not available. Certain letters from 1921, at the Exchequer and Audit Department, may be passed to the Public Record Office.

TROTT, Alan Charles (1895-1959)

Levant Consular Service from 1920. Ambassador, Saudi Arabia, 1947-51. Director, Middle East Centre for Arab Studies, Lebanon, 1953-56.

Mrs H. D. Trott (widow), 65 Arlington Lodge, Monument Hill, Weybridge, Surrey KT13 8RD, has a collection of diaries (1922-56; lacking 1943, 1944, 1947). These diaries are largely a record of day-to-day life, and touch only indirectly on political matters. There are a few letters interleaved in the diaries.

TROUBRIDGE, Vice-Admiral Sir Thomas Hope (1895-1949)

Naval career. Served European War, 1914-18; War of 1939-45. Naval Attaché, Berlin, 1936-39. 5th Sea Lord (Air), 1945-46. Flag Officer (Air), Home, 1946-47, and Flag Officer (Air) and Second in Command, Mediterranean Station, 1948.

The Vice-Admiral's son, Sir Peter Troubridge, Bt., The Manor House, Elsted, Midhurst, Sussex, has a collection of unsorted papers and press cuttings kept by his father.

TROUP, Sir (Charles) Edward (1857-1941)

Permanent Under-Secretary, Home Office, 1908-22. Chairman, Safety in Mines Research Board, 1923-39; Health Advisory Committee (Mines Department); Special Grants Committee, Ministry of Pensions, 1929-38.

Efforts to trace the family and executors were not successful.

TROUTBECK, Sir John Monro (1894-1971)

Assistant Under-Secretary, Foreign Office, 1946-47. Head of British Middle East Office, Cairo, 1947-50. Ambassador, Iraq, 1951-54.

Lady Troutbeck has no papers kept by her late husband during his career.

TRUEMAN, Sir Arthur Elijah (1894-1956)

Academic career. Chairman, University Grants Committee, 1949-53.

It was not possible to contact Lady Trueman.

TUDOR, Major-General Sir (Henry) Hugh (1871-1965)

Military career. Served South Africa; European War, 1914-18. Chief of Police, Ireland, 1920.

A collection of papers can be found at the Royal Armoured Corps Tank Museum.

TUKER, Lieutenant-General Sir Francis Ivan Simms (1894-1967)

Military career, with long service in India. Director of Military Training, G.H.Q., India, 1940-41. G.O.C., Ceylon, 1945. G.O. C.-in-C., Eastern Command, India, 1946-47.

A number of private and personal papers (1914-67), mainly relating to the North African campaign, to Indian defence and to the post-war period, are held at the Imperial War Museum. Some of this material is not open for inspection.

TURNBULL, Sir Richard Gordon (1909-   )

Colonial Service in Kenya from 1931. Governor and C.-in-C., Tanganyika, 1958-61. Governor-General, 1961-62. High Commissioner for Aden and the Protectorate of South Arabia, 1965-67.

Tapes and transcripts of his work in Kenya, 1931-58, are in Rhodes House Library, Oxford.

TURNER, Vice-Admiral Sir Frederick Richard Gordon (1889-   )

Naval career. Engineer-in-Chief of the Fleet, 1942-45.

Most of the Vice-Admiral's papers were stolen.

TURNER, Sir George Wilfred (1896-1974)

Civil Service career. Permanent Under-Secretary, War Office, 1949-56.

Some of Sir George's papers, and those of Engineer Vice-Admiral Sir Harold Brown, relating to munitions production in the War Office and Ministry of Supply (1936-45), are at the Liddell Hart Centre for Military Archives. The papers include memoranda, day-to-day diary entries and a good deal of published material.

TURNER, Vice-Admiral Sir Robert Ross (1885-   )

Naval career from 1900. Served in Submarine service during World War I, and later commanded H.M.S. *Leander*, 1933-35. Admiral Superintendent, Portsmouth Dockyard, 1935-40. Director-General of Shipbuilding and Repairs, India, 1941-44. Senior British Naval Officer, Greece, 1945-46.

A small box of material, relating to the Government of India publication *History of Directorate-General, Shipbuilding and Repairs, 1942-45,* has been donated to the Imperial War Museum.

TURNER, Lieutenant-General Sir William Francis Robert (1907-   )

Military career. Served in Great Britain and India, 1928-39. Commanding Officer during World War II in North West Europe and Middle East. General Staff Officer I, Middle East and Great Britain, 1947-50. Colonel, British Military Mission to Greece, 1950-52. G.O. C.-in-C., Scottish Command, 1961-64.

According to information supplied to the Imperial War Museum, no papers have been kept.

TUSON, Alan Arthur Lancelot (1890-1968)

China Consular Service, 1913-42. Minister, Haiti, 1943-46.

Mrs G. D. Tuson (widow) says that A. A. L. Tuson kept no relevant papers.

TWEEDSMUIR, 1st B
Sir John Buchan (1875-1940)

Novelist. Director-General of Information under the Prime Minister, 1917-18. M.P. (Con.) Scottish Universities, 1927-35. Governor-General, Canada, 1935-40.

A substantial collection of correspondence, speeches, writings, press clippings, tape recordings, photographs, scrapbooks and posthumous material is available in the Douglas Library, Queen's University, Kingston, Ontario, Canada. The papers cover the whole of Tweedsmuir's adult life and career (1895-1940), with posthumous material up to 1950. A small collection of 37 letters from Tweedsmuir to Lord Beaverbrook is located in the library of the University of New Brunswick. These cover the years 1918-35, and deal mainly with Tweedsmuir's desire for an Honour. Access to these is restricted.

TWINING, Baron
Sir Edward Francis Twining (1899-1967)

Colonial Service. Governor and C.-in-C., North Borneo, 1946-49; Tanganyika, 1949-58.

A collection of papers remains in private hands, but is not available for research.

TWYNAM, Sir Henry Joseph (1887-1966)

Governor, Central Provinces and Berar, 1940-46. Acting Governor, Bengal, 1945.

The India Office Library holds a microfilm of Twynam's papers (1913-46). This includes correspondence with the Viceroy, tour programmes, speeches, personal diaries and other official papers. A further MS. collection includes two printed volumes of speeches (1940-42), addresses and press cuttings, and a typescript of Twynam's memoirs, *Golden Years and Times of Stress.*

TYRRELL, 1st B
Sir William George Tyrrell (1866-1947)

Private Secretary to Foreign Secretary, 1907-15. Assistant Under-Secretary, Foreign Office, 1919-25; Permanent Under-Secretary, 1925-28. Ambassador, France, 1928-34.

A collection of papers at the Public Record Office (F.O. 800/220) includes correspondence with Sir Charles Mendl, Foreign Office News Department Representative and later Press Attaché in France. About 50 letters (1926-30) written by Tyrrell are housed at the National Library of Scotland.

TYRRELL, Air Vice-Marshal Sir William (1885-1968)

Service in Royal Air Force Medical Services. Served European War and War of 1939-45, and in Somaliland, Palestine, Iraq, etc.

The Imperial War Museum has Tyrrell's collection of private and official papers covering the years 1914-45. The material consists mainly of scientific and administrative papers concerning army medical services (1914-18) and R.A.F. medical care (1918-45); studies of trench warfare (1914-18); papers on medical service in the Middle East (1920-29), and on R.A.F. hospital administration; and papers on Technical and Training Commands (1930-45). Some of this material is closed.

TYRWHITT, Admiral of the Fleet Sir Reginald Yorke, 1st Bt (1870-1951)

Naval career. Served World War I. C.-in-C., Cluna Station, 1927-29; The Nore, 1930-33.

A collection of papers is preserved by Lady Agnew, Pinehurst, South Ascot, Berks. It consists largely of letters, particularly from Tyrwhitt to his family during World War I.

TYTLER, Lieutenant-Colonel Sir William Kerr-Fraser- (1886-1963)

Indian Political Service. Minister, Afghanistan, 1935-41.

The surviving unsorted papers are in the care of Lady Fraser-Tytler, The Quoit Green, West Saltoun, Pencaitland, East Lothian. They will be placed in due course in the Middle East Centre at St Antony's College, Oxford. Further papers may be found in the Walton collection at the India Office Library.

UNIACKE, Lieutenant-General Sir Herbert Crofton Campbell (1866-1934)

Served in Royal Artillery from 1885. Chief Instructor, Royal Horse and Royal Field Artillery, 1913-14. Deputy Inspector-General of Training, British Armies in France and Flanders, 1914-18. G.O.C., 1st Indian Division, 1920-24. G.O. C.-in-C., Northern Command, India, 1924. Colonel Commandant, Royal Regiment of Artillery, 1927-30.

A collection of papers relating to Uniacke's work is preserved at the Royal Artillery Institution.

UPCOTT, Sir Gilbert Charles (1880-1967)

Civil Service career from 1903, Treasury. Comptroller and Auditor-General, 1931-46.

A series of personal letters (c. 1939-53) from Sir Gilbert to his daughter, Lady Rosemary Firth, have survived, together with a number of engagement diaries. The papers are not generally available, but enquiries should be addressed to Lady Firth, 33 Southwood Avenue, London N6 5SA. Certain papers, from 1921, at the Exchequer and Audit Department, may be placed in the Public Record Office.

URQUHART, Sir Robert William (1896-)

Levant Consular Service. Inspector-General of Consulates from 1939. Minister, Washington, 1947. Consul-General, Shanghai, 1948-50. Ambassador, Venezuela, 1951-55.

Sir Robert Urquhart states that he has kept no papers which could be of assistance.

VANDEPEER, Sir Donald Edward (1890-1968)

Civil Service career. Military service, European War, 1914-18. Permanent Secretary, Ministry of Agriculture and Fisheries, 1945-52.

Mrs D. Stroud, Sir Donald's daughter states that the family has no documents of importance covering her father's career.

VANSITTART, 1st B
Sir Robert Gilbert Vansittart (1881-1957)

Assistant Under-Secretary, Foreign Office, and Principal Private Secretary to the Prime Minister, 1928-30. Permanent Under-Secretary, Foreign Office, 1930-38. Chief Diplomatic Adviser to Foreign Secretary, 1938-41.

The material (1930-48) at Churchill College, Cambridge, is not open to general inspection. The official papers and copies of official papers include not only registered Cabinet papers and minutes and Foreign Office records, but also some secret official correspondence and semi-official correspondence. Only a few personal papers, for the later period, have survived.

VAUGHAN, Sir (John Charles) Tudor St Andrew- (1870-1929)

Minister, Chile, 1918-22; Latvia, Estonia and Lithuania, 1922-27; Sweden, 1927-29.

It did not prove possible to trace members of Vaughan's family. Major T. E. St Aubyn, the son of one of Vaughan's executors, had no relevant information.

VEREKER, Sir (George) Gordon Medlicott (1889-)

Minister, Finland, 1940-41. Special Service, Gibraltar, 1942. Minister, then Ambassador, Uruguay, 1943-49.

It proved impossible to contact Sir Gordon.

VILLIERS, Sir Francis Hyde (1852-1925)

Assistant Under-Secretary, Foreign Office, 1896-1905. Minister, Portugal, 1905-11; Belgium, 1911-19 (Ambassador, 1919-20).

At the Public Record Office (F.O. 800/22-4), material for the period 1883 to 1923 survives, including correspondence with Sir Charles Hardinge (1907-08), Sir Arthur Nicolson (1893-1908), and Sir Cecil Spring-Rice (1883-1905). It proved impossible to contact Villiers's family to enquire of the whereabouts of other surviving papers.

VIVIAN, Sir Sylvanus Percival (1880-1958)

Civil Service career. Registrar-General, 1921-45.

Mrs L. Silverston, Bury House, Hatfield Broad Oak, near Bishop's Stortford, Herts., has a number of papers relating to her father. These are unsorted, but the material includes press cuttings and some letters, but no diaries.

VON DONOP, Major-General Sir Stanley Brenton (1860-1941)

Commissioned in Royal Artillery, 1880. Director of Artillery, War Office, 1911-13. Master-General of the Ordnance and 4th Military Member of Army Council, 1913-16. Commander, Humber Garrison, 1917-20.

The Imperial War Museum has a collection of papers, including three binders of press cuttings, a number of medal patents and one file of official Ministry of Munitions papers (1913-16). These papers are not generally available for research. It is understood that Von Donop's other papers were destroyed.

VYSE, Major-General Sir Richard Granville Hylton Howard- (1883-1962)

Served European War, 1914-17; Palestine, etc. Head of Military Mission, French High Command, 1939-40.

Family papers are at the Buckinghamshire Record Office, but it is understood that papers of Major-General Sir Richard Howard-Vyse are still with Lady Howard-Vyse.

WADDINGTON, Sir (Eubule) John (1890-1957)

Colonial Service, Kenya, Bermuda, British Guiana. Governor and C.-in-C., Barbados, 1930-41; Northern Rhodesia, 1941-47.

Rhodes House Library has Waddington's commission of appointment to Barbados (1938) and copies of his speeches and addresses (1939-41).

WADSWORTH, Sir Sidney (1888-   )

Indian Civil Service from 1913. Judge, High Court, Madras, 1935-47.

The Cambridge South Asian Archive holds memoirs, 'Lo, the Poor Indian', covering the Madras Presidency, 1913-45.

WAKEHURST, 2nd B
John de Vere Loder (1895-1970)

Military career. 4th Royal Sussex Regiment and Intelligence Corps, World War I, 1914-19. M.P. (Con.) Leicester East, 1924-29; Lewes, 1931-36. Governor, New South Wales, 1937-46; Northern Ireland, 1952-64.

A large collection of papers, including unpublished memoirs and press cuttings, remains with Lady Wakehurst, 31 Lennox Gardens, London SW1. Certain papers have been given to the Mitchell Library, Sydney, Australia, and photocopies of other material is to be placed with this collection. It includes papers relating to his office in New South Wales and to Northern Ireland. A letter book and diary relating to Gallipoli and the Palestine campaigns (1915-18), and a memorandum on personalities of members of the Zionist Commission (1918), are held in the Middle East Centre, St Antony's College, Oxford.

WALKER, Colonel Charles William Garne (1882-1974)

Military service, Indian Army and European War. Assistant Secretary, Committee of Imperial Defence, 1921-25. Secretary, Conference of Governors of the East African Dependencies, 1925-36. Served Treasury from 1936; Civil Defence organisation, and War Cabinet, 1943-47. Secretary, Association of Consulting Engineers, 1948-50.

Rhodes House Library has a collection (5 boxes) of Walker's correspondence, minutes, etc., as Secretary to the Conference of Governors of East African Dependencies (1925-35). Contact with the family was not established.

WALLINGER, Sir Geoffrey Arnold (1903-   )

Minister, Hungary, 1949-51. Ambassador, Thailand, 1951-54; Austria, 1954-58; Brazil, 1958-63.

Sir Geoffrey Wallinger has destroyed the diary which he kept at one time, and has retained no papers relating to his official activities.

WALLIS, Major Charles Braithwaite (d.1945)

Consul-General, Liberia, 1908; Dakar, 1909-20; New Orleans, 1920-23. Minister and Consul-General, Panama, the Canal Zone and Costa Rica, 1923-31.

Certain diaries and newspaper cuttings, together with the unpublished manuscript of a book concerning American policies towards Panama, survive with Major Charles St John Wallis, Flat 2, 5 Glengariff Road, Parkstone, Poole, Dorset BH14 9LQ.

WALMSLEY, Air Marshal Sir Hugh Sydney Porter (1898-   )

Military and Royal Air Force career. Served European War, 1914-18; Iraq, 1921-23; Aden, 1935-37; War of 1939-45. Air Officer Commanding, 91 Group, 1942-43; 4 Group, Transport Command, 1945-46. Senior Air Staff Officer, Bomber Command, 1944-45. Air Officer, Transport Command, South East Asia, 1946. Air Officer C.-in-C., India, 1946-47. Deputy Chief of Air Staff, 1948-50. Air Officer C.-in-C., Flying Training Command, 1950-52.

The Imperial War Museum found that the Air Marshal has no papers.

WALSH, Major-General George Peregrine (1899-1972)

Military career, European War, 1914-19; War of 1939-45. Chief of Staff, 8th Army, 1944; Allied Land Forces, South East Asia, 1945; Southern Command, 1948-49. Director, Weapons and Development, War Office, 1949-52. Controller of Supplies (Munitions), Ministry of Supply, from 1952.

The Imperial War Museum has a collection of official papers relating to X Corps, North Africa (1942); XXX Corps, Sicily (1943); 8th Army operations in Italy (1944); and Burma (1944-45).

WALTON, Sir John Charles (1885-1957)

Assistant Under-Secretary, India, 1936-42. Deputy Under-Secretary, Burma, 1942-46.

The collection at the India Office Library dated from 1920 to 1946 consists mainly of Walton's correspondence with various officers of the Government of India. The remainder consists of typescript and printed reports, with material on Burma, Egypt, Eire and Malaya, as well as India.

WARD, Colonel Sir Edward Willis Duncan, 1st Bt (1853-1928)

Military career from 1874. Served Sudan, 1885; South Africa, 1899-1900. Permanent Under-Secretary, War Office, 1901-14.

Lady Ward, widow of the 2nd Bt, knows of no papers. There are five letters from Ward (1903-18) in the Blumenfeld papers now at the House of Lords Record Office.

WARNER, Sir George Redston (1879-   )

Minister, Switzerland, 1935-39.

Sir George Redston Warner has kept no private papers.

WARNER, Sir William Lee- (1846-1914)

Secretary, India Office (Political and Secret Departments), 1895-1903. Member, Council of India, 1902-12.

The papers at the India Office Library include letters from a wide variety of correspondents, and an album of letters, printed memoranda and newspaper cuttings relating to Lee-Warner's period at Rugby, to important stages in his career, to his writings and to official functions he attended. There are also further papers relating to Lee-Warner's published writings, and a collection of printed official papers, books and pamphlets.

WATERLOW, Sir Sydney Philip (1878-1944)

Director, Foreign Division, Department of Overseas Trade, 1922-24. Minister, Siam, 1926-28; Abyssinia, 1928-29; Bulgaria, 1929-33; Greece, 1933-39.

Very few private papers remain, but correspondence, some of it relating to the visit of Edward VIII and the Duchess of Windsor to Greece shortly before the abdication, is held by Professor J. C. Waterlow, 3 Campden Hill Square, London W8. The papers are not open for inspection. Letters to Sydney and Violet Schiff (1924-33) are in the British Library (Add. MSS. 52922).

WATNEY, Colonel Sir Frank Donney (1870-1965)

Military career. Served in Gallipoli, Egypt, France, Salonika, Palestine, 1914-19.

A collection of papers, diaries, accounts, notebooks, photographs and family papers was sold to Peter Eaton (Booksellers) Ltd, 80 Holland Park Avenue, London W11, to whom enquiries should be addressed. The papers cover both World Wars, and many relate to the work of the Territorial Army and volunteers.

WATSON, Vice-Admiral Bertram Chalmers (1887-   )

Naval Career. Served World War I (in Harwich Force). Director, Royal Naval Staff College, 1934-36. Flag Officer, Greenock, 1940-42. Commodore of Convoys, 1942-43. Admiral Commanding Iceland, 1943-45.

Preserved at the Imperial War Museum are memoirs of service under Admiral of the Fleet Sir Reginald Tyrwhitt in the Harwich Force (1914-16).

WATSON, General Sir Daril Gerard (1888-1967)

Military career. Served in India. G.O.C., 2nd Division, 1940-41. Director of Staff Duties, War Office, 1941-42. Assistant Chief of Imperial General Staff, 1942. Deputy Adjutant-General, 1942-44. G.O. C.-in-C., Western Command, 1944-46. Quartermaster-General to the Forces, 1946-47.

According to information received by the Liddell Hart Centre for Military Archives, the General destroyed his papers as being of little interest.

WATSON, Herbert Adolphus Grant- (1881-1971)

Minister, Central America, 1928-33; Cuba, 1933-35; Finland, 1935-37; Cuba, 1937-40.

It proved impossible to contact Grant-Watson's family.

WATSON, Robert William Seton- (1879-1951)

Historian and writer on Eastern Europe. Member, War Cabinet Intelligence Bureau, 1917; Enemy Propaganda Department, 1918; Foreign Research and Press Service, 1939-40; Foreign Office Political Intelligence Service, 1940-42.

A collection of R. W. Seton-Watson's papers is housed at the School of Slavonic and East European Studies, University of London. In addition to a series of box files, arranged in chronological order and by subject matter, there are a number of papers in a filing cabinet arranged by correspondent. The boxed material includes files relating to the two World Wars, to the affairs of particular countries in Eastern Europe, to the Munich crisis (1938), to the Serbian Relief Fund and other welfare matters, to students, to historians, to Seton-Watson's publications and to the academic study of Eastern Europe. The papers may be consulted by arrangement with Mr Christopher Seton-Watson, Oriel College, Oxford, or Professor Hugh Seton-Watson at the School of Slavonic and East European Studies.

WAUCHOPE, General Sir Arthur Grenfell (1874-1947)

Military career. Served South African War; European War, 1914-18, in France and Mesopotamia. Chief of British Section, Military Inter-Allied Commission of Control, Berlin, 1924-27. G.O.C., 44th Home Counties Division, Territorial Army, 1927-29; Northern Ireland District, 1929-31. High Commissioner and C.-in-C., Palestine and Transjordan, 1931-38.

According to the terms of the General's will, the papers were destroyed.

WAVELL, 1st E
Field-Marshal Sir Archibald Percival Wavell (1883-1950)

Military career. Served World War I in France, Caucasus and Egypt. Commanded Troops in Palestine and Transjordan, 1937-38. G.O. C.-in-C., Southern Command, 1938-39. C.in-C., Middle East, 1939-41; India, 1941-43. Supreme Commander, South West Pacific, 1942. Viceroy and Governor-General, India, 1943-47.

A collection of papers, including diaries, remains in the care of members of the family. The material is not generally available for research, but was used by Sir Penderel Moon for his book *Wavell: The Viceroy's Journal* (1973). The collection includes military papers, literary papers and letters, and copies of speeches. Enquiries should be addressed to the 1st Earl's eldest daughter, Lady Pamela Humphrys, Marston Meysey Grange, near Cricklade, Wilts. Field-Marshal Earl Wavell's 1909 Staff College papers on the Civil War in America, the Waterloo campaign, and on law are in the Brigadier Sir Bernard Fergusson collection at the Liddell Hart Centre for Military Archives. Correspondence with Sir Sydney Cockerell is at the British Library (Add. MSS. 52759).

WAVERLEY, 1st Vt
Sir John Anderson (1882-1958)

Secretary, Ministry of Shipping, 1917-19. Chairman, Board of Inland Revenue, 1919-22. Joint Under-Secretary to Lord Lieutenant of Ireland, 1920. Permanent Under-Secretary, Home Office, 1922-32. Governor of Bengal, 1932-37. M.P. (Ind. National) Scottish Universities, 1938-50. Lord Privy Seal, 1938-39; Home Secretary, 1939-40. Lord President of the Council, 1940-43. Chancellor of the Exchequer, 1943-45.

Members of Waverley's family retain none of his papers. However, some material may be found at the Public Record Office, viz. papers on Ireland (C.O. 904/188/1, 2); and papers on Pensions (PEN I). Papers as Lord President remain with the Cabinet Office, and a collection of Indian papers is held at the India Office Library. Further details are given by Hazlehurst and Woodland, op. cit., pp. 4-5.

WEBB, Admiral Sir Richard (1870-1950)

Naval career from 1885. Director of Trade Division, Admiralty War Staff, 1914-17. Commander, H.M.S. *New Zealand*, Grand Fleet, 1917-18. Assistant High Commissioner, Turkey, 1918-20. Head of Naval Mission to Greece, 1924-25.

A collection of papers is housed at the National Maritime Museum. These include his logs during service at sea (1885-1912).

WEBSTER, General Sir Thomas Riddell- (1886-1974)

Military career. Served European War, 1914-19. Commanding, 2 Battalion The Cameronians (Scottish Rifles), 1930-34; Poona Brigade, India, 1935-38. Director of Movements and Quartering, War Office, 1938-39. Deputy Quartermaster-General, 1939-40. G.O.C.-in-C., Southern Command, India, 1941. Lieutenant General in Charge of Administration, Middle East, 1941-42. Quartermaster-General, 1942-46.

A box of semi-official correspondence with Generals Venning, Lindsell, Gale, Auchinleck and Sir Miles Graham concerning operations in the Middle East, North Africa, Northern Europe, and conditions in India, has been given to the Imperial War Museum.

WEIR, 1st Vt
Sir William Douglas Weir (1877-1959)

Controller of Aeronautical Supplies, and Member of Air Board, 1917-18. Director-General of Aircraft Production, Ministry of Munitions, 1918. President of the Air Board, 1918. Director-General of Explosives, Ministry of Supply, 1939. Chairman, Tank Board, 1942.

The papers are held in the archives centre of Churchill College, Cambridge, and they are described in Hazlehurst and Woodland, op. cit., p. 150.

WELBY, Sir George Earle (1851-1936)

Minister, Colombia, 1898-1906.

Mrs E. Des Graz (niece) knows of no papers, nor does Sir Oliver Welby, Bt, a distant relative. It proved impossible to contact other members of his family.

WELLESLEY, Sir Victor Alexander Augustus Henry (1876-1954)

Deputy Under-Secretary, Foreign Office, 1925-36.

A collection of papers and correspondence survives in the care of Rt Hon. the Earl Cowley, c/o The House of Lords, London SW1. The papers relate to the latter part of Sir Victor Wellesley's period in the Foreign Office, and they partly concern his research work for the book *Diplomacy in Fetters* (1944).

WEMYSS, Vice-Admiral Edward William Elphinstone (1866-1938)

Naval career.

A collection of papers at the National Maritime Museum covers Wemyss's naval career to 1911, and includes two midshipman's logbooks (1881-84); news cuttings; and five photograph albums (1882-1911).

●WENLOCK, 6th B
Sir Arthur Lawley (1860-1932)

Administrator, Matabeleland, 1897-1901. Governor, Western Australia, 1901-02. Lieutenant-Governor, Transvaal, 1902-06. Governor, Madras, 1906-11.

The present (2nd) Baron Wraxall (grandson) knows of no relevant papers.

WEST, General Sir Michael Montgomerie Alston Roberts (1905-)

Military career. Served World War II. Deputy Director, Manpower Planning, War Office, 1949-50. G.O.C.-in-C., British Troops in Austria, 1950-52. Commander, Commonwealth Division, Korea, 1952-53. Director, Territorial Army, War Office, 1955-57. Commander, 1st British Corps, British Army on the Rhine, 1958-59. G.O. C.-in-C., Northern Command, 1960-62. Head of British Defence Staff, Washington, 1962-65.

Official papers, talks, press cuttings relating to West's command of the Commonwealth Division in Korea are preserved at the Imperial War Museum.

WESTER WEMYSS, 1st B
Admiral of the Fleet Sir Rosslyn Erskine Wemyss (1864-1933)

Naval career from 1877. Commodore, Royal Naval Barracks, 1911-12. Rear-Admiral, 2nd Battle Squadron, 1912-13. Commanded Squadron of troops landing in Gallipoli, 1915. C.-in-C., East Indies and Egypt, 1916-17. 1st Sea Lord, 1917-19.

A collection of Wester Wemyss MSS. is retained by Hon. Mrs Frances Cunnack, Saint-Sirliac, Ille-et-Vilaine, France. These are most valuable for Wemyss's papers as 1st Sea Lord and feature a voluminous correspondence with the C.-in-C., Grand Fleet (Beatty), and Wemyss's unpublished memoirs for 1917-19 ('Admiralty I' and 'Admiralty II'). The Library of the University of California at Irvine has a microfilm of the 1918-19 correspondence and the memoirs.

WESTON, Lieutenant-General Sir Aylmer Gould Hunter- (1864-1940)

Army career from 1884. General Staff Officer, Eastern Command, 1904-08. Chief General Staff Officer, Scottish Command, 1908-11. Assistant Director of Military Training, 1911-14. Commanded 11th Infantry Brigade of 4th Division, 29th Division, 8th Army Corps during World War I. M.P. (Con.) Ayrshire North, 1916-18; Bute and North Ayrshire, 1918-35.

The National Army Museum holds a collection of letters and documents, mainly relating to Waziristan and the Boer War. Hunter-Weston's World War I diaries are at the British Library. In addition, the family papers (Hunter of Hunterston) are preserved in Scotland; a report has been prepared by the N.R.A. (Scotland) and a copy is available in Edinburgh, and at the National Register of Archives, London. These papers appear to contain little relating to Sir Aylmer.

WHISKARD, Sir Geoffrey Granville (1886-1957)

Civil Service career. High Commissioner, Australia, 1936-41. Permanent Secretary, Ministry of Works and Buildings, 1941-43; Town and Country Planning, 1943-46.

It is understood that any surviving private papers would be with Sir Geoffrey's son, J. M. Whiskard, Bellingham Farm, Sevenhampton, Swindon, Wilts. No details are available.

WHITE, Field-Marshal Sir George Stuart (1835-1912)

Entered Army, 1853. Military Secretary to Viceroy of India, 1880-81. C.-in-C., India, 1893-98. Quartermaster-General to the Forces, 1898-99. General on Staff to command troops at Natal (Ladysmith), 1899-1900. Governor of Gibraltar, 1900-04.

A collection of Sir George White's papers was deposited on loan by his family at the India Office Library. The earlier years, particularly those in India, are covered mainly by personal correspondence with his family and, after his marriage, letters to his wife. While Military Secretary to the Viceroy, White began a diary, and this is preserved. For White's more senior posts there are reports and other documents, though little remains, only personal letters and souvenirs, for his period in Gibraltar. Besides White's own papers, the collection includes letters to Lady White from various correspondents, and a few addressed to other members of his family.

WHITE, Sir Herbert Edward (1855-1947)

Consul-General, Morocco, 1908; British Agent, 1914-21. British Representative at Madrid Conference on Internationalisation of Tangiers, 1912 and 1913.

Mr A. R. M. White (grandson), Stakers Farm, Yapton, near Arundel, Sussex BN18 0DO, has a collection of Sir Herbert White's papers. This includes books, papers, letters, diaries (chiefly relating to Morocco) and photographs dating from the late nineteenth-century.

WHITE, Sir Herbert Thirkell (1855-1931)

Lieutenant-Governor, Burma, 1905-10.

The papers (1877-1931) at the India Office Library consist mainly of private and official correspondence and printed material relating to the administration of Burma.

WHITEHEAD, Sir James Beethorn (1858-1928)

Minister, Belgrade, 1906-10.

Messrs Heppenstall Rustom and Rowbotham, solicitors in the estate, knew of no members of Whitehead's family who might have surviving papers.

WHITWORTH, Admiral Sir William Jock (1884-1973)

Naval career. Served World War I. Commanded H.M.S. *Stuart* and 2nd Destroyer Flotilla, Mediterranean Fleet, 1928-31. Director of Physical Training and Sports, 1931-33. Naval Secretary to 1st Lord of the Admiralty, 1937-39. Vice-Admiral Commanding Battle Cruiser Squadron, 1939-41. Commanded H.M.S. *Warspite* at 2nd Battle of Narvik, 1940. 2nd Sea Lord, 1941-44. C.-in-C., Rosyth, 1944-46.

Papers donated to the Imperial War Museum include material relating to Whitworth's appointment as Vice-Admiral Commanding the Battle Cruiser Squadron (1939-41); and, in particular, to operations at Narvik (1940); letters from Lord Cunningham to Whitworth (1941-42); and other miscellaneous papers.

WHYTE, Sir Alexander Frederick (1883-1970)

M.P. (Lib.) Perth, 1910-18. President, Indian Legislative Assembly, 1920-25. Political Adviser to the National Government of China, 1929-32.

Eight volumes of diaries have been given to the India Office Library. Three volumes, dated from October 1917 to June 1919, are primarily a political commentary on the last year of the European war and the subsequent armistice negotiations, based on Whyte's experience in Parliament, as a lieutenant in the Royal Naval Volunteer Reserve (1914-17) and as a special correspondent for the *Daily News* at the Paris Peace Conference. The second group of three diaries, dated from May 1922 to November 1923, deal with Whyte's work in India in connection with the Princes Protection Bill and the Police Bill of 1922, as well as general questions of constitutional development and tariff reform. The other volumes, June to October 1934, describe a visit to China, Japan, Korea and Manchuria as an independent political observer, with records of interviews given by Generalissimo Chiang Kai-shek, Koki Hirota and Mamoru Shigemitsu. Some further, more personal papers remain with Whyte's daughter, Mrs Anne Thomas, 101 Hamilton Place, Aberdeen AB2 4BD.

WIGRAM, Ralph Follett (1890-1936)

Counsellor, Foreign Office, 1934-36.

R. F. Wigram's lectures on British foreign policy (1932-36) have been deposited in the Public Record Office (F.O. 800/292).

WILES, Sir Gilbert (1880-1961)

Indian Civil Service from 1904. Chief Secretary, Bombay Government 1937-39. Adviser to Government of Bombay, 1939-40. Adviser to Secretary of State for India, 1941-46.

The Cambridge South Asian Archive has a collection of papers, relating to service in India. The assortment of material includes notes, letters, confidential telegrams (1940), and pamphlets.

WILKINSON, Major-General Sir Percival Spearman (1865-1953)

Served with Niger Expedition, 1897-98; Ashanti, 1900. Inspector-General, West African Force, 1909-13. Served World War I. Inspector of Musketry, 1918-19. Commanded No. 1 Area, 1919-23.

Documents, including correspondence and press cuttings relating to the West African Frontier Force and the 4th Ashanti War (1900-01), have been given to the National Army Museum.

WILLERT, Sir Arthur (1882-1973)

Chief Correspondent of *The Times* in United States, 1910-20. Secretary of British War Mission in United States, 1917-18. Head of News Department and Press Officer, Foreign Office, from 1921. Head of Ministry of Information Office for Southern Region, 1939-45.

Sir Arthur Willert left his papers to Yale University Library.

WILLINGDON, 1st M of
Sir Freeman Freeman-Thomas (1866-1941)

M.P. (Lib.) Hastings, 1900-06; Bodmin, 1906-10. Junior Lord of the Treasury, 1905-12. Governor, Bombay, 1913-19; Madras, 1919-24. Governor-General, Canada, 1926-31. Viceroy and Governor-General, India, 1931-36.

The papers (1918-24) at the India Office Library consist of correspondence, chiefly with the Viceroy of India, Lord Chelmsford, and with E. S. Montagu.

WILLIS, Admiral of the Fleet Sir Algernon Usborne (1889-)

Naval career from 1904. Served European War, 1914-18 (Jutland, etc.). Chief of Staff, Mediterranean Fleet, H.M.S. *Warspite,* 1939-41. C.-in-C., South Atlantic Station, 1941-42; Levant Station, 1943; Mediterranean Fleet, 1946-48; Portsmouth Command, 1948-50. 2nd Sea Lord and Chief of Naval Personnel, 1944-46.

The Admiral states that he has diaries of naval operations in the Baltic, and the voyage of H.M.S. *Renown* with the Prince of Wales to Australia and New Zealand in 1920. He also has his memoirs of World War II, and a number of letters, newspaper cuttings and his 'appreciations of the situation' dating from that period. This material is to be given to Churchill College, Cambridge. Memoirs of the six important appointments held by the Admiral (1939-45) are in the care of the Imperial War Museum.

WILSON, 1st B
Field-Marshal Sir Henry Maitland Wilson (1881-1964)

Military career. Served World War I. Commands during 1920s and 1930s. G.O. C.-in-C., Egypt, 1939. Military Governor and G.O. C.-in-C., Cyrenaica, 1941. G.O. C.-in-C., Greece, 1941; British Forces in Palestine and Transjordan, 1941. C.-in-C., Allied Forces in Syria, 1941; Persia, Iraq Command, 1942-43; Middle East, 1943. Supreme Allied Commander, Mediterranean, 1944. Head of British Joint Staff Mission in Washington, 1945-47.

Papers of Field-Marshal Lord Wilson survive in the MacMichael collection, and in the correspondence of Dr Alford Carleton, at the Middle East Centre, St Antony's College, Oxford. Very few papers remain with the Rt. Hon. Hester Lady Wilson and there is no further material in private hands.

WILSON, Lieutenant Colonel Sir Arnold Talbot (1884-1940)

Army career from 1903. Served Indian Political Department in Persia, 1907-13. Deputy Commissioner, Turko-Persian Frontier Commission, 1913-14. Deputy Chief Political Officer, Indian Expeditionary Force 'D', 1915. Deputy Civil Commissioner, Baghdad, 1916. Acting Civil Commissioner, and Political Resident in Persian Gulf, 1918-20. Chairman, Home Office Committee on Structural Precautions against Air Attack, 1936-38. M.P. (Con.) Hitchin, 1933-40.

Two volumes of papers are housed at the London Library, and include letters, programmes, and newspaper cuttings. The first relates to Sandhurst (1889-1903); the second to India, Persia and Mesopotamia (1903-21). A collection of papers survives in the British Library (Add. MSS. 52455-59). The material includes correspondence with Sir Percy Cox at Baghdad; Sir F. A. Hirtzell, Captain G. C. Stephenson, Sir J. E. Shuckburgh of the India Office; general correspondence (1915-24), memoranda and press cuttings. The Imperial War Museum has a collection of government publications relating to Iraq (1918-22). Also there are photographs, scrapbooks concerned with civil disorders in 1922, and one file of private correspondence on Iraq. Further papers are at Durham University Library.

WILSON, Sir Arton (1893-   )

Civil Service career; Ministry of Labour, etc. Permanent Secretary, Ministry of Pensions, 1948-53.

Sir Arton Wilson has not kept a diary, and has only a small collection of personal correspondence and papers.

WILSON, Brigadier Sir Eric Edward Boketon Holt- (1875-1950)

Served in Imperial Security Intelligence Service (M.I.5), 1912-40 (Chief Staff Officer, 1917-40).

Wilson's son, Commander D. S. Holt-Wilson D.S.O., says that he returned all papers to the War Office after his father's death in 1950.

WILSON, Sir Guy Douglas Arthur Fleetwood- (1850-1940)

Assistant Under-Secretary of State, War Office, from 1898. Director-General of Army Finance, 1904-08. Finance Member, Supreme Council of India, 1908-13. Acting Viceroy of India, 1912.

A collection of personal and official papers is housed at the India Office Library. Most of the papers relate to Indian affairs, and they include general correspondence, and correspondence with Lord Hardinge (1911-13), E. S. Montagu (1910-13), Lord Crewe and Lord Morley; official notes on Indian affairs and files relating to particular subjects. Other material includes newspaper cuttings, papers and notes on the civil service and on Fleetwood-Wilson's appointments, and miscellaneous printed papers.

WILSON, Field-Marshal Sir Henry Hughes, 1st Bt (1864-1922)

Military career. Deputy, later Assistant, Adjutant-General, Army Headquarters, 1903-06. Director of Military Operations, 1910-14. Assistant Chief of General Staff to Lord French, 1914. British Military Representative at Versailles, 1917. Chief of Imperial General Staff from 1918-22.

A microfilm of Wilson's valuable diaries is available at the Imperial War Museum. These (41 in number) cover his career from 1893 to 1922. They are supplemented by a very considerable collection of correspondence and papers covering his entire military service, but with special reference to his appointment as C.I.G.S. A diary (26 Jan.-2 March 1917), relating to his war-time mission to Russia, is to be given to the Bodleian Library.

WILSON, Sir Horace John (1882-1972)

Civil Service career. Permanent Secretary, Ministry of Labour, 1921-30; Treasury, 1939-42. Chief Industrial Adviser, H. M. Government, 1930-39.

Mrs D. M. Bird, Sir Horace's daughter, states that her father kept no diaries or personal records, and that all official papers were returned to the appropriate government departments.

WILSON, Sir Leslie Orme (1876-1955)

M.P. (Con.) Reading, 1913-22; Portsmouth South, 1922-23. Parliamentary Assistant Secretary, War Cabinet, 1918. Parliamentary Secretary, Shipping, 1919; Treasury, 1921-23. Governor, Bombay, 1923-28; Queensland, 1932-46.

Certain papers, collected in preparation for a book, are with Peter L. O. Wilson, Esq., Currimundi House, Moffat Beach, Caloundra, Queensland, Australia.

WILSON, Brigadier-General Sir Samuel Herbert (1873-1950).

Military career. Served General Staff, European War, 1914-18. Assistant Secretary, Committee of Imperial Defence, and Secretary, Overseas Defence Committee, 1911-14. Home Ports Defence Committee; Imperial Communications Committee, 1918-21. Governor and C.-in-C., Trinidad and Tobago, 1921-24. Captain General and Governor in Chief, Jamaica, 1924-25. Permanent Under-Secretary, Colonial Office, 1925-33.

No information was secured.

WILTON, Sir Ernest Colville Collins (1870-1952)

Minister, Estonia and Latvia, 1921-22. President, Saar Governing Commission, 1927-32.

Sir Ernest Wilton's widow and executor died in 1963. It has not proved possible to contact any heirs.

WIMBERLEY, Major-General Douglas Neil (1896-   )

Military career. Served European War, 1914-18; North Russia, 1919; India, North West Frontier, 1930; War of 1939-45. G.O.C., 46th Division, 1941. Divisional Commander, 51st Highland Division, 1941-43. Commandant, Army Staff College, 1943-44. Director of Infantry, War Office, 1944-46.

There is an unpublished biography at Churchill College, Cambridge. Major-General Wimberley has kept a collection of his own papers, together with a mass of family material. These papers consist of diaries, letters and press cuttings, and they have been used for the compilation of a five-volume typed autobiographical account entitled *Scottish Soldier*. This covers the whole of Major-General Wimberley's career, his military service and also his later work as Principal of University College, Dundee, and as Colonel of the Queen's Own Cameron Highlanders, etc. Copies will be made available in 1985 at the National Library of Scotland, at Churchill College, Cambridge, and the Library of Dundee University. There is also a fourteen-volume series of scrapbooks. Most of the material remains with the family at Foxhall, Coupar Angus, Perthshire, and is closed for the present.

WINGATE, General Sir Francis Reginald, 1st Bt (1861-1953)

Governor-General, Sudan, 1899-1916. High Commissioner, Egypt, 1917-19.

A large collection of papers has been deposited in the Sudan Archive, University of Durham. The papers include Wingate's diaries (1881-86 and 1897-99); a series of personal papers and notes (1878-1951); correspondence relating to the Sudan and Egypt; other papers concerned with Egypt, including the English translation of the diary of Abbas Bey (1883); and an assortment of papers relating to Abyssinian affairs. Other sections of the collection are concerned with the Fashoda incident (1898); Wingate's mission to Somaliland (1909); Sanuseya affairs (1912-19); the Darfur campaign (1913-19); the Sudan-Belgian Congo frontier (1916-19); Father Paolo Rossignoli; regimental records; irrigation; ecclesiastical affairs; Sir Rudolf, Baron Slatin; and the publications of Sir Reginald Wingate. Other miscellaneous papers include memoirs, notes, maps, printed material, press cuttings, correspondence, and a collection of the papers of General Sir H. M. L. Rundle. Further papers remain with Sir Reginald's son, Sir Ronald Wingate, Bt, Barford Manor, Barford St Martin, Salisbury, Wilts.

WINGATE, Major General Orde Charles (1903-1944)

Military career, Sudan, Palestine and Transjordan. Served War of 1939-45. Commander of Special Force (Chindits), India.

Major-General Derek Tulloch used Wingate's personal papers, including letters and signals sent and received during 1943-44, for his book *Wingate in Peace and War* (1972). The material was also used by Christopher Sykes for his biography *Orde Wingate* (1959). The papers remain with Wingate's widow, now Mrs Lorna Smith. Papers of J. E. B. Barton are deposited in the National Army Museum and include magazine articles, letters and papers relating to the Indian Mutiny and the role of the Punjab Frontier Force; correspondence, newspaper cuttings and other documents relating to Major-General Orde Wingate and his campaigns in East Africa, 1940-41, and with the Chindits in Burma, 1943-45; together with miscellaneous documents, including an MS. diary of the siege of Jarboiyah, Mesopotamia, 1920. Relevant material may also be found in the papers of Colonel F. O. Cave at the Imperial War Museum.

WINGATE, Sir Ronald Evelyn Leslie, 2nd Bt (1889-   )

Indian Political Service, World Wars I and II. Member of Joint Planning Staff, War Cabinet. Author.

Sir Ronald has kept a number of his papers, including the drafts of books and of numerous articles and reviews.

WINGFIELD, Sir Charles John Fitzroy Rhys (1877-1960)

Minister, Siam, 1928-29; Norway, 1929-34; Holy See, 1934-35. Ambassador, Portugal, 1935-37. Adviser on Foreign Affairs to Press Censorship at Ministry of Information, 1939-41.

Lady Wingfield states that her husband left no diaries or papers, other than those which he returned to the Foreign Office.

WINSTER, 1st B
Reginald Thomas Herbert Fletcher (1885-1961)

M.P. (Lib.) Basingstoke, 1923-24; (Lab.) Nuneaton, 1935-42. Minister of Civil Aviation, 1945-46. Governor, Cyprus, 1946-48.

Hazlehurst and Woodland, op. cit., p. 56, describe the few papers which survive with the Resident Warden, Winster Lodge, Stone Cross, Crowborough, Sussex TN6 3SJ. Other correspondence may be found in the Creech Jones papers at Rhodes House Library.

WINTER, Brigadier-General Sir Ormonde de l'Epee (1875-1962)

Military career from 1894. Served European War, 1914-18. Deputy Chief of Police and Director of Intelligence, Ireland, 1920-22. Director of Resettlement, Irish Office, 1922. Director of Communications to International Board for Non-Intervention in Spain, 1938-39.

The Public Record Office has four files of Winter's papers (1918-22).

WIPPELL, Admiral Sir Henry Daniel Pridham- (1885-1952)

Naval career. Served World War I. Commanded H.M.S. *Enterprise*, 1928-30; Destroyer Flotilla, Home Fleet, 1932-33. Director of Operations Division, Admiralty, 1933-35. Commodore Commanding Home Fleet, Destroyer Flotilla, 1936-38. Director of Personal Services, Admiralty, 1938. 2nd-in-Command, Mediterranean Fleet, 1940. Flag Officer Commanding, Dover, 1942-45. C.-in-C., Plymouth, 1945-47.

Papers (1940-44) are preserved at the National Maritime Museum and include material relating to the Mediterranean (1940-41); the Dover Command (1942-45); and a war diary.

WISEMAN, Sir William George Eden, 10th Bt (1885-1962)

Chief Adviser on American Affairs, British Delegation to the Paris Peace Conference, 1918-19.

The collection of Sir William Wiseman's papers at Yale University Library includes 131 folders on his service during World War I as liaison officer between Colonel House and the British Government and on his work at the Paris Peace Conference.

WOLFF, Sir Henry Drummond (1830-1908)

M.P. (Con.) Christchurch, 1874-80; Portsmouth, 1880-85. Ambassador, Spain, 1892-1900.

Papers were located in a number of collections. Archives of the British representative on the Eastern Roumelian Commission (1878-79) are at the Public Record Office. Cabinet papers (1885-86) on his mission to Egypt are in the Harrowby collection, a full catalogue of which is available at the NRA (List 1561). Details of the correspondence in other collections can also be seen there.

WOLSELEY, 1st Vt
Sir Garnet Joseph Wolseley (1833-1913)

Army career from 1852. C.-in-C., Expeditionary Force to Egypt, 1882; and of Gordon Relief Expedition, 1884-85. C.-in-C., Forces in Ireland, 1890-95. C.-in-C., of the Army, 1895-1900.

The main bulk of the Wolseley papers and correspondence (some 4,000 items, 1852-1913) are preserved in Hove Central Library. Certain papers are housed at the National Army Museum and other items of value are in the care of Duke University, Durham, North Carolina. The Public Record Office has a further collection of papers. (W.O. 147). Further items are detailed at the National Register of Archives.

WOOD, Field-Marshal Sir Henry Evelyn (1838-1919)

Quartermaster-General to the Forces, 1893-97. Adjutant-General to the Forces, 1897-1901. Commanded 2nd Army Corps District, 1901-05.

Certain papers are preserved at Duke University, Durham, North Carolina. The collection consists of some 205 items of correspondence (1848-1919), and contains references to the Crimean War, Ashanti War, Zulu War, Transvaal War, Egypt, the South African War and reforms in Army administration. Papers concerning service in South Africa are in the Natal Archives, Pietermaritzburg.

WOODHEAD, Sir John Ackroyd (1881-1973)

Indian Civil Service. Chairman, Palestine Partition Commission, 1938. Governor, Bengal, 1939. Adviser to Secretary of State for India, 1939-44.

The Middle East Centre found that Sir John left no papers relating to Palestine. No other papers have been located.

WOODS, Sir John Harold Edmund (1895-1962)

Civil Service career. Permanent Secretary, Ministry of Production, 1943-45; Board of Trade, 1945-51. Minister, Economic Planning Board, 1947-51.

There are four files of Board of Trade papers in the Private Office class (BT 91) at the Public Record Office. Lady Woods, Applewick, Horsted Keynes, Haywards Heath, Sussex, has a further collection of files relating to her late husband's career. The material includes letters, copies of letters and drafts of speeches.

WOOLLEY, Sir Charles Campbell (1893-   )

Colonial Service. Governor and C.-in-C., Cyprus, 1941-46; British Guiana, 1947-53.

Rhodes House Library has a collection of correspondence and papers, relating to service in Ceylon, Jamaica, Cyprus and British Guiana (1922-59).

WRAY, Sir Kenneth Owen Roberts- (1899-   )

Legal Adviser, Colonial Office, then Dominions Office, then Commonwealth Relations Office, 1945-60.

Sir K. O. Roberts-Wray has placed certain papers on the work of the Colonial Office (1948) in Rhodes House Library, and he retains other papers in his care. Many of the papers held by Sir Kenneth are closed to researchers.

WRIGHT, Sir Michael Robert (1901-   )

Staff, Special Commissioner in South East Asia, 1946-47. Assistant Under-Secretary, Foreign Office, 1947-50. Ambassador, Norway, 1951-54; Iraq, 1954-58. Delegate, Conference for Cessation of Nuclear Tests, Geneva, 1959; Ten Power and Eighteen Power Disarmament Conferences, Geneva, 1960 and 1962.

Sir Michael states that he has not kept any private papers.

WRISBERG, Lieutenant-General Sir (Frederick) George (1895-   )

Scientific Officer, Air Defence. Artillery Director and Director-General of Weapons and Instrument Production, Ministry of Supply, 1943-46. Controller of Supplies, Ministry of Supply, 1946-49.

According to information provided to the Imperial War Museum, no papers survive.

WYATT, Brigadier-General Louis John (1874-1955)

Military career, Dongola Expedition, 1896; South Africa, 1900-02; European War, 1914-18. G.O.C., British Troops in France and Flanders, 1920. Commanded 2nd North Staffs Regiment, 1921-24.

The Imperial War Museum has a collection of notes and photographs, relating to the selection of the body of the Unknown Soldier in 1920, and a souvenir album of a reunion between British and French troops at Saint-Pol (July 1920).

WYNDHAM, Sir Percy C. H. (1864-1943)

Minister, Colombia, 1911-18. British Commissioner to Poland, 1919.

Efforts to contact persons mentioned in the Will and Act of Probate proved unsuccessful.

YOUNG, Sir (Charles) Alban, 9th Bt (1865-1944)

Minister, Central American Republics, 1913-19; Yugoslavia 1919-25.

Efforts to contact members of Sir Charles Young's family did not prove successful.

YOUNG, Sir Hubert Winthrop (1884-1950)

Colonial Service, Middle East, 1915-32. Governor, Nyasaland, 1932-34; Northern Rhodesia, 1934-38; Trinidad and Tobago, 1938-42. Assistant Secretary, Relief Department, 1943-44, and in European Regional Office, UNRRA, 1944-45.

A number of papers can be found in Rhodes House Library. Material relating to Young's Middle Eastern service (1917-32) and to Palestine problems (1946-48) remains with Lady Young, Manor House, Stretford Tony, Salisbury, Wilts. Photocopies of papers, relating to the Hejaz operations (1917-18), are at the Liddell Hart Centre for Military Archives, and copies of other material can be found in the Middle East Centre, St Antony's College, Oxford.

YOUNG, Sir Mark Aitchison (1886-1974)

Colonial Service. Chief Secretary, Palestine, 1930-33. Governor and C.-in-C., Barbados, 1933-38; Tanganyika, 1938-41; Hong Kong, 1941-47 (prisoner of war, 1941-45).

Mr Brian Young states that a collection of his father's papers survives in the care of his mother, Lady Young, Long House, Winchester. The papers are not open for inspection.

YPRES, 1st E of
Field-Marshal Sir John Denton Pinkstone French, 1st Vt French (1852-1925)

Served Sudan campaign, 1884-85; South Africa, 1899-1902; etc. Chief of Imperial General Staff, 1911-14. C.-in-C., Expeditionary Forces in France, 1914-15; Home Forces, 1915-18. Lord-Lieutenant, Ireland, 1918-21.

The legal dispute concerning ownership of the French papers is described in Hazlehurst and Woodland, op. cit., p. 57. A section of French's diary (June 1919-Aug. 1920) is held at the National Library of Ireland.

ZETLAND, 2nd M of
Lawrence John Lumley Dundas, Lord Dundas and Earl of Ronaldshay (1876-1961)

M.P. (Con.) Hornsey, 1907-16. Governor, Bengal, 1917-22. Secretary of State, India, 1935-40; Burma, 1937-40.

A large collection of papers survives in the North Riding Record Office, with some further material at the India Office Library. Details are given by Hazlehurst and Woodland, op. cit., pp. 48-9.

ZULUETA, Sir Philip Francis de (1925-   )

Served War of 1939-45. Foreign Service from 1949. Private Secretary to successive Prime Ministers, 1955-64. Assistant Secretary, Treasury, 1962-64.

Certain papers are held in the Library of Aberdeen University.

Appendix I
A select list of holders of major public office, 1900-51*

Attempts have been made to locate the papers of all persons listed below. However, an entry for each individual will not necessarily appear in the main text of this *Guide*. In cases of omissions the Project's findings were negative or inconclusive, and no useful information was available for publication.

HOME CIVIL SERVICE
(Permanent Under Secretaries, Permanent Secretaries, Directors General, etc.)

Agriculture and Fisheries	Sir T. H. Elliott, 1892-1913
	Sir S. Olivier, 1st B Olivier, 1913-17
	Sir D. Hall, 1917-20
	Sir F. Floud, 1920-27
	Sir C. Thomas, 1927-36
	Sir J. D. B. Fergusson, 1936-45
	Sir D. E. Vandepeer, 1945-52
Aircraft Production	Sir A. Rowlands, 1940-43
	Sir H. Scott, 1943-45
	Sir F. N. Tribe, 1945
Cabinet Office	Sir M. Hankey, 1st B Hankey, 1916-38
	Sir E. Bridges, 1st B Bridges, 1938-47
	Sir N. Brook, 1st B Normanbrook, 1947-62
Civil Aviation	Sir W. P. Hildred, 1941-46
	Sir A. H. Self, 1946-47
	Sir A. E. Overton, 1947-53
1st Civil Service Commissioner	W. J. Courthope, 1892-1907
	Lord F. Hervey, 1907-09
	Sir S. Leathers, 1910-28
	Sir R. S. Meiklejohn, 1928-39

---

*Sources: *Foreign Office Lists; Colonial Office Lists;* D. Butler and A. Sloman (eds), *British Political Facts, 1900-1975* (1975).

Sir P. Waterfield, 1939-51
Sir A. P. Sinker, 1951-54

Board of Customs and Excise

Sir L. Guillemard, 1909-19
Sir H. P. Hamilton, 1919-27
Sir F. Floud, 1927-30
Sir P. J. Grigg, 1930
Sir E. Forber, 1930-34
Sir G. E. P. Murray, 1934-40
Sir W. G. Eady, 1941-42
Sir A. Carter, 1942-47
Sir W. D. Croft, 1947-55

Economic Warfare

Sir F. Leith-Ross, 1939-42
10th E of Drogheda, 1942-45
(Sir G. A. Mounsey, 1939-40)

Education

Sir G. Kekewich, 1900-03
Sir R. Morant, 1903-11
Sir L. A. Selby-Bigge, 1911-25
Sir A. V. Symonds, 1925-31
Sir E. H. Pelham, 1931-37
Sir M. G. Holmes, 1937-45
Sir J. Maud, Baron Redcliffe-Maud,
    1945-52

Food

Sir C. Fielding, 1918-19
F. H. Coller, 1919-21
Sir H. French, 1939-45
Sir F. N. Tribe, 1945-46
Sir P. Liesching, 1946-48
Sir F. G. Lee, 1949-51
Sir H. D. Hancock, 1951-55

Fuel and Power

Sir F. N. Tribe, 1942-45
Sir D. Fergusson, 1945-52

Health

Sir R. L. Morant, 1919-20
Sir W. A. Robinson, 1920-35
Sir G. W. Chrystal, 1935-40
Sir E. J. Maude, 1940-45
Sir W. S. Douglas, 1945-51

Home Office

Sir K. Digby, 1895-1903
Sir M. D. Chalmers, 1903-08
Sir C. E. Troup, 1908-22
Sir J. Anderson, 1st Vt Waverley,
    1922-32
Sir R. R. Scott, 1932-38
Sir A. Maxwell, 1938-48
Sir F. A. Newsam, 1948-57

Home Security

Sir T. Gardiner, 1939-40
Sir G. Gater, 1939-42

| | Sir H. Scott, 1942-43 |
| | Sir W. Brown, 1943-45 |

Information	A. Bennett, 1918-19
(later *Central Office of Information*)	Sir K. Lee, 1939
	F. Pick, 1940
	Sir C. Radcliffe, 1st Vt Radcliffe,
	1941-45
	Sir E. Bamford, 1945-46
	Sir R. B. Fraser, 1946-54

Board of Inland Revenue (Chairmen)	Sir H. Primrose, 1899-1907
	Sir R. Chalmers, 1st B Chalmers, 1907-11
	Sir M. Nathan, 1911-14
	Sir E. Nott-Bower, 1914-18
	Sir W. Fisher, 1918-19
	Sir J. Anderson, 1st Vt Waverley,
	1919-22
	Sir R. Hopkins, 1922-27
	Sir E. Gowers, 1927-30
	Sir P. J. Grigg, 1930-34
	Sir E. Forber, 1934-38
	Sir G. Canny, 1938-42
	Sir C. J. Gregg, 1942-48
	Sir E. Bamford, 1948-55

Irish Office	Sir D. Harrel, 1893-1902
	Sir A. P. MacDonnell, 1st B MacDonnell
	of Swinford, 1902-08
	Sir J. Dougherty, 1908-14
	Sir M. Nathan, 1914-16
	Sir W. Byrne, 1916-18
	J. MacMahon, 1918-22
	Sir J. Anderson, 1st Vt Waverley,
	1920-22

Labour, Labour and National Service	Sir D. Shackleton, 1916-21
	Sir J. Masterton-Smith, 1920-21
	Sir H. Wilson, 1921-30
	Sir F. Floud, 1930-34
	Sir T. W. Phillips, 1935-44
	Sir G. Ince, 1944-56

Munitions	Sir H. Llewellyn Smith, 1915
	Sir E. B. Phipps, 1916-17
	Sir W. G. Greene, 1917-20
	Sir S. Dannreuther and Sir D. Neylan,
	1920-21

Unemployment Assistance Board,	
Assistance Board and National	
Assistance Board (Chairman)	Sir H. Betterton, 1st B Rushcliffe,
	1934-41

	Sir H. Ramsbotham, 1st Vt Soulbury, 1941-48
	G. Buchanan, 1948-53
National Insurance	Sir T. W. Phillips, 1944-48
	Sir H. D. Hancock, 1949-51
	Sir G. King, 1951-53
Pensions	Sir M. Nathan, 1916-19
	Sir G. W. Chrystal, 1919-35
	Sir C. F. A. Hore, 1935-41
	Sir A. Cunnison, 1941-45
	Sir H. Parker, 1946-48
	Sir A. Wilson, 1948-53
Production	Sir F. N. Tribe, 1942
	Sir A. H. Self, 1942-43
	Sir J. Woods, 1943-45
Reconstruction	Sir N. Brook, 1st B Normanbrook, 1943-45
General Register Office	Sir B. P. Henniker, 1880-1900
(Registrar General)	Sir R. Macleod, 1900-02
	Sir W. Dunbar, 1902-09
	Sir B. Mallet, 1909-21
	Sir S. P. Vivian, 1921-45
	Sir G. North, 1945-59
Department of Scientific and	Sir H. F. Heath, 1916-27
Industrial Research (Secretary)	Sir H. T. Tizard, 1927-29
	Sir F. Smith, 1929-39
	Sir E. V. Appleton, 1939-49
	Sir B. Lockspeiser, 1949-56
Scottish Office	Sir C. C. Scott-Moncrieff, 1892-1902
	Sir R. Macleod, 1902-08
	Sir J. M. Dodds, 1909-21
	Sir J. Lamb, 1921-33
	Sir J. Jeffrey, 1933-37
	J. E. Highton, 1937
	Sir H. P. Hamilton, 1937-46
	Sir D. Milne, 1946-59
Shipping	Sir J. Anderson, 1st Vt Waverley, 1917-19
	T. Lodge, 1919-20
	Sir C. Hurcomb, 1939-41
	(Sir E. J. Foley, 1939-42)
Supply	Sir W. A. Robinson, 1939-40
	Sir G. Gater, 1940
	Sir W. Brown, 1940-42
	Sir W. S. Douglas, 1942-45
	Sir O. S. Franks, Baron Franks, 1945-46
	Sir A. Rowlands, 1946-53

Town and Country Planning (later *Housing and Local Government*)	Sir G. Whiskard, 1943-46 Sir T. H. Sheepshanks, 1946-55
Board of Trade	Sir C. Boyle, 1893-1901 Sir F. J. S. Hopwood, 1st B Southborough, 1901-07 Sir H. Llewellyn Smith, 1907-19 Sir G. Barnes, 1913-16 Sir W. F. Marwood, 1916-19 Sir S. Chapman, 1920-27 Sir H. Payne, 1919-20 Sir H. P. Hamilton, 1927-37 Sir W. Brown, 1937-40 Sir A. E. Overton, 1941-45 Sir J. Woods, 1945-51 Sir F. Lee, 1951-59
Transport (and later, *Transport and Civil Aviation*)	Sir R. F. Dunnell, 1919-21 Sir W. Marwood, 1921-23 Sir J. Brooke, 1923-27 Sir C. Hurcomb, 1927-37 (Director-General, War Transport, 1941-46 and 1946-47) Sir L. Browett, 1937-41 Sir T. G. Jenkins, 1947-59

Treasury	Sir F. Mowatt, 1894-1903
	Sir E. W. Hamilton, 1902-08
	Sir G. H. Murray, 1903-11
	Sir R. Chalmers, 1st B Chalmers,
	   1911-13 and 1916-19
	Sir T. L. Heath, 1913-19
	Sir J. Bradbury, 1st B Bradbury,
	   1913-19
	Sir W. Fisher, 1919-39
	Sir H. Wilson, 1939-42
	Sir R. Hopkins, 1942-45
	Sir E. Bridges, 1st B Bridges, 1945-56

Works	Sir R. Brett, 2nd Vt Esher, 1895-1902 Hon. Sir S. MacDonnell, 1902-12 Sir L. Earle, 1912-33 Sir P. Duff, 1933-41 Sir G. Whiskard, 1941-43 Sir F. P. Robinson, 1943-46 Sir H. C. Emmerson, 1946-56

FOREIGN OFFICE AND DIPLOMATIC SERVICE
(Permanent Under Secretaries; Ambassadors, Ministers, etc., to selected Major Powers)

Foreign Office	Sir T. H. Sanderson, 1st B Sanderson, 1894-1906

Sir C. Hardinge, 1st B Hardinge of
Penshurst, 1906-10 and 1916-20
Sir A. Nicolson, 1st B Carnock, 1910-16
Sir E. Crowe, 1920-25
Sir W. G. Tyrrell, 1925-28
Sir R. C. Lindsay, 1928-30
Sir R. G. Vansittart, 1st B Vansittart,
1930-38
Sir A. Cadogan, 1938-46
Sir O. Sargent, 1946-49
Sir W. Strang, 1st B Strang, 1949-53
(also, Heads of the German Section:
Sir W. Strang, 1947-49;
Sir I. A. Kirkpatrick, 1949-50;
Sir D. Gainer, 1950-51)

Argentine   Hon. Sir W. A. C. Barrington, 1896-1902
Sir W. H. D. Haggard, 1902-06
Sir W. Townley, 1906-10
Vice-Admiral G. le C. Egerton, 1910-11
Sir R. Tower, 1911-20
Sir J. W. R. Macleay, 1920-22 and
1930-33
Sir B. F. Alston, 1923-25
Sir M. A. Robertson, 1927-30
Sir H. G. Chilton, 1933-35
Sir N. M. Henderson, 1935-37
Sir E. Ovey, 1937-42
Sir D. V. Kelly, 1942-46
Sir R. W. A. Leeper, 1946-48
Sir J. Balfour, 1948-51

Austria-Hungary, and Austria   Sir F. R. Plunkett, 1900-05
Sir W. E. Goschen, 1905-08
Sir F. L. Cartwright, 1908-13
Sir Maurice de Bunsen, 1913-14
Sir F. O. Lindley, 1919-20
Hon. A. Akers-Douglas, 2nd Vt Chilston,
1921-27
Sir E. C. E. Phipps, 1928-33
Sir W. H. M. Selby, 1933-37
Sir C. M. Palairet, 1937-38
Sir H. W. B. Mack, 1945-48
Sir C. B. Jerram, 1948-49
Sir H. A. Caccia, Baron Caccia, 1949-54

Belgium   Sir E. C. H. Phipps, 1900-06
Sir A. H. Hardinge, 1906-11
Sir F. H. Villiers, 1911-20
Sir G. D. Grahame, 1920-28
3rd E Granville, 1928-33
Sir G. R. Clerk, 1933-34
Sir E. Ovey, 1934-37
Sir R. H. Clive, 1937-39

269

Sir L. Oliphant, 1939-40 and 1941-44
A. F. Aveling, 1940-41
Sir H. M. Knatchbull-Hugesson, 1944-47
Sir G. W. Rendel, 1947-50
Sir J. M. Le Rougetel, 1950-51

Brazil

Sir H. N. Dering, 1900-06
Sir W. H. D. Haggard, 1906-14
Sir A. R. Peel, 1915-19
Sir R. S. Paget, 1919-20
Sir J. A. C. Tilley, 1921-25
Sir B. F. Alston, 1925-29
Sir W. Seeds, 1930-35
Sir H. Gurney, 1935-39
Sir G. G. Knox, 1939-41
Sir N. H. H. Charles, 1941-44
Sir D. St.C. Gainer, 1944-47
Sir N. M. Butler, 1947-51

Bulgaria

(Sir F. E. H. Elliot, 1895-1903)
Sir G. W. Buchanan, 1903-08
Sir M. de C. Findlay, 1909-10
Sir H. G. O. Bax-Ironside, 1910-15
Sir H. G. Dering, 1919-20
Sir A. R. Peel, 1920-21
Sir W. A. F. Erskine, 1921-27
Sir R. A. C. Sperling, 1928-29
Sir S. I. P. Waterlow, 1929-33
Sir C. M. Bentinck, 1934-36
Sir M. D. Peterson, 1936-38
Sir G. W. Rendel, 1938-41
Sir W. E. Houstoun-Boswall, 1944-46
Sir J. C. Sterndale Bennett, 1947-49
Sir P. Mason, 1949-51

Chile

Sir A. C. Gosling, 1897-1902
Sir G. A. Lowther, 1902-05
A. S. Raikes, 1905-07
Sir B. Boothby, 1907
Sir H. G. O. Bax-Ironside, 1907-09
Sir H. C. Lowther, 1909-13
Sir F. W. Stronge, 1913-19
Sir J. C. T. Vaughan, 1919-23
Sir A. C. Grant Duff, 1923-24
Sir T. B. Hohler, 1924-27
Sir A. J. K. Clark Kerr, 1st B
    Inverchapel, 1928-30
Sir H. G. Chilton, 1930-33
Sir R. C. Michell, 1933-37
Sir C. M. Bentinck, 1937-40
Sir C. W. Orde, 1940-45
Sir J. H. Leche, 1945-49
Sir C. B. Jerram, 1949-51

China	Sir E. M. Satow, 1900-06
	Sir J. N. Jordan, 1906-20
	Sir B. F. Alston, 1920-22
	Sir J. W. R. Macleay, 1922-26
	Sir M. W. Lampson, 1st B Killearn, 1926-33
	Sir A. G. M. Cadogan, 1933-36
	Sir H. M. Knatchbull-Hugesson, 1936-37
	Sir A. J. K. Clark Kerr, 1st B Inverchapel, 1938-42
	Sir H. J. Seymour, 1942-46
	Sir R. C. S. Stevenson, 1946-49
	Sir J. C. Hutchison, 1949-51
Czechoslovakia	Sir G. R. Clerk, 1919-26
	Sir J. W. R. Macleay, 1927-29
	Sir J. Addison, 1930-36
	Sir C. H. Bentinck, 1936-37
	Sir B. C. Newton, 1937-39
	Sir R. H. Bruce Lockhart, 1940-41
	Sir F. K. Roberts, 1941
	Sir P. B. B. Nichols, 1942-47
	Sir P. J. Dixon, 1948-50
	Sir P. M. Broadmead, 1950-53
Denmark	Sir W. E. Goschen, 1900-05
	Hon. Sir A. Johnstone, 1905-10
	Sir W. Conyngham Greene, 1910-12
	Sir H. C. Lowther, 1913-16
	Sir R. S. Paget, 1916-18
	Sir C. M. Marling, 1919-21
	3rd E Granville, 1921-26
	Sir M. Cheetham, 1926-28
	Sir T. B. Hohler, 1928-33
	Sir H. Gurney, 1933-35
	Hon. Sir P. W. M. Ramsay, 1935-39
	C. H. Smith, 1939-40
	Sir A. W. G. Randall, 1945-52
Egypt	[1st E of Cromer, 1883-1907
	Sir E. Gorst, 1907-11
	Field Marshal, 1st E Kitchener, 1911-14]
	Lt. Col. Sir A. H. McMahon, 1914-16
	Gen. Sir F. R. Wingate, 1917-19
	Field Marshal 1st Vt Allenby, 1919-25
	1st B Lloyd, 1925-29
	Sir P. L. Loraine, 1929-33
	Sir M. W. Lampson, 1st B Killearn, 1934-46
	Sir R. I. Campbell, 1946-50
	Sir R. C. S. Stevenson, 1950-55
France	Sir E. J. Monson, 1896-1904
	Sir F. Bertie, 1st Vt Bertie of Thame, 1905-18

271

17th E of Derby, 1918-20
1st B Hardinge of Penshurst, 1920-22
1st M of Crewe, 1922-28
Sir W. G. Tyrrell, 1928-34
Sir G. R. Clerk, 1934-37
Sir E. C. E. Phipps, 1937-39
Sir R. H. Campbell, 1939-40
A. Duff Cooper, 1st Vt Norwich, 1944-48
Sir O. C. Harvey, 1st B Harvey of
    Tasburgh, 1948-54

Germany   Sir F. C. Lascelles, 1895-1908
Sir W. E. Goschen, 1908-14
Baron Kilmarnock, 21st E of Erroll,
    1920
1st Vt D'Abernon, 1920-26
Sir R. C. Lindsay, 1926-28
Sir H. Rumbold, 1928-33
Sir E. C. E. Phipps, 1933-37
Sir N. M. Henderson, 1937-39
(Military Governors and High
    Commissioners)
Field Marshal Sir B. Montgomery, Vt
    Montgomery of Alamein, 1945-46
Marshal of the RAF Sir S. Douglas, 1st
    B Douglas of Kirtleside, 1946-47
General Sir B. Robertson, 1st B
    Robertson of Oakridge, 1947-50
Sir I. A. Kirkpatrick, 1950-53

Greece   Sir E. H. Egerton, 1892-1903
Sir F. E. H. Elliot, 1903-17
3rd E Granville, 1917-21
Sir F. O. Lindley, 1922-23
Sir M. Cheetham, 1924-26
Sir P. L. Loraine, 1926-29
Hon. Sir P. W. M. Ramsay, 1929-33
Sir S. P. Waterlow, 1933-39
Sir C. M. Palairet, 1939-43
Sir R. W. A. Leeper, 1943-46
Sir C. J. Norton, 1946-51

Hungary   Sir T. B. Hohler, 1920-24
Sir C. Barclay, 1924-28
2nd Vt Chilston, 1928-33
Hon. Sir P. W. M. Ramsay, 1933-35
Sir G. G. Knox, 1935-39
Sir P. St.C. O'Malley, 1939-41
Sir A. D. F. Gascoigne, 1945-46
Sir A. K. Helm, 1947-49
Sir G. A. Wallinger, 1949-51

Iran (Persia)   Sir A. H. Hardinge, 1900-05
Sir C. A. Spring Rice, 1906-08

272

Sir G. H. Barclay, 1908-12
Sir W. B. Townley, 1912-15
Sir C. M. Marling, 1915-18
Sir P. Z. Cox, 1918-20
H. C. Norman, 1920-21
Sir P. L. Loraine, 1921-26
Sir R. H. Clive, 1926-31
Sir R. H. Hoare, 1931-34
Sir H. M. Knatchbull-Hugesson, 1934-36
Sir H. J. Seymour, 1936-39
Sir R. W. Bullard, 1939-46
Sir J. H. le Rougetel, 1946-50
Sir F. M. Shepherd, 1950-52

Iraq

Sir H. W. Young, 1932
Sir F. H. Humphreys, 1932-35
Sir A. J. K. Clark Kerr, 1st B
Inverchapel, 1935-36
Sir M. D. Peterson, 1938-39
Sir B. C. Newton, 1939-41
Sir K. Cornwallis, 1941-45
Sir F. H. W. Stonehewer-Bird, 1945-48
Sir H. W. B. Mack, 1948-51

Israel

Sir A. K. Helm, 1949-51

Italy

Sir P. H. W. Currie, 1st B Currie,
1898-1902
Sir F. L. Bertie, 1st Vt Bertie of
Thame, 1903-05
Sir E. H. Egerton, 1905-08
Sir J. Rennell Rodd, 1st B Rennell of
Rodd, 1908-19
Sir G. W. Buchanan, 1919-21
Sir R. W. Graham, 1921-23
Sir J. E. Drummond, 16th E of Perth,
1933-39
Sir P. L. Loraine, 1939-40
Sir N. H. M. Charles, 1944-47
Sir V. A. L. Mallet, 1947-53

Japan

Sir C. M. MacDonald, 1900-12
Sir W. Conyngham Greene, 1912-19
Sir C. N. E. Eliot, 1920-26
Sir J. A. C. Tilley, 1926-31
Sir F. O. Lindley, 1931-34
Sir R. H. Clive, 1934-37
Sir R. L. Craigie, 1937-41
Sir A. D. F. Gascoigne, 1946-51

Mexico

Sir G. Greville, 1900-05
Sir R. T. Tower, 1906-10
Sir F. W. Stronge, 1911-13
Sir L. E. G. Carden, 1913-14

273

Sir T. B. Hohler, 1914-16
E. W. P. Thurston, 1917 and 1918
H. A. C. Cummins, 1918-20
Sir N. King, 1925
Sir E. Ovey, 1925-29
Sir E. St.J. D. J. Monson, 1929-34
J. Murray, 1935-37
Sir O. St.C. O'Malley, 1937-38
T. I. Rees, 1941
Sir C. H. Bateman, 1941-47
Sir T. C. Rapp, 1947-50
Sir J. W. Taylor, 1950-54

Netherlands

Sir H. Howard, 1896-1908
Sir G. W. Buchanan, 1908-10
Hon. Sir A. Johnstone, 1910-17
Sir W. B. Townley, 1917-19
Sir R. W. Graham, 1919-21
Sir C. M. Marling, 1921-26
3rd Earl Granville, 1926-28
Hon. Sir O. Russell, 1928-33
Sir C. H. Montgomery, 1933-38
Sir G. N. M. Bland, 1938-48
Sir P. B. B. Nichols, 1948-51

Norway

Sir A. J. Herbert, 1905-11
Sir M. de C. Findlay, 1911-23
Sir F. O. Lindley, 1923-29
Sir C. J. F. R. Wingfield, 1929-34
Sir C. F. J. Dormer, 1934-40
Sir L. Collier, 1941-50
Sir M. R. Wright, 1951-54

Poland

Sir H. Rumbold, 1919-20
Sir W. G. Max Muller, 1920-28
Sir W. A. F. Erskine, 1928-34
Sir H. W. Kennard, 1935-41
Sir C. F. J. Dormer, 1941-42
Sir O. St.C. O'Malley, 1942-45
V. F. W. Cavendish-Bentinck, 1945-47
Sir D. St.C. Gainer, 1947-50
Sir C. H. Bateman, 1950-52

Portugal

Sir H. G. Macdonnell, 1893-1902
Sir M. Gosselin, 1902-05
Sir M. W. E. de Bunsen, 1905-06
Sir F. H. Villiers, 1906-11
Sir A. H. Hardinge, 1911-13
Hon. Sir L. D. Carnegie, 1913-28
Sir C. Barclay, 1928-29
Sir F. O. Lindley, 1929-31
Sir C. F. W. Russell, 1931-35
Sir C. J. F. R. Wingfield, 1935-37
Sir W. H. M. Selby, 1937-40

274

	Sir R. H. Campbell, 1940-45
	Sir O. St.C. O'Malley, 1945-47
	Sir N. B. Ronald, 1947-54
Romania	Sir J. G. Kennedy, 1897-1905
	Sir W. Conyngham Greene, 1905-10
	Sir W. B. Townley, 1910-12
	Sir G. H. Barclay, 1912-19
	Sir A. R. Peel, 1919-20
	Sir H. G. Dering, 1920-26
	Sir R. H. Greg, 1926-29
	Sir C. M. Palairet, 1929-35
	Sir R. H. Hoare, 1935-41
	Sir I. H. le Rougetel, 1944-46
	Sir A. Holman, 1946-49
	Sir W. St.C. H. Roberts, 1949-51
Russia, and the Soviet Union	Sir C. S. Scott, 1898-1904
	Sir C. Hardinge, 1st B Hardinge of Penshurst, 1904-06
	Sir A. Nicolson, 1st B Carnock, 1906-10
	Sir G. W. Buchanan, 1910-18
	(Sir R. H. Bruce-Lockhart, 1918)
	(Sir F. O. Lindley, 1918-19)
	Sir R. M. Hodgson, 1924-27
	Sir E. Ovey, 1929-33
	2nd Vt Chilston, 1933-38
	Sir W. Seeds, 1939-40
	Sir R. Stafford Cripps, 1940-42
	Sir A. K. Clark Kerr, 1st B Inverchapel, 1942-46
	Sir M. D. Peterson, 1946-49
	Sir D. V. Kelly, 1949-51
Saudi Arabia	W. L. Bond, 1929-30
	Sir A. Ryan, 1930-36
	Sir R. W. Bullard, 1936-39
	Sir F. H. W. Stonehewer-Bird, 1939-43
	S. R. Jordan, 1943-45
	Sir L. B. Grafftey-Smith, 1945-47
	A. C. Trott, 1947-51
Spain	Sir H. M. Durand, 1900-03
	Sir E. H. Egerton, 1903-05
	Sir A. Nicolson, 1st B Carnock, 1905-06
	Sir M. W. E. de Bunsen, 1906-13
	Sir A. H. Hardinge, 1913-19
	Sir E. W. Howard, 1st B Howard of Penrith, 1919-24
	Sir H. G. M. Rumbold, 1924-28
	Sir G. D. Grahame, 1928-35
	Sir H. G. Chilton, 1935-38
	Sir O. St.C. O'Malley, 1938-39
	Sir R. M. Hodgson, 1939

Sir M. D. Peterson, 1939-40
Sir S. Hoare, 1st Vt Templewood,
  1940-44
Sir V. A. L. Mallet, 1945-46
Sir D. F. Howard, 1946-49
Hon. R. M. A. Hankey, 2nd B Hankey,
  1949-51

Sweden
(and Norway until 1904)

Hon. Sir F. J. Pakenham, 1896-1902
Hon. Sir W. A. C. Barrington, 1902-04
Sir Rennell Rodd, 1st B Rennell of Rodd,
  1904-08
Sir C. A. Spring Rice, 1908-12
Sir E. W. Howard, 1st B Howard of
  Penrith, 1913-19
Sir C. Barclay, 1919-24
Sir A. C. Grant Duff, 1924-27
Sir J. C. T. Vaughan, 1927-29
Sir H. W. Kennard, 1929-31
Sir A. J. K. Clark Kerr, 1st B
  Inverchapel, 1931-35
Sir C. M. Palairet, 1935-37
Sir E. St.J. D. J. Monson, 1938-39
Sir V. A. L. Mallet, 1940-45
Sir C. B. Jerram, 1945-48
Sir H. L. Farquhar, 1948-51

Switzerland

Sir W. C. Greene, 1901-05
Sir G. Bonham, 1905-09
Sir H. G. O. Bax-Ironside, 1909-10
Sir E. W. Howard, 1st B Howard of
  Penrith, 1911-13
Sir E. Grant Duff, 1913-16
Sir H. Rumbold, 1916-19
Sir O. Russell, 1919-22
Sir M. Cheetham, 1922-24
Sir R. A. C. Sperling, 1924-27
Sir C. F. W. Russell, 1928-31
Sir H. W. Kennard, 1931-35
Sir G. R. Warner, 1935-40
Sir D. V. Kelly, 1940-42
Sir C. J. Norton, 1942-46
T. M. Snow, 1946-49
Sir P. S. Scrivener, 1949-53

Turkey, and the Ottoman Empire

Sir N. R. O'Conor, 1898-1908
Sir G. H. Barclay, 1908
Sir G. A. Lowther, 1908-13
Sir L. Mallet, 1913-14
Sir H. G. M. Rumbold, 1920-24
Sir R. C. Lindsay, 1924-26
Sir G. R. Clerk, 1926-33
Sir P. L. Loraine, 1933-39
Sir H. M. Knatchbull-Hugessen, 1939-44

Sir M. D. Peterson, 1944-46
Sir D. V. Kelly, 1946-49
Sir N. H. H. Charles, 1949-51

United States of America

Sir J. Pauncefote, 1st B Pauncefote,
    1889-1902
Hon. Sir M. H. Herbert, 1902-03
Sir H. M. Durand, 1903-06
James Bryce, 1st Vt Bryce, 1907-13
Sir C. A. Spring-Rice, 1913-18
Sir R. D. Isaacs, 1st M of Reading,
    1918-19
Sir E. Grey, 1st Vt Grey of Falloden,
    1919-20
Sir A. C. Geddes, 1st B Geddes, 1920-24
Sir E. W. Howard, 1st B Howard of
    Penrith, 1924-30
Sir R. C. Lindsay, 1930-39
11th M of Lothian, 1939-40
1st E of Halifax, 1941-46
1st B Inverchapel, 1946-48
Sir O. S. Franks, Baron Franks,
    1948-52

Yugoslavia and Serbia

Sir G. Bonham, 1900-05
Sir J. B. Whitehead, 1906-10
Sir R. S. Paget, 1910-13
Sir C. L. Des Graz, 1914-19
Sir C. A. Young, 1919-25
Sir H. W. Kennard, 1925-29
Sir N. M. Henderson, 1929-35
Sir R. H. Campbell, 1935-39
Sir R. I. Campbell, 1939-41
Sir G. W. Rendel, 1941-43
Sir R. C. S. Stevenson, 1943-46
Sir C. B. P. Peake, 1946-51

THE COMMONWEALTH
(Permanent Under Secretaries, Permanent Secretaries; Governors General, Governors, Viceroys, High Commissioners etc., to selected Dominions and Colonies)

Colonial Office

Sir E. Wingfield, 1897-1900
Sir M. F. Ommaney, 1900-07
Sir F. J. S. Hopwood, 1st B
    Southborough, 1907-11
Sir J. Anderson, 1911-16
Sir G. V. Fiddes, 1916-21
Sir J. E. Masterton-Smith, 1921-24
Sir S. Wilson, 1925-33
Sir J. L. Maffey, 1st B Rugby, 1933-37
Sir A. C. C. Parkinson, 1937-40 and
    1940-42
Sir G. Gater, 1940 and 1942-47
Sir T. Lloyd, 1947-56

Dominions Office	Sir C. T. Davis, 1925-30
	Sir E. J. Harding, 1930-40
	Sir C. Parkinson, 1940
	Sir E. G. Machtig, 1940-47
Commonwealth Relations Office	Sir E. G. Machtig, 1947-48
	Sir A. Carter, 1947-49
	Sir P. Liesching, 1949-55
Australia	E of Hopetoun, 1st M of Linlithgow, 1900-02
	2nd B Tennyson, 1902-04
	1st B Northcote, 1904-08
	2nd E of Dudley, 1908-11
	3rd B Denman, 1911-14
	Sir R. C. Munro-Ferguson, 1st Vt Novar, 1914-20
	1st B Forster of Lepe, 1920-25
	Sir J. L. Baird, 1st Vt Stonehaven, 1925-30
	Sir I. A. Isaacs, 1931-36
	Brig-Gen. 1st E Gowrie, 1936-44
	D of Gloucester, 1945-47
	W. J. McKell, 1947-53
Canada	4th E of Minto, 1898-1904
	4th E Grey, 1904-11
	1st D of Connaught, 1911-16
	9th D of Devonshire, 1916-21
	1st Vt Byng of Vimy, 1921-26
	1st M of Willingdon, 1926-31
	9th E of Bessborough, 1931-35
	Sir J. Buchan, 1st B Tweedsmuir, 1935-40
	1st E of Athlone, 1940-46
	1st E Alexander of Tunis, 1946-52
Ceylon	Sir J. W. Ridgeway, 1896-1903
	Sir H. A. Blake, 1903-07
	Sir H. E. McCallum, 1907-13
	Sir R. Chalmers, 1st B Chalmers, 1913-16
	Sir J. Anderson, 1916-18
	Brig-Gen. Sir W. H. Manning, 1918-25
	Sir H. C. Clifford, 1925-27
	Sir H. J. Stanley, 1927-31
	Sir G. Thomson, 1931-33
	Sir R. E. Stubbs, 1933-37
	Sir A. Caldecott, 1937-44
	Sir H. Moore, 1944-49
	Sir H. Ramsbotham, 1st Vt Soulbury, 1949-54
Cyprus	Sir W. F. Haynes Smith, 1900-04
	Sir C. A. King Harman, 1904-11

Maj. Sir H. J. Goold-Adams, 1911-14
Maj. Sir J. E. Clauson, 1915-20
Sir M. Stevenson, 1920-26
Col. Sir R. Storrs, 1926-32
Sir R. E. Stubbs, 1932-33
Sir H. R. Palmer, 1933-39
Sir W. D. Battershill, 1939-41
Sir C. C. Woolley, 1941-46
Sir R. T. H. Fletcher, Baron Winster,
    1946-48
Sir Andrew Barkworth Wright, 1949-53

Gibraltar

Field Marshal Sir G. J. White, 1900-04
Gen. Sir F. W. E. F. Forestier Walker,
    1905-10
Gen. Sir A. Hunter, 1910-13
Lt-Gen. Sir H. S. G. Miles, 1913-18
Gen. Sir H. L. Smith-Dorrien, 1918-23
Gen. Sir C. Monro, 1923-28
Gen. Sir A. J. Godley, 1928-33
Gen. Sir C. Harington, 1933-38
Sir Edmund Ironside, Field Marshal 1st
    Vt Ironside, 1938-39
Lt-Gen. Sir C. G. Liddell, 1939-41
Field Marshall 6th Vt Gort, 1941-42
Lt-Gen. Sir F. N. Mason-Macfarlane,
    1942-44
Lt-Gen. Sir T. R. Eastwood, 1944-47
Gen. Sir K. A. N. Anderson, 1947-52

Gold Coast

Sir M. Nathan, 1900-03
Sir J. P. Rodger, 1903-10
J. J. Thorburn, 1910-12
Sir H. C. Clifford, 1912-19
Brig. Gen. Sir F. G. Guggisberg, 1919-27
Sir A. R. Slater, 1927-32
Sir T. S. W. Thomas, 1932-34
Sir A. W. Hodson, 1934-41
Sir A. C. Burns, 1941-47
Sir G. H. Creasy, 1947-49
Sir C. N. Arden-Clarke, 1949-57

Hong Kong

Sir H. A. Blake, 1897-1903
Sir M. Nathan, 1903-07
Sir F. D. Lugard, 1907-12
Sir F. H. May, 1912-19
Sir R. E. Stubbs, 1919-25
Sir C. Clementi, 1925-30
Sir W. Peel, 1930-35
Sir A. Caldecott, 1935-37
Sir G. A. S. Northcote, 1937-40
E. F. Norton, 1940-41
Sir M. A. Young, 1941-47
Sir A. W. G. H. Grantham, 1947-57

Ireland	(Lord-Lieutenants) 5th E Cadogan, 1895-1902 2nd E of Dudley, 1902-06 7th E later 1st M of Aberdeen, 1906-15 2nd B later 1st Vt Wimbourne, 1915-18 1st Vt French, 1st E of Ypres, 1918-21 1st Vt Fitzalan, 1921-22
Irish Free State	T. M. Healy, 1922-28 J. McNeill, 1928-32 D. Ua Buachalla (D. Buckley), 1932-36
Jamaica	Sir A. W. L. Hemming, 1898-1904 Sir J. A. Swettenham, 1904-07 Sir S. Olivier, 1st B Olivier, 1907-13 Brig. Gen. Sir W. H. Manning, 1913-18 Sir L. Probyn, 1918-24 Brig. Gen. Sir S. Wilson, 1924-26 Sir R. E. Stubbs, 1926-32 Sir R. Slater, 1932-34 Sir E. Denham, 1934-38 Sir A. Richards, 1st B Milverton, 　1938-43 Sir T. Huggins, 1943-51
Kenya	Sir C. N. E. Eliot, 1900-04 Sir D. W. Stewart, 1904-05 J. H. Sadler, 1905-09 Col. Sir E. P. Girouard, 1909-12 Sir H. C. Belfield, 1912-18 Maj-Gen. Sir E. Northey, 1918-22 Sir R. T. Coryndon, 1923-25 Lt-Col. Sir E. W. M. Grigg, 1st B 　Altrincham, 1925-31 Brig-Gen. Sir J. A. Byrne, 1931-37 Air Chief Marshal Sir R. Brooke-Popham, 　1937-39 Sir H. Moore, 1940-44 Sir P. E. Mitchell, 1944-52
Malta	Field Marshal Sir F. W. Grenfell, 　1st B Grenfell, 1899-1903 General Sir C. M. Clarke, 1903-07 General Sir H. F. Grant, 1907-09 General Sir H. M. L. Rundle, 1909-15 Field Marshal 3rd B Methuen, 1915-19 Field Marshal Sir H. C. O. Plumer, 1st 　Vt Plumer, 1919-24 General Sir W. N. Congreve, 1924-27 General Sir J. P. Du Cane, 1927-31 General Sir D. Campbell, 1931-36 General Sir C. Bonham-Carter, 1936-40 General Sir W. G. S. Dobbie, 1940-42 Field Marshal 6th Vt Gort, 1942-44

	Lt-General Sir E. C. A. Schrieber, 1944-46
	Sir F. C. R. Douglas, 1st B Douglas of Barloch, 1946-49
	Sir G. H. Creasy, 1949-54
Mesopotamia (Iraq)	Sir P. Z. Cox, 1914-17 and 1920-23
	Sir A. T. Wilson, 1917-20
	Sir H. R. C. Dobbs, 1923-29
	Brig-Gen. Sir G. F. Clayton, 1929
	Sir F. H. Humphreys, 1929-32
New Zealand	5th E of Ranfurly, 1897-1904
	5th B Plunket, 1904-10
	1st B Islington, 1910-12
	2nd E of Liverpool, 1912-20
	1st E Jellicoe, 1920-24
	General Sir C. Fergusson, 1924-30
	1st Vt Bledisloe, 1930-35
	8th Vt Galway, 1935-41
	Marshal of the RAF, Sir C. L. N. Newall, 1st B Newall, 1941-46
	Sir B. Freyberg, 1st B Freyberg, 1946-52
Nigeria	Sir F. D. Lugard, 1914-19
	Sir H. Clifford, 1919-25
	Sir G. Thomson, 1926-31
	Sir D. C. Cameron, 1931-35
	Sir B. H. Bourdillon, 1935-42
	Sir A. C. M. Burns, 1942-43
	Sir A. F. Richards, 1st B Milverton, 1943-47
	Sir J. S. MacPherson, 1948-55
Northern Rhodesia	Sir L. Wallace, 1911-21
	Sir D. Chaplin, 1921-23
	Sir R. Goode, 1923-24
	Sir H. J. Stanley, 1924-27
	Sir J. C. Maxwell, 1927-32
	Sir R. Storrs, 1932-34
	Maj. Sir H. W. Young, 1934-38
	Sir J. A. Maybin, 1938-41
	Sir E. J. Waddington, 1941-47
	Sir G. M. Rennie, 1948-54
Palestine	(General Sir L. J. Bols, 1919-20)
	Sir H. L. Samuel, 1st Vt Samuel, 1920-25
	Field Marshal, 1st Vt Plumer, 1925-28
	Sir J. Chancellor, 1928-31
	General Sir A. G. Wauchope, 1931-38
	Sir H. A. MacMichael, 1938-44
	Field Marshal 4th Vt Gort, 1944-45
	General Sir A. G. Cunningham, 1945-48

Singapore (Straits Settlements)	Sir F. A. Swettenham, 1899-1904
	Sir J. Anderson, 1904-11
	Sir A. H. Young, 1911-19
	Sir L. N. Guillemard, 1919-28
	Sir H. C. Clifford, 1928-30
	Sir C. Clementi, 1930-36
	Sir T. S. W. Thomas, 1936-42
	Sir F. C. Gimson, 1946-52
South Africa	Sir H. J. Gladstone, 1st Vt Gladstone, 1910-14
	1st E Buxton, 1914-20
	Prince Arthur of Connaught, 1920-24
	1st E of Athlone, 1924-31
	6th E of Clarendon, 1931-37
	Sir P. Duncan, 1937-43
	N. J. de Wet, 1943-46
	G. Van Zyl, 1946-51
Southern Rhodesia	Sir W. H. Milton, 1897-1914
	Sir D. Chaplin, 1914-23
	Sir J. Chancellor, 1923-28
	Sir C. H. Rodwell, 1928-34
	Sir H. J. Stanley, 1935-42
	Sir E. Baring, 1st B Howick of Glendale, 1942
	Admiral Sir W. E. C. Tait, 1945-46
	Sir J. N. Kennedy, 1947-53
Sudan	H. H. Kitchener, 1st E Kitchener, 1899
	Sir F. R. Wingate, 1899-1916
	Sir L. O. F. Stack, 1916-24
	Sir G. F. Archer, 1924-26
	J. L. Maffey, 1st B Rugby, 1926-34
	Sir G. S. Symes 1934-40
	Sir H. J. Huddleston, 1940-47
	Sir R. G. Howe, 1947-54
Tanganyika	Sir H. A. Byatt, 1916-24
	Sir D. Cameron, 1925-31
	Sir G. Stewart Symes, 1931-33
	Sir H. A. MacMichael, 1933-37
	Sir M. A. Young, 1938-41
	Sir W. E. F. Jackson, 1942-45
	Sir W. D. Battershill, 1945-49
	Sir E. F. Twining, Baron Twining, 1949-58
Trinidad	Sir C. A. Maloney, 1900-04
	Sir H. M. Jackson, 1904-08
	Sir G. R. Le Hunte, 1908-15
	Sir J. Chancellor, 1916-21
	Brig-General Sir S. H. Wilson, 1922-24
	Sir H. A. Byatt, 1924-29

Sir A. C. Hollis, 1930-36
Sir A. G. M. Fletcher, 1936-38
Maj. Sir H. W. Young, 1938-42
Sir B. E. H. Clifford, 1942-46
Sir J. V. W. Shaw, 1947-50
Maj. General Sir H. Rance, 1950-55

India Office (India and Burma)   Sir J. A. Godley, 1st B Kilbracken,
        1883-1909
Sir R. T. Ritchie, 1910-12
Sir T. Holderness, 1912-19
Sir F. W. Duke, 1919-24
Sir A. Hirtzel, 1924-30
Sir S. F. Stewart, 1930-41
Sir D. T. Monteath, 1941-47
Sir R. H. Carter, 1947.

India   1st M Curzon, 1898-1905
4th E of Minto, 1905-10
1st B Hardinge of Penshurst, 1910-16
1st Vt Chelmsford, 1916-21
1st M of Reading, 1921-26
1st B Irwin, 1st E of Halifax, 1926-31
1st M of Willingdon, 1931-36
2nd M of Linlithgow, 1936-43
Field Marshal Sir A. P. Wavell, 1st E
        Wavell, 1943-47
Admiral of the Fleet, 1st E Mountbatten
        of Burma, 1947

Burma   Sir F. W. R. Fryer, 1897-1903
Sir H. S. Barnes, 1903-05
Sir H. T. White, 1905-10
Sir H. Adamson, 1910-15
Sir S. Harcourt-Butler, 1915-18 and
        1923-27
Sir R. H. Craddock, 1918-22
Sir C. A. Innes, 1927-32
Sir H. L. Stephenson, 1932-36
Hon. Sir A. Douglas Cochrane, 1936-41
Sir R. H. Dorman-Smith, 1941-46
Sir H. F. Knight, 1946
Maj. General Sir H. E. Rance, 1946-48

Bengal   Sir J. Woodburn, 1898-1902
Sir A. H. Leith Fraser, 1903-08
Sir E. N. Baker, 1908-11
Sir T. D. Gibson-Carmichael, 1st B
        Carmichael, 1912-17
E of Ronaldshay, 2nd M of Zetland,
        1917-22
2nd E of Lytton, 1922-27
Sir F. S. Jackson, 1927-30
Sir H. L. Stephenson, 1930-32

Sir J. Anderson, 1st Vt Waverley,
1932-37
5th B Brabourne, 1937-39
[Sir J. A. Woodhead, 1939]
Lt-Col. Sir J. A. Herbert, 1939-43
Sir R. G. Casey, Baron Casey, 1944-46
Sir F. J. Burrows, 1946-47

Bombay

Sir H. S. Northcote, 1st B Northcote,
1899-1903
2nd B Lamington, 1903-07
Sir G. S. Clarke, 1st B Sydenham, 1907-13
Sir F. Freeman-Thomas, 1st M of
Willingdon, 1913-18
Sir G. A. Lloyd, 1st B Lloyd, 1918-23
Sir L. O. Wilson, 1923-28
Maj. General Sir F. H. Sykes, 1928-33
5th B Brabourne, 1933-37
Sir L. R. Lumley, 11th E of Scarborough,
1937-43
Sir D. J. Colville, 1st B Clydesmuir,
1943-48

Madras

2nd B Ampthill, 1900-1904
Hon. Sir A. Lawley, 6th B Wenlock,
1906-11
Sir T. D. Gibson-Carmichael, 1st B
Carmichael, 1911-12
Sir J. Sinclair, 1st B Pentland,
1912-19
Sir F. Freeman-Thomas, 1st M of
Willingdon, 1919-24
2nd Vt Goschen, 1924-29
Lt-Col. Hon. Sir G. F.Stanley, 1929-34
Viscount Erskine, 1934-40
Hon. Sir A. Hope, 2nd B Rankeillour,
1940-46
Lt-Gen. Sir A. E. Nye, 1946-48

THE DEFENCE FORCES

(Permanent Under Secretaries, Chiefs of the Imperial General Staff, 1st Sea Lords,
Chiefs of Air Staff, etc.)

Admiralty

Sir E. MacGregor, 1884-1907
Sir I. Thomas, 1907-11
Sir W. G. Greene, 1911-17
Sir O. Murray, 1917-36
Sir R. Carter, 1936-40
Sir H. V. Markham, 1940-46
Sir J. G. Lang, 1947-61

Air Ministry	Sir W. A. Robinson, 1917-20
	Sir W. Nicholson, 1920-31
	Sir C. Bullock, 1931-36
	Sir D. Banks, 1936-39
	Sir A. Street, 1939-45
	Sir W. Brown, 1945-47
	Sir J. Barnes, 1947-55
Defence Ministry	Sir H. Wilson Smith, 1947-48
	Sir H. Parker, 1948-56
War Office	Sir R. H. Knox, 1897-1901
	Sir E. W. D. Ward, 1901-14
	Sir R. Brade, 1914-20
	Sir H. J. Creedy, 1920-39
	Sir P. J. Grigg, 1939-42
	Sir F. Bovenschen, 1942-45
	Sir E. Speed, 1942-49
	Sir G. W. Turner, 1949-56
Army	Field-Marshal 1st E Roberts of Kandahar, 1901-04
	General Sir N. G. Lyttleton, 1904-08
	Field-Marshal Sir W. G. Nicholson, 1st B Nicholson, 1908-12
	Field-Marshal Sir J. French, 1st E of Ypres, 1912-14
	General Sir C. Douglas, 1914
	General Sir A. J. Murray, 1915
	Field-Marshal Sir W. R. Robertson, 1915-18
	Field-Marshal Sir H. H. Wilson, 1918-22
	Field-Marshal 10th E of Cavan, 1922-26
	Field-Marshal Sir G. Milne, 1st B Milne, 1926-33
	Field-Marshal Sir A. A. Montgomery Massingberd, 1933-36
	Field-Marshal Sir C. Deverell, 1936-37
	Field-Marshal 6th Vt Gort, 1937-39
	Field-Marshal 1st Vt Ironside, 1939-40
	Field-Marshal Sir J. G. Dill, 1940-41
	Field-Marshal Sir A. Brooke, 1st Vt Alanbrooke, 1941-46
	Field-Marshal Sir B. L. Montgomery, 1st Vt Montgomery of Alamein, 1946-48
	Field-Marshal Sir W. J. Slim, 1st Vt Slim, 1948-52
Royal Air Force	Marshal of the Royal Air Force Sir H. Trenchard, 1st Vt Trenchard, 1918 and 1919-30
	Maj-Gen. Sir F. Sykes, 1918-19
	Marshal of the Royal Air Force Sir J. M. Salmond, 1930-33

Air Chief Marshal Sir W. G. H.
Salmond, 1933
Marshal of the Royal Air Force Sir
E. L. Ellington, 1933-37
Marshal of the Royal Air Force Sir
C. L. N. Newall, 1st B Newall,
1937-40
Marshal of the Royal Air Force Sir
C. Portal, 1st Vt Portal, 1940-45
Marshal of the Royal Air Force Sir
A. W. Tedder, 1st B Tedder,
1946-50
Marshal of the Royal Air Force Sir
J. Slessor, 1950-53

Royal Navy

Admiral of the Fleet Lord W. T. Kerr,
1899-1904
Admiral of the Fleet Sir J. A. Fisher,
1st B Fisher of Kilverstone, 1904-10
and 1914-15
Admiral of the Fleet Sir A. K. Wilson,
1910-11
Admiral Sir F. Bridgeman, 1911-12
Admiral of the Fleet Prince Louis of
Battenberg, 1st M of Milford Haven,
1912-14
Admiral of the Fleet Sir H. B. Jackson,
1915-16
Admiral of the Fleet Sir J. R. Jellicoe,
1st E Jellicoe, 1916-17
Admiral of the Fleet Sir R. E. Wemyss,
1st B. Wester Wemyss, 1917-19
Admiral of the Fleet Sir D. Beatty,
1st E Beatty, 1919-27
Admiral of the Fleet Sir C. E. Madden,
1927-30
Admiral of the Fleet Sir F. L. Field,
1930-33
Admiral of the Fleet Sir E. Chatfield,
1st B Chatfield, 1933-38
Admiral of the Fleet Sir R. Backhouse,
1938-39
Admiral of the Fleet Sir D. Pound,
1939-43
Admiral of the Fleet Sir A. Cunningham
1st Vt Cunningham of Hyndhope, 1943-46
Admiral of the Fleet Sir J. Cunningham,
1946-48
Admiral of the Fleet 1st B Fraser of
North Cape, 1948-51

Appendix II
Notes on specialist libraries, archives projects and record repositories

This *Guide* has drawn heavily on the work done by a number of related archives projects, and the researchers have enjoyed the help and co-operation of the staff at a number of specialist libraries and record repositories. The wide field of diplomats and civil servants had not been the subject of any earlier project, but much work had been done by others with regard to colonial administrators and military personnel. The research work resulting in this *Guide* has, therefore, been concentrated on the former categories.

Inevitably, the information given in this *Guide* is subject to alteration. Owners of papers may change their addresses, and collections may be placed in the care of a library. Further collections of papers will also come to light, while others may be lost or destroyed. Corrected reports and new information will be made available at the *National Register of Archives*, where detailed lists of many of the papers briefly described in this *Guide* may be consulted. H. M. Stationery Office publishes for the Royal Commission on Historical Manuscripts an annual *List of Accessions to Repositories*, which should also be consulted. The Annual Report of the Keeper of the Records of Scotland provides a similar service in Scotland.

In the research for this book, contacts with the Civil Service Commission were established at an early stage, and a standard letter of enquiry sent out to former officials or their families was approved by the Commission's representatives. Often, individuals referred in their replies to papers which were handed back to government departments at the time of retirement or some later stage. In many cases, these collections are now to be found in the appropriate Private Office classes of documents at the *Public Record Office*. Through the co-operation of the staff at the Public Record Office, a survey was made of archives still held in government departments, and in a few instances further 'Private Office' collections were located. Often, however, so called 'private' collections have been absorbed into registered files and these are not generally described in this *Guide*. Private Office papers, and others which may subsequently come to light, will be transferred in due course to the Public Record Office. Particular enquiries were addressed to the appropriate officer at the Ministry of Defence, the Cabinet Office (Historical Section), the Library and Records Department of the Foreign and Commonwealth Office, the India Office Library, and several other government departments and institutions such as the Post Office and the Bank of England. Readers should consult the *Guide to the Contents of the Public Record Office*, 3 vols (H.M.S.O., 1963-), and the typescript supplements which are available in the Search Rooms of the Public Record Office. The Public Record Office's annual reports describe all recent transfers and acquisitions. The handbooks and annual reports of the Scottish Record Office and the Public Record Office of Northern Ireland should also be consulted.

Much work has been done by related archives projects in particular fields, and much of the information collected by them is not repeated in this *Guide*. Researchers would save much time and trouble by consulting the publications and examining the files of appropriate institutions. The *India Office Library and Records* publishes an annual report, and the staff pursue an active policy for acquiring private papers relating to the Government of India and to Indian affairs prior to independence. Also, a very large number of the private papers of Indian civil servants and army officers (mainly of a rank lower than those persons covered in this *Guide*) have been collected at the Centre of South Asian Studies at Cambridge: see Mary Thatcher (ed.), *Cambridge South Asia Archive* (Cambridge, 1973).

Sources in Middle Eastern affairs are also well researched. *St Antony's College, Oxford,* began in 1961 at its Middle East Centre to make an index of private papers relating to British policy in the Middle East, and to act as custodian of such material. At the *University of Durham,* meanwhile, papers relating to the Sudan are collected. Recently too, a survey of papers relating to the British Mandate in Palestine was set up under the auspices of the British Academy and the Israeli Academy.

In the wider field of imperial affairs, the *Oxford Colonial Records Project* began work in 1963 to search for and to preserve those privately owned papers likely to be of value for research into the history of the British Colonial period. The work which was undertaken at the Institute of Commonwealth Studies, Oxford, covered papers concerned with all the territories administered by the Colonial Office as reconstituted in 1925.* Many papers were subsequently offered to the project; these have now been placed in the custody of the Rhodes House section of the Bodleian Library, Oxford. Here too may be found the archives of the Colonial Records Project itself, giving information about many papers which still remain in private hands. Persons contacted included not only former administrators, but doctors, educationalists, police officers, farmers, missionaries and others who worked in the colonial territories.

The papers of some civil servants mentioned in this *Guide*, and many others of lesser rank who have not appeared here, have been dealt with by the *Archives of British Men of Science* project which began in 1969 at Sussex University. This survey covered the private papers of a wide range of British scientists who flourished between 1850 and 1939, and it included many individuals whose careers took them into public service as government advisers and in other capacities. *Archives of British Men of Science* has been published on microfiche by Mansell. Other civil servants fall within the scope of the *Archive Sources in the History of Economic Thought*, a project undertaken at the Institute of Historical Research at the University of London.

Only a selection of the private papers known to exist relating to twentieth-century British military and naval history are described in this *Guide*. This selection was necessitated by the multiplicity of archival collections in this field. Further information regarding other papers which remain in private hands or in local record

---

However, records relating to Ceylon were the concern of the Institute of Commonwealth Studies of the University of London.

offices and regimental museums will be available at the various specialist libraries and repositories mentioned below.

The Centre for Military Archives at King's College, London (now the *Liddell Hart Centre for Military Archives*) was set up in 1964 to meet the need for a repository to which private owners of documents bearing on twentieth-century military affairs could send them in the knowledge that they would be preserved for posterity under conditions which would respect the confidential nature of their content. In this context the term 'military' is used in its widest sense as referring to defence matters and the armed forces generally. The Centre now holds a large number of important collections and pursues an active policy to locate other papers in private hands. Many collections of papers have been promised, by gift or bequest, to the Centre.

King's College does not seek to compete for papers with other repositories such as the museums of the individual services, with which it works in close co-operation. The *Imperial War Museum*'s Department of Documents has in its files and on index cards a mass of information regarding records relating to warfare in the twentieth century, held in private hands and in the care of European and American archives and research institutes. The Museum's own documentary collections fall into two main groups, one consisting largely of captured German material, and the other of British private papers. These private collections cover a wide range of military personnel, from policy makers at the highest level to men and women in the lower ranks and to civilians who recorded their experiences of war. Also of importance are the records held by the *National Army Museum*, which are of particular relevance for the pre-1914 period and for the history of the British army in India.

The *National Maritime Museum* at Greenwich is also rich in its collections of papers, and in the information available there regarding further sources in naval history. The *Royal Air Force Museum* at Hendon has established an Aviation Records Department, to which important collections of papers kept by top-ranking Royal Air Force commanders, aircraft designers, etc., have already been given. The department aims to collect not only documentary archives, but books, films, photographs and sound recordings.

As with other categories of public servant, some private papers of military and naval personnel find their way into the Public Record Office, and some others may still be located in the libraries and record departments of the Ministry of Defence. Other collections are absorbed into regimental archives as they are given to the appropriate regimental museum. Many of these regimental museums have only recently been able to start sorting their archival holdings, and very little information regarding such collections was available for inclusion in this *Guide*. Researchers should address specific enquiries regarding papers to the Curator of the appropriate regimental museum.

The records of societies and organisations, as described in Volume 1 of this *Guide*, will often include papers of persons who are mentioned here. The archives of the Royal Institute of International Affairs at Chatham House, the Fabian Society, and the Royal Commonwealth Society are just three such sources. Finally, readers are referred to the official Cabinet and departmental papers at the Public Record Office, the Royal Archives at Windsor, and the private papers described by C. Hazlehurst and C. Woodland, *A Guide to the Papers of British Cabinet Ministers, 1900-1951* (Royal Historical Society, 1974) (referred to throughout this volume as Hazlehurst and Woodland, op. cit.).

Among published works which describe further sources in British Political History after 1900, the following may be mentioned:

Britain

Guide to the Records of Parliament, M. Bond (1971)
Guide to the India Office Library (1967)
National Library of Scotland. Catalogue of MSS., vols 1-3, and handlists (1938-   ). Also *Accessions of MSS.*
National Library of Wales. Handlist of MSS., vols 1-3, and further handlists (1943-   )
A Guide to the Sources of British Military History, R. Higham (ed.) (1972)
A Guide to Archive and other Manuscript Sources for the History of British and Irish Economic Thought, R. P. Sturges (1975)

Africa

A Guide to Manuscripts and Documents in the British Isles relating to Africa, Noel Matthews and M. Doreen Wainwright (compilers), edited by J. D. Pearson (Oxford 1971)
An index to authors of unofficial, privately-owned MSS relating to the history of South Africa, 1812-1920, Una Long (1946)
A Select Bibliography of South African History: a guide for historical research, F. J. Muller, F. A. Van Jaarsveld and T. Van Wijk (jt eds) (Pretoria, 1966)
Guide to the Archives and Papers at the University of Witwatersrand (Johannesburg, 1970)
Union List of MSS in South African Libraries (forthcoming: SA Library, Queen Victoria Street, Cape Town)

Asia

Guide to Western MSS and Documents in the British Isles relating to South and South East Asia, M. D. Wainwright and Noel Matthews (eds) (1965)
'Guide to Western MSS and Documents in the British Isles relating to the Far East', J. D. Pearson (unpublished MS at School of Oriental and African Studies, London)

Australasia

Concise Guide to the State Archives of New South Wales (Sydney, 1970)
MSS in the British Isles relating to Australia, New Zealand and the Pacific, P. Mander-Jones (ed.) (Canberra, 1972)
Catalogue of MSS of Australasia and the Pacific in the Mitchell Library (Series A and B, 1967 and 1969).
Quarterly list of special accessions, 1954 to date
Report of the Council (annual report), Library of New South Wales
Guide to collections of MSS relating to Australia (Canberra: National Library of Australia, 1965)

Canada

General Inventory of Manuscripts, vol. 5, *Papers of Prime Ministers and Political Figures, 1867-1950* (MSS. groups 26 and 27; Ottawa, 1972), Public Archives of Canada, *Union List of MSS in Canadian Repositories* (Ottawa, 1968)

Latin America and the Caribbean

A Guide to manuscript sources for the history of Latin America and the Caribbean in the British Isles P. Walne (ed.). (1973).

United States   *Guide to Archives and MSS in the United States*, Philip M. Hamer (ed.). (New Haven, 1961).

National Union Catalog of MSS Collections (Library of Congress, Washington D.C., 1959).

The Southern Historical Collection — A Guide to MSS, University of North Carolina Library (Chapel Hill 1970)

New York Public Library, Research Libraries, *Catalog of the MSS Division* (Boston, 2 vols, 1968).

Catalog of the Albert A. and Henry W. Berg collection of English and American Literature (Boston), 2 vols.

Guide to MSS relating to America in Great Britain and Ireland, B. R. Crick and Miriam Alman (eds) (Oxford, 1961) and supplements.

Appendix III
Postal addresses of libraries and record offices cited in the text

The following is an alphabetical list of libraries mentioned in the text. At the time of writing, the most up-to-date list of relevant libraries was that produced by the Royal Commission on Historical Manuscripts, *Record Repositories in Great Britain* (5th ed., H.M.S.O., 1973). Since this was published the reorganisation of local government areas (operative from April 1974) has resulted in a reorganisation of record and library authorities. This list has attempted, where possible, to provide the most up-to-date list of addresses. Where a now redundant name has been used in the text, this will be found in its alphabetical position in the list below, with the current title and address alongside it.

Aberdeen University Library, Manuscript and Archives Section, University Library, King's College, Aberdeen AB9 2UB
Airborne Forces Museum, Browning Barracks, Aldershot, Hants.
Army Museums Ogilby Trust, Whitehall, London, SW1
Balliol College, Oxford
Berkshire Record Office, Shire Hall, Reading RG1 3EY
Black Watch Regimental Museum, Dalhousie Castle, Perth
Birmingham University Library, P.O. Box 363, The University, Edgbaston, Birmingham B15 2TT
Bodleian Library, Oxford OX1 3BG
British Library, Department of Manuscripts, Great Russell Street, London WC1B 3DG
British Library of Political and Economic Science (BLPES), London School of Economics, Houghton Street, Aldwych, London WC2A 2AE
Brotherton Library, University of Leeds, Leeds LS2 9JT
Buckinghamshire Record Office, County Offices, Aylesbury, Bucks. HP20 1UA
Bury St Edmunds and West Suffolk Record Office, now Suffolk Record Office, Bury St Edmunds Branch, School Hall Street, Bury St Edmunds IP33 1HA
Cambridge South Asian Archive: see Centre of South Asian Studies
Cambridge University Library and Archives, West Road, Cambridge CB3 9DR
Central Zionist Archives, PO Box 92, Jerusalem, Israel
Centre of South Asian Studies, University of Cambridge, Laundress Lane, Cambridge
Christ Church, Oxford
Churchill College, Cambridge CB3 0DS

Customs and Excise Library, Museum and Records, H.M. Customs and Excise, King's Beam House, Mark Lane, London, EC3

Dorset Military Museum, The Keep, Dorchester, Dorset

Douglas Library, Queen's University, Kingston, Ontario

Duke University Library, Durham, North Carolina, 27706, U.S.A.

Durham County Record Office, County Hall, Durham DH1 5UL

Durham University Library, Palace Green, Durham DH1 3RN

Durham University Library, Oriental Section (Sudan Archive), Elvet Hall, Durham DH1 3TH

East Riding County Record Office, now Humberside County Record Office, County Hall, Beverley

East Sussex Record Office, Pelham House, Lewes BN7 1UN

Edinburgh University Library, Department of Manuscripts, George Square, Edinburgh EH8 9LJ

Essex Record Office, County Hall, Chelmsford CM1 1LX

Foreign and Commonwealth Office Library, Cornwall House, Stamford St, London SE1

Glamorgan County Record Office, County Hall, Cathays Park, Cardiff CF1 3NE

Hampshire Record Office, 20 Southgate Street, Winchester, Hants. SO23 9EF

Harvard University Library, Cambridge, Mass., 02138, U.S.A.

Hereford County Record Office, now Hereford and Worcester County Record Office, Hereford Branch. The Old Barracks, Harold Street, Hereford HR1 2QX

Hertfordshire County Record Office, County Hall, Hertford SG13 8DE

House of Lords Record Office, House of Lords, London SW1A 0PW

Hove Central Library, Church Road, Hove BN3 2EG

Hull University Library, The Brynmor Jones Library, The University, Hull, Humberside HU6 7RX

Imperial War Museum, Department of Documents, Imperial War Museum, Lambeth Road, London SE1 6HZ

India Office Library, European Manuscripts Section, Foreign and Commonwealth Office, 197 Blackfriars Road, London SE1 8NG

Institute of Commonwealth Studies Library, University of London, 27 Russell Square, London WC1

Ipswich and East Suffolk Record Office, now Suffolk Record Office, Ipswich Branch, County Hall, Ipswich, Suffolk IP4 2JS

Kent Archives Office, County Hall, Maidstone, Kent ME14 1XQ

King's College Library, University of London, Strand, London WC2R 2LS

Liddell Hart Centre for Military Archives, King's College, Strand, London WC2R 2LS

Light Infantry Museum (Somerset), 14 Mount Street, Taunton, Somerset

Lincolnshire Archives Office, The Castle, Lincoln LN1 3AB

London Library, 14 St James's Square, London, SW1

London University Institute of Education Library, 11/13 Ridgmount Street, London, WC1

London University Library, Senate House, Malet Street, London WC1E 7HU

Manchester: John Rylands University Library of Manchester, Deansgate, Manchester M3 3EH

Middle East Centre, St Antony's College, 137 Banbury Road, Oxford OX2 6JF

Mitchell Library, Macquarie Street, Sydney, New South Wales 2000, Australia

National Army Museum, Royal Hospital Road, London SW3 4HT

National Library of Australia, Canberra, ACT 2600 Australia

National Library of Ireland, Department of Manuscripts, Kildare Street, Dublin 2, Ireland

National Library of Scotland, Department of Manuscripts, George IV Bridge, Edinburgh EH1 1EW

National Library of Wales, Department of Manuscripts, Aberystwyth, Dyfed SY23 3BU

National Maritime Museum, Greenwich, London SE10

National Register of Archives, Historical Manuscripts Commission, Quality House, Quality Court, Chancery Lane, London WC2A 1HP

National Register of Archives (Scotland), General Register House, Edinburgh EH1 3YY

Naval Library, Ministry of Defence, Empress State Buildings, Lillie Road, Fulham, London

Newcastle upon Tyne University Library, Queen Victoria Road, Newcastle upon Tyne, Tyne and Wear NE1 7RU

North Riding County Record Office, now North Yorkshire County Record Office, County Hall, Northallerton, North Yorkshire DL7 8SG

Northamptonshire Record Office, Delapré Abbey, Northampton NN4 9AW

Northumberland Record Office, Melton Park, North Gosforth, Newcastle upon Tyne NE3 5QX

Nottingham University, Manuscripts Department, University of Nottingham Library, University Park, Nottingham NG7 2RD

Nuffield College Library, Oxford OX1 1NF

Pembroke College, Cambridge

Pierpont Morgan Library, 29 East Thirty-Sixth Street, New York, NY 10016, U.S.A.

Public Archives of Canada, 395 Wellington Street, Ottawa, Ontario, K1A 0N3

Public Record Office, Chancery Lane, London WC2A 1LR

Public Record Office of Ireland, Four Courts, Dublin, Ireland

Public Record Office of Northern Ireland, 66 Balmoral Avenue, Belfast BT9 6NY

Rhodes House Library, Oxford

Royal Air Force Museum, R.A.F. Hendon, The Hyde, London NW9 5LL

Royal Archives, Windsor Castle, Windsor

Royal Armoured Corps Tank Museum, Bovington Camp, Wareham, Dorset

Royal Army Medical Corps Museum, Royal Army Medical College, Millbank, London SW1

Royal Artillery Institution, Old Royal Military Academy, Woolwich, London SE18 4JJ

Royal Commonwealth Society Library, Northumberland Avenue, London WC2N 5BJ

Royal Institute of International Affairs, The Library, Chatham House, 10 St James' Square, London SW1Y 4LE

Royal Marines Museum, Eastney, Portsmouth

Royal Military College Museum, Sandhurst, Camberley, Surrey

Royal Norfolk Regimental Museum, Britannia Barracks, Norwich

Royal Signals Museum, Cheltenham Terrace, Chelsea, London SW3 4RH

Rutgers State University Library, New Brunswick, New Jersey 08903, U.S.A.

St Deiniol's Library, Hawarden, Clwyd

School of Oriental and African Studies Library, University of London, Malet Street, London WC1E 7HP

Scott Polar Research Institute Archives, Cambridge CB2 1ER

Scottish Record Office, P.O. Box 36, H.M. General Register House, Edinburgh EH1 3YY

South African Government Archives, Transvaal Archives Depot, Pretoria, South Africa

South African Government Archives, Orange Free State Archives Depot, Bloemfontein, South Africa

South African Library, Queen Victoria Street, Cape Town, South Africa

Southport Public Library, Lord Street, Southport, Lancs.
Staffordshire Record Office, Eastgate Street, Stafford ST16 2LZ
Sussex University Library, Brighton BN1 9QL
Texas University Library, Humanities Research Center, Box 7219, Austin, Texas 78718, U.S.A.
Trinity College, Cambridge
University College London Library, Gower Street, London WC1E 6BT
Wellcome Institute of the History of Medicine Library, 183 Euston Road, London NW1 2BP
Westfield College, University of London, Kidderpore Avenue, London NW3
West Sussex Record Office, West Street, Chichester, PO19 1RN
Worcestershire Record Office, Shirehall, Worcester WR1 1TR

Appendix IV
Index of name changes

No attempt is made here to provide a comprehensive index for this volume. The main body of the text is set out in alphabetical order, under the last known name of the person concerned, or in the case of hyphenated surnames, under the last part of the name. It is therefore to a large degree self-indexing. In a number of cases, however, names changed during the course of a career (usually through elevation to or in the peerage) and this list is intended to provide a guide to such changes. It also includes cross-references to certain persons who preferred to be listed under the first part of a hyphenated surname.

HOARE, Sir Samuel John Gurney, 2nd Bt: see TEMPLEWOOD, 1st Vt
HOPE, Sir Arthur Oswald James: see RANKEILLOUR, 2nd B
HOPETOUN, 7th E of: see LINLITHGOW, 1st M of
HOPKINSON, Sir Henry Lennox d'Aubigné: see COLYTON, 1st B
HOPWOOD, Sir Francis John Stephens: see SOUTHBOROUGH, 1st B
HOUGHTON, 2nd B: see CREWE, 1st M of
IRWIN, 1st B: see HALIFAX, 1st E of
ISAACS, Sir Rufus Daniel: see READING, 1st M of
JEBB, Sir Hubert Miles Gladwyn: see GLADWYN, 1st B
KERR, Sir Archibald John Kerr Clark: see INVERCHAPEL, 1st B
KERR, Philip Henry: see LOTHIAN, 11th M of
KILMARNOCK, Baron: see ERROLL, 21st E of
KNATCHBULL, Hon. Michael Herbert Rudolph: see BRABOURNE, 5th B
LAMPSON, Sir Miles Wedderburn: see KILLEARN, 1st B
LAW, Colonel Cecil Henry: see ELLENBOROUGH, 6th B
LAWLEY, Sir Arthur: see WENLOCK, 6th B
LODER, John de Vere: see WAKEHURST, 2nd B
LUMLEY, Lawrence Roper: see SCARBROUGH, 11th E of
MACKAY, Sir James Lyle: see INCHCAPE, 1st E of
MAFFEY, Sir John Loader: see RUGBY, 1st B
MAUD, Sir John Primatt Redcliffe: see REDCLIFFE-MAUD, Baron
MILLAR, Sir Frederick Robert Hoyer: see INCHYRA, 1st B
MORLEY, Sir James Wycliffe Headlam-: see HEADLAM-MORLEY
MOUNTBATTEN, Admiral of the Fleet Louis Alexander: see MILFORD HAVEN,
    1st M of
NICOLSON, Sir Arthur, 11th Bt: see CARNOCK, 1st B
PONSONBY, Sir Vere Brabazon: see BESSBOROUGH, 9th E of
POWELL, Sir Robert Stephenson Smyth Baden-: see BADEN-POWELL, 1st B
POYNDER, Sir John Poynder Dickson-: see ISLINGTON, 1st B
RAMSBOTHAM, Sir Herwald: see SOULBURY, 1st Vt
RICE, Sir Cecil Arthur Spring-: see SPRING-RICE
RICHARDS, Sir Arthur Frederick: see MILVERTON, 1st B
RODD, Major-General Francis James Rennell: see RENNELL OF RODD, 2nd B
RODD, Sir James Rennell: see RENNELL OF RODD, 1st B
RONALDSHAY, Earl of: see ZETLAND, 2nd M of
RUTHVEN, Sir Alexander Gore Arkwright Hore-: see GOWRIE, 1st E
SINCLAIR, John: see PENTLAND, 1st B
STANLEY, Baron: see DERBY, 17th E of
THESIGER, Hon. Frederic John Napier: see CHELMSFORD, 1st Vt
THOMAS, Sir Freeman Freeman-: see WILLINGDON, 1st M of
VANNECK, Sir William Charles Arcedeckne: see HUNTINGFIELD, 5th B
VEREKER, John Standish Surtees Prendergast: see GORT, 6th Vt
VINCENT, Sir Edgar: see D'ABERNON, 1st Vt
WEMYSS, Admiral of the Fleet Sir Rosslyn Erskine: see WESTER WEMYSS, 1st B
WEST, Charles John Sackville-: see SACKVILLE, 4th B
WOLMER, Viscount: see SELBORNE, 2nd E of
WOOD, Edward Frederick Lindley: see HALIFAX, 1st E of